Roberto Clemente:

The Great One

Roberto Clemente:

The Great One

---

by
Bruce Markusen

SPORTS PUBLISHING, LLC.
www.sportspublishing.llc.com

Director of production: Susan M. Moyer
Cover, photo insert design: Julie L. Denzer,

ISBN: 1-58261-312-5

Sports Publishing LLC.
www.SportsPublishingLLC.com

Printed in the United States.

This book is dedicated to the memory of my mother, Grace Markusen (Rodriguez), who was born in Santurce, the home of Roberto Clemente's first professional team. Although my mother held no special interest in baseball, she never discouraged me from pursuing my own passion.

Thank you, Mom, for reminding me of my roots, while always being there to defend and support me.

CONTENTS

Introduction vii
Acknowledgments ix
Foreword xi

1	Beginnings to Brooklyn	1
2	Hidden in Montreal	17
3	This is Pittsburgh, Not Puerto Rico	37
4	Frustration in the Fifties	55
5	What if the Dodgers Had Kept Clemente?	69
6	The Arm	73
7	The Breakthrough	79
8	World Series Mismatch	87
9	Silver Bats	107
10	Fallback	115
11	A Challenge From the GM	121
12	The Hat	133
13	A Push for Power	145
14	The Hat Falls Off	159
15	A Troubled Summer	171
16	Bowie, Boos, and Bandits	179
17	The Irishman Returns	189
18	Integration's Team	207
19	Slaying the Giants	241
20	Clemente's Showcase	249
21	Game Seven	271
22	The March to 3,000	289
23	A Rematch With the Machine	301
24	The Fates of Winter	307
25	Aftershocks	329
26	Honors	339
27	The Sports City	345
28	The Legacy	349
Index	....	355

INTRODUCTION

Few baseball fans even knew his real name during his lifetime. It wasn't Roberto Walker Clemente, as many believed, but Roberto Clemente Walker. As per Puerto Rican custom, Roberto had two surnames; the first one represented the father's last name (Clemente) and the second one came from the mother's maiden name (Walker). There were many other things that people misunderstood about this man—such as characteristics of his personality—that were far more important than the ordering of his name. When asked to compare himself with other great players, Roberto often responded: "For me, I am the best." Most writers interpreted this as sheer braggadocio, as if Clemente were arrogantly proclaiming that he was better than Willie Mays, or Mickey Mantle, or Hank Aaron. That wasn't what Clemente meant at all. He was trying to communicate in English a saying that originated in Spanish—a statement that had no literal translation, but reflected pride in his accomplishment and effort. "I am doing a good job and I am doing my best." That is what Clemente was trying to say.

His best produced the following accomplishments: 3,000 base hits, a .317 lifetime average, 240 home runs, 15 All-Star Game selections (including 14 actual All-Star appearances), 12 Gold Glove awards (all won consecutively), two world championships, a World Series MVP Award, and a National League MVP Award. Having said all of that, Roberto Clemente was not the greatest player in the history of the game. He was probably not even the greatest player of his era, what with fellow legends like Aaron and Mays patrolling rival outfields. Yet, there has been no player in my lifetime who has played the game with more dynamism or passion. There has been no player who exhibited more selfless concern for others—to the point of heroism—away from the field of play. If for no other reasons than those two, Clemente deserves to be remembered. In fact, we *need* to remember him—at a time when the actions of modern day athletes have often disappointed us.

When I received an offer to write a book about Roberto Clemente, I had realized a lifetime dream. After all, Clemente was my favorite player; he still is. He was a full Puerto Rican; I am half-Puerto Rican, on my mother's side. Roberto Clemente is one of many reasons why I am proud to inform people of my heritage.

In accepting the offer to write about Clemente, I also understood the challenge at hand. Since so many books have been written about "The Great One," how would I make mine different?

My goal was to write the most accurate and comprehensive book that has ever been done about Clemente. The readers will have to decide whether I have achieved that aim. I also wanted to write a book that measured Clemente's legacy and impact in the years that have passed since he played his last game. Most of the Clemente books were written in the immediate aftermath of his death. This book was written in 1998—twenty-five years after his election and induction to the National Baseball Hall of Fame. The natural lapse of time has provided an invaluable sense of historical perspective, one that could not have been achieved in the early to mid 1970s. Furthermore, in the 25 years that have come and gone since Clemente's enshrinement, his stature in American society has not decreased—it has only grown. Simply put, Clemente's legacy is more powerful than it has ever been. This book attempts to capture that legacy with the written word.

ACKNOWLEDGMENTS

The Great One could not have been written without the assistance of others. Two men, in particular, emerge as stars in the upcoming chapters. Nellie King, a teammate and friend of Clemente, and Luis Mayoral, Roberto's friend and a lifelong baseball contributor, provided in-depth thoughts about this special man. They also provided key research materials and fact-checking assistance. In addition, Sally O'Leary, formerly of the Pirates' public relations department, welcomed us into her home, allowed us to interview her, and helped provide contacts with numerous other interview subjects. Jill Renwick of the National Baseball Hall of Fame Library proved invaluable in transcribing interviews and proofreading the manuscript.

Special thanks to researcher, writer and Pirates' expert Andrew O'Toole, who provided dozens of pages of primary source material along with transcripts of the many interviews he conducted with former teammates and acquaintances of Clemente. Andrew's contributions have added much to the accuracy and detail of *The Great One*. As a fellow author, I appreciate the sacrifices he made in consolidating his research with mine.

Thank you to the following individuals for granting interviews to Andrew O'Toole and the author: Joe Black, Steve Blass, Bobby Bragan, Marcos Breton, Nellie Briles, Joe Brown, Jose Cardenal, Dave Cash, Joe Christopher, Donn Clendenon, Dave Giusti, Bill Guilfoile, Richie Hebner, Art Howe, Nellie King, Bowie Kuhn, Vernon Law, Luis Mayoral, Roy McHugh, Bill Nunn, Sally O'Leary, Al Oliver, Bob Robertson, Willie Stargell, John Steadman, John Steigerwald, Clyde Sukeforth and Bob Veale.

Thanks to these people who helped in research and development of the manuscript:

Sue Bartow, Bill Burdick, Gene Carney, Jim Gates, Darci Harrington, Greg Harris, John Horne, Lesley Humphreys, Jeff Idelson, Milton Jamail, Pat Kelly, Susan MacKay, Scot Mondore, John Ralph, Corey

Seeman, Milo Stewart, Jr., Helen Stiles, Ron Visco, Joe Wallace and Tim Wiles. I'd also like to offer special recognition to the terrific staff and abundant resources of the National Baseball Hall of Fame Library.

And finally, thanks to Mike Pearson, Susan Moyer and Joanna Wright of Sports Publishing, Inc.

List of Sources
Publications and Miscellaneous:

Associated Press
Baltimore Herald
Baltimore Sun
Baseball America
Baseball Digest
Boston Globe
Chicago Sun-Times
Cleveland Plain Dealer
Ebony
Houston Chronicle
Houston Post
Icon
Inside Sports
Knight-Ridder Newspapers
Los Angeles Herald Examiner
Los Angeles Times
McKeesport Daily News
Montreal Star
National Baseball
   Hall of Fame Library
New York Daily News
New York Post
New York Times
New York World Telegram
Oneonta Daily Star
Philadelphia Bulletin
Pittsburgh Pirates Media Guide
Pittsburgh Pirates Yearbook
Pittsburgh Post-Gazette
Pittsburgh Press
Pittsburgh Sun-Telegraph

San Juan Star
Sport
Sports Collectors Digest
Sports Illustrated
The Diamond
The Sporting News
The Sporting News'
   Official Baseball Guides
Time
United Press International
USA Today
USA Today Baseball Weekly
WIIC-TV

Books:

Baseball with a Latin Beat, Peter
   Bjarkman, McFarland, 1994
Clemente, Kal Wagenheim, Praeger,
   1973.
Numero Uno: Roberto, Bill Christine,
Stadia Sports, 1973.
Remember Roberto, Jim O'Brien,
   1994.
Sports Encyclopedia: Baseball, David
Neft and Richard Cohen,
St. Martin's, 1997
The Baseball Encyclopedia, Macmillan,
1996.
Total Baseball, Penguin Group,
   1997
Who Was Roberto? Phil Musick,
   Doubleday, 1974.

1

Beginnings to Brooklyn

At about three o'clock in the afternoon on August 18, 1934, the life of a Hall of Famer and a humanitarian began. A boy named Roberto was born to Luisa Walker Clemente and Melchor Clemente in a large wooden house located in the San Anton barrio of Carolina, Puerto Rico. Dark-skinned like the others in his family, Roberto was the last of eight children, five of whom had been born to Luisa and Melchor. The succession of children included three brothers—Matino, Andres and Osvaldo—and a sister—Ana Iris, who died a horrifying death at the age of five after her dress accidentally caught fire.

Luisa had also raised three children by a previous marriage: two sons, Luis and Oquendo, and a daughter, Rosa Maria. Luisa's first husband had died, leaving her a widow before she eventually met and married Melchor. Unfortunately, tragedy would become a recurring theme in the Clemente family.

Roberto's mother was a dignified woman, yet warm and friendly in demeanor, someone who brought a cheerful quality to the Clemente household. Luisa attended church regularly, bringing Roberto with her to Baptist services in Carolina. Although her youngest son would eventually marry in the Catholic church, the Baptist upbringing would help lay the groundwork for Roberto's strong set of values.

Luisa worked hard as a laundress and in a variety of jobs assisting the workers at a local sugar cane plantation called the Victoria Sugar Mill. "My mother have to really work," Clemente said in a 1972 interview with Sam Nover of WIIC-TV. "My mother used to get up at one o' clock in the morning. She had to work and make lunches for these people that used to work in the sugar cane plantation where my father worked. Now, my mother never went to a show. My mother, she didn't [even] know how to dance."

At the time of Roberto's birth, Melchor was already 54 years old. As a serious man who carried a strong work ethic, Melchor preached discipline and loyalty in a strict Clemente household. Melchor worked as a foreman for the plantation, which was located in Carolina, a land of sugar cane fields and dairies. For his labor, Melchor earned about 45 cents a day. Although the salary sounds meager, it was not considered a poor salary; given the economic standards of the 1930s and forties in Puerto Rico, the average income might have been 30 cents a day.

Still, Melchor was not bringing in a large sum, especially with so many mouths to feed and bodies to clothe in his massive household. As a result, the Clementes had little extra income at their disposal, usually enough to pay for the basic essentials, but nothing more. To supplement his income, Melchor rented his truck to a local construction company, helping them with the deliveries of gravel and sand to various building sites.

Luis Mayoral, a friend of Clemente and a baseball career man for 30 years, assesses the Clemente family's economic status in the forties and fifties. "I would say that they could have been a little bit below middle-income then," Mayoral says. "They weren't poor poor because one thing [Roberto] was proud of, and he said it all the time, 'I always wore clothing and I always had food at the table at home.' They made ends meet. But then, a family with that income could never have compared with the [incomes of the] overall population in the states for obvious reasons."

During his career as a sportswriter, broadcaster, and public relations official, Mayoral met both Mr. and Mrs. Clemente. Although the large differences in age between he and the Clemente parents posed a natural roadblock in getting to know them well, Mayoral did observe their close relationships with Roberto. "They were individuals that Roberto loved and admired not only because they were his parents, but for the fact that they had to struggle so much in life. Working in the cane fields like Melchor did was not easy. [Nor was] being a housewife like Dona Luisa was for so many years when there were so many hardships on the island.

"Plus the fact that they were black. You know, there is racism in Puerto Rico, too. Racism in Puerto Rico is worse than here because it's hypocritical, it's hidden. Here [in the United States] it's open."

Clemente's sense of humor and appreciation of life were also aided by his parents, who created a loving atmosphere in the home. Although the Clementes lived a hard life in Carolina, Luisa and Melchor made it enjoyable. At night, the Clementes often spent time telling jokes and laughing among themselves. "I owe so much to my parents," Clemente once said. "They did so much for me. I never heard my father or mother raise their voices in our home. I never heard hate in my house."

Roberto greatly respected his mother and father, to whom he felt a binding loyalty. Unlike other young children who don't appreciate their parents until adulthood, Roberto understood fully the ways that they cared for him and his brothers and sisters. For example, when World War II affected the already unfavorable Puerto Rican economy, the Clemente parents made sure that their children came first. "During the war, food was hard to get," Clemente once said, "but my parents always fed us first before they ate."

Luisa hoped that Roberto would pursue a full education and a career in engineering, rather than in sports. "We wanted him to be an engineer," his mother explained in a 1960 interview with Emilio Carmona of the *San Juan Star,* "because in that way he could help society. But God wished it differently." In watching him during his youngest days as a child, Luisa realized that Roberto wanted to become a professional baseball player.

Her son's love of baseball and softball was evident by the time he turned five. "I started playing baseball in the neighborhood before I was old enough to go to school," Clemente told Dan Donovan of the *Pittsburgh Press* in a 1972 interview. "We would play all day and I wouldn't care if we missed lunch. We played until it got so dark that we couldn't see." As Clemente looked back on his childhood, he realized that his destiny was to become a ballplayer. "The more I think about it," Roberto told Sam Nover in 1972, "I convinced that God wanted me to play baseball."

"Roberto was born to play baseball," Luisa said, recognizing what Roberto would come to know. "I can remember when he was five years old. He used to buy rubber balls every time he had a chance." Roberto constantly carried rubber balls in his hands; he squeezed them tightly, strengthening his hands and fingers. Roberto loved to bounce balls off the ceilings and walls of the family's large, five-bedroom home. "When I was a little kid," Clemente remembered, "the only thing I used to do was play ball all the time. With a paper ball, with a rubber ball, with a tennis ball; we used to make our own balls, and stuff like that."

In the absence of his favored rubber balls, Roberto occasionally substituted the tennis balls, which didn't bounce quite as high and lost some of their bounce when they got wet. When he ran out of money to buy new rubber balls, Roberto adopted an innovative approach. He took old magazines and newspapers, and crunched them into the shape of a ball. Sometimes he took old pairs of stockings and wrapped them tightly to form another kind of ball. Either way, the makeshift ball would serve as a crude and temporary replacement, until enough money could be secured to purchase one of the high-grade rubber balls.

The necessity to buy rubber balls, among other boyhood desires, forced Roberto to adopt an early work ethic. One day, the youthful Clemente eyed a bicycle, one that he felt he had to have. He told his father about it; predictably, Melchor told him he would have to work to achieve his goal. The opportunity would soon come. A neighbor promised to give Roberto one cent a day for carrying a large milk can one-half mile from the country store to the man's home. Although he was skinny and hardly looked capable of lifting heavy items, Roberto accepted the offer. Three years later, Roberto had finally accumulated enough money to purchase the second-hand bicycle.

Roberto also worked at other jobs, especially those that helped his father in particular. He frequently assisted Melchor in loading construction trucks with shovels. The work was not easy, but Roberto approached it with enthusiastic and dedicated respect to his father. In later years, Clemente remembered the ways that his father repeatedly instilled his work ethic in his children, especially himself. "My father used to say, 'I want you to be a good man; I want you to learn how to work. And I want you to be a serious person.' I grew up with that in my mind."

Melchor saw to it that his youngest son worked and learned the value of loyal and consistent labor, but he also made sure that he attended school. Roberto was not an exceptional student, but he was above average. The teachers found his deportment exemplary; he was very quiet and well-behaved, and respected his teachers in much the same way that he did his parents.

When Roberto wasn't attending class, or helping his father, or working for his second-hand bicycle, he was consumed by his greatest interest—baseball. On weekends, he frequently made his way to the ballparks in Puerto Rico, where he watched the Negro League teams that toured the island during the winter months. "It was hard to go to the ball game and watch the game because we didn't have the money," Clemente told WIIC-TV in 1972. "It was Saturday that my father gave me 25 cents. That's exactly what it cost me to go from my house to the ballpark; 10 cents for the bus and 15 for the ballpark."

Clemente quickly adopted a favorite player, a powerful Negro League outfielder who played for the San Juan Senators during the Puerto Rican Winter League season. "The first hero that I have, I would say was Monte Irvin, when I was a kid," recalled Clemente. "And I used to watch Monte Irvin play when I was a kid. I idolized him. I used to wait in front of the ballpark just for him to pass by so I could see him."

Roberto worshipped Irvin, a black player from Columbus, Alabama, whose batting style and powerful throwing arm excited the young Carolinian. At first, Roberto felt so nervous and awkward around Irvin that he hesitated to even look him in the eye, much less attempt to talk to him. After several visits to the ballpark, Clemente eventually garnered enough nerve to ask Irvin for an autograph. Though separated by age and culture, the two baseball aficionados soon developed a special relationship. Clemente would carry Irvin's glove for him; Monte would reward Roberto by giving him baseballs that he could keep for his own collection. When Roberto couldn't make it to one of Monte's games, he would listen intently to the play-by-play description of Irvin's team on local radio.

Luisa still harbored an outside hope that her son might opt for a career in engineering. More and more, though, she realized that Roberto had found his calling. At times, Roberto's obsession with the game concerned his mother. "There were times he was so much in love with baseball that he didn't even care for food," Luisa explained to the *San Juan Star*. On one occasion, Luisa became so exasperated with Roberto's fixation on baseball that she tried to burn his bat! Luckily, the bat survived, as did Roberto's love for the sport.

At the age of eight, the youngest of the Clemente sons joined his first neighborhood softball team. Roberto's first set of baseball equipment represented ingenuity and improvisation at its finest. His first bat was constructed from a large tree branch; his first glove was fashioned from an old coffee bean sack. He owned no special set of baseball shoes, no sophisticated baseball uniform.

By 14, Roberto had joined his first full-fledged league—a group of "slow-pitch" softball teams, where pitchers tossed the ball slowly on a high arc toward batters. A part-time high school teacher named Roberto Marin had recruited Clemente after watching him play a pick-up game in his neighborhood. "I met Roberto Marin, I knew him fairly well," says Luis Mayoral. "Roberto Marin was a salesman; he sold rice for the Sello Rojo company. And as a salesman for Sello Rojo rice, he would travel to different parts of the island. In 1948, Roberto was driving around barrio San Anton, and he told me many times that he saw a group of kids playing baseball, with guava tree limbs as bats. Guava tree limbs are very hard; that's what they used to play with. Also, with broomsticks. And they used, let's say cans, like for spaghetti or other foods, as baseballs—the kids would crush them, and that would be the ball. One day driving around San Anton, he stopped to take a look at the kids. He saw this one kid in particular, who turned out to be Roberto, and just by watching him for a few minutes, he saw the athletic abilities that Roberto had. And that led Roberto Marin to contact Roberto and ask him to play softball on the team sponsored by Sello Rojo Rice."

Clemente eagerly joined the team, which was organized and managed by Marin and sponsored by the local rice factory. As one of the benefits in playing in an organized league, Marin supplied Roberto with his first playing uniform. It was the start of a special relationship between the two, with Marin providing an early jump-start to Clemente's aspiring career. "I think that more than [being] instrumental," Mayoral says of Marin's role in Clemente's development, "Roberto Marin and Roberto Clemente became compadres. Roberto Clemente's first son was baptized by Roberto Marin and that makes them compadres, in Spanish. And when you select someone to be your compadre, to be the godfather of one of your sons, well you know there is something to that relationship.

"I think that overall that along the road of Roberto's baseball career, he appreciated Roberto Marin's friendship, plus the fact that he was the one who really gave him the opportunity to leave his surroundings in barrio San Anton and start playing softball, and hence, going into playing baseball as an amateur, and baseball as a professional player."

Marin's team needed help on the infield. He inserted Clemente at shortstop, where Roberto made a number of fine plays and dazzled spectators with his long, powerful throws to first base. Clemente played so well in his first season for Marin that he earned selection to a special "Future Stars" competition, the equivalent of Little League or Babe Ruth League play in the United States. That local coaches and managers considered him talented enough to make the "Future Stars" level was impressive enough. It became even more noteworthy when one looked at Roberto's birth certificate. Roberto was still only 14; most of the other boys selected for the competition were already 16 years old. Somehow, Roberto had closed the enormous two-year gap, at an age when even a one-year difference could give an older boy a huge advantage.

Some days Roberto played endlessly. "I loved the game so much," Clemente wrote in a personal album that he kept, "that even though our playing field was muddy and we had many trees on it, I used to play many hours every day." Clemente once played a marathon game that started in the morning and lasted until the evening. Although the game dragged ridiculously long, it provided him the chance to showcase his batting skills at a ball field known for its shallow dimensions. "The fences were about 150 feet away from home plate and I used to hit many homers. One day I hit 10 home runs in a game we started about 11 a.m. and finished about 6:30 p.m."

After two seasons, Roberto Marin decided to switch his softball team to a "fast-pitch" league, where pitchers wound up and windmilled balls toward home plate with ferocious underhand motions. As the eighth-place hitter, Roberto struggled to hit the rapid offerings of the fast-pitch league, where many games were played under poor lighting, but continued to play well in the field. Still, Marin felt Roberto was playing out of position. He considered the 16-year-old Clemente too slow to play the infield, especially shortstop. Marin decided that Roberto's future would rest in the outfield, where that unusually strong throwing arm would truly prosper.

During one of his softball tournaments, Clemente's play caught the eye of some scouts from another local league. This wasn't a softball league, but a baseball league: the prestigious Double-A amateur league, considered by some scouts the equivalent of play in the lower minor leagues. Shortly after the tournament, Clemente joined a team owned by Ferdinand Juncos, one of the best teams in the Double-A League.

As a student-athlete at Vizcarrondo High School, Clemente excelled in sports other than softball and baseball. He performed marvelously in track and field, in particular three events: the javelin, the high jump, and the 400 meters. With Roberto especially adept in the javelin—sometimes throwing it as far as 190 feet—speculation arose that he might be picked to represent Puerto Rico in the 1952 Olympic Games in Helsinki. Baseball now had some competition among the sporting options for the multi-talented Clemente.

Clemente's expertise in throwing the javelin aided him in playing baseball. He may not have known it at the time, but the footwork, release, and general dynamics employed in throwing the javelin coincided with the skills needed to throw a baseball properly. The more that Clemente threw the javelin, the better and stronger his throwing from the outfield became.

After his junior year in high school, Roberto made an important decision regarding his sporting future; he elected to pursue a career in professional baseball. He would forego the Olympics, instead focusing his efforts toward the refinement of his ballplaying skills. Clemente's hitting soon improved with Juncos, as he made better contact and began to pull the ball more frequently. Believing strongly that Clemente could play ball professionally, Roberto Marin took his teenage protege to Pedro "Pedrin" Zorrilla, a wealthy man who owned one of the teams in the Puerto Rican Winter League. Heavy set in appearance and humble by nature, Zorrilla would come to be known as "Mr. Baseball" in Puerto Rico. "Pedrin Zorrilla was a great human being, to begin with," says Luis Mayoral. "He grew up in a well-to-do family, financially speaking. But Pedrin Zorrilla had a touch of Gandhi in him, where, even though he was in a position of certain advantages in Puerto Rican society, he cared for the people who were less fortunate. Prior to the Clemente days, he had been like a big father to most of the African-American players who had played winter ball in Puerto Rico, since the 1938-39 season in winter baseball. That was the official first season of professional baseball in Puerto Rico. And I'm talking he was like a father to guys like Willard Brown, Lucious Easter, you name it, all those black players."

Zorrilla would also help major league teams discover Puerto Rican stars like Orlando Cepeda, Ruben Gomez and Juan Pizarro. He would continue to uncover Puerto Rican baseball talent until the last days of his life. In 1981, the 75-year-old Zorrilla passed away while serving the Chicago Cubs as their chief scout in the Caribbean.

"Zorrilla was the father to so many players," says Mayoral. "Puerto Ricans and African Americans. He, in fact, was a turning point and an inspirational point, a mentor, in the life of Roberto Clemente." In the early 1950s, Zorrilla would fulfill a critical role in the major leagues' discovery of Clemente.

The founder of the Santurce Cangrejeros (which means Crabbers) in 1939, Zorrilla continued to operate the franchise in 1952. He had also managed to establish good working relationships with a number of major league teams, including the Brooklyn Dodgers of the National League. One day, 72 players gathered at Santurce's Sixto Escobar Stadium for a tryout camp that was sponsored by both the Dodgers and Zorrilla's Santurce Crabbers. Alex "Al" Campanis, the Dodgers' chief scout in the Caribbean, didn't expect much; most tryout camps produced a collection of hungry, but untalented athletes who had no business playing professional baseball at any level.

The group of young hopefuls included the 17-year-old Clemente, who showed up wearing a plain T-shirt, wrinkled baseball pants and an awkward-looking duck-billed cap. Campanis watched all 72 players as they participated in the first phase of the workout. "The first thing we do at the tryout is ask the kids to throw from the outfield," Campanis told Dick Young of the *New York Daily News* in 1971. "This one [kid] throws a bullet from center on the fly. I couldn't believe my eyes."

Campanis asked the youngster to make another throw, estimated at nearly 400 feet. "'Uno mas [one more],' I shout," said Campanis. "And he does it again. I waved my hand, that's enough." It was Clemente who made the throw. By far, Clemente's arm would prove the most accurate and powerful of the group, as evidenced by the pair of eye-opening strikes he had hurled toward the infield.

During the workout, Clemente informed Campanis that he had played several positions in Puerto Rico: the outfield, shortstop, and even catcher. Clemente remembered Campanis' subsequent words of advice. "When I was through, Campanis said, 'Forget any of those other positions, kid. You're an outfielder.'" Campanis had recognized what many scouts would come to call the greatest throwing arm they had ever seen exhibited by a baseball player.

The second stage of the tryout involved the 60-yard dash, the equivalent of running the lengths of two bases, but without the turn in between. Up stepped Clemente, as Campanis prepared his stopwatch. "The first time I clock him in 6.4, I couldn't believe it," Campanis told Dick Young. "That's in full uniform."

Clemente had run the dash in 6.4 seconds, at a time when the world record was only 6.1.

"Uno mas," said Campanis, repeating his refrain from the throwing exhibition. Clemente ran 60 yards once again. The time? Six point four seconds. There was nothing wrong with Campanis' watch.

Campanis sent the other 71 players home; none of them had impressed the Dodgers' scout. Clemente, however, was a different story, a remarkable athlete. Thoroughly convinced of Roberto's speed and throwing ability, Campanis now wanted to know if he could swing the bat. "The only one I asked to hit was this boy," said Campanis, "who told me his name was Roberto Clemente."

As a veteran Dodger scout, Campanis had seen many superior athletes who could field and run, but lacked the bat speed and fundamental techniques required of good hitters. Campanis wondered whether Clemente fell into this category, one that had so often frustrated major league scouts. "I'm saying to myself, 'We gotta sign this son-of-a-buck if he can just hold the bat in his hands.'"

Campanis asked Clemente to take batting practice against an accomplished minor league pitcher named Jose "Pantalones" Santiago, a legendary hurler in Puerto Rican Winter League play. Clemente ripped several line drives, some to center field, many to right, and a few to left field. Noticing that Clemente liked to stand far away from home plate, Campanis doubted that the youngster could reach pitches on the outer half of the strike zone. Campanis instructed Santiago to throw the next series of pitches, preferably curve balls, toward the outside corner. Santiago obliged; Clemente responded by ringing another set of line drives. "The kid swings with both feet off the ground and hits line drives to right and sharp ground balls up the middle," marveled Campanis. Clemente also showed power during the batting exhibition. By Clemente's own estimate, he hit 10 balls over the fence.

The 20-25 minute batting display convinced Campanis that he had found a prospect. In fact, Campanis realized he had discovered much more than that. "He was the greatest natural athlete I have ever seen as a free agent," Campanis told Dick Young in 1971. By this time, Campanis had seen thousands of free agents during his long tenure as a scout and executive with the Dodgers.

Unfortunately, Campanis could not sign Clemente—at least not yet. Since Roberto, who was still in high school, was only 17 and considered underaged, no major league team could legally offer him a contract. Any offers would have to wait until Roberto's 18th birthday. In the meantime, Roberto continued to play his second season for Juncos.

Shortly after the workout for Campanis, Roberto Marin invited Pedrin Zorrilla to watch Juncos play one of its league games in person. Playing against a team in Manati—near Zorrilla's upper class home, Clemente impressed the Santurce owner by cracking a double and making two fine catches in the outfield. After watching Clemente excel for Juncos, Zorrilla told Marin that he was interested in signing the young outfielder to play for his Santurce team in the Puerto Rican Winter League. Zorrilla could offer a bonus of $400 and a weekly salary of $40 to $45 during a 72-game season that lasted about 10 weeks. Marin took the offer to Clemente, who was excited by the news but knew that he needed to have his father's approval.

When Melchor learned of the offer, he immediately went to a neighbor's house, asking him for his opinion. Believing that Zorrilla had made what amounted to only an initial offer, the neighbor advised Roberto's father to ask for more money. Melchor agreed and instructed Marin to make Zorrilla a counter-offer, but the Crabbers' owner refused to raise the ceiling. Not wanting to lose out on the opportunity, the young Roberto told Marin that he wanted to sign the contract as it was. Melchor finally approved. On October 9, 1952, with a friend standing by as a witness, Melchor signed his underage son's first professional contract.

The owners of each winter league team were limited in the number of American players they could sign, but could have as many Latinos on the roster as they wanted. Partly due to the restrictions on signing American players, many of which also played in the major leagues, there existed an imbalance in each team's salary structure. The American players tended to receive the highest salaries, while the Latinos rounded out the bottom of the payroll. The highest-paid American major leaguers received as much as $1,000 a month, in addition to housing expenses. The lowest paid players in the winter league earned anywhere from $400 to $500, with no additional money to pay for renting apartments or houses.

As a young Latino with little leverage, Clemente settled for the low end of the pay scale. He received a contract that would pay him $40 a week, plus a signing bonus of $400. Zorrilla also threw in a new glove, replacing the ragged model that Roberto had been using. Most of the veteran players on the Crabbers earned considerably more money; yet, Clemente's salary figures were respectable numbers for a teenager who had never played professional ball, or proven himself against major league competition.

Clemente joined a Santurce team that would eventually feature another Puerto Rican teenager of considerable talent, an infielder also discovered by Zorrilla. The youngster was named Jose Pagan, who would play shortstop and third base. Many years later, the two native Puerto Rican prodigies would become inexorably linked on another notable team.

As was customary with clubs operated by Pedrin Zorrilla, Clemente spent most of his first season watching games from the dugout. Zorrilla simply did not believe in playing young, inexperienced players, especially in a league that featured numerous veterans of both the major leagues and the Negro Leagues. At the start of the season, Clemente rode the bench, appearing only as a pinch-hitter. By the end of the schedule, he had come to bat only 77 times, batting a mere .234. Although Clemente bristled at the lack of exposure, there were additional reasons for the sparse playing time. In 1952-53, Santurce had several outfielders of high caliber: Willard Brown, a former Negro League star who had played 21 games for the St. Louis Browns in 1947, and Bob Thurman, who would make his major league debut in 1955.

The Crabbers also featured an intriguing player named James Buster Clarkson. Known alternately by his middle name and by the nickname "Buzz," Clarkson had played only briefly in the major leagues, appearing in 14 games in 1952 for the Boston Braves, but had starred in the Negro Leagues in the years prior to Jackie Robinson's shattering of the color barrier. Clarkson had also become a fixture in the Puerto Rican Winter League, playing shortstop and driving in runs by the cartload. By the winter of 1952-53, Clarkson had taken on the additional responsibilities of managing the Santurce club.

As player-manager, Clarkson wanted to play Clemente regularly, but had to yield to the wishes of the more cautious Zorrilla. Although Clemente didn't play very often his first season with Santurce, Clarkson immediately recognized his talent. "He came to me right out of high school," Clarkson recalled in a 1973 interview with Donald Hall. "I could see he was going a long way. Some of the old-timers didn't think so, but I could see great ability in Clemente."

The lack of playing time frustrated Clemente, who was used to playing everyday and being one of the centerpieces of his team. Clarkson recognized the depletion of Clemente's ego. "The main thing I had to do," said Buzz, "was to keep his spirits up. He didn't realize how good he was. But I could see his potential."

Clarkson encouraged his young center fielder, telling him that he would eventually become a star in the United States. "I told him he'd be as good as Willie Mays someday," Clarkson said, referring to the New York Giants' young superstar. "And he was." Clarkson also gave him some sage advice. Noticing that Roberto tended to drag his left foot backward as part of the "bailing out" process, Buster placed a bat behind Clemente as he stood in the batter's box during batting practice. If Clemente continued to drag his foot, he would step on the bat. "He had a few rough spots," Clarkson acknowledged, "but he never made the same mistake twice. He was baseball savvy and he listened. He listened to what he was told and he did it." Listening to Clarkson's advice about dragging his foot, Roberto began to stride slightly more directly toward the pitcher, as opposed to the direction of the third base dugout.

As Clemente's first manager in professional baseball, Clarkson made a special effort to nurture the talents and psyche of a young, unproven player, at a time when veteran teammates often shunned rookies, making them feel worthless. In turn, Clemente recognized the effort of the former Negro League star. "I played for Clarkson's team and I was just a kid," Clemente said later in his career. "He insisted the other players allow me to take batting practice and he helped me."

The learning process of Clemente's first winter league season began to yield dividends during the winter of 1953-54. Although still a teenager, Roberto moved into the starting outfield. "Some of the old pros didn't take too kindly to a kid breaking into the lineup," Clarkson admitted, "but Clemente was too good to keep out." The recipient of regular playing time, Clemente continued to field brilliantly and showed vast improvement at the plate. In 219 winter league at-bats, he batted a highly respectable .288 and exhibited occasional power.

The increase in playing time, coupled with his upgraded level of play, prompted visitations from a cache of major league scouts. The interested parties included National League scouts like Andy High from the Brooklyn Dodgers, Luis Olmo of the Milwaukee Braves, Tom Sheehan of the New York Giants, and Quincy Trouppe of the St. Louis Cardinals. From the American League, the New York Yankees sent Harry Craft to take a look at the Puerto Rican phenom. Scouts from a total of nine teams approached Clemente about the possibility of signing a contract. Bids began to trickle in, creating options for the native of Carolina.

While slow to integrate their major league roster with black players, the Yankees had decided to aggressively pursue players in the Puerto Rican Winter League. In particular, two players on the island interested the Yankees: Clemente and an American first baseman named Frank Leja, whom the Yankees considered the more appealing of the two prospects. Yankee scouts regarded Leja, a left-handed batter, as the more accomplished hitter, one who was capable of reaching the right field seats at Yankee Stadium; they had their doubts, however about Clemente's ability to handle the bat.

The Yankees offered Leja a bonus approaching $150,000, which left them with little money to offer Clemente—about $3,000. Roberto knew that he could fare better financially with a number of teams, even if they lacked the appeal of baseball's most storied franchise. In fact, he had already received a more substantial offer from another team. Clemente rejected the offer from the Yankees, who ended up signing Leja and bringing him to the Bronx in 1954. New York soon realized what Clemente already knew. "He could hit and that was it," Clemente told Pat Livingston of the *Pittsburgh Press* in 1972. Leja was a one-dimensional player who couldn't field or run, and even his hitting was suspect at the major league level. During a three-year career that lasted only 26 games with the Yankees and Los Angeles Dodgers, Leja accumulated one hit in 23 at-bats.

The New York Giants had actually been the first team to make Clemente an offer. Although Santurce owner Pedrin Zorrilla enjoyed an informal working relationship with the Brooklyn Dodgers, he encouraged Brooklyn's rivals to bid and bid heavily for the mercurial Clemente. (Curiously, Zorrilla would go to work for the

Giants as their chief scout in 1957.) Zorrilla whispered his insider's knowledge to Giants' owner Horace Stoneham, but New York's scouts expressed concern over Clemente's undisciplined approach to hitting. Listening to his chief talent-seekers, Stoneham became preoccupied with Clemente's frequent strikeouts. As a result, Stoneham made a bid for Clemente, but one that was tempered by financial restraint.

If the Giants had been slightly more aggressive in their negotiating approach, they might have tempted Clemente with the opportunity to play with his boyhood hero. Monte Irvin, the former Negro League star, had joined the Giants in 1949, two years after the termination of baseball's color line. If the Giants had been able to sell Roberto on the joys of playing with his idol, he might have been willing to take a bit less in up-front bonus money.

Thanks to their friendship with Zorrilla, the Dodgers already knew about Roberto's many talents. Not wanting their principal rivals to add Clemente to an outfield that already included a star like Irvin and a young superstar in Willie Mays, the Dodgers quickly moved in and bettered the Giants' proposal. The Dodgers offered Clemente a signing bonus of $10,000, a nice supplement to an annual salary of $5,000. If Clemente were to accept the offer, it would represent the largest bonus the Dodgers had doled out since signing Jackie Robinson to a minor league contract in 1945. Both the money, and the prospect of playing in New York City, where thousands of fellow Puerto Ricans had immigrated, intrigued Clemente. He gave the Dodgers a verbal commitment that he would sign with them.

Shortly after the Dodgers raised the stakes, scouts from the Milwaukee Braves swooped in on Clemente. "Next day, the Braves offer me $27,500," Clemente recalled in a 1962 interview with Les Biederman of the *Pittsburgh Press*. "I say, 'Where were you yesterday?'" Estimates of the monetary sum offered by the Braves varied according to different reports, anywhere from $28,000 to $40,000. In other words, the Braves had offered a package three to four times the size of the Dodgers' bonus.

The contractual waters now muddied, Clemente faced a dilemma. Should he accept the offer from Milwaukee, which was by far the best deal financially, but play in a town that he had never heard of? Or should he play for the Dodgers, near the city that some called the most glamorous in the United States? "I do not know much then about Milwaukee," Clemente told Bill Christine of the *Pittsburgh Press* in a 1969 interview. "Brooklyn was a famous team. I wanted to play for the Dodgers."

Indeed, the Dodgers, who had won the National League pennant in 1953, boasted a lineup of well-known players: National League RBI champion Roy Campanella, power-hitters like Gil Hodges and Duke Snider, the versatile and dynamic Jackie Robinson, National League batting champion Carl Furillo, and 20-game winner Carl Erskine. Although their nucleus of players was aging, the Dodgers figured to be a good team—maybe a great one—for two or three more years.

Clemente also took note of Brooklyn's aggressiveness in recruiting and signing black players. In 1947, the Dodgers had become the first major league team in 20th century history to sign an African-American player. After importing Jackie Robinson, the Dodgers had added several other black players, including Campanella, infielder Junior Gilliam and pitchers Dan Bankhead, Joe Black and Don Newcombe. The Dodgers had also signed a black Latino, Sandy Amoros, who seemed on the cusp of cracking the Brooklyn lineup. Cities and teams aside, Clemente faced an even more important consideration in his choice of major league clubs. Although he had not officially signed a contract with the Dodgers, he had given them a promise that he would do so. Still confused over what he should do, Roberto sought out his parents. Luisa Clemente quickly and sternly advised her son. He had given the Dodgers his word; it would be improper to back out of a promise. Although Luisa ultimately left the decision up to Roberto, he had now made up his mind. His parents, good and caring people, had always given him sound advice. Influenced by the words of his mother, Clemente explained to the Braves that he could not sign with them; he had already committed to the Dodgers.

Pedrin Zorrilla sent a telegram to Brooklyn, indicating that Roberto had made his decision. On February 19, 1954, with his father standing by, Clemente signed a one-year, $5,000 contract with the Dodgers. With a signing bonus of $10,000, the total package reached $15,000. The days of lugging milk cans across town for a penny a day seemed like a distant memory.

2

Hidden in Montreal

Although Clemente felt he had done the right thing by signing with Brooklyn, he eventually came to the conclusion that the Dodgers had misled him during negotiations. "I was just a youngster and believed everything everybody told me," Clemente told Les Biederman of the *Pittsburgh Press* in a 1962 interview. "The Dodgers told me a big bonus was no good and they said other players would resent it. Better for me to take small amount of money and work my way." If Clemente had been older and more accustomed to business negotiations, he might have been able to extract a much larger bonus from the Dodgers.

While the Dodgers' bonus paled in comparison with the offer from the Braves, it was still the first bonus contract the Dodgers had arranged since the major leagues had adopted a rule meant to limit the amount of bonus money that could be given to rookie players. "You see, under the rule that year," Pirates scout Howie Haak explained to the *Associated Press*, "any player who got more than a $4,000 bonus and was put on a minor league team had to remain frozen on that team and go through the major league draft." Under the new rule, any team signing a rookie to a contract whose bonus and salary exceeded $4,000 would have to keep that player on its 25-man major league roster for the entire season. If the player were to be sent to the minor leagues at any time during the season, he would become eligible for an off-season draft and could be taken by any other team. The drafting team would then have to pay $4,000 for that player.

Even though he had full knowledge of the rule, Dodgers vice president Buzzie Bavasi decided to sign Clemente to a minor league contract, assigning him to play for Brooklyn's top affiliate at Montreal. Al Campanis, who by now was managing a Cuban team in winter ball, told Bavasi he should give Clemente a major league contract and guarantee his inclusion on the Brooklyn Dodgers' 1954 roster. Campanis warned his boss that he was taking a huge gamble; he might lose the heralded prospect after only one minor league season.

After wrapping up his winter league season for Santurce, Clemente arrived in Vero Beach for his first spring training with the Dodgers. From there, he would report to the Montreal Royals of the International League. Clemente's teammates at Montreal would include another budding Latin American prospect and fellow outfielder, Sandy Amoros, a slick-fielding shortstop named Chico Fernandez, and former Brooklyn Dodger pitcher Joe Black.

When in Clemente's presence, Black quickly took note of the young outfielder's confidence and passion for the game. "I was impressed," says Black, "because he was 18 years old, just turning 19, but he had a lot of desire to play." Black also recognized Clemente's raw athletic skills, particularly his unusual but powerful batting style. "The thing that amazed me, is that sometimes one of his legs would be up in the air and he'd he hitting, and it'd still go out of the ballpark. He was just *strong*."

The Dodgers had known full well about Clemente's ability to hit line drives to all fields, especially to center and right, but had seen little direct evidence of his sheer power—at least up until now. During the opening week of the International League season, Clemente impressed not so much with his speed or throwing, but with a measure of that previously unseen power potential. Clemente ripped a monstrous, 400-foot home run over the left field wall at Delorimier Downs, Montreal's home ballpark. Clemente became the first player in Royals' history to clear the left field wall—and the stadium—at such a point. Considering the depth of the fences at Delorimier Downs—where it required a 340-foot blast just to reach the left field foul pole—the home run was impressive by usual standards. It became even more noteworthy when one realized that a hearty wind was gusting straight in from left field toward home plate. In the past, few Montreal players had managed to overcome the left field fence at Delorimier, even under ideal weather conditions.

Strangely, Clemente found himself on the bench next day. Perhaps Dodger management simply wanted to bring Clemente along slowly, considering that this was his first exposure to the minor league game. One week later, the Royals played a game against Richmond, and Clemente found himself in the starting lineup. In the first inning, the Royals loaded the bases, setting the stage for Clemente to come to bat. Unbelievably, Montreal manager Max Macon called Clemente back to the bench, lifting him for a pinch-hitter.

Later in the month, Clemente collected three triples in one game. The next day, Clemente rode the bench again. The pattern continued for most of the season. One impressive game, followed by a stint on the Royals' bench. Bewildered by the irregularity of his playing time, Clemente frequently approached Macon in his office, both before and after games. "He wasn't conceited," says Joe Black, "but he had a lot of self-confidence and couldn't understand why he couldn't play." Macon told Roberto that he was simply doing what was best for a young rookie playing at the minor leagues' highest level. Macon also pointed out that Montreal had many other fine outfielders, including future major leaguers like Amoros and Gino Cimoli, and a former big leaguer in Dick Whitman.

In spite of the explanations, the sporadic playing time annoyed and frustrated Clemente, just as it had during his first winter league season in Santurce. In addition to his inconsistent playing time, Roberto reportedly encountered other problems. He spoke a little bit of English, a language he had studied in high school, and no French, making communication with some teammates and many fans extremely cumbersome. Other than Amoros, Black and Fernandez, none of his Montreal teammates spoke Spanish.

Just how much English Clemente spoke during his season in Montreal remains a debatable point. According to Hall of Fame manager Tommy Lasorda, one of the pitchers on the 1954 Royals, Clemente spoke only Spanish. "I had to take care of him because he couldn't speak one word of English," Lasorda told Phoenix Communications in 1993. "He couldn't go get anything to eat. So he would wait for me in the morning until I woke up. And then, when I would come down to the lobby, he would be sitting there waiting for me. He was hungry. And I'd have to take him to the restaurant and order his meals for him."

The recollections of Joe Black differ greatly from Lasorda's. During a recent All-Star Game, Black confronted Lasorda over his version of the story. "I saw him on the field and I said, 'Tommy, why did you tell that story,'" Black says. "He said, 'What do you mean?' I said, 'One, Clemente didn't hang out with you. Second, Clemente speaks English. There's some Puerto Ricans who speak English.'"

Although Black spoke Spanish, he says his conversations with Clemente were never in that language. "No, he did speak English," Black reiterates. "[Orlando] Cepeda speaks English. Puerto Rico, you know, is part of the United States. So, over there, youngsters have the privilege of taking English in classrooms." As Black recalls, Clemente showed himself quite capable to handle basic conversations in English. "He wouldn't give a speech like Shakespeare, but he knew how to order breakfast and eggs. He knew how to say 'it's a good day,' 'let's play,' or 'why I don't play.' He could say, 'Let's go to the movies.'"

Other players on the Royals, like Cuban outfielder Sandy Amoros, were less versed in English than Clemente. "I played with guys," says Black, "like when Sandy got on the Dodgers, he knew maybe 20 words of English. That's whey they roomed with me because I spoke a little Spanish from playing in Cuba. But that wasn't [the case] with Clemente." As Black recalls, Clemente picked his spots in deciding when to speak English. "Clemente was able to communicate with those he wanted to communicate with."

Clemente also experienced a cultural phenomenon that he had seen little evidence of during his days in Puerto Rico—racial segregation.

At the time, the International League consisted of three Canadian franchises, Montreal, Ottawa and Toronto, a Latin American entry in Havana, and four American cities: Buffalo, Richmond, Rochester and Syracuse. When the Royals traveled on road trips that included stopovers in Richmond, they had to venture into the South, where segregation of hotels, restaurants and other public places infested the American culture.

On his first road trip to Richmond, Clemente encountered segregation for the first time. He could not eat in the same restaurant as his white Montreal teammates, nor could he stay in the same hotel with them. Black teammates, players like Amoros, Black and Fernandez, endured a similar plight. To make matters worse, few of Roberto's white teammates—who considered him cocky and arrogant, perhaps even a "hot dog"—offered any sympathy for the second-class treatment that he and the other black players received.

An American player like Black came to expect segregation in the South. For Latin American blacks, such social policies were far more confusing. "See, when I first went to a Latin country," Black says, "I went to Caracas, Venezuela, [and] I was shocked that some families—some looked white, some dark as me, some were [Roy] Campanella's color, you know. I said to [two Latin brothers], 'If you two guys go to the states, they're gonna separate you. They said, 'What do you mean? We're brothers.' I said, 'No they're gonna send you to the colored part of town, and he's gonna have to go to the white part of town.' I mean, families were just mixed like that, but they didn't pay any attention to it [in Latin America]." In Puerto Rico, light-skinned residents sometimes received advantages not given to those with darker skin. Yet, there existed little segregation of restaurants, hotels and public buses.

"The segregation only came when they hit these borders," says Joe Black. "And they couldn't understand. Like in the Negro Leagues, we had three Puerto Ricans on our team. They could not understand [segregation] when we went to the South; they wanted to go downtown to the stores to buy some clothes." Black and other African-American players had to warn their Latino teammates about the new and unfair American rules. "'Wait a minute,'" Black told Latin players on more than one occasion, "'Let somebody go with you cause you just can't walk in all these stores.' We'd let them know that they're not gonna let you try on those clothes. It was shocking to them to realize that there are some stores you can't go in, and if you could go in to buy a coat, you can't try the coat on. And they couldn't understand that."

Roberto found solace from racism when the Royals played at home. In the mid-1950s, Montreal existed as a place relatively free from overt racism and segregation. "They had a couple of night clubs that were owned by Americans that had moved up there and there were a lot of blacks that catered to them," Black explains, "but they were mixed clubs. I don't know if they had a section that was all black." Other than having some difficulty finding a barber who would cut the hair of African-Americans, Black found few examples of segregated treatment or existence in Montreal. "There wasn't a colored section, per se."

Except for one incident outside of Delorimier Downs, where a racist fan chastised Clemente for talking to a white woman, Roberto found the community to be fair and receptive. In fact, a white family invited Clemente and Fernandez to live in their home in one of Montreal's French residential neighborhoods. The two Latinos accepted the invitation and lived in the family's house. On the road, Clemente and Fernandez continued to share a room.

For the most part, Clemente socialized with only two of his Royals teammates. "Chico Fernandez, Roberto and myself, the three of us palled around," Joe Black says. "We went out to eat, we went to movies together, we laughed and we joked." Clemente's keen sense of humor helped make their conversations more enjoyable. "Oh yeah, he was funny," says Black. "The three of us, we just laughed all the time. See, we joked amongst ourselves."

Due to concerns over racial stereotyping, Black and Clemente did not usually feel comfortable showing their senses of humor around white players. And when they did joke among themselves, they preferred a more subtle form of comedy. "Some people think because if you're colored they've got the stereotype that we're like those guys back in the old days, always cracking jokes. I'm not a joke cracker, Clemente wasn't either, but we could say things now and then that were funny and we could ad lib things."

By 1954, Clyde Sukeforth, a well-liked baseball man who split his time between coaching and scouting, had earned a reputation as one of the game's most fair-minded and color blind thinkers. In 1945, while working as a coach with the Dodgers, Sukeforth had received a special assignment from president Branch Rickey, who told him to scout a Negro League prospect named Jackie Robinson. Although an injured shoulder prevented Robinson from playing, Sukeforth interviewed the infielder for two hours after the game, and came away impressed with the young man's character, intelligence, and determination. Perhaps encouraged by Sukeforth's findings, Rickey signed Robinson to a minor league contract within the next three days.

After the 1951 season, Sukeforth left the Dodgers and rejoined Rickey as a coach and part-time scout in the Pirates' organization, where "The Mahatma" had become general manager. In July of 1954, Rickey instructed Sukeforth to temporarily vacate his coaching duties with the Pirates and scout Joe Black, who had been demoted to the Dodgers' affiliate at Montreal after being overworked by Brooklyn the previous summer. Rickey was considering a trade that would send hard-hitting outfielder-third baseman Sid Gordon—who was in the midst of a .306 season—to the Dodgers in exchange for Black. Before making the deal for Black, Rickey wanted to know about the condition of the right-hander's arm.

Sukeforth stayed to watch a long, five-game International League series between Montreal and Richmond, but Black did not pitch. Prior to one of the games, Sukeforth observed batting and outfield practice and noticed the powerful throwing arm displayed by the Montreal right fielder, who made two particularly outstanding 300-foot heaves toward the infield. "I get there just in time to see the Montreal club take the field for batting practice," Sukeforth tells researcher Andrew O'Toole. "I noticed in right field they had a colored boy with a great arm."

The right fielder did not play in the game—until the seventh inning. "Max Macon, the Montreal manager, put in a pinch-hitter to hit," recalls Sukeforth. "Montreal was a run or so behind, and he sent up this right fielder, this black player with the good arm, up to hit. He hit a sharp, routine ground ball to the shortstop, and would you know it, it was a very close play at first base. I said, 'There's talent there. There's two things that he can do super.'" The player who could throw and run so well was the youthful Roberto Clemente.

Since Sukeforth hadn't heard of Clemente prior to his visit to Richmond, he had started asking questions around the ballpark. According to Joe Black, Sukeforth had initially mistaken Clemente for one of the Royals' pitchers. "Roberto Clemente took batting practice with the pitchers," recalls Joe Black, "because they knew he had capabilities and they were trying to hide him from scouts. Rickey had sent Sukeforth to Richmond to see me pitch to see if I could still throw. He got there early because he knew pitchers practiced early, so when I got there, he came to me and said, 'Who's that pitcher, who hits all those balls out?' I said, 'What pitcher?'" After the initial confusion, Black informed Sukeforth that the player's name was Clemente—an outfielder, not a pitcher.

"I learned he was a bonus player," Sukeforth revealed in an interview with *The Sporting News*, "and would be eligible for the draft." Clemente, whose bonus and salary of $15,000 far exceeded the $4,000 limit, fell into the category of unprotected minor league players. Since the Pirates were playing miserably that summer and seemed destined to complete a last-place finish in 1954, they would almost certainly have the No. 1 pick in the draft.

Sukeforth observed Clemente in batting practice over the next four days. Sukeforth noticed several extreme tendencies on the part of Clemente, who liked to stand deep in the batter's box and far away from home plate. Clemente preferred an unorthodox style at the plate, often hitting off his front foot, the result of striding so early. Yet, Sukeforth liked the power stroke that Clemente displayed, the way that balls resonated off his bat. As he prepared to leave Richmond, Sukeforth approached the Royals' manager and dropped a hint about the Pirates' intentions. "I told Montreal manager Max Macon to take good care of 'our boy' and see that he didn't get hurt," Sukeforth recalled in a 1955 interview with *The Sporting News*. Pleasantries exchanged, Sukeforth wrote a letter to Rickey. "Before I signed the letter, I wrote, 'I haven't seen Joe Black, but I have seen your draft pick.'"

As Joe Black recalls, Sukeforth told him almost immediately about his interest in Clemente. "He says to me, 'You haven't been pitching, but I'm gonna tell the old man, Joe can still pitch, but let's work on a guy named Roberto Clemente.'"

Although intrigued by Sukeforth's enthusiasm, Rickey wanted a second opinion. After all, if Clemente was as talented as Sukeforth claimed, why was he so unknown to the Pirates' organization? There must have been a problem with Clemente, a fatal flaw in his game. Rickey assigned Howie Haak, another one of his top scouts, to follow up on the Sukeforth report. "I went to Rochester to see him play and the strangest thing happened," Haak told the Associated Press in 1971. "Clemente got two triples and a double, and when they removed the southpaw pitcher, Clemente was taken out for a pinch-hitter. The Dodgers were trying to hide Clemente." In other words, the Dodgers' real intention in not playing Clemente was to prevent other teams' scouts from finding out about his talent. In so doing, the Dodgers hoped that Clemente would not be taken in the post-season draft of minor league players who had exceeded the $4,000 bonus limit.

At first, Clemente hadn't understood the reasons behind the sporadic dispersal of playing time. Frustrated by Macon's lineup policies, Clemente didn't know how the bonus rules and the draft affected him. At one point, Clemente became so unhappy that he sought out Al Campanis, whom he knew spoke Spanish. When Clemente said that he wanted to leave the team and return to Puerto Rico, Campanis explained why Macon had been keeping him tied to the bench. Campanis assured him that there would soon be a resolution to the problem, hinting that Roberto would find himself in the major leagues by the following season.

When Macon pinch-hit the lefty-swinging Dick Whitman for Clemente—after he had so easily handled Rochester's starting pitcher and seemed deserving of a crack at the ensuing reliever—Roberto became infuriated. "Roberto was disgusted all of 1954 with the Montreal Royals," says Luis Mayoral, "because he'd have a good day and then he'd be back on the bench and so forth. That happened repeatedly. Well into the season, Roberto got frustrated and abandoned the ballpark, went to his residence, which I understand was a small hotel room, to pick up his gear, abandon the team and go back to Puerto Rico."

Having returned to his room at the Powers Hotel, Clemente seemed determined to leave the team once and for all. Fortunately for Clemente, Howie Haak had arrived in town. "It so happened that Howie was there," says Mayoral. "When Howie asked where Clemente was, they told him he had abandoned the club. So Howie, having received this information, found Roberto in his room at the hotel. And he told him, 'Hey, go back to your ballclub. I promise you we'll pick you up in the November draft. And in 1955, you're going to be the starting right fielder with the Pirates.'"

Although Haak spoke little Spanish, he tried to ease the confused youngster's mind. Haak, who had roomed with Max Macon as a minor leaguer in 1935, confirmed what Al Campanis had hinted at earlier in the season: the Dodgers had been trying to hide him all season, in an effort to deter his selection in the post-season draft. Up until then, Clemente had believed he would be a member of the Brooklyn organization for life. "His thing was, he was going to play with the Dodgers," says Joe Black. "He had no inkling that somebody was going to draft him."

When Clemente told Haak that he wanted to leave the team, the Pirate scout warned him about the consequences, which could affect his career. If Clemente were to leave the team without permission, the parent Dodgers could place him on the suspended list, rendering him ineligible for the draft. No other major league team, including the Pirates, would then be able to take Clemente. Clemente might have to return to Montreal in 1955, buried in an organization that boasted proven outfielders like Jackie Robinson, Duke Snider and Carl Furillo, and a seeming "can't miss" prospect like Sandy Amoros. Thanks to the counsel of Haak, Roberto remained with Montreal.

Having heard about attempts at "hiding" him from scouts both inside and outside of the Brooklyn organization, Roberto was now convinced that Macon and the Dodgers had an ulterior motive in benching him. "The idea was to try to make me look bad," Clemente would say repeatedly during his life. Clemente claimed that whenever he enjoyed a profitable streak of hitting, Macon would bench him. Conversely, an unproductive 0-for-4 performance at the plate would merit another start the next day. To make matters worse, Macon didn't explain to Clemente why he played him so sporadically. "If they had talked to me, I would never have been so mad," Clemente said in a 1972 interview with Pat Livingston of the *Pittsburgh Press*. "But it came to where they never told me anything that was going on."

The Dodgers' alleged attempt at subterfuge might have had nothing to do with any efforts to "hide" him from other teams. Instead, the Dodgers may have had a more sinister desire—albeit a legal one—which would have made Clemente completely ineligible for the upcoming draft. Perhaps the Dodgers thought that they could treat Clemente so poorly and unfairly that the exasperated youngster would have no other choice but to bolt the team in mid-season and go home to Puerto Rico. As Haak had warned Roberto: if he were to jump the team without their permission, the parent Dodgers would have the right to suspend him, making him unavailable for the draft. That way, the Dodgers could keep Clemente in their organization, bringing him to the major leagues in 1955 or beyond.

Mayoral disagrees with this theory of Dodger subterfuge. "No, I don't think so," says Mayoral. "I know Al Campanis well." Mayoral doesn't believe that Campanis would have allowed such mistreatment of Clemente, as a way of trying to force him to bolt the team. "Al Campanis is the guy, who thanks to Pete Zorrilla, was able to sign Roberto for the Dodgers. I don't think there was anything behind that thought."

Up until his death in 1989, Max Macon repeatedly denied the allegation that the Dodger brass had ordered him to "hide" Clemente by restricting his playing time. Macon insisted that Buzzie Bavasi had given him but two directives: win games and draw fans; nothing was ever said about keeping Clemente on the bench as a way of preventing other teams from scouting him. According to Macon, the decision to play or sit Clemente was the manager's—and the manager's alone.

Although Macon recognized Clemente's abilities, especially with regard to his running, fielding and throwing, he harbored concerns about his hitting. Macon said that Clemente swung wildly, showing little discipline in taking pitches out of the strike zone. He almost always took the first pitch, which frequently put him behind in the count, making him more likely to swing at bad pitchers later in an at-bat. At times, International League pitchers made Clemente look so bad that Macon felt he had to take him out of the lineup.

Macon could also point to a few season-ending statistics for his other outfielders as evidence to support his claims. While with the Royals, Sandy Amoros batted .352, before earning a call-up to Brooklyn. Jack Cassini, who led all Montreal outfielders in games played, batted .286. Gino Cimoli hit .306, while playing in over 100 games. Dick Whitman batted a respectable .278, 21 points higher than Clemente. Although Roberto had the most physical talent of the top Montreal outfielders, the others had all posted better offensive numbers.

Even when Macon joined the Pirates organization as a territorial scouting director, he continued to refute the existence of a Clemente "cover-up." Whenever the two men met, usually during spring training, Macon insisted that he had not tried to make him look bad, or prevent other scouts from watching him play. To his credit, Clemente harbored no grudge against Macon, but still didn't believe him. Others, like Clyde Sukeforth and Howie Haak, didn't either.

Nor does Luis Mayoral. "I didn't meet the manager," Mayoral says of Macon and his protestations against the accusations of hiding, "but I think that was a public relations answer. I think that everyone knows that they had the draft in those days, which I guess is similar to what happens nowadays with the Rule Five draft."

Joe Black never talked to Macon about his handling of Clemente, but has no doubts that the Dodgers were trying to hide him. "Everybody knew it," says Black, who asked other players and scouts about the situation. "I said, 'Why is he practicing with the pitchers?' They said, 'Well, you know, they're trying to hide him from the scouts.'" One of Macon's policies in playing Clemente lends further support to the theory. "He started second games of doubleheaders," Black says. "Of course, some scouts—most scouts—never stayed for two games of doubleheaders."

The routine of scattered playing time continued for the rest of the season, worsening during the final month of the season, when

Clemente failed to play in the team's final 25 games. Even though Clemente would come to bat only 148 times for Montreal, with a mediocre average of .257, the Pirates were not fooled. Given his inconsistent pattern of playing time, his statistics meant little. The scouting reports produced by Sukeforth indicated that the Pirates should take Clemente, assuming they had the first choice in the draft.

As expected, the 1954 Pirates did their part by finishing last, with a record of 53-101 and a deficit of 44 games in the standings. Rickey realized that he needed to rebuild the organization's farm system, while populating the major league team with as much young talent as he could find. The first pick in the draft of minor league players, created by the rule limiting bonuses, would supply Rickey with at least one potential piece of the reconstruction.

"Well, we had the draft meeting at Mr. Rickey's farm outside of Pittsburgh," Sukeforth recalls. "He called the meeting to order. 'We have the first draft choice, as you know. Who are we going to draft?'

"Two or three guys spoke up. One guy wanted a fellow in the Southern League. Another wanted a fellow on the coast. Mr. Rickey said to me, 'Clyde, what would your choice be?'

"I said, 'Clemente is definitely our man.'

"In the meantime, Mr. Rickey called another of our scouts and asked him if he'd seen Clemente. He didn't like his arm. Rickey asked me, 'Did you see his arm?'

"'I sure did. One of the finest arms I've ever seen. I'd compare it favorably to Furillo.'"

Rickey was close to being convinced that he should use his No. 1 draft choice on Clemente—but not completely. Although Rickey respected the judgment of Sukeforth, "The Mahatma" still had a few doubts. He had not yet seen Clemente for himself.

Knowing that Clemente was scheduled to play a third consecutive winter ball season with Santurce, Rickey would get his chance. In the middle of the winter league campaign, Rickey flew to Puerto Rico to watch his prospective draft choice in person. With the draft still a couple of weeks away, Rickey would be able to watch Clemente play in 10 games before finalizing his decision. The timing of Rickey's visit could not have been better. At that juncture, Clemente was playing left field and hitting well over .400, battling his teammate in center field, Willie Mays, for the league batting title. Much like it had with Haak and Sukeforth, Clemente's all-round play captivated Rickey. After watching him play, Rickey prepared to question the outfielder, to measure his character and his confidence. "Can you do the same thing in the major leagues?" Rickey asked almost immediately. Still struggling with the English language and perhaps intimidated by Rickey's direct approach, Clemente offered an unsure answer. "I don't know," replied the winter league star. "I don't know if your players in the United States are better than the ones in our country."

Given the confidence—some might say arrogance—displayed by Clemente in later years, such an answer seemed inconsistent with his personality. But Roberto was still only 20 years old. He had never played against a major league team, only against winter league and minor league teams that had some major leaguers. In giving such an unclear response to Rickey, Clemente was simply being honest and respectful. The major leagues were an entity that he did not yet know or fully understand.

Rickey might have been disturbed by Clemente's lack of bravado, but if he was, he didn't let it affect his draft strategy. On November 22, 1954, after the initial urgings of Clyde Sukeforth, the follow-up work of Haak, and his own first-hand scouting trip, Branch Rickey drafted Roberto Clemente from the Brooklyn Dodgers' organization for the bargain price of $4,000.

According to Luis Mayoral, the Dodgers had simply made a calculated gamble, only to come up short. "Hey, they took a chance," says Mayoral philosophically. "They figured, 'If we have him down there [in Montreal], and we play him occasionally, well then there may be an opening in '56 or '57, whenever.' They just took the chance, and they lost it."

Other teams settled for the leftovers provided by the bonus draft. The Kansas City Athletics, baseball's newest team, selected pitcher Cloyd Boyer, the older brother of future major league third basemen Clete and Ken. The Chicago Cubs tabbed a journeyman outfielder named Jim King. The New York Giants, who could have had Clemente had they been more aggressive just one winter ago, settled for a journeyman catcher named Mickey Grasso. None of these selections were legitimate prospects. Not like Clemente.

Timing had played a big part in the Pirates' landing of Clemente. If it had been any other season, Clemente would have remained Dodger property. "That particular draft rule lasted only one year," Al Campanis explained to Dick Young, referring to the $4,000 maximum bonus rule that was put in place after the 1953 season. "If we had signed Clemente the year before or the year after, he would have played his lifetime with the Dodgers."

On the surface, losing a player who had hit in the mid-.250s with virtually no power and had accumulated only one outfield assist seemed like a non-story to Dodger followers. But Dodger insiders knew better. Max Macon knew, as did Al Campanis. So did Buzzie Bavasi, even though he refused to concede that the Dodgers had made a mistake.

New York Giants manager Leo Durocher claimed that the Dodgers' primary purpose in originally signing Clemente had involved a desire to keep the talented youngster away from his team, Brooklyn's cross-town rivals. In the July 1955 edition of *Baseball Digest*, Buzzie Bavasi would back up Durocher's claim about the Dodgers' "preemptive strike." "Leo's right," said Bavasi. "We didn't want the Giants to have Willie Mays and Clemente in the same outfield and be the big attraction in New York. The main point was to keep the Giants from claiming him...The main point is that the Giants don't have him."

Bavasi retraced the history of the Dodgers' pursuit of Clemente. "We were very friendly with the fellow who owned Clemente's contract in Puerto Rico," Bavasi explained, referring to Pedrin Zorrilla. "[We] had to give Clemente what he wanted because the Braves were after him also." Bavasi's recollection differed from that of Clemente, who claimed that he had fulfilled a promise he made to the Dodgers before the Braves had even entered the negotiation.

"The Giants wanted him badly," Bavasi told *The Sporting News*, "but didn't want to make him a bonus boy and have him sit on the bench. But we didn't care as long as we nailed him." Even though the Dodgers had laid out $15,000 for Clemente, they had thought they could get their money back after another team drafted him. "We put him on the Montreal roster, exposing him to the unrestricted draft, figuring we could get back our original investment. We have a letter from the commissioner's office to the effect that we could get back our investment if he were drafted, but then we later learned all we could collect was $4,000. So, all right. It cost us $6,000 actually, but the Giants didn't get him, which was the important thing." In actuality, the loss of Clemente cost the Dodgers more than $6,000. They had also paid Roberto a salary of $5,000 for a year of non-contribution at Montreal, bringing the total tab to $11,000.

A reporter asked why the Dodgers had played Clemente so little at Montreal. "We knew we were going to lose him in the draft," Bavasi responded, "so why should we spend the time developing him for another team. We used the players who would belong to us [in the long run], and Clemente played defense in the late innings or went up as a pinch-hitter." If that was truly the Dodgers' approach with regard to Clemente, it contradicted what Max Macon would say over and over again: that he was under no such orders from Brooklyn to keep Clemente tied to the bench.

Bavasi continued to react to the loss of Clemente philosophically, almost matter-of-factly. Yet, others in baseball disagreed with Bavasi's contentions, claiming that he was simply trying to explain away a huge mistake by the Dodgers' front office. Those skeptics explained that the Dodgers could have held on to Clemente if they had signed him to a major league contract—and not a minor league deal with Montreal—and placed him on Brooklyn's 25-man roster. Why hadn't the Dodgers done just that?

The Dodgers argued that they already had three terrific starting outfielders in 1953: Jackie Robinson in left, Duke Snider in center, and Carl Furillo in right field. Although Robinson had played all four infield positions in 1953, he had played the majority of his games—76—in the outfield and had batted .329 with 17 stolen bases. Snider had enjoyed a spectacular season as the starting center fielder, batting .336 with 42 home runs and 126 RBIs. Although Furillo was the least heralded of the starting outfielders, he had led the National League in hitting with a .344 mark and owned, like Clemente, a cannon-like arm.

The Dodgers also possessed outfield depth. Left-handed hitters George Shuba and Don Thompson were decent backups capable of pinch-hitting and filling in on a short-term basis. The same could be said of the right-handed hitting Dick Williams (the future major league manager). Brooklyn also had a fine left field prospect in Sandy Amoros, who had played the 1953 season at Montreal, leading the International League in hitting with a .353 mark. With such depth, and such talents in the starting outfield, the Dodgers felt they had no room for Clemente. If they had rushed Clemente, a player with no minor league experience, to Brooklyn in 1954, he would have wasted away on the bench.

On the surface, the Dodgers' arguments made sense. Yet, if they truly felt that Clemente was such a great talent, a player whom they did not want to see teamed with Willie Mays in New York, they could have found room for him at the major league level in 1954. By the end of the 1953 season, Brooklyn's starting third baseman, Billy Cox, had turned 34 years old. Still an excellent defensive player on the infield, Cox had always been a mediocre hitter and had now been set back by injuries, which limited him to 100 games in 1953. If the Dodgers wanted to make room for Clemente, they could have traded Cox or demoted him to a utility role and moved Jackie Robinson to third base full-time. Such a move would have been neither unrealistic or impractical, considering that Robinson had actually played 44 games at third base in 1953.

Even if the Dodgers didn't think Clemente was ready for an everyday role in the major leagues, they could have inserted Sandy Amoros in left field and used Roberto as a fourth or fifth outfielder. Such a role would have seemed a natural for a player like Clemente, whose speed and defensive ability were already proven commodities. If a fourth or fifth outfielder could run, play defense and throw, he could be used as both a pinch-runner and a late inning defensive player; even at the age of 19, Clemente could have excelled in those areas. And with his hitting potential, Roberto might have been an option as a right-handed pinch-hitter against left-handed pitching. A major league team could have done far worse than have Clemente as a fourth or fifth outfielder.

So why didn't the Dodgers make more of an effort to find space on their roster for a player as talented as Clemente, a player whom they had already mentioned in the same breath with Willie Mays? The skeptics had their own theory: the Dodgers had reached their limit of blacks on the major league roster. In 1953, Roy Campanella, Jim Gilliam, Jackie Robinson and Joe Black had populated the Dodger roster with four blacks, which at the time was considered a substantial number. With Sandy Amoros scheduled for a promotion to Brooklyn and Don Newcombe set to return from military service in 1954, that would give the Dodgers potentially six blacks overall, including as many as four in the regular lineup. The addition of Clemente would stretch the quota to unthinkable bounds.

In 1954, the Dodgers operated under an unstated quota system of no more than four blacks in the lineup at any one time. On the days that Newcombe was scheduled to pitch, one of the black regulars might be benched. The Dodgers would supply some ambiguous reason for the lineup change, citing some mysterious "injury" or a particular difficulty that the player had against the other team's starting pitcher. It would be relatively easy to explain why a rookie like Amoros—who played in 70 games in 1954—wasn't playing on a given day, but the explanations became somewhat far-fetched when the benchings involved established stars like Campanella, Gilliam and Robinson.

Although a quota may have existed, some authorities don't believe that it had an impact on Clemente's exclusion from the Dodgers' major league roster in 1954. "I don't think it was because they had reached their quota of black players. I think they had a team all set up," contends Luis Mayoral, referring to the presence of Robinson, Snider and Furillo in an all-star outfield. Clemente's youth and lack of experience also played a part in the Dodgers' thinking. "Roberto was a rough diamond," Mayoral says, "but with another team he might have stayed up at the major league level." A last-place team, like the Pittsburgh Pirates.

After his scattered 1954 season in Montreal, Clemente had anxiously returned to Santurce for his third season of winter ball. The lack of playing time with the Royals had given Roberto extra motivation to play with the Crabbers, where he would surely play everyday in front of his native fans. Yet, changes had taken place in Santurce. New teammates included fellow major leaguers like infielder Don Zimmer, the future manager who had made his playing debut with Brooklyn in 1954, and power-hitting first baseman George Crowe. James Buster Clarkson was no longer the Santurce manager, having been replaced by New York Giants' coach Herman Franks.

That winter league campaign also afforded the fans of Puerto Rico the rare opportunity to watch two future Hall of Famers playing side-by-side in the same outfield. Crabbers' owner Pedrin Zorrilla had managed to lure New York Giants' star Willie Mays, who would play center field for Santurce, next to Clemente in left. "The first and only year that Clemente and Mays played together was 1954, right after Mays won the batting championship and the MVP Award in the National League," says Luis Mayoral. "November '54 through January of '55. And how this came to be is the fact that Zorrilla had many friends. Zorrilla is the guy who had contacts with so many major league clubs."

One of Zorrilla's contacts could be found in the front office of the Giants, where team owner Horace Stoneham had presided since 1936. "Zorrilla loved his Santurce baseball club," Mayoral says. "He had befriended Mr. Stoneham, the owner then of the Giants. It was during a party in New York prior to that 1954-55 winter season that they were having drinks. And Pete would always say laughing that he got Mr. Stoneham drunk, and that's the only way Stoneham gave him permission to have Willie Mays go and play in Puerto Rico."

While Clemente and Mays grabbed most of the attention because of their youthful promise, Santurce also owned another terrific outfielder, one who lacked youth but boasted talent and experience. Veteran Negro League star Bob Thurman rounded out the Santurce outfield, while also providing the Crabbers with some much needed thump from the left side of the plate. Although Thurman was already 37 years old, he still retained the speed and power that had made him one of the perennially dynamic players in winter league play. Thurman would hit 14 homers during the winter of 1954-55, a substantial amount for a season that lasted approximately 70 games. With Thurman, Mays and Clemente patrolling the outer reaches of Sixto Escobar Stadium together, some winter league fans called Santurce's threesome the best outfield combination they had ever seen—major league or otherwise.

With Mays as his teammate, Herman Franks in place as his manager, and a former major league outfielder named Luis Olmo providing a substantial influence, Clemente enjoyed one of his finest winter league seasons. Clemente also adopted a facet of outfield play that would become his trademark: the basket catch. The origins of Clemente's basket catch would also become the focus of long-standing dispute.

Nellie King, a former Pirate pitcher and broadcaster, once asked Clemente how he learned to catch the ball in his unusual style. Through his conversations with Clemente, King recalls the origin of the basket catch. "He said, 'I used to play with a tennis ball when I'd go to bed, and I was a young kid, you know. I'd love to play ball. I would get a tennis ball and I would throw it up over the bed right near the ceiling and try to catch it while you're laying down. If you try to catch a tennis ball the way most guys catch a ball in the outfield with their glove facing up, you cannot see the ball. You hold the glove down around the belt, then you can watch the ball all the way into the glove, you know.' It makes sense. You're a little kid and you're laying in the bed, and you keep throwing it up like that. That's why he started catching fly balls that way."

Some baseball historians claimed that Clemente borrowed the basket catch from Willie Mays, who had been making such waist-level catches in the major leagues since his rookie season of 1951. Clemente insisted otherwise. "No, I don't learn the basket catch from Mays," Clemente would tell John Carroll of United Press in later years. "It was Luis Olmo and Herman Franks who teach me when I in Dodger chain. That back in 1954 winter league." Clemente's reasoning finds support in the voice of Luis Mayoral. "I do recall, that way before Clemente, before Willie Mays came up," Mayoral says, "the man people in Puerto Rico said was the greatest fielder, and the man that people in Puerto Rico pinpoint the basket catch to—that was Luis Olmo. If Roberto copied the basket catch from anyone, it was Luis Olmo, not from Willie Mays."

Although an American outfielder might have been influenced by Mays, and a Puerto Rican player like Olmo, who used the basket catch on occasion during his days as an outfielder, neither had been the original inventor of the unique style of snaring fly balls. That honor went to former major league infielder Bill Rigney, who had begun his eight-year career with the New York Giants in 1946. Splitting his time between second and third base, Rigney sometimes caught high pop-ups with his palms up and his hands near his waist.

During his early professional career, Clemente had approached the catching of fly balls like most other outfielders, with his hands outstretched above his head. "I miss fly ball many time because I try to catch too high," Clemente revealed to the United Press. Realizing his difficulty, which may have been caused by depth perception, Franks and Olmo told Clemente to try keeping his hands at chest-level. Clemente accepted the suggestion, finding the method a more comfortable way to make catches. He eventually dropped his hands even further, making catches at his waistline. Unlike Mays, he sometimes made catches even lower, at his thighs or just above his knees. The basket catch also supplied an unintended benefit. "It make it more easy for me to throw, too, after I make the catch."

In spite of such benefits, critics of Clemente and Mays chided the superstars for the basket catch, calling it a "showoff" or "hot dog" play, which they felt set a bad example for youngsters learning to play the outfield. Late in his career, Clemente defended the play when he claimed that he had never dropped a fly ball while executing the basket catch. "It work good for me and I just keep doing it."

In addition to developing and refining his own basket catch, Clemente hit marvelously in winter league play. After teasing the

.400 mark—and convincing Branch Rickey to take him in the draft—Roberto settled at a season-ending .355.

Spearheaded by the dream outfield of Clemente, Mays and Bob Thurman, Santurce captured the Puerto Rican Winter League championship. The regular season title qualified Santurce for the Caribbean World Series, an annual event that, from 1949 to 1960, featured the champions of winter league play in Cuba, Panama, Puerto Rico and Venezuela.

The four representatives played in a round-robin tournament. In one of the early round games, Santurce played Magallanes, the champions of the Venezuelan League. The two clubs matched each other through 10 innings. In the 11th, Clemente faced Ramon Monzant, a major league pitcher who had hurled for the New York Giants in 1954. Clemente reached base against Monzant, bringing Willie Mays to the plate to face his Giants teammate. Mays, in an 0-for-12 Caribbean World Series slump, smashed a gargantuan home run against Monzant, scoring Clemente with the game-winning home run. Lifted by the dramatic victory that had been provided by Clemente and Mays, the Crabbers went on to win the Caribbean World Series. For the third straight year, a team from Puerto Rico had claimed the winter leagues' crowning event.

Although Clemente and Mays spent the entire winter league regular season and Caribbean World Series together, they did not forge a particularly strong relationship. "Roberto and I spoke about Mays several times," recalls Luis Mayoral. "I don't think they were friend friends; they were teammates. But I don't think they were really too close. I don't think they were buddy-buddy. I never got that impression from Roberto."

3

This is Pittsburgh, Not Puerto Rico

In 1955, Roberto Clemente joined a struggling Pittsburgh Pirates' team that featured only a handful of notable players. First baseman Dale Long and outfielder Frank Thomas, who led the Pirates in home runs and RBIs in 1954, represented the only run producers in the everyday lineup. Young pitchers like Bob Friend and Vernon Law had struggled, but would soon become winners. Promising shortstop Dick Groat and young reliever Elroy "Roy" Face would also begin to display their talents. The aforementioned group of players would provide the Pirates with a smattering of bright spots on an otherwise dismally talent-barren and aging roster.

The offseason of 1954-55 brought not only the good news of a new team destination—with the Pirates figuring to afford Clemente a regular job at the major league level—and a winter league championship, but resulted in misfortune, as well. Roberto's older brother Luis fell ill, victimized by a brain tumor. Doctors could not treat the tumor, which they deemed inoperable. On New Year's Eve, 1954, Luis died in a hospital bed in San Juan. Although the family realized that Luis' condition was serious, they did not expect him to die so quickly.

After one of his final visits to Luis' hospital bed, Roberto drove home through the streets of San Juan. While maneuvering his car through a busy intersection, Roberto's vehicle was struck broadside by a drunk driver, who had run a red light at the speed of 60 miles per hour. The impact of the crash jarred three of Clemente's spinal discs, causing him recurrent back pain for the rest of his career. The damage would limit Clemente's playing time occasionally, especially when he reached his mid-thirties. As a result of his back's weakened condition, Clemente would develop a ritual both before and during many of his at-bats. He would rhythmically rotate his head and neck, sometimes flicking his neck side to side. The movements became part of his habitual effort to loosen the muscles in his back.

In the meantime, Clemente's new team needed loads of help. Not only had the Pirates finished last in 1954, enabling them to pick up Clemente, they had also ruled the cellar in 1952 and '53.

Roberto reported to spring training in Fort Myers, Florida, where the Pirates were training for the first time. Like the team's other rookies and minor leaguers, Clemente dressed in a section of the clubhouse called the "outhouse." Racial prejudice played no part in the Pirates' decision to place Clemente in this second-class back room; even young white players had to locker there. The group included an unknown minor league second baseman named Bill Mazeroski, who joined Clemente in the "outhouse."

Clemente did encounter racism, however. It happened almost immediately. The initial dose came from the local media in south Florida. "The first day that I get to Fort Myers," Clemente recalled in a 1972 interview with Sam Nover, "there was a newspaper down there. The newspaper said, 'Puerto Rican hot dog arrives in town.' So now, these people never knew nothing about me, but they know I was a Puerto Rican. As soon as I got to camp, they tell me I'm a Puerto Rican hot dog." The label irritated Clemente, who rightly felt that he was being derogatorily stereotyped.

Clemente approached the other Latin American players in camp, a group that included outfielders Felipe Montemayor and Roman Mejias. "I talked to some of the Latin players and they told me, 'Roberto, you better keep your mouth shut, because they will ship you back [to the minors.]' I said, 'I don't care one way or the other. If I am good enough to play, I have to be good enough to be treated like the rest of the players. So I don't want to be put in the bathroom because I came from here from Puerto Rico.'"

Racism also manifested itself in an even uglier form when the Pirates played the Baltimore Orioles in an exhibition game at Birmingham, Alabama. Due to the sports segregation ordinance adopted by the city in 1954, the Pirates' three dark-skinned players—Clemente, Roman Mejias and Curt Roberts—could not dress for the game. For the first time in his life, Clemente had been told he could not play because of the color of his complexion.

As a 26-year-old right-handed pitcher vying for a spot on the Pirates' pitching staff, Nellie King first met Clemente during the spring of 1955. "I don't think anybody understood this," says King, "but he never had to deal with racial prejudice because they didn't deal with that in Puerto Rico. Race was something he did not have to contend with in Puerto Rico," says King. "This, coupled with his native personal pride, created deep emotional problems for him."

Yet, racism ranked as only one of several hurdles. As King points out, Roberto faced a number of other first-year obstacles, some of which had not even affected the pioneering Jackie Robinson during his historic integration of major league baseball eight years earlier. While Robinson had dealt with monumental problems of race and ethnic abuse, he did not have to overcome the kinds of cultural differences experienced by Clemente.

"Number one, Roberto did not speak the language," says King. "Number two, he was in a cultural twilight zone." In contrast, Robinson did not have to acclimate himself to playing in a foreign country, with its differing sets of behaviors and expectations. Robinson also had the benefit of added years of wisdom. By the time he debuted for the Dodgers, Robinson had already turned 28. When Clemente stepped onto a major league field for the first time, he was barely past his teenage years. "You can imagine," King says, "what a change it was for a kid of only 20 years of age playing at that level of sports having to deal with those things."

An eight-year veteran of minor league pitching, King was attending his second major league spring training in 1955. Although much older than Clemente, King was faced with a similar chore: trying to crack the Opening Day roster and establish himself as a major leaguer. "I was unaware of him or others, as I was trying to stay afloat in the big ocean of competition among pitchers," King admits. "It was just like you're in the ocean, you're trying to swim, you don't notice anybody else around you, you're just trying to stay afloat. I really didn't know Roberto very much."

While absorbed in his own baseball struggles, King did emerge from spring training with some distinct impressions of Clemente—the player. "He was inexperienced," says King, "but you could see the natural talents of speed, powerful body and a magnificent throwing arm. He just knocked your eyes out with the things he could do. Physically, he threw the ball so well. Wasn't as accurate as he was later. He was just an enthusiastic ballplayer who put the ball in play."

Like most other Pirates, King did not know much about Clemente personally. He did not socialize with Clemente away from the ballpark. "I was married," says King. "He was not. I never saw much of Roberto, to be honest with you, on the social scene." Those experiences would come much later for the future Pirate broadcaster.

As spring training progressed, manager Fred Haney began to shape plans for his revamped outfield. Left field appeared to be the property of veteran Frank Thomas, who had hit .298 with 23 home runs and 94 RBIs in 1954. Two other players, Tom Saffell and Earl Smith, figured to platoon in center field.

In right field, Haney hinted that he might also institute a platoon. The left-handed hitting Felipe Montemayor, who had batted .309 for New Orleans in 1954, would play against right-handed pitchers. That would leave Roberto Clemente "against the other type of pitching," as indicated by Pirate beat writer Jack Hernon in the April 13th edition of *The Sporting News.*

The list of outfield contenders also included Roman Mejias, a young Cuban who batted .355 in his first 45 spring training at bats. In 1954, Mejias had compiled a startling 55-game hitting streak for Waco of the Big State League. After finishing the minor league season with a .355 mark, and continuing to impress Haney and Branch Rickey in the spring, the Pirates decided to reward Mejias with a major league contract.

Clemente also hit superbly in the spring, compiling what Jack Hernon described as a "sound" .395 average in March and April. It might have been the first time in baseball history that an average so close to .400 had been described in such minimalist terms. Curiously, Hernon would criticize Clemente much later in his career, calling him both a poor hitter in the clutch and a malcontent. Hernon remained a critic up until his death from cancer in 1966. During the final year of the 48-year-old writer's life, Hernon and Clemente did not speak.

Although his spring training hitting had been categorized as merely "sound," a breakdown of Clemente's 17 hits revealed much more than that. The tally included two home runs, two triples and a double.

Yet, Mejias had impressed Haney even more. The manager decided to make the hard-hitting Cuban his Opening Day right fielder. Tom Saffell won the center field job, beating out Earl Smith. Veteran holdover Frank Thomas remained in left field. That left Clemente and Smith as the odd men out.

Just prior to the start of his first major league season, Roberto came upon an unusual way to select the uniform number that he would wear for the Pirates. Roberto and a new-found friend went to see a movie in the city's downtown section. Moments prior to the start of the film, Roberto picked up a piece of scrap paper that he saw on the movie house floor. He took a pen and proceeded to write out the letters of his full name:

R-O-B-E-R-T-O C-L-E-M-E-N-T-E-W-A-L-K-E-R.

Roberto counted the letters, which totaled 21. He had found the uniform number that he would wear for the rest of his playing career.

Contrary to some revisionist history, Clemente did not begin his major league career in full-fledged stardom. He did not even crack the starting lineup penned by Fred Haney. Clemente possessed all the requisite talents, but they were raw, far from their refined stages. With only one year of minor league experience tucked into his resume, Clemente still had much work to do, and abilities to prove. Stardom would have to wait, for a much longer time than Clemente and the Pirates would anticipate.

On Opening Day, Clemente felt a series of mixed emotions. While he had made it to the major leagues, he would have to sit on the bench, watching his future roommate play right field. Batting out of the third spot, Mejias went 1-for-3 on Opening Day in Brooklyn. Roberto did not get a chance to play, not even as a pinch-runner or defensive replacement, as he had so often been used in Montreal. Mejias went 1-for-4 in his next game, and then looked bad in an 0-for-4 performance. Clemente did not leave the bench in any of the three games, all losses for the Pirates.

On April 17, as the Pirates prepared to play a traditional Sunday doubleheader at Forbes Field, manager Fred Haney made a lineup change. The Pittsburgh skipper replaced Mejias' name with that of Clemente's. After three seasons of winter league baseball, a disjointed campaign in the International League, a full spring training in Fort Myers, and three more games of idling on the bench, Roberto Clemente found himself in a major league starting lineup for the first time in his life.

Ironically, Haney called on Clemente to play his first game against his original organization—the Brooklyn Dodgers. Left-hander Johnny Podres, who had won 11 games for the second-place Dodgers in 1954, quickly disposed of Earl Smith and second baseman Gene Freese to start the first inning. Batting out of the prestigious No. 3 position in the order—often reserved for the team's best pure hitter—Clemente rapped a hard, bounding ball toward the left side of the infield. Brooklyn's shortstop, the nifty-fielding Harold "Pee Wee" Reese, knocked down the smash with his glove. By the time Reese retrieved the ball and threw to Gil Hodges, the hard-running Clemente had already reached first base. The official scorer ruled the play a base hit—the correct call. Clemente was now 1-for-1 as a major leaguer.

Clemente's single would prove profitable, as he came around to score on a triple by Frank Thomas, giving the Pirates a 1-0 lead. The Pirates would expand the lead to two runs, only to lose their fourth straight game, a 10-3 blasting at the hands of the Dodgers. Still, Clemente had impressed Haney enough to merit a start in the second game of the doubleheader.

Even though the Dodgers would throw tough right-hander Clem Labine in the nightcap, Haney inserted Clemente into the leadoff spot. Now playing center field in place of Earl Smith, Clemente collected two more hits in game two—a single and a double—giving him a total of three hits for his inaugural day in the major leagues. Unfortunately, Clemente's offensive outburst could not prevent a difficult 3-2 loss, and a sweep at the hands of the mighty Dodgers.

The next day, Haney returned Clemente to the No. 3 hole in the lineup, while also switching him back to right field. The newfound starting outfielder continued to show off his speed and hitting skills, while adding a dash of power to the recipe. Playing at the oddly-configured Polo Grounds against the Giants—yet another team that had missed its opportunity to lasso Clemente's services as a player—Roberto rounded the bases for an inside-the park home run. Roberto also picked up another hit, and threw out his first runner from the outfield. Although the Pirates would lose the game, 12-3, Clemente's initial major league blast, struck in the fifth inning against diminutive left-hander Don Liddle, wrapped up all of his offensive abilities into an attractive display lasting less than 20 seconds; the home run exhibited Clemente's strength as a line drive hitter capable of reaching the gaps, while showing off the speed that had so glaringly caught the eye of Brooklyn talent-seeker Al Campanis only three years earlier.

Haney continued his lineup juggle in the next game, a road affair at Philadelphia, as he moved Clemente back to the leadoff spot and the center field position. Roberto enjoyed his least productive game to date, but still managed a triple in five at-bats. Much to the displeasure of Clemente, the Pirates blew a four-run lead in the bottom of the ninth. The defeat gave the Bucs seven straight losses to start the season.

Playing an afternoon game on Saturday after their Friday night matchup with the Phillies, Haney gave Clemente the day off. Tom Saffell played center and Felipe Montemayor remained in right field. The two young outfielders combined to go 1-for-8. The Pirates lost again, an incompetent 8-0 setback to Phillies' starter Murry Dickson. There would be no more rest for Clemente, who would play both ends of the doubleheader on Sunday.

Inserted in center field, Roberto rapped out two hits and two RBIs in the first game, and first baseman Dale Long posted a four-hit day, spearheading the Bucs to their first win of the season. Finally, after eight consecutive defeats, one short of tying the modern day National League record to start the season, the Pirates had posted a 6-1 win.

In the nightcap, Clemente went 1-for-4 before Pennsylvania curfew laws suspended play in the eighth inning. The curfew temporarily stopped Clemente's hitting, whereas National League pitchers had not. He had picked up nine hits in his first full week as a regular, while playing against some of the National League's finest pitching. Opposing hurlers like Johnny Podres, Clem Labine, and Don Liddle did not quite know how to approach such an aggressive hitter in their pitching patterns. Roberto not only swung at any pitches thrown over the plate; he offered at any pitches in the general vicinity of the strike zone determined by the senior circuit's arbiters. Unlike other free swingers who chopped at pitches and missed often, Clemente could reach deliveries thrown well off the plate and hit them hard in all directions.

When Clemente didn't make contact with stray pitches, he showed his anger. After striking out, Roberto often fired his helmet to the ground. The display of temper prompted a quick lecture from the usually soft-spoken Fred Haney, who fined him $25 on the spot and warned him that he would have to pay for any broken equipment, including helmets. By his own estimate, Clemente cracked 22 plastic hats during his rookie season. With each helmets costing $10, Roberto owed the Pirates $220 at season's end.

On April 27, Clemente had little reason to pound his helmets off the grass and dirt of Forbes Field. Roberto enjoyed the fourth two-hit game of his young career, while driving in two more runs out of the leadoff spot. The parade of hits against the Chicago Cubs pushed Clemente into the National League's list of top 10 hitters. Since moving into the lineup 10 days earlier, he had accumulated 11 hits in 30 at-bats, including a home run and six RBIs. Clemente's .367 average nudged him past the Giants' Willie Mays, who was hitting .362. Although the season was still very early, Clemente appeared to be one of the best first-year players in the National League.

After his first seven games in the lineup, Clemente's hitting cooled off. It was not until April 28, in a game against the Cincinnati Reds, that Clemente failed to notch at least one hit. The next day, Fred Haney slid Clemente back to right field, where he would play almost exclusively the rest of the season. Although Clemente played center field adequately, he seemed more comfortable in right. More importantly, his supreme throwing ability mandated a move to right field, a position that required a strong arm to deter runners from advancing too frequently from first to third base.

In right field, Clemente's defensive play truly shined. In his first 50 games, he would register a whopping 10 assists—including four in a five-game stretch—a season's worth for some of the league's finest defensive outfielders. His throwing capacity impressed the most, but his other fielding skills ranked only a bit behind. A preseason scouting report had indicated that Clemente struggled in retreating for fly balls hit over his head, but Fred Haney and the Pirate coaches quickly found that report to be flawed. Relishing the challenge of playing the spacious right field environs at Forbes Field, Clemente ran with abandon, covering ground like a wide-ranging infielder. Unlike his brethren on the infield, Clemente had to track baseballs over a far larger strip of land, which he did exceptionally, whether they be ground ball singles, line drives in the gaps, or fly balls to the depths of the warning track.

On May 4, the Pirates staged their most dramatic victory of the season, a game that saw Clemente at his fielding worst—and best. The Pirates led the Wednesday evening tilt at Forbes Field, 5-3, to start the ninth inning. With one out, the Milwaukee Braves put runners on first and second. Fred Haney lifted his tiring starting pitcher, Max Surkont, and called upon his best reliever, Bob Friend. Pinch-hitter Andy Pafko grounded into a force play for the inning's second out. Right fielder Hank Aaron followed with a single, scoring a run. After fielding Aaron's single cleanly in right field, Clemente threw wildly, allowing both Pafko and Aaron to move up a base. Partly due to Clemente's overly aggressive throw—which typified his early career inability to hit the cut-off man—the Braves had placed the tying run on third, and the potential go-ahead run at second.

With the Pirates clinging to the 5-4 lead, Friend faced left-handed-hitting first baseman George Crowe. The Milwaukee slugger, one of Clemente's teammates during the winter league season, lofted a high drive toward right field. Judging by the force of his swing and the height of the ball, Crowe's drive appeared to have enough distance to clear the fence for a three-run homer. Clemente backed up, and backed up some more, eventually planting himself in front of the right field stands. Timing his leap rhythmically with the trajectory of the ball, Clemente stretched his glove over the fence into the bleachers. Clemente's one-handed grab of Crowe's apparent home run ended the game, preserving the lead—and the win—for the Pirates. Thanks to Clemente's brilliant glovework, the Bucs had won their fourth straight game.

Clemente didn't like the right field territories at either of the New York ballparks—Ebbets Field and the Polo Grounds—because of the unpredictable bounces that rang off their outfield and corner walls. In contrast, Clemente enjoyed playing the open-spaced right field at Forbes Field, Even though the right field walls featured a mix of wire screening and concrete, Clemente learned to play the caroms through study and repetition. The fans at Forbes also made his experiences at home games more palatable; they loved the exciting style that he featured, especially his dynamic array of throwing and fielding plays. So quickly popular that he had become in Pittsburgh, Clemente regularly stepped to the plate amidst a background of standing and cheering fans.

Part of Clemente's popularity stemmed from his willingness to interact with the fans. Made to feel unwelcome by some of his insensitive veteran teammates—some of whom didn't like him because he was black—Clemente often spent two to three hours signing autographs after home games. In between games of doubleheaders, some fans rewarded Clemente by bringing him sandwiches and other snacks.

Clemente's good looks also contributed to his status as a fan favorite. Pirates' executive Joe L. Brown, who encountered Clemente for the first time in the spring of '55, says the right fielder's striking physical features left an immediate impression. "I thought he was physically a very attractive man, facially. And in uniform, of course, he always looked good," says Brown. "He was very attractive to women of a certain age, just at first sight," says former *Pittsburgh Press* writer Roy McHugh. "He was without flaw physically." With his handsome face, broad shoulders, marvelous chest and lean torso, Clemente found himself besieged by teenage girls and young ladies in their twenties. They often approached him after games, asking for autographs. He even accepted dates with a few of the young ladies, but none became steady girlfriends. Roberto had no time for that; his first priority was playing baseball.

After a fast start at the plate, which had him leading all Pirate regulars at one juncture in April, Roberto started to struggle. On May 12, Fred Haney made a lineup change affecting Clemente. Haney dropped Clemente from the leadoff spot, a position that did not suit him to begin with because of his extreme aggressiveness in swinging at pitches. Roberto would now bat out of the more appropriate third slot in the batting order, at least for a few games.

Clemente also had to sit out a smattering of games in May, but for reasons other than his inconsistent bat. In making a fine catch against the St. Louis Cardinals, Clemente jammed a finger against the outfield wall at Sportsman's Park. The sore finger forced Clemente to miss a game. The injury, while a relatively minor one, would represent the first of many ailments for the fragile outfielder. On May 26, Clemente's spikes caught in the turf during a pre-game workout at Forbes Field. The slightly sprained ankle shelved Clemente for four games. Later in the season, Clemente would miss an occasional game with back pain, an offshoot from the off-season car wreck that had damaged his spinal discs.

After spraining his ankle, Roberto returned to the lineup for the second game of a doubleheader on May 29. He hit like he never had before in a single major league game, collecting five straight hits against the Phillies. The barrage included three doubles, helping the Bucs to an 8-3 lead. A cautious Fred Haney interrupted Clemente's performance in the seventh inning, lifting him for a pinch-running Roman Mejias. Moments later, Pennsylvania's curfew law interrupted the game for all of the participants.

Clemente would accumulate a sixth consecutive hit the next day. Batting out of the leadoff spot, Roberto singled against Brooklyn's Russ Meyer in his first at-bat. Clemente went hitless the rest of the game, before bouncing back with two hits against right-hander Don Newcombe in the second game of the twinbill. Considering Newcombe's tough, side-winding motion and hard fastball, not to mention his 8-0 record, Clemente's hitting ranked as even more noteworthy.

In June, Clemente fumbled through a spotty stretch of batting, picking up just one safety in eight games. For the first time all season, Roberto found himself wading through a legitimate batting slump. He hit the ball hard at times, but right at opposing fielders. A hitless effort against the Cardinals on June 14 dropped his season average to .275. Only 10 days earlier, Clemente had been hitting 40 points higher.

Prior to his slump, Clemente had hit safely in 37 of his first 44 games. He had been leading the team in hitting. His defensive play in right field remained spectacular throughout. Yet, Roberto chafed at the quality of his overall play. "I no play so gut yet," said Clemente, as quoted as saying by Les Biederman of the *Pittsburgh Press.* "Me like hot weather, veree hot. I no run fast cold weather. No get warm in cold. No get warm, no play gut. You see."

Aside from explaining his preference for warmer weather, the quotation illustrated subtle racism toward Clemente, and all Latin American players. Biederman tried to quote Clemente phonetically, substituting unusual spellings for words as a way of conveying the distinctive accent of the Latino ballplayer. Writers like Biederman may have been striving for accuracy—Clemente didn't say the word "good," but rather something that sounded like "gut," they might have argued—but when read from the written page, such quotations made Latin American players sound unintelligent, almost primitive, and proved distracting to the reader. Without the benefit of actually hearing the player speak, made-up words like "gut" and "veree" served to exaggerate the crudeness of the language. As a result, the Latino player sounded worse in the newspaper or magazine story than he might have in person.

Such journalistic habits angered Clemente. "Of course, it pissed him off to the day he died," says Luis Mayoral. "To the day he died. He felt that they were making fun of him. He would always say to me, 'Those SOB's know only one language [English]; I know good Spanish and my English is getting better everyday.'"

"He resisted the writers' practice," says Marcos Breton, a senior writer for the *Sacramento Bee* and an expert on Latin American baseball. "There's been throughout the course of baseball history, the Latin player—all you have to do is go and read the clips and you'll see the making fun of the way that they talked. The big joke, 'Baseball has been berry, berry good to me.' It became a comedy routine on Saturday Night Live and that has stuck in people's minds. But Clemente was a man who refused to play the clown and wanted to be judged on his own terms, as somebody who should be recognized for the things that he did on the field."

Latino players like Clemente may have wondered why writers didn't phonetically account for the pronounced accents of other players, such as those who hailed from the South, or Brooklyn, or Boston, or anyone of a number of geographic regions. Since those players spoke English that was far from perfect, why didn't those same writers see fit to change the spellings of certain words to reflect the unusual sound of their language? The writers, it seemed, had enforced a double standard on the Latin American player.

"I think it was ignorance on the part of people then," says Nellie King of the writers' tendencies to report quotations phonetically. "They never had to deal [with Latinos]. They were white guys, and for the first time, they're finally dealing with black people, you know. The culture at that time in this country was difficult. You had to be white and you had to speak English." Yet, King doesn't believe that the culture of the 1950s should excuse the practices of the writers. "I still don't understand why people did quote that way. They should have corrected the guy's grammar rather than writing it the way he said."

Difficulties with the language made Clemente feel less than comfortable in Pittsburgh. He had learned additional English since his days in Montreal, but not enough to put him at ease with many of his teammates, fans, or baseball writers. "Language naturally was a problem," Nellie King says of Clemente's early relationship with the media. "With a very limited vocabulary in English, misconceptions between him and the media were at times embarrassing and almost constant." Few, if any writers, made any efforts to learn Spanish, even though the Pirates now had three Latin American players on their roster.

The language barriers also created problems in game situations. During a spring training game against the Baltimore Orioles on April 9, both Clemente and Roman Mejias had run through stop signs costing the Pirates two big scoring innings. After the game, Fred Haney held a meeting with the two rookies, whose inability to fully understand their coaches' words had contributed to their baserunning mistakes. To his credit, Haney took the initiative, buying a Spanish-language dictionary that would help him communicate with his confused rookies.

Other major league managers of the day held a less sympathetic view toward their Latin American players. In April, Washington Senators' skipper Chuck Dressen had coldly instructed the four Cuban players on his roster to learn English—and do it quickly. "I can't send over to the United Nations for an interpreter every time I want to give a sign," Dressen snapped sarcastically. "I want the Cubans to learn English good enough to get the signs and talk some baseball," Dressen told *The Sporting News.* "They don't seem to have any trouble picking up enough English to order their meals." Yes, life in the major leagues could have been worse for Roberto Clemente. He could have had Chuck Dressen as his first manager.

Although Haney made some effort to communicate with Clemente in Spanish, few of his teammates extended olive branches. The Pirates of 1955 consisted of several fragmented units. Fading veteran players wanted to hold on to their tenuous positions with the ballclub; therefore they made little effort to help rookies, like Clemente, who posed a threat to their playing time. "I think the guys in '55—most of them were in their waning years," recalls Nellie King, himself one of the team's young, unproven players. "They were just trying to grab another year out of the game, and I can't blame them. There was not a whole lot of effort made to say, 'Let me help you. I'll show you how to take my job.'" In turn, the younger players felt less secure, making them more concerned with their own plights and less apt to sympathize with their fellow teammates who were also unproven and unsure of themselves. In addition, several white players felt little inclination to associate with black players, a group that included the dark-skinned Clemente.

"He always stated—not particularly about 1955—he always stated that since he came to play professionally in the United States, he always fought for being treated fairly," says Luis Mayoral, who now serves as a liaison for Latin American players with the Texas Rangers. "If he was a major league player, he had to be treated like a major league citizen. The problem there, you gotta remember it was only eight years after [Jackie] Robinson broke the color barrier. So, Roberto had his struggles. There was not, like me with Texas, a guy to help him bridge, and vice versa, help the Anglos bridge with the Latinos. And remember he was alone. He was alone in a country he didn't know."

Clemente did find an ally, but one who did not play baseball. "Now there was a guy who really helped him out a lot," Mayoral explains. "His name was Phil Dorsey. Phil Dorsey was a postal employee. He was also a member of the National Guard in the same unit as Bob Friend, the Pirates pitcher. Bob Friend told Phil Dorsey, who's African American, 'Hey, we have this guy on the team. He's Puerto Rican, he's black; maybe you can help him.' And to the day of his death, Roberto's best friend in Pittsburgh was Phil Dorsey."

During a pre-game workout held at Forbes Field near Opening Day, Friend had introduced Clemente to Dorsey. The two struck up a quick conversation. When Dorsey found out that Clemente did not own a car, he invited him to go to dinner at a local restaurant before dropping him off at his hotel. The two men hit it off immediately, with Dorsey fast becoming a combination of chauffeur, confidant, business manager, and most of all, a valued friend to Clemente.

"Roberto was a young kid, black, looking for some association," Nellie King explains. "This guy was a good friend for him when he first came up. Roberto never forgot people. As I've said, he never forgot where he came from, and he never forgot this kid, I'm sure, because you're 20 years old in a strange country and you finally meet somebody who's really helpful and kind. I guess Phil was that way—Roberto liked him."

At the start of the season, Clemente had lived in a dilapidated hotel called Webster Hall, with its oppressively hot rooms. The aging, uncomfortable residence afforded Clemente a short commute to Forbes Field, but little else. When Dorsey found out how much the hotel was charging in rent, he suggested that Roberto move out. Clemente soon found a place to stay in a home owned by Mr. and Mrs. Stanley Garland, a friendly middle-class couple who lived in Schenley Heights. Roberto shared a room there with teammate Roman Mejias. Dorsey often stopped by, becoming a de facto third roommate to the rookies from Latin America. Dorsey paid Roberto many visits during the morning hours, reminding him that it was time to wake up and get ready for the day. The two friends then walked to Forbes Field together.

During his rookie season, Clemente spent much of his time attending movies with Dorsey. The American cinema provided Clemente with opportunities to observe actors like Errol Flynn and Tyrone Power speaking the English language. Roberto often dined with Mejias, who spoke practically no English, even less than Roberto. On trips to New York, they often ate at a Puerto Rican restaurant located near the Commodore Hotel, where the Pirates always stayed. Clemente and Mejias often dined on fried bananas, beans, rice and steaks, the kinds of food that Roberto preferred from his days growing up in Puerto Rico.

Other than Mejias, Clemente had only one other Latin American teammate during his first season, Mexican outfielder Felipe Montemayor. He had only one teammate of African-American descent, light-hitting second baseman Curt Roberts, who had been the first black player in the history of the Pirates' franchise. Clemente didn't like the way that opposing players taunted Roberts. Accomplished "bench jockeys" shouted racial slurs from the other dugout, loud enough for Roberts to hear. Sometimes Clemente walked to the far end of the dugout, so he wouldn't have to hear words like "nigger." At other times, Clemente stood up and glared at the other team's dugout, or at his own white teammates, who said nothing to defend the honor of their minority brethren.

Clemente also burned over the way some of his own Pirate teammates treated Roberts. Rather than let such behavior pass without comment, Clemente took a stand. "I didn't like some of the things the white players said to Roberts," Clemente recalled in a 1971 interview with Milton Richman of United Press International, "so I said some things to them they didn't like."

Racism was not limited to the playing field, or the clubhouse. Some fans treated Clemente ignorantly. One asked him if he wore a loin cloth in his native Puerto Rico. Other, more mean-spirited fans mailed him letters of hate, warning him that he should return to his "jungle." On one occasion, a local police officer spotted Clemente talking to two white girls, who had asked him for an autograph. Referring to him as a "boy," the policeman told Clemente to leave the girls alone.

Clemente also faced the typical anxieties that plague most major league rookies. In later years, Clemente detailed his first-year fears for Nellie King.The former Pirate pitcher and broadcaster remembers Clemente's clear portrayal of his own anxious feeling. "I was so afraid of making a mistake in right field," Clemente told King,"that I had tunnel vision. I would concentrate so much on the hitter, I never even saw the pitcher, first or second baseman between me and the hitter. I saw only the hitter."While such a singular approach made sense for a hitter in facing a pitcher, it prevented an outfielder from anticipating certain pitches and detecting defensive shifts among the infielders.

Fortunately for Clemente, the tunnel vision soon eroded."After a couple of weeks," Clemente explained to King, "I began to relax and noticed the first baseman, the second baseman, and then the pitcher. As I became more comfortable, I started to see the shortstop, the third baseman, then the left fielder and center fielder." As King relived his conversation with Clemente, he marveled at Roberto's eloquence in describing the changes in his own vision and outlook."I began to relax and gain confidence," said Clemente. "Now instead of being outside the picture, I was in the picture, and could see it all."The playing field, at first limited and filled with tension, had become serene and familiar, a stage for Clemente to perform and excel.

By season's end, the difficulties experienced by a rookie who was playing in a new country, unfamiliar with the language, and uncomfortable with the racism surrounding him, had taken their toll. The Pirates' unyielding habit of losing games didn't help either. Clemente's final average came to rest at .255, a far cry from the blazing averages that he had posted in April and May.

Some members of the Pirates' organization had their doubts about Clemente's staying power in the major leagues. Was he ready? Had he been rushed? Would he be able to make the needed adjustments in his struggle to hit major league pitching? In later years, Clemente would admit that he had been brought to the major leagues too quickly. "I wasn't ready for the majors when I joined the Pirates in 1955," Clemente told Les Biederman of the *Pittsburgh Press* nine years later. "I was too young and didn't know my way around."At times, Roberto sought the advice of his older brother Matino, who had starred in amateur baseball before having his career interrupted by the Korean War. Roberto asked him for help on how to handle inside pitches.

National League pitchers had come to realize two distinct, but related flaws in Clemente's hitting approach. First, he swung at too many pitches, regardless of their proximity to home plate. After his prosperous start, pitchers began taking advantage of his free-swinging tendencies; one writer said Clemente's expansive strike zone stretched from one dugout to the other, a description that explained his paltry total of 18 walks. Second, Clemente habitually and needlessly bobbed his head during his swing, which pulled his eyes away from the pitched ball, resulting in a cascade of strikeouts.

Clemente's power numbers weren't much better. The unsavory proportions of Forbes Field, with its long dimensions in left-center and right-center field, hadn't helped a gap hitter like Clemente. Still, the Pirates had hoped for more than a mere five home runs and 47 RBIs, coming from a position—right field—that was expected to produce a fleet of runs for his team. Since Roberto hadn't stolen many bases or scored many runs, either, he had failed in almost all of the major offensive categories. Only his defensive play in the field ranked as above average. That, of course, smacked of star quality.

As Pirates' executive Joe Brown recalls, Clemente's lack of experience hindered his first season. "I would say that it was obvious that he had not played much professional baseball, that he had things to learn," says Brown. "But it was even more obvious that he had great talent. There wasn't anything he couldn't do; he just had to learn by playing more on the major league level." While Clemente's final statistics reflected his offensive shortcomings, he had certainly flashed enough physical talent to give the Pirates hope. He had also helped the team improve slightly, from a 53-win season in 1954 to a 60-win campaign in 1955. Yet, the Pirates had not improved enough in the standings to lift themselves from last place. They had finished 38 and a half games back of the first-place Dodgers. Even the second-to-last place Cardinals owned an eight-game advantage on the Pirates.

The repeated last-place finish cost the soft-spoken Fred Haney his job. Bobby Bragan replaced him in the manager's office. Even team president Branch Rickey had seen enough of the perennial rebuilding project in Pittsburgh. "The Mahatma" retired from the Pirates' presidency, opting to become the club's "Chairman of the Board." The baseball decisions would now be made by young executive Joe Brown.

4

Frustration in the Fifties

C lemente became the last of the Pirates to sign his 1956 contract. After the briefest of hold-outs, which lasted about a day, he negotiated a small raise with Branch Rickey, Jr., the son of "The Mahatma," who served as the organization's minor league director.

On Opening Day, Bobby Bragan sent a message to his players that he would have little tolerance for mental mistakes. With Johnny O'Brien on third and one out, Bragan instructed Clemente to lay down a squeeze bunt. O'Brien broke for home, but Clemente took a full swing and fouled the pitch off. Bragan fined Clemente $25 for missing the sign. Bragan also docked first baseman Dale Long $25 for erroneously cutting off a throw from the outfield in the ninth inning.

In addition to cracking down on his mental lapses, the Pirates realized that they needed to do some work with Clemente as a hitter. Conceding that he owned an unorthodox batting style, the coaching staff allowed him to stand nearly 20 inches from home plate and continue his tendency of striding toward third base. But the club did want him to make some changes. While acknowledging his natural aggressiveness, the Pirates believed that his habit of swinging at almost any pitch in sight had reached the point of foolishness. He needed to show some restraint at the plate. The Pirates also sought to eliminate his incessant head-bobbing, which served no benefit to his batting. Pirates' management called upon batting instructor George Sisler, a Hall of Fame first baseman, to provide Clemente with the necessary counsel about the art of hitting.

"He was moving his head around," Sisler told Jack Hernon of the *Pittsburgh Post-Gazette*. "It was up in the air most of the time when he swung. That's why he was troubled so much by curves. Now after one bit of instruction, he is holding his head steady." Yet, Sisler did like other aspects of Clemente's approach to hitting. "A thinking hitter, the kind I like," Sisler told Al Abrams of the *Post-Gazette*. "I don't like guess hitters."

Under the tutelage of Sisler, Clemente's early-season batting average ballooned. In the first game of a June 10 doubleheader against the Cardinals, he enjoyed his first three-hit day of the season. On June 12, he homered to extend his hitting streak to 12 games, pushing his average to a gaudy .357, the third-best figure in the National League. Thanks in large part to the early returns of his sophomore engagement, the Pirates owned first place. Although the Pirates—and Clemente—would slump shortly thereafter, the second-year right fielder had given warning to pitchers throughout the National League.

Although he had been hired by the Pirates only months before, Joe Brown quickly proved his expertise as a procurer of baseball talent. In his first major move as general manager, Brown acted aggressively. On May 17, he traded journeyman pitcher Dick Littlefield and one of the organization's top prospects, minor league outfielder Bobby Del Greco, to the St. Louis Cardinals. In return, Brown acquired center fielder Bill Virdon, the National League's "Rookie of the Year" in 1955.

The move smacked of brilliance. Virdon was only 24 years old, just one year the elder of Del Greco. Del Greco was a terrific prospect, but Virdon had already proved he could play at the major league level. He had batted .281, collected 17 home runs and played center field with precision and finesse. Who knew if Del Greco, who had played most of his professional career in the minor leagues, would be able to hit National League pitching?

The acquisition of Virdon provided Clemente with a suitable dance partner in the outfield. The move also insured that Roberto would remain in right field, and would no longer have to move to center at the whim of his manager. Yes, Clemente could play center field, but not nearly at the level of his mastery of right field. Furthermore, the demands of chasing fly balls in center field figured to drain Clemente, making him weaker, more injury-prone, and more susceptible to batting slumps.

As Nellie King recalls, the atmosphere surrounding the Pirates of 1956 was far different than that of the 1955 team, for which Clemente had debuted. "I think 1956 saw an unbelievable change in the team," King says. "I really enjoyed that [team]. They went with an all-young team; they got rid of the older ballplayers on the team. They went with the Branch Rickey crew that he had scouted: Clemente, Mazeroski, [Dick] Groat, [Bob] Skinner, Virdon, Friend, [Vernon] Law. We were in first place in June, just enjoying it, and Clemente was a very important part of that."

Clemente also felt more comfortable living in Pittsburgh. Improved in his ability to handle the language, Clemente spoke more easily and more often with fans and teammates. His relationships with some of the Pirates blossomed. One veteran teammate, in particular, made a special effort to improve the lockerroom atmosphere, while also connecting with Clemente. "It was a great clubhouse," King says. "There was great leadership. And the guy that provided it first was Dale Long." The 30-year-old first baseman kidded Clemente good-naturedly, unlike the mean-spirited treatment some of the Pirates had given Roberto in his first season. Long made Clemente feel relevant in the Pittsburgh clubhouse. For the first time, Roberto felt that his presence and his feelings mattered in the context of the Pirate lockerroom.

With Long taking a leadership role, Clemente felt more secure about his stature with the Pirates. "There was no talking behind the back of anybody," King says in describing Long's law. "Everything was done right out front. And nobody was [considered] better than anybody in the clubhouse." Pirate players, at least when speaking in the public setting of the clubhouse, no longer regarded Latino players like Clemente as second-class citizens.

With Clemente feeling more comfortable, his play improved. In early July, Clemente made one of the finest fielding plays of his early career. In the third inning, Dusty Rhodes of the New York Giants vaulted a drive toward right field. Clemente gave chase, running hard to the right-center field gap. As he neared the wall, he reached out with his left arm, snaring the ball with a backhand grab.The running catch snuffed out a New York rally, and drew the admiration of Giants' outfielder Willie Mays, who tipped his helmet in Clemente's direction.

Clemente's outstanding defensive play throughout the season actually created a minor controversy. According to Nellie King, a writer approached Clemente during the 1956 season and complimented him on his fielding and throwing.The writer called him the best defensive right fielder in the game. Instead of responding with false modesty, or even sincere humility, Clemente seconded the opinion of the writer. "Yes, I feel I am very good and have dedicated myself to being the best right fielder in baseball," Clemente said.

"His response reported in the media," says King, "brought comments from players, media types and fans. 'Who does this guy think he is?' said some people. 'He's been in the league only two years and he thinks he's the best right fielder in the game.' It came off as bragging and arrogance."

In this particular situation, a cultural difference between the United States and Puerto Rico had created a misunderstanding. "In Puerto Rico, if someone pays you a compliment, you are expected to accept the compliment and thank them," King says.As Clemente once explained to the Pirate broadcaster and former teammate, "If a fellow tells you that you are the best plumber in Puerto Rico, you are supposed to respond to him, 'Thank you. I feel I have learned my trade and I am proud of the work I do and am the best in the trade.' In Puerto Rico, it is expected for you to accept a compliment."

Such a reaction contrasted with how an American might respond to a compliment. "In the United States," King said, "if someone pays you a compliment, you shuffle your feet and say, 'Aw shucks, I'm not that good,' and the person will tell you two or three times more how good you are. In America, you are expected to be humble."

When Clemente reacted in the way that a typical Puerto Rican might have, with honesty and pride, the media roasted him for perceived arrogance. "It was not meant that way," King says, "but it was a cultural difference that created misunderstandings between these groups.Americans, I believe, are [actually] more arrogant. We expect everyone to have the same feelings and beliefs that we have."

Clemente once explained to King some of the general characteristics of Puerto Ricans. "'Nellie,' he said, 'Puerto Rican people, they're the nicest people. They will give you the shirt off your back. If they love you, they will give you anything. But I'll tell you something, if they do not like you and tell you not to come around, [then don't]. They wear their emotions on their sleeves; there's no bull— with those people.'"

As the season progressed, Clemente became even more popular with the fans. On July 24, he contributed a home run and triple, the big hits in a 6-2 win over the Cubs. During the game, Roberto received a louder ovation each time he came to the plate. As Charles Doyle wrote in the *Pittsburgh Sun-Telegraph,* "the fans discovered a new hero—right fielder Roberto Clemente."

Clemente did suffer setbacks, however, especially in terms of public perception. In one game, Roberto came to the plate in the ninth inning, the Pirates down to their last out. With the Pirates needing a run, preferably a home run to tie the game, Clemente opted for some odd strategy. He tried, but failed, to beat out a bunt, bringing an unexpected ending to the game.

Moments later, Bobby Bragan approached Roberto. The manager asked him why he had decided to bunt, when the Pirates really needed a longball, or at least an extra base hit. According to Bragan, Clemente responded with the following explanation: "Boss, me no feel like home run today."

Pirate beat writers jotted down the comic quotation, using it to illustrate the naivete of a young player. Whether or not Clemente actually said those words, in that exact sequence, remains a debatable point. Regardless, the attribution made him sound stupid, both in terms of baseball logic and general intellect. Once again, the insistence on attaching Clemente's words to broken, grammatically incorrect English embellished the stereotyped notion of the Latin American player's primitive thinking skills.

Clemente's early baserunning also become a source of consternation. An incident in 1956 underscored his naivete on the basepaths. On July 25, Clemente stepped to the plate in the ninth inning against Cubs' pitcher Jim Brosnan. Although the Pirates had loaded the bases with no out, they still trailed Chicago, 8-5. "We get up in the ninth inning, and Turk Lown's pitching," recalls Nellie King, who had entered the game in the top half of the ninth, throwing one pitch to end the inning. "[Lown] gives up a hit, walks two and loads the bases. They bring in Brosnan, who takes his warm-up pitches." Clemente stepped in against the 26-year-old right-hander and promptly powered a hanging slider into the gap, scoring all three runners to tie the game. "Clemente's at bat, with three on, nobody out," says King, "and he hits the ball near the light tower in the ballpark, just next to the scoreboard in left-center. [The ball's] in play, and they try to hold Clemente at third base." As he approached the base with what appeared to be a stand-up triple, Roberto eyed his manager Bobby Bragan, who doubled as third base coach. With the heart of the Pirates' order coming up, Bragan held up his arms, signaling Clemente to stop. "He runs through the sign, and he's just safe at home plate," King recalls. "We won the ballgame. Clemente just ran through the sign."

After the game, someone asked Bragan whether he thought Clemente was going to stop at third. "No, sir," Bragan told Jack Hernon of the *Pittsburgh Post-Gazette.* "When I got a look at him coming past the shortstop's position, I knew my signal didn't mean a thing. He was just then shifting into high gear."

Clemente both heard and saw Bragan's stop sign, but deliberately ran through it. "I say to Bobby [Bragan]: 'Get out of my way, and I score,'" Clemente explained to the Associated Press. "Just like that. I think we have nothing to lose, as we got the score tied without my run, and if I score, the game—she is over and we don't have to play no more tonight." The Pirates didn't have to play any more, as Clemente slid into home plate ahead of the tag. The unusual inside-the-park, grand slam home run against Brosnan gave the Pirates 9-8 win over the Cubs. As Brosnan wrote in the October 24, 1960 edition of *Life Magazine,* Clemente's feat "excited fans, startled the manager, shocked me and disgusted my club."

Although Clemente had committed a fundamental error—trying to score a run on a potentially close play with no one out—Bragan handled the mistake appropriately. Given Clemente's hustle on the play and its ultimate success, Bragan excused the mistake. The manager added that there would be no $25 fine, usually a standard punishment for a player who had missed a sign.

Clemente's overzealous romp against the Cubs typified the recklessness of his early baserunning. In later years, Clemente admitted to his errors on the basepaths, poking fun at himself in the process. As Nellie King recalls, Clemente occasionally tried to repair his baserunning mistakes by duping the umpires. "He used to tell me, 'You know, Nellie, when I was young I would run on fly balls hit to the outfield.' He says, 'I'd go round second base and I suddenly realize the ball is going to be caught. Sometimes I would run across the infield and never re-touch second base. Sometimes the umpires wouldn't notice it if the players wouldn't. I didn't know how to run the bases well the first couple of years.'" Clemente would eventually become a more accomplished baserunner. Though still aggressive and daring, he would learn to recognize the limits of his own speed while coming to respect the abilities of other outfielders.

After the Pirates' season came to a close, Clemente showed few limitations with regard to his hitting in winter league play. Despite being sold by the Santurce Crabbers to the Caguas Criollos in mid-season (a move that was prompted by Pedrin Zorrilla's decision to sell the Crabbers), Clemente flirted with a .400 batting average. He entered the final game of the season at .398, but went 1-for-4 to finish with a .396 mark. Still, Clemente won the Puerto Rican Winter League batting title by an overwhelming 63 points.

The benefits of major league life began to pay dividends in the off-season. Clemente's much improved second season earned him a raise from Joe Brown, who was far more generous handing out checks than his notoriously thrifty predecessor, Branch Rickey. Armed with a more substantial major league salary, Clemente bought his parents a new $12,500 suburban home in Puerto Rico. Rather than spend new-found money on himself, Roberto thought first of paying back his parents for their years of loyalty and love. It was typical Clemente.

Clemente had started complaining of a sore back in July of 1956, during a series against the Reds. The pain eventually went away, only to return after the first three or four days of spring training. He felt discomfort in the lower left side of the back when he tried to run or throw, two frequent occurrences for a professional baseball player. In fact, he felt jabs to his lower back whenever he tried to do anything that required shifting his weight to the left side of his body.

In response to the problem, the Pirates' medical staff suggested a number of remedies: heat, ultrasound, whirlpool sessions, even injections. The latter treatment seemed to concern Clemente. "I don't know [about] this injections," Clemente told George Kiseda of the *Pittsburgh Sun-Telegraph.* "I never feel like this before. Oh, my head. Dizzy, dizzy."

The mysterious back problems caused some Pittsburgh writers to write about an alleged division between Clemente and his manager, Bobby Bragan. A few scribes speculated that Bragan considered Clemente's back pain a "mental" problem, rather than a physical one. They wrote that Bragan questioned the sincerity of any back difficulties, suggesting that the manager thought the root of the pain might be psychosomatic in nature.

The writings of the press called into question the relationship between player and manager. Clemente disputed that contention. "He know I like to play," Roberto insisted in an interview with George Kiseda, before explaining that he had never had trouble with Bragan. "Never in my life. I say he's best manager I ever play for." In turn, Bragan enjoyed having Clemente on his team. "He was likable, you know, very easy to get along with," Bragan tells researcher Andrew O'Toole. "Never a problem at all for the manager. Always on time."

The recollections of players like Nellie King support the notion of a strong relationship between Clemente and Bragan. "He [Bragan] loved the guy," King says emphatically. "He let him play, and [Roberto] flowered under him as a young kid." While some players resented Bragan's ego and starvation for acclaim, Clemente seemed to appreciate the manager's all-out desire to win. "Bragan was a unique guy," says King. "He loved attention. He wanted to get attention himself. He was a colorful guy. He played each game like it was the last game you were ever gonna play all year. He used everybody [to win a game]. If a guy was going good, he used him, you know. I remember, he used to take Mazeroski out [of the game] before he even got a chance to bat. He'd pinch-hit for him the first time that he came up with a runner in scoring position."

Clemente also tried to refute the idea that he was sitting out games for reasons other than an actual injury. "I get sick when I see somebody play and I can't play," Clemente told the *Pittsburgh Sun-Telegraph.* In spite of his denials, several writers questioned his motivation. One scribe speculated that Clemente might have made the injury up as a means of showing his displeasure with playing in Pittsburgh. "The story's all over town that he wants to get away from the Pirates in the worst way," Davis J. Walsh wrote in the April 12 edition of the *Pittsburgh Sun-Telegraph.* "Is Roberto Clemente's back trouble real or imagined?" pondered Ray Kienzl, another writer for the *Sun-Telegraph.* Insinuations of hypochondria had begun.

According to general manager Joe Brown, questions about Clemente's injuries resulted from two factors. "There was a lack of communication. Clemente didn't speak English [then] as well as he does now," Brown said in a 1970 interview with Charley Feeney of the *Pittsburgh Post-Gazette.* "Second, when he is hurt, he can do a lot of things better than most players can do when they are healthy. Then people wonder: 'How can he do that when he is hurt?'"

The Bucs' team physician ordered a set of X-rays to be taken on Clemente's back, but the examination showed no specific cause of the problems. As a result of the spring back pains, Clemente sat on the bench to start the new season. He deferred the right field position to Roman Mejias, who remained a perennial prospect in the Pirates' scheme of things.

Back pains persisted through July. Whenever he swung hard, the pains became especially excruciating. Clemente became so discouraged that he talked of retiring. "No one knows what it is," a confused Roberto told the United Press. "I run, I throw, I move, it hurts. It goes away and comes back. Someday it hurt, someday no. If it doesn't cure, I quit baseball. No fool around."

The Pirates sent Clemente to Presbyterian Hospital for a series of tests on his back. After a 10-day stay, a doctor suggested another possible origin of the back problem. Having examined Roberto's tonsils, the doctor noticed that they had become slightly infected. He felt the tonsils may have been causing the pain in his lower back, and ordered their immediate removal.

Unfortunately, the backaches persisted. One doctor talked about the possibility of an operation. Clemente didn't like that idea; a brother and a sister had died while undergoing surgery. "I don't think my mother and father let me take operation," Clemente told George Kiseda of the *Pittsburgh Sun-Telegraph.*

Clemente also raised the possibility of early retirement. "I won't play ball in the winter," Roberto predicted. "I gonna rest. If the pain is still there, I won't come back to spring training." His back pains had become such a problem that they had led to him dropping a nearly routine fly ball in a recent game against the Reds. "I don't want to play the way I play now. I can't do nothing. That's like I steal money from the club."

Clemente's injuries prevented him from aiding a ballclub that needed all too much help. On August 3, with the Pirates' record a miserable 36-66, Joe Brown decided to fire Bobby Bragan. Three days earlier, the unpredictable Bragan had infuriated the National League office by returning to the field after an ejection and offering the umpires a sip from a small carton of orange juice that he had carried onto the field.

Several players defended Bragan's work as manager, including team captain Dick Groat, pitcher Vernon Law and Clemente himself."How you gonna win when everybody play bad?" Clemente asked George Kiseda."How you gonna manage if players can't play? He's good manager."

When Brown first made the decision to fire Bragan, he offered the managing job to team scout and Clemente finder Clyde Sukeforth. At the beginning of the 1947 season, the suspension of Brooklyn Dodgers manager Leo Durocher had elevated Sukeforth to the post of interim manager.The timing had proved intriguing, allowing Sukeforth to become the first major league manager in the career of Jackie Robinson. That brief managerial stint had apparently sufficed for Sukeforth. Preferring the security of a scouting position to the hassles of managing a rebuilding ballclub, Sukeforth turned down Brown's offer to become Pirate skipper.

Brown's next choice? Pirates' coach Danny Murtaugh, a former major league second baseman who figured to bring grit and determination to the Pittsburgh dugout.While the selection of Murtaugh would benefit the Pirates in the long run, it would also result in problems between the manager from Chester, Pennsylvania and the star player from Carolina, Puerto Rico.

Clemente's mediocre performance in his third season—the worst year of his major league career—prompted trade rumors in the spring of 1958. In the March 30th edition of the *Pittsburgh Sun-Telegraph*, Davis J.Walsh reported the Milwaukee Braves' interest in trading for a right-handed hitting outfielder, either Clemente or Roman Mejias. In exchange, the Braves reportedly offered young left-hander Juan Pizarro, one of Puerto Rico's best home grown talents.

"I think other teams were interested in him, but we never had any intent of trading him," says Joe Brown."[Even] if we wanted to trade him, we wouldn't have gotten what his potential was. And to trade away a player with his kind of potential before he had reached it, you'd be selling really at a pretty discounted price, which would be foolish."

On April 30, Clemente made a snap sidearm throw in a game against the LosAngeles Dodgers."I hear it crack," Clemente explained two years later in an interview with Joe King of the *World Telegram*. The force of the sudden throw led to the development of a bone chip in his right elbow."It feels like needles in there," said Clemente. "I do not throw hard until it is needed." Clemente could still unleash bombastic throws from the right field corner; he just needed to be more selective in doing so.

Injuries such as bone chips in his elbow would cause problems between Clemente and Danny Murtaugh. Although Murtaugh would prove a sagacious managerial choice for the Pirates overall, he did not mesh well with his budding star in right field. Whereas Clemente enjoyed a common approach to the game with Bobby Bragan, he and Murtaugh differed in backgrounds and personalities. Murtaugh, a toughened Irishman from a poor neighborhood in Chester, Pennsylvania, felt players should continue to perform even when hurt; Clemente believed that playing with injuries could embarrass himself and hurt the team. "Danny came up the hard way," explains Nellie King. "You know, those guys who chew tobacco and spit on their injuries. I think there was quite a misunderstanding between Clemente and him with regard to [playing hurt]. Roberto had a bad back that one year in '57 or '58, and Danny never quite understood that. Murtaugh said, 'Get out and play.' Clemente responded, 'No, I'm not going to play.' So they never got together very well at all." Clemente believed that Murtaugh had labeled him a hypochondriac, a tag he would have difficulty shaking over the balance of his career.

In spite of his problems with Murtaugh, Clemente's continuing defensive brilliance, coupled with his offensive rebirth, helped the Pirates improve to second in the 1958 National League pennant race. Only the Milwaukee Braves of Hank Aaron, Eddie Mathews, Lew Burdette and Warren Spahn finished higher in the standings.

While Clemente's play remained somewhat inconsistent in quality, it did not waver in excitement. With runners on base, any ball hit to right field became a source of anticipation for fans, who wondered if Clemente might unleash one of his patented powerful throws. Drives to the gap and bloopers to short right field often resulted in a furious chase by Clemente, who repeatedly ran out from underneath his poor-fitting cap. Even on routine plays, Clemente entertained fans with his delightfully unorthodox basket catch.

On the basepaths, Roberto sometimes made poor decisions and ran through stop signs, but his style of running stamped him differently from any other player. Unlike fast runners who appeared to move effortlessly, Clemente churned his body with the force of an engine. He huffed as he ran, kicking his knees high and flailing his elbows furiously. Yet, he also exhibited grace with his distinct form of motion. Clemente's legs and arms appeared to be flowing in a myriad of directions, frenetically but gracefully. Watching him run, he offered observers and fans a strange mix of pounding effort and athletic finesse.

When Clemente stepped onto the field, his charismatic presence drew a unique response from those who had gathered at Forbes Field. Many fans hailed Clemente with a unique chant, which had originated with former Negro League pitcher Lino Donoso and Pirate broadcaster Bob Prince. Donoso, who played for the Pirates in 1955 and '56, had nicknamed Clemente "Arriba," a Spanish word that has several translations in English. Literally, it means "upstairs," but also carries the connotation of "lifting" or "arising." When Clemente stepped to the plate, lashed out a hit, or made a standout play in the field, Prince—a lover of nicknames—raised his voice with the pleasure of emphasis and purred, "Arriba." In essence, Prince was asking the fans to rise up, much like a modern day scoreboard encourages fans with words like "Charge!" or "Let's Go!" Pittsburgh fans soon caught on, serenading Clemente with their own recurrent chants of "Arriba." Many fans didn't know what they were saying, but the lyrical Spanish word seemed to fit the dynamic playing style of Clemente.

At first intimidated by his foreign culture surroundings, Clemente gradually adjusted to the ways of life in the states, and in Pittsburgh. He learned to relax by listening to classical music in his Pittsburgh apartment. There he kept some of his favorite records, which he had transported from the extensive collection of classical music that he maintained in his Puerto Rican home. Clemente also enjoyed reading, which helped him improve his understanding of the English language. Clemente's tastes varied, from the basic grammar of popular comic books to the more sophisticated selections of American history. "The comics are for laughs," Clemente told Harry Keck of *The Sporting News*, "and the history for the improvement of the mind." In contrast to the stereotype of the unintelligent athlete, and the even more unfortunate notion of Latin American illiteracy, Clemente wanted to learn—both about the language and the American culture.

As a key member of the Pirates front office, Joe Brown held Clemente's ability to think and reason in high regard. "I've got to mention something that very few people have mentioned," says the former Pirate general manager. "And I've mentioned it almost every time I talk to anybody when they ask about Clemente. I speak about his intelligence, and nobody ever mentions it. Nobody ever recognizes how very, very smart he was—intelligent. He was also intelligent in his business affairs, in his dealings with people. He had a perception, an intellect that was somewhat unusual." Brown respected Clemente's intelligence so much that he would call on him for advice repeatedly during his tenure as general manager.

All in all, Clemente had played well in 1958, but the spasms in his back caused him anguish. No one could have known at the time, but an upcoming stint in the U.S. Marines would prove a worthy remedy. After the season, Clemente reported to the Marine training camp in Parris Island, South Carolina, where he embarked on a six-month tour of duty. The military regimen, complete with daily sets of calisthenics, eased the soreness and pain in Clemente's back. By the time the 1959 season began, Roberto felt as if the suffering of back pains had ended.

In 1959, the Pirates made a key six-player deal, trading little-used players Whammy Douglas, Jim Pendleton and Johnny Powers to the Cincinnati Reds for catcher Smokey Burgess, third baseman Don Hoak and pitcher Harvey Haddix. Burgess, an exceptional pinch-hitter capable of reaching the seats, gave the Pirates a fine left-handed hitting catcher. Hoak provided power and defense at third base, while Haddix fortified the depth of the starting rotation. In addition, the Pirates promoted two promising hitters from the minor leagues: first baseman Rocky Nelson and outfielder Joe Christopher.

Joe Christopher, a young outfielder from the Virgin Islands, had met Clemente several years earlier but first became familiar with him in 1959. Christopher soon learned about Clemente's rapidly developing social conscience. "Well, I became friendly with him in spring training," says Christopher, "when the idea came to him that he wanted this place for kids in Puerto Rico. Actually the idea came to him when we used to look at old movies on TV about Father Flanagan and Boys Town. That's when he said he would like to do something of the same magnitude in Puerto Rico for the kids. That's when the whole idea started." The seeds of the "Roberto Clemente Sports City," an athletic complex for underprivileged children, had been sown.

Christopher learned more about Clemente when he shared hotel rooms with him during the regular season. "I really enjoyed being his roommate," says Christopher of his experiences with Clemente in '59 and '60. "I really enjoyed the man and appreciated what he had to deal with. Because deep in his heart he was a very, very sensitive, very caring individual. He was always wanting to give other people respect. Clemente, to me, was one of the nicest men I ever met."

Clemente's bat sizzled during the early part of the '59 season, but the lack of recognition from the media disturbed him. "I remember in 1959 he carried the team for the first two months of the season," says Christopher, who made his major league debut that year. "Clemente was the kind of man that wanted respect for whatever he did. All he wanted was to get the recognition for what he did. Sometimes he didn't believe he was getting that recognition. Clemente was the kind of ballplayer who liked to be told how he was doing: 'If I've done something right, tell me. If I've done something wrong, tell me.' All he was looking for was the truth."

Unfortunately, the truth included a badly swollen elbow. On May 25, Clemente paid a visit to the 30-day disabled list and saw his place taken—ironically enough—by Christopher, who had started the season in the minor leagues. Upon his return in early July, Clemente continued to hit well, but the interruption prevented him from putting together the kind of monster season that his terrific start had forewarned. Clemente finished the year with a .296 batting average, four home runs and 50 RBIs in 105 games. Another good year, but not a great one.

5

What if the Dodgers Had Kept Clemente?

The Dodgers played their final game in Brooklyn in 1957. Much to the near-hatred of Dodger fans, Brooklyn owner Walter O'Malley announced the move of the franchise to Los Angeles. In light of the exodus from New York City's greater metropolitan region, some baseball historians have pondered the following question: might the Dodgers' fate have been different, if they had somehow retained the playing services of one Roberto Clemente?

While it might be an awful burden to place on the shoulders of one man—in this case one player—Clemente's presence in a Dodgers' uniform might have functioned as a drawing card in Brooklyn. Thousands of Puerto Rican natives had moved to the borough and its surrounding regions since the end of the World War II, creating an untapped source of spectatorship for O'Malley's club. Although the Dodgers boasted several black players, who might have created interested among the black community, they had virtually no Latin American presence on their club. By the end of the 1957 season, the Dodgers had brought only one Latino to the majors: Sandy Amoros, who was Cuban, and not Puerto Rican. More importantly, Amoros had failed to live up to his minor league expectations. In his first five seasons, he had reached high-water marks of only .277 and 16 home runs. Amoros had performed decently as a sometime starter and fourth outfielder, but could hardly be expected to lure thousands of Latin American fans to Ebbets Field with his presence alone.

In contrast, New York's Puerto Rican population might have felt an attraction toward a young phenom like Clemente, who hailed from their own land, creating a common bond between player and fan. In 1955, the novelty of watching an exciting rookie like Clemente might have spurred fan interest, at least during the first half of the season, when Roberto had hit over .300 and played the outfield spectacularly. Perhaps fan sentiment toward Clemente would have tailed off in July and August, but by then attention would have shifted to the Dodger team itself, which was headed toward another National League pennant.

In 1956, Dodger fans might have enjoyed Clemente's upgraded sophomore season, when he raised his batting average 56 points, drove in a respectable 60 runs, and continued to play the outfield like few others to precede him. Although Clemente was not yet an established star, he had become a much more viable all-round player—both offensively and defensively—in his second season. Beyond that, his game was exciting, predicated on the elements of speed on the bases and in the outfield, and a ferocious, slashing style of hitting that seized the attention of the fans.

The aforementioned notion of Clemente saving Brooklyn loses steam in his third season, when Roberto slumped to a .253 average and saw his home run and RBI production cut in half. Injuries held him to 111 games, reducing his appeal as a potential gate attraction. Perhaps Clemente's reputation would have preceded him sufficiently to help bring Puerto Rican fans through the turnstiles; perhaps his stream of strikeouts and injuries would have served as a deterrent.

Of course, the argument that Clemente might have changed the fate of the Dodgers' location is based upon the assumption that Walter O'Malley ultimately moved the team for reasons of poor attendance. Given the Dodgers' history at the turnstiles throughout the 1950s, that presumption is difficult to make. In 1954, which would have been Clemente's first year in the major leagues if the Dodgers had played his situation correctly, Brooklyn drew just over one million fans to Ebbets Field. In 1955, the total increased slightly, to 1.03 million. The following summer, the year after the Dodgers won the World Series, the franchise attracted over 1.2 million fans. That figure represented the second-best number of the decade, behind only their attendance of 1.28 million fans in 1951. By 1957, the turnstile count had fallen off to 1.02 million, but much of the drop could be attributed to fan rebellion against O'Malley's intentions of moving to Los Angeles.

If Clemente had played for the Dodgers from 1954 to '57, he probably would have helped attendance at least slightly. His heritage, his dynamic style of play, and his production would have expanded the Dodgers' already rabid fan base. Would it have been enough to motivate O'Malley to keep the team in Brooklyn, in lieu of potential riches on the West Coast? Maybe, maybe not. Yet, if Clemente had brought hundreds of thousands of additional fans to Ebbets Field, as some maintained that he would have, O'Malley would have had an even more difficult time trying to justify a franchise move that had already stirred substantial debate.

A less important, but equally intriguing theory involves the potential composition of the Brooklyn outfield. If the Dodgers had retained Clemente, they could have formed a "dream" outfield of either Carl Furillo in right, Duke Snider in center, and Clemente in left, or Furillo in left, Snider in center field, and Clemente in his trademark position of right. Either way, some baseball historians have contended that the Dodgers would have boasted one of the finest outfields in history, maybe the best of all time.

Although this contention might be accurate, the reign of this great outfield would have lasted a relatively short time. From 1953 and '55, Furillo enjoyed three of his finest seasons, including the only batting title of his career. Snider was also in his prime, having reached the 40-home run mark all three years, while leading the National League in RBIs on one occasion. On the other hand, Clemente could not have joined the Dodgers until 1954 at the earliest. When he did crack the major leagues a year later, he struggled. He did not enjoy his first really good season until 1956, when he batted .311 with 60 RBIs. Furillo and Snider both played well that summer; Furillo hit .289 with 21 home runs, and Snider again reached the 40-home run, 100 RBI marks. Both players continued to shine defensively. So, in 1956, Clemente, Furillo and Snider—if they had played together—might have formed the best outfield of the day.

By 1957, such a stellar outfield would have fallen on harder times. Clemente slumped to a paltry .253 average amidst a wave of injuries and batting slumps. Snider still hit 40 home runs, but his RBIs dipped below 100 and his average fell to .274. Furillo batted .306, but played in only 119 games, which caused his run production numbers to suffer. In 1958, Clemente boosted his home runs, RBIs and batting average marks, but Furillo and Snider started to show their age in Los Angeles. The 36-year-old Furillo batted .290 with 83 RBIs but played in only 122 games. The 31-year-old Snider played a mere 106 times, with his home runs and RBIs falling off to 15 and 58, respectively.

By 1959, the alleged dream outfield would have been no more. Snider continued to play regularly for the Dodgers, but saw himself playing more frequently in right field, flanked by Don Demeter in center and Wally Moon in left. Reduced to a bench role, Furillo played in only 50 games, coming to bat a scant 93 times. In Pittsburgh, Clemente batted .296, but played in only 105 games. Although an accomplished hitter by now, Clemente was still one year away from the breakout stage of his major league career.

Still, even if only for a short time, it would have been fun to watch Clemente, Furillo and Snider patrol the outer limits of the unique configuration known as Ebbets Field. Defensively, no outfield would have compared. Although Snider played most of his prime seasons prior to the advent of the Gold Glove award, he played center field as skillfully as most of his contemporaries, with the exception of Willie Mays. Although the recognition for Clemente's defensive play came later during the 1960s, when he began a stretch of 12 consecutive Gold Gloves, he had already placed himself among the game's finest right fielders. In terms of pure throwing strength, Clemente and Furillo had few challengers among their peers, with the possible exceptions of Cleveland's Rocky Colavito and Detroit's Al Kaline. And even if one preferred the throwing arm of one of the American League stars, no team would have boasted the simultaneous presence of two firearms like Furillo and Clemente. That indeed would have been a special sight.

6

The Arm

In the late 1950s, a young boy named Art Howe regularly attended Pirate games at Forbes Field. Born and raised in Pittsburgh, Howe recalls the first time he saw Clemente play. "I remember I was sitting down the left field line in the old bleacher seats, the 50-cent seats down the left field line. It was a game against the Philadelphia Phillies, and I remember Richie Ashburn playing in the game because he was involved in the play that won me over as a Clemente fan. [Roberto] was kind of an unknown quantity at the time.

"The Pirates were leading, 4-3, in the ninth inning. In the top of the ninth, the Phillies got a rally going. And with one out, Richie Ashburn was on third base with the bases loaded. Whoever the hitter was hit a line drive to deep right field. And Clemente turned his back to the infield and caught the ball on the dead run going away from the infield, stopped on a dime, spun around and threw a rocket to home plate, and doubled up Ashburn trying to tag from third. It was the final out of the game— and the place went bananas. What a throw. It was just— no one could believe that anybody could throw a ball the way he did there. And especially Richie Ashburn. I think he was probably the most surprised person at the ballpark, because Richie could run."

As a result of his first encounter with Clemente, Howe underwent a conversion. "He became my favorite player—period," says Howe, who went on to become a major league player himself. "He was my idol. Before that, I was a big Hank Aaron fan. But when I had the chance to go see Roberto play, it was love at first sight, I'd guess you'd say. We tried to get seats out behind right field and just watch him throw."

As Howe recalls, not only did Clemente's throws intimidate opposing base runners, they struck fear in his own infielders. "Don Hoak was a real hard-nosed third baseman the Pirates had," says Howe, himself a third baseman for much of his playing career. "And Clemente would literally handcuff him with throws from right field, when guys were trying to go from first to third. He would uncork the ball and he'd throw so hard that he sometimes fell down. He put so much effort into his throws. It was like a bullet coming in there, and if it wasn't a long hop, it would eat Don Hoak up."

While Hoak owned a reputation as one of the game's most fearless players, even he yielded to intimidation when Clemente threw his way. "Oh yeah," says Howe, "You could see Don Hoak saying [to himself], 'Oh no, here it comes.' He'd just kind of tie himself down and hope he could handle the throw because man—what a rifle."

During Howie Haak's years as a scout with the Pirates, the organization had developed a rating system that attached a number grade to each player based on the strength of his throwing arm. According to Haak, a player with a 30 had an average major league arm. A 40 meant he was above average. If a player reached 50, he was considered outstanding. A 60 represented the highest grade a player could achieve—a perfect throwing arm. In the history of the organization, only two players merited a perfect score. One player, Shawon Dunston, would eventually play shortstop in the major leagues. The only other player to reach a 60? Clemente.

Who had the best throwing arm of all-time? Clemente? Carl Furillo? Rocky Colavito? Perhaps a player from an earlier era, such as "Shoeless" Joe Jackson of the Chicago White Sox? An article by Dennis Tuttle in the August 1997 issue of *Inside Sports* rated and categorized the game's "all-time greatest outfield arms." The magazine listed Clemente No. 1, describing him as a "magnificent thrower who defined the art of intimidating base runners." The article cited Clemente's mastery in grabbing caroms off the outfield wall, spinning, and throwing so quickly that he often nabbed unsuspecting runners. Rocky Colavito placed second in the survey, which claimed that his arm equaled Clemente's in terms of "pure power," but lacked the same accuracy and precision. The magazine cited Furillo as the best thrower of the 1950s, but placed him third all-time, behind Clemente and Colavito. Several outfielders from the 1970s and eighties, including Bo Jackson, "Downtown" Ollie Brown, Dave Winfield and Ellis Valentine, rounded out the top seven in the survey.

As a major leaguer, Art Howe played against some of the great outfield throwers of the 1970s and managed against many in the eighties and nineties, but says none match the ferocity of Clemente's arm. "There are some great arms around," says Howe, who has managed the Houston Astros and Oakland A's since his playing days. "I remember Ellis Valentine. When I played against him, he had a great throwing arm. Ollie Brown, they said, had a tremendous throwing arm. But I really didn't get to see him throw that much. In this day and age, to be honest with you, I can't think of anybody that comes close to [Clemente]."

What made Clemente's arm so powerful and accurate? Other than natural ability, Clemente may have been assisted by a youthful trait shared by many young Latin American ballplayers. "They start throwing when they are five and six years old," Howie Haak told Dennis Tuttle of *Inside Sports* in 1997. "They throw stones, bottle caps—whatever they can find—and they're developing arm strength." Unlike American boys, who sometimes wait until they are closer to 10 years old to start nurturing their throwing arms, Clemente had started picking up rubber balls and throwing them against walls at the age of five.

Although Clemente's shoulder and arm strength helped him fashion a reputation for throwing supremacy, he perfected the art through a ceaseless work ethic. "It was something that he worked on," observes Willie Stargell, who played with Clemente from 1962 to 1972. "First of all, he would make sure that he had good balance in throwing. Everything was [thrown] across the seams. And he knew how to throw the ball so that it could land in a certain spot and take one perfect hop to the infielder or the catcher so that it doesn't handcuff him."

Clemente used a drill to hone his throwing accuracy. "He would take a garbage can," says Stargell, "and put it at third base where the opening was facing him. He would have somebody hit him the ball in right field, he would run in, bring his body under control, pick up the ball, and throw it one-hop into the can. Tough to do. But that's what made him shine a little brighter, stand a little taller."

By the end of the 1958 season, most baseball observers recognized that Clemente's arm had surpassed that of the aging and injury-plagued Furillo as the best in the National League, and probably the finest in all of baseball. In spite of the sore arm that had resulted from making a quick throw against Furillo's Dodgers on April 30, Clemente had led major league outfielders in assists that season. He had thrown out 22 runners, most of whom had not come to fully respect the howitzer that stationed itself in Forbes Field's right field corner.

Clemente made one of his greatest throws during the late 1950s. The play took place at Forbes Field against the Giants, who had placed a runner on second base. "The ball was hit down the right field line," says Nellie King, who observed the play from his seat in the Pirate bullpen just a few feet away. "Kind of a blooper, and it spun into the Pirate bullpen, which was adjacent to some field seats. The seats near the right field bullpen were almost on the line, and he [ran] behind the seats. We could not see home plate." The seats, filled with spectators, blocked the bullpen's view of the catcher. "I was in direct line with [Roberto] as he threw the ball. And I couldn't see home plate, but he could somehow tell where home plate was by looking at third and second, and he threw it right into home plate—right on home plate."

In spite of his obstructed view of home plate, Clemente's throw landed in the catcher's mitt on the fly. "And the guy didn't score," says King. "He either got him out, or he didn't [try to] score." How did Clemente know where to throw the ball? "He told me, 'You know, Nellie, when the ball was hit to the outfield and I turned my back [to the infield], it's like a camera is going on in my mind and I can see everything behind me. I'm going to the wall, I visualize every base, and I know where every runner is when I catch the ball and make the throw to the base where I should.' I think he had an innate ability. When he got behind those box seats, he couldn't see home plate. He had to throw over the top [of them], but that son-of-a-gun threw it right on target. Right on target." The tunnel vision that had plagued a nerve-wracked Clemente during his rookie season had completely eroded, giving way to the visualization techniques that he would use both as a fielder and as a hitter.

Clemente had also adopted a trick play that made further use of his power-packed right arm. When opposing hitters hit singles toward right field, they sometimes strayed too far in rounding the first base bag and making their threatened attempt toward second. Anticipating that the Pirate right fielder would throw the ball toward second base—as did most other right fielders—a few runners became embarrassed victims when Clemente threw behind them, in the direction of first base. Art Howe remembers watching Clemente's patented play. "He was the first right fielder that I remember that would literally take balls off the right field wall in Forbes Field—it was only 300 feet down the line—and he'd take the ball off the wall and without even looking, just spin around and throw the ball in behind the runner coming around first base. He'd get the guy going back to first before he could even stop and turn around. Maybe only one time did a runner keep going to second off him, anticipating that he was going to throw behind him [to first]. He was just uncanny; those guys wouldn't even make a turn at first base when they'd hit a ball of the screen in right or off the wall."

Unlike most other outfielders who played conservatively, Clemente often picked the ball off the wall barehanded, allowing him to make the throw fractionally faster. Dale Long, the Pirates' regular first baseman, complied in the conspiracy of the play by standing inconspicuously on the first base bag, his glove and hands down, not up as if he were expecting a throw. Suddenly, Long would lift his mitt to catch Clemente's latest throw and then swipe the runner with the ball and mitt. The opposing hitter still gained credit for a single, but his presence on the bases had been duly dismissed. The play—which mixed quickness, strength and smarts—was vintage Clemente.

7

The Breakthrough

In his first five seasons in Pittsburgh, Clemente had batted as well as .300 only once, and reached a high of only seven home runs. Except for the stretch covering the 1958 and '59 seasons, he had alternated good offensive seasons with poor ones. The right fielder's lifetime average of .282 was respectable, but the lack of home run and RBI power from a position that usually featured such an offensive quality disturbed the Pirates.

Injuries had also played their part in derailing Clemente's march to stardom. Back problems, infected tonsils, bouts with the flu, and recurrences of diarrhea and an upset stomach had caused him to miss an average of nearly 29 games per season. Instead of playing a standard 154-game schedule, Clemente was trying to pack a season's worth of production into about 120 games. If Roberto could not find a way to stay healthy, he would not become the superstar the Pirates and the Dodgers had once envisioned.

On the plus side, his defensive play had become top-notch almost immediately. Four times he reached double figures in assists, twice reaching the 20-assist mark. If the Pirates wanted to quibble, they could point to his high error totals in 1956 and '59, when he committed 15 and 13 errors, respectively. Those numbers reflected his tendency to play too aggressively, throwing to bases when he had no chance to terminate a runner's life on the basepaths. Clemente sometimes hurried his throws, which bounced and skipped past Pirate infielders and catchers.

Clemente clearly needed to refine his game. He could continue to hit in the .280 to .290 range, drive in 50 to 60 runs, and make exciting plays in the outfield. If that was his game, he would be regarded as a good, contributing major league player. There was no shame in that. But he would be considered a disappointment. After all, he had been the object of a bidding war in 1954, when several teams fell over themselves trying to secure his hot-shot talent. Some people had dared to mention him in the same breath as Willie Mays, perhaps the game's best young player in the early fifties. If Clemente circa 1958 and '59 was as good as it was going to get, then many of the game's finest scouts—from Brooklyn to Milwaukee to New York to Pittsburgh—had overestimated his value as a ballplayer.

The feats of April and early May stamped Clemente as the game's hottest hitter. Some writers talked about the possibility of him hitting .400, something that had not been done by a major league hitter since Ted Williams in 1941. Clemente conceded the possibility gracefully, without boasts or guarantees. In later years, Clemente would discourage such talk. "Nobody will ever hit .400," Clemente would tell the *New York Times* in 1967. "We play too many games. We don't rest enough. Got to be strong to hit .400, but nobody can be strong enough with this schedule."

In 1960, Clemente cited other problems that he believed were holding him back from further greatness. He continued to complain of a series of physical ailments. He spoke with frustration about the condition of his back and elbow. "I am always mad at myself," Clemente told Joe King of the *World Telegram*. "I am mad at my back and my arm when they hurt, and I am worrying very much." Characterizations of him as a chronic complainer hurt the sensitive Clemente. "I hear that people say I do not want to play because I beef so much," said Clemente, continuing his outpouring. "When people say that, I tell myself, there is something wrong with me [physically], because it is my wish to play baseball. I see all the players trying very hard and I say they will think I am faking it if I do not play. Now I run into the wall and hurt my knee—I play. My arm hurts—I play. My back hurts—I play."

As sportswriter King observed, Clemente tried to offer proof of his bad back. "Listen," said Clemente, lifting his left leg, "and you will hear it." Clemente then shifted his lower back, creating an audible but "muffled click." The sound was produced by one of Clemente's loose spinal discs, which had been injured in the 1954 car accident outside of a San Juan hospital.

Although Clemente had been hitting well to start the season, he charged umpires with treating him unfairly. "Other players throw their hat into the dugout when they strike out and it is all right," Clemente reasoned. "When I throw it, the umpire says that's all, you go out, and then I have a letter for a $50 fine." Just as writers had treated Spanish-speaking players unfairly in interview settings, Clemente felt that such on-field episodes exhibited how umpires imposed a double standard against the Latino player.

Baseball writers and broadcasters rewarded Clemente's fine start by naming him the National League's "Player of the Month" for May. Clemente received 24 of a possible 40 votes, a nice acknowledgment for his .336, 39 hits and 25 RBIs in 27 games during the month. Prior to the Pirates' game on June 23, Clemente received his award in a ceremony at home plate. Hall of Fame third baseman Pie Traynor presented Roberto with an engraved desk set, courtesy of the office of National League President Warren Giles.

By June of 1960, Clemente had begun to earn praise from some of the game's greatest players. St. Louis Cardinals' first baseman Stan Musial, one of the National League's most respected stars, responded to a reporter's question about Clemente. "He's a fine player," Musial told Harry Keck of *The Sporting News.* "Good defensively and maturing at bat." While Musial's words may have seemed grudging and understated, one must consider the protocol of the era. In the days before the advent of the Players Association, rivals from other teams rarely showered excessive praise on their opponents, even those playing at an All-Star caliber.

Stars from older generations joined in the acknowledgment of Clemente. "He's a four-letter man. He can hit, run, field and throw," former Pirate great Pie Traynor told *The Sporting News.* "You won't find many with all of those qualifications. Some have two or three, but not many have all four." Traynor knew of what he spoke. Unlike some old-time players who had lost touch with the current-day game, Traynor continued his involvement with baseball as a member of the Pirates' scouting staff.

For the first time in his career, others had begun to compare Clemente to outfield stars from previous generations. Traynor mentioned Clemente in the same group as one-time Pirates' great Kiki Cuyler, former Cardinal and Red outfielder Charles "Chick" Hafey and National League legend Edd Roush. All three would gain election to the Hall of Fame in the sixties and seventies. Traynor went so far as to compare Clemente to one man who had already attained Cooperstown, New York Yankee icon Joe DiMaggio.

A mild offensive slump interrupted Clemente's season in early June. His average dropped from .360 to .346 in the span of a week. In the first game of a doubleheader at St. Louis, Clemente came to bat with a runner on first. He pounded out a ground ball, then jogged to first, barely escaping a double-play attempt. A few hundred Cardinal fans booed Clemente for what they perceived as a lack of effort. Danny Murtaugh removed Clemente from the second game lineup, explaining that Clemente needed a "rest." In the next day's edition of the *Pittsburgh Press*, Les Biederman speculated that the Irishman may have benched Clemente as punishment for his supposed failure to run hard on the ground ball.

Some teammates claimed that Clemente occasionally failed to run out routine grounders or pop-ups. "When he first came up, he had great ability, played well, played hard, but he was somewhat of a "hot dog," former Pirate pitcher Bob Purkey told Phoenix Communications in 1993. "Maybe he didn't run out a ball. He was known for that when he first came up. Then, as he matured, he became the leader of the club and the 'hot dog' was gone."

According to such a line of thought, Clemente did not become an all-out hustler—running hell-bent on every play—until a few years later in his career. Other teammates, like Bill Mazeroski, refuted the characterization of the young Clemente as an occasional loafer. "I don't think he ever jaked," Bill Mazeroski said in a 1972 interview with Phil Musick of the *Pittsburgh Press*. "Nobody plays the game harder."

"I don't think so," says Nellie King, when asked if he ever saw Clemente not hustle on the field. "I don't think so at all—not to my knowledge. I can't remember that. To my mind, he hustled all the time, maybe too much. In fact, he told me that he would make some of the dumbest running mistakes. You gotta remember, this guy didn't start playing baseball until he was 16 years of age—he played softball."

Did Joe Christopher, his onetime roommate, ever notice Clemente not hustling? "Not when I played with him," Christopher responds without hesitation. "Clemente was the kind of man that I'd like to have on my team. We were playing one time in St. Thomas, an exhibition game. This [game] was for nothing and here's a guy making over $100,000 bucks a year. Somebody hit a short fly ball into right field. Here's Clemente, he took off for the ball, and there was a whole pile of rocks there, and the guy made a helluva diving catch. How many guys are gonna do that making the kind of money he was making? When he put a baseball uniform on, there was only thing that Clemente thought: 'Give my best and give my all.' When he played with the Pirates, that's all he did."

In August, with Clemente in the midst of his finest season, a conversation with an out-of-town writer proved most discouraging. A reporter who covered the Los Angeles Dodgers showed Clemente a letter he had received from a Pittsburgh scribe. In the letter, the Pirates' beat writer had told the Los Angeles reporter to register his National League Most Valuable Player vote for Pirates' shortstop Dick Groat, not Clemente. Roberto found it distasteful that a Pittsburgh writer would openly and actively campaign for one player over another. He also couldn't believe that a writer had already made up his mind about the MVP Award, when over a month of regular season play remained.

Thanks to such unpleasant experiences, Clemente developed contempt for some writers. "I tell you the truth. I don't like lots of writers," Clemente told Sam Nover in 1972. "I never criticize a writer that I think is sincere on what he's writing. But lots of these writers, they go up to you and they put the interview in a way that [make it] sound like you have said that, when you don't say exactly that."

"For the first few years that I was writing a column, every time I'd go to him I'd have to listen to a denunciation of sportswriters," says former *Pittsburgh Press* writer Roy McHugh. "It was embarrassing because you'd be the center of attention in the clubhouse with Clemente shouting at you and the other ballplayers looking over. I said, 'Well, have I ever written anything unfair about you?' and he said, 'No.' He just wanted to get his point across. He had some genuine grievances because when he first came up, the writers would quote him phonetically." Clemente, who held no animosity toward McHugh himself, usually settled down after the first few minutes. "Then, he'd sit there and stay with you as long as you wanted him to and he'd answer any question," says McHugh. "He was absolutely open about everything."

On September 25, the Pirates played the Milwaukee Braves. Needing a win against the Braves or a Cardinal loss to the Cubs to clinch the National League pennant, Clemente came to bat late in the game against Warren Spahn. As he stepped into the batter's box, the scoreboard at Milwaukee's County Stadium flashed a brief but important message. The neon words brought good tidings to the Pirate players, who erupted at the sight of the news. Unable to determine the reasons behind his teammates' ruckus, Clemente asked Dick Stuart, the next scheduled batter, what had happened. From the on-deck circle, Stuart told Clemente that the Cardinals had lost to the Cubs, wrapping up the pennant for the Pirates. Clemente hurried back to the plate and promptly lined a single to center field. Hal Smith followed with a double, third base coach Frank Oceak signaling Clemente to stop at third. Clemente would have none of it. Anxious to return to the dugout and partake of the Pirates' pennant celebration on the bench, Clemente rounded third and slid home safely.

The Braves scored two runs in the tenth to post a 4-2 win, but the outcome meant nothing to the Pirates. Thanks to the Cubs' handiwork against the Cardinals, the Pirates spent more than a few post-game minutes reliving the regular season accomplishments that had pushed them to a championship.

Upon their return to Pittsburgh, the newly crowned pennant winners enjoyed a salute from an estimated crowd of 125,000 fans, who appreciated a persistent team that had posted 21 of its 95 victories in the ninth inning. For Pirate fans, the pennant had also been long in waiting. The franchise had not won a National League championship since 1927.

Another important development had taken place in 1960. The find uncovered by Roberto Marin and Pedrin Zorrilla, the budding professional scouted by Al Campanis, Howie Haak and Clyde Sukeforth, the raw minor leaguer drafted by Branch Rickey had begun to blossom. Clemente hit a career-best .314, edging his previous high—set in 1956—by three points. That ranked as nice improvement, but it paled when compared to the lifting of his power numbers. Clemente finished the summer with 16 home runs and 94 runs batted in. Compared with his personal best of 1956, those statistics represented a jump of nine home runs and 34 RBIs.

Clemente's numbers compared favorably with those of his teammates. His .314 average rated second-best on the Bucs, only 11 points behind Dick Groat. His home run total tied him for second on the club, behind only the 23 hit by mammoth first baseman Dick Stuart. In perhaps the most meaningful statistic of the group, Clemente's 94 RBIs placed him first among the Pirates, eight better than hard-hitting outfielder Bob Skinner. In terms of all-around offensive production, Clemente had contributed as much as any Pirate batter.

8

World Series Mismatch

I n the October 24, 1960 edition of *Life Magazine*, pitcher-turned-author Jim Brosnan wrote a concise but accurate scouting report of Clemente. "High fastball hitter, fair on breaking stuff. Power on inside strikes. Pushes bunt occasionally. Dislikes knockdown by close pitches. Runs well, takes risks on bases. Excellent defensive right fielder. Frequently bluffs fumble of ground balls to dare opposing runners to try for extra base."

In the next paragraph, Brosnan fleshed out his thumbnail sketch a bit further. He said that Clemente exhibited a "Latin American variety of showboating." Although Brosnan probably meant no real harm in penning such a remark, one might have wondered why the words "Latin American" needed to be included in the description. Imagine someone writing of a "black variety of showboating." Such a remark might have created a racial stir in the 1960s and almost certainly would in the 1990s. But in the early sixties, when describing someone from the Latino culture, such a characterization was considered acceptable.

Brosnan also referred to Clemente's "hard-headed reputation," which resulted from an incident that took place in a game between the Pirates and Brosnan's Reds several years earlier. Early in the game, Clemente had slid hard into Cincinnati second baseman Johnny Temple in an effort to break up a double play grounder. Two innings later, Clemente again bore down on Temple on an infield grounder. Like most second baseman, Temple threw overhand after completing the double play pivot. This time, Temple dropped his right arm and threw sidearm toward first base. The low throw pegged Clemente in the head, just above the nose and between the eyes. In the words of Brosnan, Clemente "didn't even blink."

The Pirates figured to need such aggressive play in the upcoming World Series. Few fall classics of recent vintage seemed as one-sided as this impending matchup between the favored New York Yankees and the underdog Pirates. Las Vegas bookmakers preferred the Yankees at relatively modest odds of 5-to-7, but the consensus of veteran baseball writers leaned even more heavily in the direction of New York.

Although the Yankees had won only two more games than the Pirates—97 to 95—they had claimed the American League pennant with far more emphasis than their National League counterparts. Fifteen straight wins to end the season, coupled with a powerhouse lineup headlined by Mickey Mantle, Roger Maris and Bill "Moose" Skowron, convinced the baseball media that the Yankees would win—and win easily. Unlike the Yankees, who had three players with at least 20 home runs, the Pirates had only one, first baseman Dick Stuart. The Bombers owned three players with 90 or more RBIs; the Pirates had only one, named Clemente. And even he wasn't known for his RBI production as much as his ability to hit for average.

Yet, the experts seemed to ignore the comparisons of the pitching staffs. Whitey Ford had won only 12 games, in spite of the ample support offered by a lineup that led the American League in runs scored. Right-hander Art Ditmar had pitched well, winning 15 games, but his repertoire of pitches offered little intimidation to opposing hitters. The Yankees' third-best starter, Jim Coates, had allowed over four runs per nine innings.

In contrast, the Pirates featured a 20-game winner in Vernon Law, who had led all National League starters in complete games. Another right-hander, Bob Friend, had won 18 games and posted 16 route-going efforts. Two effective left-handers with loads of experience, Harvey Haddix and Wilmer "Vinegar Bend" Mizell, rounded out the rotation. And then there was the bullpen, headed by the diminutive but durable intimidator, ElRoy "Roy" Face. The owner of a devastating forkball, the five-foot, eight-inch Face had saved 24 games in pitching a league-leading 68 times.

At least one member of the Yankees had publicly expressed concerns over facing the Pirates. In mid-September, former Pirate Dale Long had forewarned his teammates not to underestimate the Pirates, should they win the National League pennant. Long, a mid-season acquisition by the Yankees, had seen the Pirates up close and personal as a member of the NL's San Francisco Giants. Long listed the Pirates' pitching staff, shortstop Dick Groat—who was out with a broken wrist at the time—and one other player as Pittsburgh's most dangerous assets. The other player? None other than Clemente, whom Long praised for his determination and hustle. "What makes Clemente tick?" Long asked himself out loud in an interview with Dan Daniel of the *World Telegram*. "First, experience. Second, gameness and drive." Long also praised Clemente's physical talents. "Clemente makes fantastic catches, has a remarkable arm, can run and hits .320."

Referring to Clemente's early seasons in the major leagues, Long remembered a player who sometimes allowed his concentration to wander. "There was a time when he was inclined to lose interest," Long said. By 1960, Clemente had changed his approach to the game. "Right now Roberto is one of the most hungry of the hungry Pirates." As proof of the transformation, Long recalled an incident involving Clemente earlier in the season, when Long was still playing for San Francisco. "He crashed into a concrete wall against the Giants," said Long, referring to a play where Clemente had severely cut his chin while making a game-saving catch against Willie Mays. "They took six stitches in his face and three days later he was back in the lineup."

Although Clemente had recovered from the facial injury, the summer had taken its toll. He had lost 20 pounds during the course of the season, leaving his playing weight at 165 pounds. Clemente was tired after playing in 144 games, but he needed to muster some energy for the first post-season games of his major league career.

A crowd of 36,676 fans piled into Forbes Field for Game One. The gathering included some friendly faces for Clemente, in particular his mother and brother. Yet, when Clemente ran out to right field to start the game, he felt differently. During the regular season, the fans in right field usually showered Clemente with verbal appreciation when he ran out to his position to start a game. With most season ticket holders shut out of the World Series, the Game One crowd featured a host of celebrities and business types who failed to send applause Clemente's way. Clemente didn't understand the pall of silence until a sportswriter explained the situation.

Writers from Pittsburgh and New York streamed into the press box for what some considered a formality—a Pirate stomping at the hands of the Yankees. The early developments of Game One seemed destined to fulfill the prophecy. In the first inning, Roger Maris came to bat against Vernon Law with two outs and no one on. After seeing the count run to 1-and-1, Maris blasted a discouraging home run into the highest deck in right field. The 1-0 lead confirmed what the inhabitants of the press box had suspected.

Not willing to concede the Series to the consensus of the media, the Pirates stormed back with three runs in the bottom half of the first. Taking advantage of Art Ditmar, Casey Stengel's surprising choice to start Game One, Bill Virdon walked and pulled off a delayed steal of second base. When shortstop Tony Kubek failed to handle Yogi Berra's throw from home plate, Virdon moved up to third. Dick Groat, using the opposite field stroke that had helped him win the National League batting title, followed with a run-scoring double to the right field corner. Bob Skinner rammed a single past Bobby Richardson at second base, bringing Groat home. After a Dick Stuart lineout, Skinner stole second base, continuing the Pirates' plan of aggression against Berra. With another runner in scoring position, Clemente hacked a hard, high-hopping grounder past Ditmar into centerfield, giving the Bucs a 3-1 advantage.

Law held the Yankees scoreless in the second and third before running into trouble in the fourth. Maris led off with a single into right-center field, past the reach of the wide-ranging Bill Mazeroski. A walk to Mantle put runners on first and second. Berra assaulted a Law delivery, deep into right field. At Yankee Stadium, the drive would have easily landed in the right field bleachers, giving the Yankees three runs—and the lead—with one swing. But the unfavorable dimensions of Forbes Field gave the Pirates hope. Virdon and Clemente ran toward right-center field, converging near the fence, almost 420 feet from home plate. Both men called for the ball, but the loudness of the crowd made their cries inaudible. The two outfielders collided, with Virdon stepping on the back of Clemente's right shoe, but Virdon held on to the ball, completing a spectacular catch. Maris tagged up and moved to third, eventually scoring on a Bill Skowron single to left. After a Gil McDougald foul out, the inning ended when Richardson flied out to Virdon. The Yankees had scored one run, but felt they should have had more.

In the bottom of the fourth, the Pirates again extended their lead. After retiring leadoff man Smokey Burgess, Art Ditmar issued a one-out walk to Don Hoak. Ditmar jumped ahead of Mazeroski 0-and-2, but left his next pitch too vulnerable. Mazeroski, not known as a power hitter, cleared the scoreboard in left field. The Pirates, who only a half-inning earlier came close to trailing the game on an apparent home run by Berra, now led the Yankees, 5-2.

In the sixth inning, Mazeroski scored again, this time on a double by Virdon. The Pirate lead remained 6-2 until the ninth. Roy Face, who had succeeded Law in the eighth, allowed a single to leadoff batter Gil McDougald. After Mazeroski and Groat teamed up on a forceout at second base, Yankee manager Casey Stengel called upon Elston Howard as a pinch-hitter for Ryne Duren. Going with the pitch, Howard served a home run into the lower deck in right field. The pinch-hit blast brought the Yankees within two runs. Tony Kubek followed with a single, bringing Hector Lopez to the plate as the tying run. The owner of nine regular season home runs, Lopez hit a stiff grounder that Mazeroski fielded before flipping to Groat, who scraped second for one out and then fired to Stuart at first base. The double play ended the heart-palpitating Yankee rally, sealing an unlikely 6-4 win for the Bucs.

Groat and Mazeroski had played major roles in the upset victory. In addition to their nifty work around the middle of the diamond, each infielder had picked up two hits and scored one run. In tandem, they had totaled eight bases. Clemente had also helped, albeit in more subtle fashion. His first inning single had plated the Pirates' third run. On the flip side, Clemente had almost interfered with Virdon's miraculous catch in the fourth inning; fortunately, his bumping of Virdon had not prevented the Pirates' center fielder from making a game-saving play.

Encouraged by the surprising results of the Series lidlifter, a crowd of 37,308 fans (a boost of 632 fans from the first game) crammed into Forbes Field for the Game Two matchup. Clemente did his part, smacking a first inning single into right-center and reaching on a slow tapper to Gil McDougald in the third, but little else went right for the Pirates. As Branch Rickey watched glumly from the first row behind the Yankee dugout, the New Yorkers gathered 19 hits against a half-dozen Pirate pitchers. Mickey Mantle crushed two home runs, one estimated at 450 feet to straightaway center field, the other an even 400 feet. Although the Pirates themselves bundled 13 hits against the combined efforts of Bob Turley and Bobby Shantz, they managed to score runs in only two different innings. The end results added up to a 16-3 rout—the Pirates' worst loss of the season—in front of a shell-shocked gathering at Forbes Field.

The World Series schedule permitted a day off between the second and third games, giving the Pirates and Yankees ample time to travel to New York. During the off-day workout at Yankee Stadium, Pirates' third base coach Frank Oceak snared a fungo bat and smacked balls off the walls in left field. Oceak and his outfielders observed the way that balls tended to spin around the curve of the outfield wall, much like pucks would hug the dasher boards of a hockey rink.

As Oceak and the Pirates worked out at Yankee Stadium prior to Game Three, Clemente conducted his own experiments in the right field corner. He had never before played in baseball's shrine, having only heard about its short right field porch and "death valley" depth to left-center field. Yankee Stadium would have suited Clemente's offensive game just fine; he pulled inside pitches, but preferred driving the ball into the right field gap. At Forbes Field, some of those drives landed for doubles and triples, but some ended up being caught by fleet-footed outfielders. At the Stadium, many of those opposite field drives would have landed in the lap of a Yankee fan seated in the right field bleachers. Since most pitchers tended to work the outside corner against Clemente, he might have bombarded a steady stream of right field home runs over the short porch at the Stadium. Instead of hitting his usual 14 to 16 longballs a season, Clemente might have regularly topped the 20-home run plateau.

On this day, Clemente didn't dwell on the dream of hitting home runs into the seats. Rather, Clemente had more immediate work to do, like learning to play the caroms in Yankee Stadium's right field corner. Asking a teammate to accompany him, Clemente took a ball with him as he ran onto the outfield grass. Instead of trusting Oceak or one of his teammates to throw balls off the right field wall, Roberto did it himself. He threw ball after ball against the fence, much like he used to bounce rubber balls against the walls of his boyhood home in Puerto Rico. Sometimes he threw the ball on a short hop, sometimes on a bounce, sometimes on a fly. Each time, his teammate retrieved the ball and threw it back to him. Clemente tried to spin the ball as he threw it, creating a different bounce, coming off a different angle, as the ball separated itself from the wall. Each time, Clemente noticed how the ball caromed, and how it varied from the previous bounce.

After years of playing the corners of Forbes Field, the Polo Grounds and Ebbets Field, Clemente wanted to be ready for the unusual tendencies of the Yankee Stadium walls. "I don't want them to play no dirty tricks on me," Clemente told Dick Young of the *New York Daily News,* using the word "them" to refer to the unfamiliar walls. It was as if Clemente felt the walls at Yankee Stadium had minds of their own.

After sitting in the Yankee dugout during the first two games of the Series, Whitey Ford finally took the mound. As he talked with reporters before Game Three, Ford listed Clemente and Groat as the two most dangerous Pirate hitters because of their judicious ability to drive pitches to right field. Since Ford liked to work the outside corner, he knew he would have to alter his strategy against Pittsburgh's right fielder and shortstop.

Ford's presence on the mound once again raised the issue of Casey Stengel's selection of starting pitchers. Even Stengel's most ardent supporters had questioned the manager's decision to use Art Ditmar and Bob Turley in games one and two. While Ditmar had been the Yankee's most effective pitcher during the regular season, Ford had proven himself in World Series competition above and beyond all other pitchers. Furthermore, if Stengel had pitched Ford at the start of the Series, he could have used him again in Game Four, and if needed, in Game Seven. By waiting to use Ford in the third game, Stengel had reduced the number of Series starts he could give Ford from three to two.

Critics of Stengel loaded more ammunition after watching Ford in Game Three. Deftly mixing his pitches between the inside and outside corners, the left-hander held the Pirates to four hits. Ford limited the Pirates' two most accomplished hitters to one hit in eight at-bats. In his first three at-bats, Clemente struck out, bounced out to Gil McDougald and flied to Yogi Berra in right. Groat fared even less successfully. He grounded out all four times: once to Richardson, a tapper to Ford, once to McDougald and another to Skowron.

The short hit list against Ford including a meaningless ninth inning single to center by Clemente. By that time, any Pirate fans had probably left Yankee Stadium, disgusted by New York's 10-0 lead. Six more Pirate pitchers had caved in against New York's crippling batting attack. Mickey Mantle's third home run of the Series and Bobby Richardson's grand slam had fueled the Yankee explosion, spoiling Danny Murtaugh's 43rd birthday.

Pirate players showered quickly and returned to the Commodore Hotel, their usual accommodation on road trips to New York. As they neared the entrance of the hotel, groups of Yankee fans taunted them with shouts and insults. They reminded them of what the writers had been saying, only far less politely. Most of the Pirate players remained silent as they entered the hotel lobby. Clemente did not. He turned back, looking at some of the fans who had authored such derision. Clemente reminded them to come back for Game Four.

Vernon Law faced Ralph Terry in the Yankee Stadium rematch. Law had pitched capably in the first game, lasting until the eighth inning. He pitched just as well in the fourth game, giving up two runs in six and a third innings. When he gave way to Roy Face in the seventh inning, the Pirates held a 3-2 lead. Pittsburgh had scored all of its runs in the fifth inning, thanks in large part to Law's hitting. A two-out double by the pitcher off the left field wall had scored Gino Cimoli with the first run, and set the table for two more. Law himself scored a run on Bill Virdon's single.

After striking out in his first two at-bats, Clemente led off the sixth against Terry. Clemente singled to right—once again confirming the Whitey Ford scouting report—giving him hits in all four Series games. Roberto moved up on groundouts by Dick Stuart and Cimoli, only to be stranded at third. The failure to score an insurance run didn't hurt the Pirates, as Face held the Yankees scoreless over the final two and two-thirds innings. Another whirlwind catch by Bill Virdon in right-center field, robbing Bob Cerv of extra bases on a 400-foot drive, helped the Pirates claim a tense 3-2 victory.

The win ensured the Pirates of a return to Forbes Field for Game Six. Most of the writers had predicted a Yankee victory in four or five games. In that sense, Pittsburgh had already scored an upset. Law had pitched efficiently, perhaps brilliantly when considered in the context of facing such a powerful Yankee lineup. Virdon's defensive play had minimized two Yankee rallies. Clemente had filled a supplementary role, racking up five hits in four games and handling eight chances without an error. Although Clemente hadn't registered any assists, Yankee runners weren't exactly taking chances against his throwing arm. On base hits to right field, they took it one base at a time; on fly balls, they held their ground. The Yankees had read the scouting report of pitcher-writer Jim Brosnan, along with the reports filed by their own scouts.

In Game Five, Art Ditmar and Harvey Haddix pitched scoreless first innings. In the top of the second inning, Smokey Burgess nailed a one-out double into the right field corner, pushing Gino Cimoli to third. Don Hoak bounced a grounder to shortstop, scoring Cimoli. Instead of throwing to first base for the sure out, Tony Kubek wisely flipped to Gil McDougald at third in an attempt to nail the snail-paced Burgess. Kubek's throw beat Burgess, but McDougald dropped the ball for an error. The miscue allowed Burgess to reach third safely, while also paving the way for some attentive baserunning. Nicknamed "The Tiger" for his relentless style of play, Hoak smartly hustled his way into second base, giving the Pirates two runners in scoring position. That brought Bill Mazeroski, one of the heroes of Game One, to the plate. Maz bounced a ball down the third base line, a high hopper that eluded the leap of McDougald. Hugging the left field line, the double scored Burgess and Hoak, and knocked a luckless Ditmar from the game.

The Yankees came back with single runs in the second and third, while the Pirates added a fourth run in their next at-bat. In that third inning, Dick Groat led off against Yankee reliever Luis Arroyo by doubling into the left field corner. Clemente came to bat against Arroyo, a fellow Puerto Rican. Feeling little sympathy for his countryman, Clemente banged a hard ground ball between Clete Boyer and Tony Kubek on the left side of the Yankee infield. The single to left scored Groat, ending Arroyo' tainted—and only—appearance in the Series. Clemente's second RBI of the Series gave the Pirates an insurance run, setting the stage for another fine stint of relief pitching by Roy Face. The forkballing right-hander stymied a Yankee rally in the seventh and kept the Bombers scoreless the rest of the day. A 5-2 Pirate win put the underdogs within one game of the world championship.

Unfortunately for the Pirates, they had to face Whitey Ford in the Game Six return to Forbes Field. Clemente pushed a single to right in the first, and five innings later, crossed up Ford by driving a single to center. Other than Clemente's safeties, however, the Pirates managed only five hits. Ford fired his second straight shutout, despite pitching with a blister. Five Pirate pitchers—a beleaguered group that included starter Bob Friend—gave up 17 hits.   In a contest similar to the blowouts suffered in the second and third games, the Pirates lost, 12-0.

In his two best offensive games, Clemente had seen his team lose by a combined score of 28-3. In the games that the Pirates had won, Clemente had managed respectable batting displays, but he yearned to do more. He hoped that Game Seven would bring both a Pirates' title and a brilliant individual performance.

The Pirates could comfort themselves with two facts: The Yankees had used their best pitcher in the sixth game; Pittsburgh had not. The Bucs would have Vernon Law available to start the seventh game. In addition, the Pirates would play that game at Forbes Field, giving them the security of the final at-bat, should they need it.

Bob Turley, the Yankees' third best starter and the winner of Game Two, retired the first two Pirate batters routinely. A Bill Virdon fly out to Yogi Berra and a Dick Groat pop-up to Tony Kubek brought Bob Skinner to the plate. Skinner drew a walk, bringing first baseman Rocky Nelson to the plate. A journeyman major leaguer who had spent part or all of 12 seasons in the minor leagues, Nelson had started only one other Series game. That was Game Two, also against Turley. Nelson had picked up two hits in five at-bats, all against Turley. Danny Murtaugh had a hunch that the left-handed hitting Nelson could handle the Yankee right-hander better than his usual first baseman, Dick Stuart.

Nelson lofted a high fly ball toward right field. Roger Maris backed up, stationing himself in front of the 32-foot screen that separated the shallow part of the right field stands from the playing field. At first, Maris appeared ready to make the catch. He looked up, waiting for the ball to come down. It didn't. Nelson's high-arcing fly ball barely cleared the tall screen. Skinner and Nelson scored on the unlikely home run, giving the Pirates a 2-0 lead.

The Pirates scored two more runs in the second, knocking out Turley in the process. Bill Stafford came in and allowed a walk and a bunt single, before starting a bases-loaded double play. But Stafford could not handle Virdon, who delivered a two-out, two-run single to right-center field. The timely base hit gave the Bucs a 4-0 advantage.

The Yankees finally dented Law in the fifth inning. Bill Skowron homered into the lower section of the right field stands, barely keeping the ball inside the foul pole. Still, the Pirates led by three runs, with their best starting pitcher on the mound.

That scenario changed in the sixth. Bobby Richardson led off by singling to center and moved up to second on a walk to Tony Kubek. Given the gravity of a seventh-game situation, Danny Murtaugh yanked Law earlier than usual and replaced him with Roy Face. Maris hit a foul pop wide of third, which Don Hoak snared for the inning's first out. Needing a double play to escape the inning, Mantle obliged by hitting a ground ball up the middle. Unfortunately for the Pirates, the ball eluded Face and scooted into center field. Richardson scored, bringing the Yankees within two. With runners on first and third, Yogi Berra connected on a soaring drive down the right field line. Clemente did not move from his position, knowing that the ball would land in the seats, fair or foul. Either way, the ball had home run distance. Berra's drive landed in the upper deck—just inside the foul pole. A three-hit rally had resulted in four runs, giving the Yankees a sudden 5-4 lead.

The Pirate dream seemed to have been crushed, especially when the Yankees tacked on two more runs against an ineffective Face in the eighth. The three-run lead left the Pirates with only two more cracks at the Yankee bullpen. Standing in against left-hander Bobby Shantz, Gino Cimoli pinch-hit for Face to start the bottom of the eighth. Cimoli singled to right-center, giving the Pirates faint hope. Hope seemed to end when Bill Virdon followed with a hard grounder to shortstop, a routine double play ball. As Tony Kubek prepared to field the ball on its last hop, the ball caromed unexpectedly. Instead of bouncing away from Kubek, it bounced into Kubek, plugging him in the neck. The ball struck Kubek's Adam's apple, leaving him gasping for air. As Cimoli steamed into second and Virdon landed at first, the Yankees' training staff attended to the fallen shortstop. Kubek recovered his breath somewhat, and pleaded to stay in the game, but Casey Stengel ordered him to leave the field. From there, Kubek went to Pittsburgh's Eye and Ear Hospital. Stengel called upon backup infielder Joe DeMaestri to take Kubek's place on the Yankee infield.

Although concerned for their teammate, the Yankees had sufficient worry on the field. With two runners on and no one out, Dick Groat singled past Clete Boyer at third base. Cimoli scored, Virdon stopping at second. With the left-handed hitting Bob Skinner scheduled to bat, Stengel made a puzzling move. He removed the southpaw Shantz, replacing him with tall right-hander Jim Coates.

Murtaugh decided to play for the tie. He instructed Skinner, his No. 3 hitter, to lay down a sacrifice. Skinner obliged by pushing a bunt to Boyer, who watched both runners advance. Coates now faced Nelson, the architect of the early inning home run. As he did in the second inning, Nelson pulled a pitch in the air toward right field. This time the ball didn't have home run distance. In fact, it didn't fly far enough to score Virdon from third. Maris made the catch, both runners holding.

Coates needed one more out to escape the inning. Up came Clemente, who had been held hitless in three previous at-bats. Determined to keep the ball away from the aggressive Clemente, Coates targeted the far corner of the plate. He threw three consecutive outside pitches, which Clemente fouled off each time. Then came a fourth. Swinging hard and embarrassingly off-stride, Clemente weakly tapped a grounder between the pitcher's mound and first base. Instead of conceding the out and consuming himself with anger, Clemente ran hard from the start. Moving to his right, Skowron fielded the ball wide of first base. Coates ran to first base to receive the toss from Skowron. The Yankee first baseman waited for Coates to near the bag and made an accurate throw to his pitcher.

Coates could not match the stride of Clemente, who arrived at first base a full beat ahead of the throw. "I can still remember that, Clemente beating that play out, just an infield bloop, you know," says Nellie King, by now retired as a player and reporting the World Series for a radio station in Latrobe, Pennsylvania. "It should have been an easy third out, but it wasn't the third out. Coates got a late start and Clemente beat the play to first base."

But did Coates *really* make a late break from the pitching mound, as King and many other eyewitnesses have contended over the years? A close and repeated examination of the film replay shows Coates breaking for first base at *virtually* the same moment Clemente made contact with the ball. Coates actually lost time, not because of a late start, but because he failed to maintain a direct path between the mound and first base. Instead of running a straight line, Coates veered slightly toward the second base side of the first base bag. Why did Coates take a roundabout route to first base? He may have feared running into his first baseman, Bill Skowron. In fact, Coates came so close to meeting his teammate that Skowron could have handed him the ball and let *him* run to first. If Skowron had made such a transfer, Coates likely would have beaten Clemente to the bag.

In reality, Clemente, by maintaining a straight and hard path, had outrun Coates, even though the pitcher had far less distance to travel in running to first base. A batter must run 90 feet (or about 92 feet for a right-handed batter) in going from home to first; a pitcher needs to navigate about two-thirds that distance—63 and a half feet—from the mound to the same destination. Coates, a right-handed pitcher, enjoyed the added benefit of his weight naturally shifting toward the first base side of the mound after his delivery to the plate. In contrast, Clemente had swung so hard as to lose his balance at home plate. Yet, in spite of the circumstances dictating otherwise, Clemente had managed to win the race to first base. Through sheer hustle from the moment he stepped out of the batter's box, coupled with the extraordinary speed that Al Campanis had first witnessed nearly a decade before, Clemente had kept the inning alive.

Virdon had scored on Clemente's infield single, cutting the Yankee lead to one, 7-6. Groat, the potential game-tying run, had advanced to third. The next scheduled batter? Platoon catcher Hal Smith, who had entered the game after Smokey Burgess had been removed for a pinch-runner one inning earlier. Although Smith was considered the Pirates' second best catcher after Burgess, he did have power. Playing mostly against left-handed pitching, Smith had clubbed 11 home runs in 258 regular season at-bats.

Smith faced an additional challenge now. Since Coates was still in the game, he would have to hit against a right-handed pitcher. Coates and Smith battled, working the count to 2-and-2. Smith hammered the next pitch deep to left. The drive sent Yogi Berra to the left field wall. Berra looked up at the 400-foot drive as it sailed into the bleachers. A two-out, three-run homer by a part-time player had placed the Pirates in the lead, 9-7.

Groat crossed home plate, soon to be followed by Clemente. As Roberto rounded third and galloped home, he repeatedly leapt in the air, his arms outstretched. Clemente jumped on home plate, then turned to greet Smith. Roberto hugged his teammate, the platoon catcher who had made Clemente's dash toward first base that much more meaningful.

Groat, Smith and Clemente continued their celebration as they jogged from home plate toward the dugout. When they arrived near the top step of the Pirate dugout, the rest of their teammates joined in. Yet, more work needed to be done. Although the Pirates now led by two, they needed to retire three more Yankee batters in the ninth.

Danny Murtaugh summoned Bob Friend, usually one of his starters, to pitch the ninth. The Pirates' second most winningest pitcher in 1960, Friend had pitched only one game in relief. Still, he was the most logical choice. After all, Roy Face had already been used, and had left the game in the eighth for a pinch-hitter.

Bobby Richardson, the Yankees' best hitter throughout the Series, immediately singled to left-center field. Dale Long, the former Pirate who had befriended Clemente in 1956, came up as a pinch-hitter for Joe DeMaestri. Long tortured his former teammates with a single to right. Having seen enough of Friend, Murtaugh called upon left-hander Harvey Haddix to face the soul of the Yankee order: the left-swinging Roger Maris and the switch-hitting Mickey Mantle.

Maris lofted a foul pop behind home plate, which Smith handled easily for the first out. Mantle would not fall so quietly. The Yankee center fielder singled into right-center field, chasing Clemente and Virdon into the gap. Richardson scored easily and Long, the potential tying run, stopped at third. Stengel called Long over from third, replacing him with a pinch-runner, Gil McDougald. Yogi Berra then rapped a sharp grounder down the first base line. Rocky Nelson made a nifty back-hand stop and stepped on the bag to retire Berra. To Nelson's surprise, Mantle tried to return to first base—a strange decision—instead of making a conventional run for second. As Mantle slid headfirst into the bag, the force play having been removed, McDougald neared home plate. Nelson missed Mantle with a swipe tag, preserving the inning as McDougald scored the tying run.

As the teams headed to the bottom of the ninth, deadlocked at 9-9, Stengel made some necessary defensive changes. He placed McDougald at third and moved Boyer to short, replacing DeMaestri. But Stengel kept Ralph Terry, who had replaced Coates in the eighth, on the mound.

Terry's first batter? The No. 8 hitter, Bill Mazeroski.

Mazeroski looked at the first pitch—a fastball—which rode high and inside. Terry didn't want to walk Mazeroski, the inning's leadoff batter, so he threw another fastball. Seconds later, at 3:36 p.m. Eastern time, Mazeroski's drive landed in a cluster of maple trees located beyond the 406-foot mark in left-center field. As Mazeroski rounded first and headed toward second, he removed his helmet with his right hand and windmilled his arm, over and over. As Pirate fans streamed onto the field, Mazeroski's teammates waited for him, less than patiently, at home plate. A World Series first—a Series-ending home run, in Game Seven no less—had given the Pirates their first world championship in 35 years.

As Mazeroski completed his route around the bases, Clemente rejoiced with his teammates on the field, continuing the celebration that he had started one inning earlier—after Hal Smith's eighth-inning home run. A few moments later, Pirate players doused each other, and a few writers, with a mixture of beer and champagne. Dick Stuart led the effort, pouring anyone in sight with suds of beer. One Pirate, however, could not be found in the clubhouse celebration.

After shaking hands and slapping the backs of his teammates, Clemente had dressed quickly in the clubhouse. He grabbed one of Bill Mazeroski's gloves as a remembrance of the victory and left the locker room almost immediately, before the post-game revelry had even begun to boil. Where did Clemente go? Fitted in his street clothes, Clemente walked into the mid-afternoon sunshine that enveloped Forbes Field. In a 1966 interview with Myron Cope of *Sports Illustrated*, Clemente detailed his post-game itinerary. "The biggest thrill was when I come out of the clubhouse after the last Series game and saw all those thousands of fans in the streets. I did not feel like a player at the time. I feel like one of those persons, and I walked the streets among them."

The way that Clemente told the story, he made his way across the street, through the crowds of fans that had begun to gather around the ballpark, and into a nearby park. "I went to Schenley Park to celebrate with the fans," Clemente told Charley Feeney of the *Pittsburgh-Post Gazette* many years later. "We hugged each other. I felt good being with them." According to Clemente, he rejoiced with some of the one million fans who poured into the city—the people who honked on car horns, beat on the tops of garbage cans, threw baskets full of paper, and laughed and yelled outside of his little kingdom of Forbes Field.

The testimony of at least one observer brings into question whether Clemente actually did take time to celebrate with the fans. "I drove Clemente to the airport right after that World Series because he did not want to be a part of it [the clubhouse celebration]," says former *Pittsburgh Courier* writer Bill Nunn in an interview with researcher Andrew O'Toole. "Unless he did not get on the plane [to Puerto Rico]. I was in the dressing room afterward and he said, 'Hey, how about getting me out of here?'"

If Clemente did celebrate with the fans, he had certainly done something unusual—almost unheard of for a professional athlete—whether it be in the 1960s, the 1920s, or today. At least based on his public comments—through a story he told repeatedly—Clemente had expressed a preference for the company of his fans, the people who faithfully served him and the Pirates with their loyalty and support.

Clemente's version of the story does find some support among members of the electronic media. Nellie King believed Roberto when he told him that he had celebrated with the fans. He also understood why Clemente had decided to abandon the clubhouse so quickly. "Everybody misunderstood that he was mad or something," says King. "But it wasn't that. He just enjoyed the average guy, you know."

This much is certain. Clemente did draw widespread criticism when he refused to participate in the clubhouse celebration after the seventh game. Clemente repeatedly explained his decision to stay apart from his teammates, "When we win in 1960, the noise, I stay away from," Clemente told Harold Kaese of the *Boston Globe* in 1971. "I go off by myself. I dress, go off with fans [and celebrate with them]. I'm quiet fella. I try to keep piece of mind."

Still, some writers refused to buy Clemente's line of reasoning. They perceived his fast departure from the clubhouse as a sign of his aloof personality. Others claimed that Clemente's actions revealed the tension that existed between him and the other players in the clubhouse. Some writers speculated that Clemente was upset with his teammates.

Although former *Pittsburgh Press* writer Roy McHugh doesn't know if anger had motivated Clemente in leaving the clubhouse so quickly, he does recall a general tension between the right fielder and his teammates during the early 1960s. "He was sort of an outsider on the team," says McHugh. "He didn't mix well with the older players. After Groat and Hoak and some of the others left Pittsburgh, and Clemente became the acknowledged team leader, then the new players looked up to Clemente and the whole atmosphere changed."

Controversy aside, Clemente had played no small role in the World Series upset. Hitting consistently against Yankee pitching, Clemente became only the 13th player in history to pick up hits in each game of a seven-game World Series. For the Series, he batted .310 with nine hits, three RBIs and a run scored. And in the opinion of at least one World Series manager, Clemente's ability to beat out the infield grounder in the eighth inning represented the key to the game. "The ball that Clemente hit could have got [Jim Coates] out of the inning," observed Yankee manager Casey Stengel in an interview with Bob Drum of the *Pittsburgh Press.* "That play on Clemente was the one."

Clemente did not win the MVP—that award went to the Yankees' hot-hitting Bobby Richardson—nor did he receive much acclaim, what with Bill Mazeroski's home run grabbing a stranglehold of fan and media attention. Given the circumstances, Clemente probably understood that Mazeroski and Richardson deserved the recognition they received.

A month later, Clemente *would* feel neglected. In fact, he would become the recipient of what he considered the most grievous snub of his career. Prior to the World Series, each member of the Baseball Writers Association of America had cast a vote for his choice as National League MVP. Since the vote had actually taken place prior to the Series, no post-season accomplishments could be taken into account in the selection of the MVP. Still, Clemente's regular season performance had placed him among the leading contenders for the award. Having reached career highs in home runs, RBIs and batting average, Clemente had ably assisted the Pirates in winning the National League pennant.

On November 17, the writers announced the results of the vote. Clemente didn't hear about the awarding of the MVP until the next day, when he picked up a newspaper in San Juan. Given his revealing conversation with the Los Angeles sportswriter in August, the choice for MVP did not completely surprise him. The writers had selected a member of the world champion Pirates as the National League winner, only it wasn't Clemente. With 16 of 22 first-place votes, shortstop Dick Groat earned MVP honors, despite missing almost the entire month of September with a broken wrist. (The injury, suffered on September 6, kept him out of action until September 30.) Another Pirate, third baseman Don Hoak, picked up five first-place ballots and finished second in the voting.

The selection of Groat as MVP fulfilled the campaign that Clemente believed had been conducted by Les Biederman in mid-season. "When Dick Groat won the MVP in '60, Clemente was really ticked off at Les Biederman," says former Pittsburgh Courier writer Bill Nunn. "Biederman pushed for Dick Groat over Clemente. I heard this from some white reporters at that time." In the November 17th edition of the Pittsburgh Press, Biederman wrote: "Groat truly deserved this much coveted award." Biederman also laid out the order of his personal voting for the award: Groat first, followed by Hoak second, and Clemente third.

Clemente actually fared better with Biederman than he did in the overall voting. Receiving only one first-place vote, Clemente didn't even finish as high as fourth or fifth. In fact, Clemente's name could not be found until eighth place, well after superstars like Willie Mays and Ernie Banks. Even players like Lindy McDaniel, Ken Boyer and a third Pirate, Vern Law—very good players all, but not at the superstar level—finished higher than Clemente. In other words, the writers regarded Clemente as no better than the eighth most important player in the league and the fourth most valuable player on the 1960 Pirates.

The results of the balloting infuriated Clemente, who understood why Groat had won and harbored no resentment toward his teammate, but felt that he himself should have finished higher than eighth in the voting. Clemente cited "political reasons," code words for his belief that racism against Latin American players had played a part in the writers' thinking. "He was convinced that it was due to that," says Luis Mayoral, referring to possible racism on the part of the writers. "To the day of his death, he was convinced of that."

Although the low finish gnawed at Clemente, he did not allow it to affect his relationship with Groat. "Roberto and Dick Groat got along well," Mayoral says. "It was not a personal struggle, or a fight as to who was MVP or not. What hurt Roberto was the fact that he ended up eighth in the MVP voting, and even Don Hoak, the third baseman, got more votes than him."

While the selection of Groat as MVP was justifiable in some respects, given his league-leading batting average and reliable fielding at arguably the most demanding of defensive positions, Hoak's higher finish over Clemente remains mystifying. Hoak's defenders might point to his spirited leadership and durability, specifically his fire-and-brimstone style of play and his ability to play a full regular season schedule, even with injuries. After suffering an eight-inch cut to his foot in a swimming pool accident, Hoak had told a doctor to stitch the injury without an anesthetic. Unbelievably, Hoak didn't miss a game. Clemente played hard—when he played—but had missed a few games in 1960 with nagging injuries. Hoak played in all 155 games, while Clemente appeared in 144. On the issue of durability, Hoak rated the edge.

Hoak supporters might also point to his brilliant defensive play at third base, but the fielding comparison to Clemente doesn't hold much significance. The 32-year-old infielder was no more dominant at his position than Clemente, who threw out 19 runners from his post in right field. Both fielded their positions extremely well, although neither captured a Gold Glove Award. In terms of offensive production, Hoak and Clemente hit the same number of home runs—16—but other key offensive statistics showed a large disparity in favor of the Pirate right fielder. Clemente easily distanced Hoak in batting average, outhitting him by 32 percentage points. Clemente also topped Hoak in RBI production, 94 to 79. Clemente was also a much faster, and therefore, more dangerous baserunner. Given the evidence, Hoak's second-place finish and Clemente's eighth-place finish seem incongruous.

Upset by his embarrassingly low finish in the MVP tally, Clemente refused to wear his 1960 World Championship ring. His teammate, Joe Christopher, joined him in a pact, agreeing not to wear his World Series ring either. To this day, Christopher has never worn the ring.

Clemente would instead wear an All-Star ring that would come his way the next summer. "That is true," says Luis Mayoral. "What he wore was the 1961 All-Star Game [ring]. Now remember, it was nothing against Dick Groat. It was against the fact that he ended up eighth in the MVP balloting." In 1961, National League pitchers would have to pay heavily for that oversight by the writers.

9

Silver Bats

In the early days of spring training, Roberto Clemente made a daring change in the equipment he had used to post his best offensive season. Clemente switched from a 31-ounce bat to a much weightier version, which he hoped would allow him to control his swing and hit with even more authority to right field. Clemente had hopes of winning a batting title; a spring training conversation with batting coach George Sisler encouraged him further. Sisler told him that he believed he could become the best hitter in the National League. Clemente confirmed Sisler's confidence by racing out to a league-leading .359 batting average through the second All-Star break and earning selection to both midsummer All-Star games.

On July 31, standouts from the American and National Leagues participated in the season's second All-Star Game. Fenway Park provided the setting for a game that would be smeared by a controversial call at first base.

The disputed ruling involved Clemente. In the top of the fourth, with the American League leading 1-0 on a Rocky Colavito home run, the National League attempted to rally. Maury Wills reached on a leadoff single to center field. One out later, Willie Mays blooped a single to left. Orlando Cepeda—like Clemente, a native of Puerto Rico— popped up for the inning's second out. Needing a two-out single to tie the game, Clemente came up and banged a hard grounder to the left side of the infield. Shortstop Luis Aparicio fielded the ball cleanly, but decided to forego the force play on Mays at second base. Aparicio fired across the diamond, but threw too low, the ball landing well in front of first baseman Norm Cash. Using his over-sized first baseman's mitt, Cash attempted to scoop the throw, which had beat Clemente to the bag. Cash bobbled the scoop twice, the ball nestling into a space between his glove and his chest. By the time Cash corralled the ball and held it in his glove, Clemente had crossed first base.

Fans, broadcasters and writers saw the play clearly. Clemente was safe, loading the bases. First base umpire Frank Secory saw it differently. Blocked by Cash's broad-shouldered back, Secory didn't see the first baseman bobble the ball and called Clemente out. Home plate umpire Larry Napp enjoyed a better viewpoint, but didn't overrule the call because Secory elected not to ask him for help. Even though the call aided the cause of the American League stars— the game being played at an AL stadium—many of the fans at Fenway Park booed the decision. Others laughed at a call so blatantly wrong.

If the play had occurred during a meaningful regular season game, Clemente would have argued—long and loudly. Given the exhibition nature of the All-Star Game, Clemente and most of his National League teammates decided to let it pass. Only first base coach Elvin Tappe put up a protest, and a mild one at that.

The National League managed to tie the game with a single run in the sixth. At the end of nine innings, with the game still deadlocked at 1-1 and rains falling on Fenway, the umpires stopped play. After a brief 21-minute wait, Commissioner Ford Frick called off the game. For the first and only time in major league history, an All-Star Game had ended in a tie. It was also an unproductive game for Clemente—hitless in two at-bats— especially compared to his performance at the earlier All-Star Game in San Francisco, where he had driven in the winning run with a tenth-inning single.

In August of 1961, Clemente talked at length with Pirate beat writer Jack Hernon on a team flight. During a 45-minute interview, Clemente expounded on issues ranging from his health to finan-cial matters. When Hernon informed him that Ralph Kiner had made the highest salary in Pirates' franchise history—$90,000—

Clemente exclaimed, "That much!" By comparison, Roberto's salary seemed like a pittance. Yet, Clemente went on to describe general manager Joe Brown as a fair man during contract negotiations, while acknowledging Brown for making several loan arrangements. "Joe Brown, he's OK with me when I need money to buy house and he's OK when I sign my contracts," Clemente told Hernon. Clemente explained that he had supplemented his income by buying four apartment houses in Puerto Rico and renting them unfurnished for $90 a unit.

Clemente also discussed one of his most-asked topics—injuries. He talked about the bone chip that he had complained about during the 1960 season. "You can still feel bone chip in my elbow," Clemente told Hernon. "That's why I throw the ball underhand sometimes. If I throw real hard lots of times overhand in game, the elbow hurts and swells up."

Clemente bristled at the criticisms that came from others, those who had questioned the severity, or even existence, of his ailments. "Sometimes I get mad at people," Clemente told Hernon. "But only once here in Pittsburgh. That when I was hurt and everyone call me 'Jake.'" The less-than-flattering nickname represented a play on the slang word "jaker" or "jaking," referring to someone who refused to play because of minor inconveniences or slight injuries.

"He would not play certain days when he didn't feel good," says former teammate Nellie King. "It became kind of a sign that he was a malingerer or didn't have enough [guts], so to speak. [Others said], 'He didn't want to play today because so and so was pitching,' [Bob] Gibson or [Johnny] Antonelli. It got whispered around that he didn't want to play; he's jaking it."

Unlike some of his teammates, King understood why Clemente missed games. "He said, 'If I cannot play well, I will embarrass myself and my family, and I will embarrass the team.' If he didn't feel like he could play well that day, he wouldn't play." As with many aspects of his life, self-esteem played a great part in Clemente's decisions about playing. "Clemente's pride would not allow him to give a bad performance," King says.

Another cultural difference between the United States and Latin America, specifically Puerto Rico, created problems for Clemente. "In the United States," King explains, "if you don't feel good, you're supposed to go out there, put some tobacco juice on it and [say], 'Let's get going.' We expect that from everybody. Teammates did not understand why he was acting the way he was, or why he didn't play. It wasn't an act; it was just a sincere belief on his part. It's hard for anybody to understand that unless you understand the pride and culture he came from. 'You should not embarrass yourself, or your parents, or your team.'"

Misunderstandings of Clemente's cultural mindset about playing hurt stirred feelings of resentment from a few of the Pirate players, especially ElRoy Face, one of Clemente's harshest critics. "That became a big, big problem between the players on the team when he first came up—til the mid-sixties, when most of them left," says King. "They never understood that."

Some teammates failed to understand why Clemente didn't socialize with them at nightclubs after games. "Clemente was not that type of individual," says Joe Christopher. "ElRoy Face and all those different guys, they're partying types. And if they're the partying type, would you expect a man [like Clemente] who was a sedentary individual to get involved? No.

"These individuals were drinking, they were out, having parties, they have fun. Clemente said, 'If I'm here to do a job, the job must take precedence. Now after the season is over, I can have all the parties I want. But if I'm here to do a job—I'm signing a contract to do a job.' But the American mentality is not that way."

In an effort to get himself healthy, Clemente revealed to Jack Hernon that he had been in contact with a friend, a man who was not legally a doctor, but had helped his back nonetheless. "I have a friend in Puerto Rico who studied to be a doctor but not finished," Clemente told the *Post-Gazette*. "He had lots of money now and just likes to work as doctor sometimes. He fixed me up." Clemente had also been in touch with a chiropractor in St. Louis, a doctor who had been recommended by Cardinals' beat writer Bob Broeg.

In spite of his health problems, Clemente finished the season with a .351 batting average. The mark ranked him first among National League batters, eight points ahead of Cincinnati's developing young star, the 23-year-old Vada Pinson. Now 26 years old, the once-raw Clemente had evolved into legitimate National League stardom of his own.

In dissecting the reasons for his career-best batting average and hitting title, an examination of his 1961 statistics showed a remarkable discrepancy between day games and night games. In 68 games played during the afternoon hours, Clemente batted .411. In his last 13 day games, Clemente tortured pitchers at a .484 rate. At night, he compiled a .301 average—a good mark, but 50 points below his final season average.

While Clemente hit capably at Forbes Field during the day-time, he reached his offensive peak playing on the road against the Cubs. In games played at Wrigley Field, where the absence of ballpark lights dictated that all games be played during the day, Clemente achieved a .478 rate of success. Poor Cubs' pitching—the second worst in the National League—combined with the sightlines of Wrigley made Chicago a hitter's haven for Clemente.

Roberto tried to explain his achievements in daytime base-ball. "My brother keeps my records and he call me a weekend hitter," Clemente told Les Biederman of the *Pittsburgh Press*, referring to the day games that National League teams almost always played on Saturdays and Sundays. "I like to hit better in daylight than at night. I like sunshine. It makes me feel good. And I can see ball better than at night."

A breakdown of Clemente's 1961 season also typified his style of power hitting. Of his career-high 23 home runs, 15 traveled to right field and two went to straightaway center field. Clemente pulled only a half dozen longballs to left field. When Clemente drove the ball with his utmost power, it was usually to the alley in right-center field.

By winning the batting championship in 1961, Clemente be-came the first native Puerto Rican to own a major league hitting crown. He also became the first Latin American to claim a National League hitting championship. Roberto "Bobby" Avila, a second baseman from Veracruz, Mexico, had captured the 1954 batting title by hitting .341, but he had done so for the Cleveland Indians, an *American League* team.

Luis Mayoral believes that the 1961 batting crown may have marked a turning point in Clemente's career, empowering him as an accepted and respected figure in the Pirate clubhouse. "I would say early sixties, maybe right after his first hitting championship in 1961," Mayoral says. "That hitting championship meant a lot to him. You gotta remember that during the 1960 season, he helped the Pirates immensely in getting to the World Series. Then, when the MVP voting came out for the 1960 season, Dick Groat, the short-stop got the award."

Motivated by the ridiculously low finish in the MVP ballot-ing, Clemente had embarked on a personal mission of excellency. "So in 1961," says Mayoral, "and this he told me many times, he went out there to try to be the best ballplayer in the National League." With the batting championship in hand, Clemente also became more credible as a social spokesman, one who would be heard by both the fans and the media. "Right after then," Mayoral contends, "people started seeing the true Clemente as a ballplayer and the true Clemente coming out of the shell, speaking out for his rights. Not only for his rights, but for Latinos and African-Americans who had grown up and still grow up in the states—people being slapped on one side of the face and putting up the other side to get slapped. Roberto was not afraid to speak. But he had to reach a level of stardom where people would say, 'Hey, we gotta listen to this guy.'"

While Clemente had started to become a champion for social rights, his presence as a clubhouse leader had not yet fully developed. "I know when I first got there, Clemente had not assumed the role," says Donn Clendenon, who made his major league debut in 1961. "I think that Clemente had developed something of a shell around him. It might have been a protective mechanism, I don't know. But I noticed as time progressed that he became the leader he was supposed to be."

The 1961 season also represented a breakthrough for Puerto Rican baseball, in general. While Clemente had won the first of his batting titles, another Puerto Rican National League had dominated the other two Triple Crown categories. "Roberto's hitting championship in '61," Mayoral points out, "coincided with [Orlando] Cepeda of the Giants winning the National League home run and RBI championships." Splitting his time between first base and the outfield, the 23-year-old Cepeda hit 46 home runs and drove in 142 runs. Cepeda's closest pursuers in those categories, teammate Willie Mays and Reds' outfielder Frank Robinson, weren't really close at all. Mays finished six home runs behind Cepeda, while the 25-year-old Robinson drove in 124 runs, nearly 20 behind the pace set by the "Baby Bull." In the past, no Puerto Rican player had led the league in either home runs or RBIs.

In a sense, two Puerto Rican players had captured the Triple Crown, Clemente leading the league in hitting and Cepeda topping all contenders in home runs and RBIs. The combined accomplishment was not overlooked by natives of the island, or the Caribbean. According to Mayoral, "the exploits of Clemente and Cepeda served as a source of great pride to Puerto Ricans and Latinos—the Triple Crown in the National League for two Puerto Ricans." Bolstered by its two greatest hitting stars, Latin America had achieved a special niche in the consciousness of baseball fans, even for those born and raised in the states.

The feelings of pride didn't merely exist in the minds of hopeful Latino ballplayers or sportswriters. When the season came to an end, Clemente and Cepeda flew back to Puerto Rico together. After arriving at San Juan International Airport, the two men rode in a motorcade to Sixto Escobar Stadium in Santurce. Along the way, an estimated crowd of more than 18,000 fans welcomed Clemente and Cepeda, bathing them in rhythmic applause. An additional gathering of 5,000 fans waited for the two stars at Sixto Escobar Stadium. On the small island of Puerto Rico, over 23,000 fans, had taken time to see two of their most cherished baseball stars.

During the season, Roberto had seen a doctor about the continuing pain in his right elbow. Dr. Richard Bennett of Johns Hopkins had ordered X-rays, which showed a floating bone chip. Dr. Bennett said that Clemente could continue to play with the bone chip, but would need an operation after the season. After the Pirates' final game, Clemente returned to the hospital to have the chip surgically removed. According to one version of the story, Dr. Bennett opened up Clemente's elbow, but couldn't find any bone chips. Some of Clemente's harshest critics refueled their notions of hypochondria, claiming that his elbow had been fine from the start.

In a 1970 interview with the *Pittsburgh Post-Gazette*, the recollections of Joe Brown placed the bone chip story in a different light. According to Brown, there had definitely been a bone chip, which had either moved from the elbow to another spot within the arm, or had completely dissolved. Either way, the bone chip had *not* been the figment of Clemente's imagination.

Even though the Pirates had endured a disappointing season after their world championship, Clemente received better recognition from the writers than he had the previous year. Roberto finished fourth in the MVP voting, four spots better than his placement in the 1960 tally. Local honors began to pour in, too. Pittsburgh's Dapper Dan Club, a charitable sports organization, honored Clemente at a dinner on February 6. Clemente received the annual "Dapper Dan Award," given to the Pittsburgh-area athlete who did the most to publicize the city.

The next day, Clemente signed his name to a monetary reward—a new contract paying him a salary of $50,000 for the upcoming 1962 season. "We reached an agreement with no trouble," Pirate general manager Joe Brown informed UPI. "Obviously, Roberto felt it was a fair offer because he signed readily." As was becoming the custom, Clemente felt that Brown had treated him justly at the contract table.

10

Fallback

When Clemente reported to spring training, he disclosed that his stomach had been bothering him. He had lost 10 pounds from a frame that was already lean and fragile. The ailment did not bode well for the upcoming season. After hitting an Opening Day grand slam against the Phillies, Clemente struggled in the summer's early months, hitting in the .260s with little power. "I just don't feel good," Clemente complained to *The Sporting News* in late May. "I have no pep, no get-up-and-go. Last year I felt good, but this year it seems like such an effort."

Clemente's relationships with certain writers also required an effort—one that Roberto was not always ready to give. Clemente disliked the way that some reporters asked him negative questions about teammates. "I remember a story," says Nellie King, "1962, it must have been, when the Mets came into the league." At the time, San Francisco and Los Angeles represented the best of the National League, while teams like the Cubs and the expansion New York Mets dragged the bottom of the league's barrel. "One of the sportswriters came in [to the clubhouse]," King says.

"He said [to Roberto], 'You know, Bob Friend just can't beat the Giants and the Dodgers. The only teams he can beat are the Mets and the Cubs.' Instead of diplomatically trying to sidestep the question, Clemente put the writer on the spot. 'Why are you talking [over] here, talking to me? Bob Friend is over there. You can go tell him.'"

As King describes, Roberto decided to carry his point further. "'I will tell him for you,'" Clemente instructed the writer. 'Bob, he does not think you can beat the good teams, you can only beat the bad teams.'" Clemente's demonstration angered the writer, who inquired, "'What the hell are you doing that for?' Roberto shot back, 'Hey, if you want to talk to him, you go talk to him. Don't talk to me about him.'" As King recalls: "Although the exchange embarrassed the writer, Clemente had made his point," says King. "If you have something say about someone, tell him directly. If you have a question to ask, do it face-to-face. Clemente didn't like people—writers, or anyone else for that matter—talking about others behind their back."

Clemente did not appreciate another practice of the media. Some writers and broadcasters insisted on calling him "Bob" or "Bobby." Several teammates used similar names in addressing or referring to him. Even most of his baseball cards listed him as "Bob Clemente," a trend that continued as late as 1969. Clemente did not encourage such Americanization of his given name, a disrespectful practice that had occurred mostly during the late fifties and early sixties. "Roberto made it clear from the first that his name was 'Roberto,' not 'Bobby,'" says Luis Mayoral. "He didn't like that. He didn't like that at all. He said, 'My name is 'Roberto Clemente,' not 'Bobby Clemente' or 'Robby Clemente.' My name is 'Roberto Clemente.'" If his teammates insisted on using a nickname, Roberto preferred that they call him "Momen," an untranslatable Spanish moniker that he had acquired as a youngster.

After his poor start at the plate, Clemente's batting surged in June and July. He raised his average to .336 by mid-season, earning selection to the National League All-Star team. Clemente picked up three hits in three at-bats during the first of the two midsummer classics, helping the Nationals to a 3-1 victory over the American League.

Willie Stargell made his major league debut for the Pirates in 1962, appearing in 10 late-season games. The following year, he became a regular for the Bucs, playing primarily in left field. It didn't take long for Stargell to realize what made his neighbor in right field a Gold Glove defender. "He worked at it," Stargell says of Clemente. "One of the things that he taught me was every time we'd go into a stadium—or even at home—to spend a little extra time working on things: have balls hit to you, not just fly balls or ground balls, but hit 'em off the wall at different angles. Find the sun, hit the ball into the sun and be able to shield the sun in such a way that you don't lose the ball in the sun."

While Stargell had natural home run power, his own defensive play did not come so smoothly. By watching Clemente, he learned that he would have to work at his fielding to make himself a competent left fielder. He also realized that Clemente's defensive talents, while more ample than his own, were not simply God-given. "His ability was no accident," says Stargell. "He put a lot of time and effort and intelligence into his game. And what people saw was the finished product."

Clemente finished the 1962 season at .312, the eighth best batting average in the league. He might have fared even better, if not for another weight loss brought on by anxiety and stomach trouble. Clemente's late-season slump, coupled with his early hitting woes, had some wondering what he might do if he could only sustain his strength over a full season.

Prior to the 1963 season, general manager Joe Brown made two major trades, one with the Philadelphia Phillies and the other with the St. Louis Cardinals. In two of his least sagacious deals, Brown sent the entire left side of his infield—shortstop Dick Groat and Don Hoak—to National League rivals for the meager return of first baseman Juan "Pancho" Herrera, infielder Julio Gotay, outfielder Ted Savage and pitcher Don Cardwell. On the plus side, Brown did make two favorable trades, acquiring outfielder Manny Mota from the San Francisco Giants and catcher Jim Pagliaroni from the Boston Red Sox. From within their farm system, the Pirates also promoted young infielder Gene Alley, who would become the team's regular shortstop within two years.

In May, Clemente's confrontations with National League umpires became a recurring theme. In one game, he strongly argued a call at first base, but the ruling stood. On May 28, Clemente's dissatisfaction with umpires reached a head. In the fourth inning, arbiter Bill Jackowski called out Donn Clendenon on a close play at first base, stifling a potential Pirate rally. In the fifth inning, Jackowski called Clemente out on a similar play, capping off a ground ball double play. Clemente justifiably argued the play, as did Pirate manager Danny Murtaugh. Clemente badly overreacted, however. When first base coach Ron Northey intervened, Clemente tried to move him out of the way. In so doing, Clemente bumped Jackowski—twice. The umpire ejected Clemente from the game, and the National League supported his decision by announcing a $250 fine and a five-day suspension.

National League president Warren Giles justified the length of the suspension by describing Clemente's offense as "the most serious reported to our office in several years." Giles admonished Clemente for failing to control his temper with the umpires. Although Clemente acknowledged his own wrongdoing in making contact with the umpire, he insisted it was unintentional. "This was an accident," Clemente told Bill Christine of the *Pittsburgh Press* several years later. "I hit him with my open palm, not my fist, but this was because I was trying to get away from the coach." Clemente considered the fine justifiable, but felt the suspension was unfair given his lack of intent.

Clemente even hinted at being the victim of a kind of conspiracy conducted by National League umpires. "I lose 15 to 20 points every year on close plays and I never argue unless I feel umpire is wrong," Clemente told Les Biederman of the *Pittsburgh Press*. "I have good record in NL office, but this is the worst year I have ever seen for umpiring."

The umpires and league rulings provided only some of Clemente's sources of discontent. Another was supplied by manager Danny Murtaugh. During a West Coast trip, Roberto ate a meal that combined steak and shrimp. He became so ill that he had to visit a nearby hospital to have his stomach pumped. When Clemente reported to Dodger Stadium in a weakened state the next day, he appeared to be in no condition to play. Murtaugh kept him in the lineup anyway, and watched him strike out twice against Dodgers' ace Don Drysdale.

The Pirates traveled from Los Angeles to Houston. Clemente complained of feeling dizzy and asked to be taken out of the lineup. The request angered Murtaugh, leading to a nasty pre-game argument. Clemente sat out the next three games.

Later in the season, Murtaugh questioned the right fielder's hustle and desire. In an at-bat against the Phillies, Clemente swung and hit a ground ball. As soon as he hit the ball, he fell at home plate, unable to run out the routine grounder. Clemente said he had a bad ankle, but the manager didn't believe him. Murtaugh told Clemente to take his uniform off and head for the clubhouse. Insulted by such a request, Clemente refused and shouted back at his manager. The two men continued to argue, with Murtaugh announcing a fine that eventually escalated to $650.

Clemente's disagreements with Murtaugh and the umpires may have contributed to one of his more habitual problems—insomnia. He had experienced episodes of sleep deprivation in the past, but they became worse in 1963. The presence of a snoring roommate, Pirates' coach Gene Baker, did not help the situation. "With this coach, I could not sleep at all," Clemente told Red Smith in 1964. "I keep asking them to let me sleep alone, but they say 'no, can't do it.'"

Yet, even when Clemente slept alone, he found himself distracted. "Anything makes noise while I'm in bed," Clemente told *Time* magazine in 1967. "I hear it—a truck outside the hotel, a footstep in the hall."

Clemente's insomnia had prevented the Pirates from making baseball history several years earlier. When white-skinned Dick Hall had joined the team, Pittsburgh's traveling secretary asked Clemente if Hall could room with him. Clemente said no. Clemente didn't care about rooming with a white player; he preferred having no one as a roommate, black, white or otherwise because of his problems sleeping. If not for Clemente's incessant insomnia, the Pirates might have become the first team in major league history to feature interracial roommates.

In spite of his many problems, Clemente played in 152 games and won his third straight Gold Glove. His final offensive numbers also looked good, highlighted by his .320 batting average, second-best in the National League. Yet, some in the organization did not regard the season as vintage Clemente. "This isn't a good year for Clemente," general manager Joe Brown told Les Biederman of the *Pittsburgh Press* during the off-season. "He can be better, much better. With his ability, I feel any time he bats under .350, it isn't a good season."

Brown believed Clemente capable of reaching the hitter's magic circle. "When they talk of potential .400 hitters," Brown told Biederman, "they never mention Clemente. Yet, he has all the tools to reach that figure. He hits line drives, he hits to all fields and he has power. And he can run." Brown talked of Clemente's potential. As much as his right fielder had accomplished, Brown felt he could do more—much more.

The Pirates *needed* Clemente to do more. They had finished eighth out of 10 teams in the National League. With Dick Groat and Don Hoak gone, clubhouse and on-field leadership had taken a major hit. Given his star status, no player was better equipped to set an example than Clemente.

After the season, Clemente returned home to Puerto Rico. As he was driving by Landrau's Pharmacy, he noticed an attractive young woman walking across the plaza. "He was driving and he passed by me," said the woman, "and he kept looking at me. And I just kept on walking, looking very serious." She walked into the drugstore, as did Clemente. Roberto talked with her briefly, but did not ask for a date, as she made a hasty retreat from the store. When Clemente returned home, he informed his mother that he had met his future bride.

Vera Cristina Zabala had attended college at the University of Puerto Rico. She had studied pre-law, graduating first in her class. She then went to work as a secretary at the Government Development Bank. A few days after their first encounter, Roberto saw her again and asked her to go to lunch. Being a conservative Catholic girl, she declined the invitation. A mutual friend then arranged for the two to meet at a small house party. Roberto talked to the young woman before asking again for a date. This time she said yes, agreeing to go to a game with Roberto in San Juan. The ballpark in San Juan—Hiram Bithorn Stadium—served as the backdrop for their first official date.

11

A Challenge From the GM

C lemente missed the first 20 games of the 1963-64 Puerto Rican Winter League season. When he did begin his winter league schedule, he soon established himself as one of the league's top hitters. His batting average soared into the .330 range, as line drive after line drive landed in the outfield gaps. By season's end, Clemente's average had risen to .345, the fourth best figure in the league. Roberto found himself in good company. Of the three players who posted better marks, all were heralded young major leaguers: Walter Bond, who would hit 20 home runs for the Houston Colt 45s in 1964; Tony Oliva, who would bat .323 as a rookie for the Minnesota Twins; and San Francisco Giants' star Orlando Cepeda.

In January of 1964, general manager Joe Brown planned a trip to the Dominican and Puerto Rico to talk to several of his top young players, including the impressive 13-game winner Alvin McBean. Brown also planned to talk contract with Clemente. "That was not an unusual thing for me to do," Brown recalls. "I went every year. I went to Latin America to talk about things [contracts]. I didn't believe it was fair to have players whose basic language was not English try to negotiate their contracts by letter. If I didn't understand what he said in a letter, I couldn't ask him what he meant. But in a face-to-face conversation, we could exchange opinions and exchange ideas."

Brown also hoped that by meeting with his best player in person prior to the 1964 season, he could encourage him to push himself harder, to raise his level of play higher. "Clemente can do so much for the Pirates," Brown told Les Biederman, corresponding for *The Sporting News*. "He has as much ability as anybody in the game, yet, great as he is, he could be greater."

As much as Brown liked Clemente's on-field results, he wanted his star to become more of a presence in the clubhouse. "He could be our leader, the man we need to show the way," Brown said. "Clemente is very emotional and sometimes he's controlled by the way the team is going. If we're winning, he's hitting and doing everything expected of him. But when we hit a slump, Clemente's spirit gets down, too."

Brown met with Clemente for four hours, terming it an upbeat and productive conversation. "Clemente told me he never felt better," Brown reported happily to *The Sporting News*. "In other seasons, he has always had a stomach ailment and trouble sleeping—even in the winter. But he said he has had no pains."

In addition to the optimism created by Clemente's physical state, Brown came away impressed with Roberto's attitude. Brown told him how much the Pirates needed him, how he expected him to lift his game further. According to Brown, Clemente seemed agreeable to the challenge of leading the Pirates both on and off the field.

Perhaps motivated by his winter sit-down with Brown, Clemente hit safely in 23 of his first 24 games. The .398 average represented the best and most consistent start of Clemente's 10-year career. For that, Clemente credited a productive and peaceful off-season. "Last year and the year before, I had trouble sleeping," he said, referring to his recurring nocturnal problems. "But not now," a relieved Clemente told Les Biederman of the *Pittsburgh Press*.

As a skinny right-hander from Canaan, Connecticut, Steve Blass made his major league debut in the summer of 1964. He noticed that Clemente was beginning to evolve into a stronger presence in the clubhouse. "When I came up to the Pirates in '64," Blass recalls, "Clemente was just kind of emerging in terms of being a leader and asserting himself more." During his rookie season, Blass felt some natural intimidation when he neared Clemente and other team veterans. "When I came to the Pirates," Blass says, "I was very much aware of what Clemente was doing every minute, what [Bill] Mazeroski was doing, what [Willie] Stargell was doing. Maybe as much Clemente as any of the three of them because he was the quieter one, he was the stern-looking one at times."

After awhile, Blass felt more comfortable about striking up a conversation with Clemente. "It's almost like you had to be around him for awhile and watch him play, until you felt you were qualified to be his teammate. In other words, I had him up on a pedestal. Until I was a teammate of his for awhile and had pitched in front of him and had contributed some. Then I felt it was OK to approach him." In time, Blass developed a special appreciation for the artistry of Clemente. "It passes into a phase where it was just such a delight to watch him play, and a delight to have him in right field when you're pitching. He had that gift; he was an exciting enough ballplayer that he could turn a 10-year veteran into a 10-year-old kid watching baseball."

Blass says that in games in which he pitched he tries to focus his energies on the opposing team's batters. When Clemente came to the plate, however, Blass transformed into the role of a spectator. "Most times in between innings, when I'd come off the field from pitching, I'd go into the clubhouse and wander around because I was always kind of high strung. But when Clemente was going to bat, I'd make sure I was out on the bench watching."

On July 1, Clemente experienced one of the most interesting pitcher-hitter confrontations of his career. With one out and the bases loaded in the fifth inning, Clemente came to bat against San Francisco's Juan Marichal. Protecting a 2-0 lead, Marichal worked carefully to Clemente, filling the count. As Clemente pawed at the dirt in the batter's box with his feet, his head looking downward as he smoothed the soil, Marichal decided to deliver a quick-pitch. Clemente heard a shout from his third base coach, warning him that Marichal had already thrown the ball. An unprepared Clemente looked up suddenly and swatted at the ball with one hand. Somehow Clemente made contact, the ball caroming off his bat onto home plate and then bounding high into the air toward first base. By the time Giants' first baseman Orlando Cepeda fielded the high chopper, Clemente had crossed first base and the Pirates had scored their first run of the game. Although the Pirates would end up losing the game, 2-1, Clemente had denied the future Hall of Famer another shutout. The ultimate bad-ball hitter had done it again.

In July, for one of the first times since joining the Pirates, Clemente talked at length about the struggles faced by Latin American players in making the transition to professional baseball in the states. In responding to a reporter who wondered why some talented Latinos didn't live up to expectations, Clemente offered a number of reasons. "I've heard American scouts tell me about Latin players they have signed," Clemente told *The Sporting News*, "and when they see these kids in the United States, they can't believe it's the same boy." Clemente expressed frustration with some scouts' lack of understanding. "Maybe this is puzzling to Americans, but it isn't puzzling to any of us from Latin America who have gone through this ordeal."

According to Clemente, cultural differences lengthened the period of adjustment for most Latino players. "We lead different lives in America," Clemente explained. "The language barrier is great at first and we have trouble ordering food in restaurants." The overt racism of American society also posed a problem. "Even segregation baffles us," said Clemente, who had witnessed little of that racial practice in his native Puerto Rico.

Clemente called for scouts and managers to show more patience with Latin American players, especially those who had come to the United States for the first time. "It takes time for us to settle down emotionally," Clemente said. "Once we're at peace with the world, we can do the job." Clemente was a perfect example of a player who had made a slow, but successful transition. After the struggles of his first five seasons, he had become one of the game's best all-around players by 1960.

His outstanding performance during that watershed season, coupled with his fine play in the World Series, had vaulted him to a new level of respect in the Caribbean. Clemente then began seizing opportunities to sound off on issues of concern to the Latino player. "I guess right after the 1960 World Series," reasoned Luis Mayoral, "he had become sort of like the leader of Latinos in baseball. To me, he had the intestinal fortitude to become the spokesman for Latinos in the game. There have been other Latinos prior to him like Minnie Minoso and Chico Carrasquel—great players, great individuals—but they didn't have that makeup to really take the flag and lead Latinos in searching for recognition and respect in major league baseball."

Carrasquel and Minoso had starred in the 1950s, at a time when minority players still felt great discomfort in speaking out against racism. The major leagues had integrated only a few years earlier, making blacks and dark-skinned Latinos less secure about their ability to hold employment in either of the established leagues. Most didn't want to complain publicly, for fear that they might be branded as malcontents and given their outright releases. When combined with natural inhibitions in speaking the English language, Latin American players of the fifties felt even less inclined to speak out about issues of racism and respect. They didn't want to discuss even the most remotely controversial topics, lest they say the wrong thing and irritate the powers-that-be in the managers' offices and the general managers' chairs.

Unfortunately, few of Clemente's Latino contemporaries joined him in speaking out for the rights and concerns of Hispanic players. According to some Latin American baseball experts, the absence of outspoken leadership continues to be felt in the 1990s. Even in recent years, with many Latin American players far more skilled in their command of the English language, few have taken the aggressive approach that Clemente did in speaking out for his Hispanic brethren. "In the quarter century since Clemente passed away, no one has really stepped in to fill the moral void—the moral role—that he held when he played the game," says Marcos Breton. "While Latin players are making such a big impact now, the void is still there in that there isn't anybody of Clemente's moral stature coming out of Latin America, nobody who is arguing and advocating on behalf of Latin players."

In the mid-sixties, a little-known encounter with one of the country's most famed civil rights leaders provided Clemente with a further education on the subject of racism. "Something interesting happened that not too many in the states know," reveals Luis Mayoral. "Somewhere along the road in his major league career, he befriended Martin Luther King. I think that was also a key relationship, in relation to the development of Roberto Clemente, the fighter for social equality."

Clemente and King held their first meeting in 1964. "They met in Puerto Rico," says Mayoral, "when Martin Luther King went down there to a little farm that Roberto had in the outskirts of Carolina. In that little farm, Roberto would build a restaurant and recreational area for families, called 'El Carretero [which means Man of the Road].' In that little farm, that's where they had that meeting."

Although one was African-American and the other Latino, the

two men found common grounds of interest. "They became friends," Mayoral says. "I do remember that around 1970 there was an all-star game—it could have been '69—in Los Angeles at Dodger Stadium, where blacks and Latinos played to raise funds for the Martin Luther King Foundation. And one of the most prized possessions or awards that Roberto got was a Martin Luther King medallion for playing in that game." In later years, Vera Clemente lent the medallion to Mayoral, who in turn passed it on to the Texas Rangers' museum located at the Ballpark in Arlington. The medallion is displayed in a booth commemorating Clemente.

Clemente's own words showed his support for King, a man who had fought principally for African-Americans, but also for other groups of minorities. "I believe that this man not only changed the lifestyle of the American black, he changed the life of everybody," Clemente said in a 1972 interview with Sam Nover of WIIC-TV.

In Clemente's early days with the team, the Pirates' black players had traveled together with the white players on the team bus. Although the practice appeared to foster unity between the white and black players, it also created feelings of awkwardness whenever the team stopped at a restaurant to eat. On many occasions, restaurants simply refused to serve the black players on the team. The segregationist practice was mostly evident in spring training, since the Pirates trained in the south. "Now we are in Florida, not too far from Puerto Rico," Clemente said, setting the scene. "You see the white players go to a restaurant, and they said, 'Fellas, do you want anything to eat?' Now we are sitting inside the bus, and I remember I told one of the players, 'Look, if you ever accept anything from anybody from that restaurant, you and me we going at it.' We're gonna have a fight because I think it's unfair."

"We didn't give it [segregation] a lot of thought," Vernon Law tells researcher Andrew O'Toole. "Or at least I didn't. I felt bad for Roberto, but he, just like us, accepted those kinds of things because that was the way it was. Even though it wasn't right, there was nothing we could do to change it, to make things any easier on him or the other black players."

But Clemente refused to accept this kind of segregation. He protested to general manager Joe Brown, who provided the Pirates' black players with a compromise solution. "After a year or so, we got a couple of cars from a local car dealer," Brown says. "We would only take enough black players on the road that would fill those two cars. They'd get their meal money and they'd drive their own cars and go to the games so they could stop wherever they knew they would be served." The alternative plan gave the Pirates' minorities a more comfortable ride, while sparing them the embarrassment of having to wait on the team bus while the white players dined comfortably in restaurants.

The segregationist practices of many Florida hotels in the late fifties and early sixties also created problems for black players like Clemente. "They had a law in effect—or at least it was a custom—in Fort Myers where we trained that the blacks could not live in the white hotels," says Joe Brown. "And we had a hotel downtown [where] they would not or could not take the blacks, so we put them in a very nice home owned by one of the top black men in town, a gentleman by the name of Mr. Earl." Mr. Earl lived on Evan Street, a predominantly black neighborhood in Fort Myers.

In time, Brown came up with a more formidable tactic to combat the segregation of the south. "After a few years, we found a motel that we could rent for the spring and we took the motel over ourselves," Brown explains, referring to the Edisonian Hotel, which the Pirates occupied beginning in 1963. "In as much as we owned the motel, we could put anybody we wanted in there. So we had all our players in there—black and white."

On the field, the Pirates continued to face obstacles of a different sort. A 12-inning loss to the Dodgers on September 2, capping off a three-game sweep, proved most exasperating—especially to Clemente. As he sat in the clubhouse at Forbes Field, Clemente talked glumly about the team's woes with Les Biederman. "Losing takes too much out of a team," complained Clemente. "Takes too much out of me. I don't like it. I'd give up the bat title if we could win the pennant."

Clemente went on to target specific reasons for the Pirates' summer of failure. "We give too many runs away. We're not good defensively, and this hurts our pitching, which isn't too strong but needs defense to make it look better. We make too many mistakes." Although Clemente was in the midst of his best statistical season, he found little solace in batting average, home runs and RBIs when they seemed to mean so little in the context of winning and losing.

In 1964, Clemente's season exceeded that of his 1960 performance. He accomplished career highs in three significant categories: hits (211), doubles (40), and walks (51). He won his second National League batting title. He even found a way to hit his pitching nemesis, Bob Purkey, a onetime Pirate teammate. By pitching him inside repeatedly and mixing in a masterful knuckleball, Purkey had owned Clemente in their previous pitcher-hitter confrontations. With six hits against Purkey in 1964, Roberto exceeded the total that he had accumulated against the Cincinnati Reds' right-hander over the previous half-dozen campaigns.

Although the Pirates finished a mediocre 80-82—tied for sixth place in the standings—Clemente's well-rounded season figured to place him in contention for MVP honors. Few expected Clemente to win the award, which went to the Cardinals' Ken Boyer, but a top five finish seemed in order. In a vote reminiscent of the mystifying 1960 tally, Clemente placed a disappointing ninth in the latest MVP tabulation.

Award voters added another blow to Clemente's chin when United Press International announced its 1964 All-Star team. UPI selected three outfielders from the two leagues combined: the Yankees' Mickey Mantle, the Giants' Willie Mays and the Cubs' Billy Williams. Clemente's .339 average and status as the game's premier defensive right fielder failed to sway the wire service's voting. Once again, Clemente's lack of home run power hurt him in gaining postseason recognition. Although Clemente's batting average easily exceeded the marks of all three UPI stars, his home run and RBI numbers lagged well behind.

Disappointment over the UPI and MVP snubs didn't discourage Clemente from pursuing a busy off-season schedule. Roberto staged several baseball clinics for underprivileged children in his native Puerto Rico. Clemente received no money for this voluntary duty, which would become an annual winter rite for the civic-minded baseball star. "You should learn the fundamentals. Work on them," Clemente often told youngsters who aspired to play the game. "This is a great game. It can do a lot for you, but only when you give it all you can."

Clemente made another important commitment during the winter of 1964. On November 14, about a year after they had first met, Roberto and Vera Zabala exchanged their wedding vows in the large San Fernando Catholic Church, which faced the plaza in Carolina. Fifteen hundred people attended the service. The event drew thousands of other well-wishers, not surprising given Clemente's celebrity status. Vera recalled the circumstances of the day. "I remember they closed the main street of Carolina. The plaza was full of people," Vera told Phoenix Communications in 1993. "The celebration [reception] was in Rio Piedras. That was an event—I will never forget it."

Luis Mayoral first met Vera Clemente within a few years of the wedding. "Vera, to this day, is one of my best personal friends," Mayoral says. "Vera, a bright lady—very quiet. Vera has always been the [faithful] wife and widow of Roberto Clemente." From the start, Mayoral noticed that Mrs. Clemente preferred a background role, rather than a place in the spotlight. "She was low-key [back then], even though I learned over the years that she is, in fact, a very bright lady. But very low-key." Vera would serve as a calming influence on Roberto, who would enjoy eight of his best seasons after their marriage.

"I heard a story about Vera," says Sally O'Leary, a longtime employee in the Pirates' public relations office who began working for the team in 1964. "It took place in the early sixties. This young man who came to see me works in the Pirate office now. He went someplace to get Roberto's autograph. It was at a church function somewhere. He stood in line with his dad for so long to get this autograph. And he finally got up to him and Roberto was signing it. And his father's taking photographs and his sister's taking autographs and all these flash bulbs are going off. After about five or six flashes, Roberto stopped and he looked at the people, and he said, 'Don't do that again. The flash bothers my eyes.'

"Then they went off and mingled with the crowd. Pretty soon, Vera Clemente came up to his mother and dad and to [the boy] and she took them back to the kitchen of this church. She said, 'Can I get you some coffee and some cake? I just wanted to apologize for my husband's behavior out there. He gets a little uptight at times and he doesn't mean it. But sometimes he just goes off and says something he doesn't mean.' That really impressed me about Vera."

The newlyweds purchased a villa located atop a large hill, replete with a view of San Juan Bay. Shortly after the wedding, Phil Dorsey found the Clementes a new apartment in the Homewood section of Pittsburgh. The next year, the couple moved to a new apartment complex in Pennley Park, where teammates like Matty Alou, Jose Pagan, Andre Rodgers, Manny Sanguillen stayed. In later years, newly acquired players like Juan Pizarro—a fellow Puerto Rican—would move into the Pennley Park complex. Clemente truly felt at home there, living with his wife, while also being close to his friends on the Pirates—players who shared a Latin American bond.

On December 21, 1964, Clemente embarked on a new phase of his ever-widening life. With his winter league team, the San Juan Senators, struggling to stay in the race, general manager Pepe Sada decided to make a change. In an unexpected move, Sada fired manager Cal Ermer. A veteran of managing in the Puerto Rican Winter League, Ermer had also served as a major league scout and was scheduled to become a manager in the Minnesota Twins' farm system. Ermer seemed eminently qualified for the position of managing San Juan, but Sada felt differently.

Ermer's replacement? Sada picked Clemente, the team's best player. Ironically, Clemente had played an indirect role in helping Ermer win the job in the first place. In the spring of 1964, rumors had floated that the Senators might tab Clemente as their next manager. Clemente happened to run into Ermer, informing him that he had no interest in the position. "I'm too young for the job," Clemente told Ermer. "It makes an old man of you." Clemente then dropped a surprise on Ermer. "I'm going to nominate you for it." With Clemente on his side, the Senators picked Ermer.

Now that Ermer was out, Clemente accepted the job reluctantly. "I'm only doing this until they get someone else," Clemente told Miguel J. Frau, a correspondent for *The Sporting News*. Sada had different plans, telling Clemente that he wanted him to play and manage the rest of the season.

In his managerial debut, Clemente helped his own cause by doubling twice against Mayaguez starter Denny McLain, the Detroit Tigers' young right-hander. Clemente drove in two runs with his second double, then raced home on an errant throw. Unfortunately, Clemente twisted his left ankle while scoring and had to depart the game. In spite of Clemente's productive, injury-shortened day, the Senators lost his debut, 6-4. They also lost the next game, 2-0, to Santurce left-hander Juan Pizarro, as Clemente sat out with the bad ankle. Although Roberto returned for the next game, the Senators lost their third straight, 6-3 to Arecibo. On December 27, San Juan lost its fourth straight game, dropping the opener of a doubleheader. (If Clemente didn't like managing to begin with, he probably liked it even less now.) In the nightcap, the Senators finally squeezed out a 4-3 decision over Arecibo, giving Clemente his first win as a manager. After the initial managerial travails, Clemente guided San Juan to a fourth-place finish and a berth in the playoffs. The Senators then lost their first-round matchup to powerful Santurce, which featured accomplished major league slugger Orlando Cepeda and future star Tony Perez.

Aside from the expected playoff ouster, the winter also brought Clemente an array of unanticipated physical setbacks. Earlier in the off-season, Clemente had suffered an attack of food poisoning. Another day, he found himself mowing the lawn outside the family's home. As he pushed the mower across the grass, a rock became tangled within the mower's machinery. The mower spit out the rock, which struck Clemente in his upper right thigh, near his hip.

At first, the injury seemed mild, merely a bruised hip. Clemente stopped playing briefly before returning to play in the winter league All-Star game. Roberto delivered a pinch-hit single to right field, but struggled to run to first. When he reached the base, his right leg gave out completely.

Coagulated blood had swelled up so badly within the bruise that Clemente had to be rushed to the hospital, where an examination determined that he needed to have the area near his hip drained. Three days later, doctors removed the blood clot from his upper thigh. During the surgery, doctors discovered that a small muscle tear in the thigh had caused the bruising, and eventually the clotted blood. How serious was the tear? That soon became a matter of debate—and special concern for the Pirates.

Joe Brown became alarmed when he read a story in the *San Juan Star,* which detailed the extent of Clemente's thigh injury. According to the newspaper, the surgical procedure had revealed a partially severed ligament in his upper right thigh. The story also claimed that the ligament was held together by the mere strength of a thin strand. Brown quickly placed a call to Clemente, asking him if the injury was as bad as the *Star* had alleged. To Brown's delight, Clemente informed him that the reporter had exaggerated the injury. A muscle in his thigh had been cut, but no ligament had been severed, partial or otherwise. Clemente assured Brown that he had begun light workouts with little difficulty. He felt only slight soreness when he ran hard, but no pain during light jogs.

Although Clemente's physician, Dr. Roberto Buso, revealed the clot to be less serious than originally thought, he advised Clemente to stay in the hospital for a full week. He also told Roberto to forget about playing baseball until the start of spring training with the Pirates. As a result, Clemente's winter league season had ended.

The off-season brought more physical problems. As spring training approached, Clemente became ill with a combination of nausea, headaches and extreme fever. He vomited repeatedly. On March 2, he entered a hospital in San Juan with what doctors called a "systemic infection." Clemente felt so nauseous that he could not eat, instead relying on intravenous feeding. After a day or two, he felt well enough to resume eating normally, but a slight fever persisted. After initial difficulties in finding a specific cause to Clemente's problems, doctors finally diagnosed the problem with a case of malarial fever.

How had Clemente contracted malaria? There were two possibilities. He might have been exposed to the disease on a recent barnstorming trip to Santo Domingo. Or he might have contracted the fever while raising hogs on a small farm he owned on the outskirts of Carolina. Or perhaps both experiences had contributed to the infection. Whatever the origin, Clemente would lose 20 pounds while battling the rages of the disease.

After his stay in the hospital, Clemente decided to try to regain his strength by taking long walks on the sands of a nearby beach. The walks gradually built up the stamina in Roberto's legs. Clemente's doctor also placed him on a special diet and prescribed special vitamin pills in an effort to restore his weight to its previous level.

Joe Brown wanted to talk to Clemente directly about his rehabilitation but couldn't do so because his star remained in the hospital. When Brown suggested to Dr. Buso that Clemente continue his recuperation in Ft. Myers, where the Pirates would open spring training on March 1, he received an immediate rebuttal from the physician. Dr. Buso informed Brown that Clemente probably wouldn't be able to make the trip to the mainland until March 20, at the earliest. Dr. Buso said that Clemente would not be allowed to travel off the island until he tested negative for malaria.

By early March, Clemente had regained six of the 20 pounds that he had lost. Dr. Buso told Brown that Roberto would be able to report to the Pirates' spring training camp in Fort Myers on March 25. By then, the Pirates would have completed several weeks of training camp, but at least they would have Clemente before the start of the regular season.

The winter of 1964-65 had proved torturous to Clemente. The list of injuries and illnesses included a bout with food poisoning, an ankle sprain, a deep thigh bruise and hemorrhaging of his leg, and now malaria. In addition, Clemente had been given a managerial position he really didn't want. Spring couldn't arrive soon enough.

Roberto's first winter league season. Here he is pictured with Junior Gilliam (on the left), one of his teammates on the 1952-53 Santurce Cangrejeros (Crabbers). Note: Clemente is wearing No. 39; he would not adopt the No. 21 until he joined the Pittsburgh Pirates in 1955.

Clemente, early in his major league life.

During the 1950s, Clemente batted .282, with a high of .311 in 1956.

At the finish of one of his unorthodox swings, Clemente contorts his body awkwardly while flashing a grimace.

Clemente strikes a batting pose.

Playing in a game against the Cubs, Clemente slides
safely into third. Chicago's Ron Santo awaits the throw.

Standing deep in the batter's box, Roberto recoils as the pitch is delivered.

Clemente with Bill Mazeroski, his longest running teammate on the Pirates. The perennial Gold Glove winners played together from 1956 to 1972.

From 1960 to 1967, the "Pride of the Pirates" never batted lower than .312.

A relaxed spring training moment. Clemente with fellow Hall of Famer Willie Stargell (No. 8), who first joined the Pirates in 1962.

Roberto with his wife, Vera. They married in 1964.

Roberto stretches
the muscles in his
chronically fragile
back, which he
originally injured in
a 1954 car accident.

Holding two bats, Clemente displays his deceptively powerful bicep.

Classic Clemente at the plate.

Roberto shares an enjoyable moment with Hall of Famer Casey Stengel, the first manager in the history of the rival New York Mets.

In 1966, Clemente won the MVP; the following year he hit a career-high .357.

Standing by his locker at
Forbes Field, Roberto
handles the Pirates'
classic 1960s uniform.

Clemente, circa 1970.
Note the new uniform
style adopted by the
Pirates, along with
Roberto's flowing signa-
ture on the right.

Clemente finishing
another violent swing.

Cutting the base perfectly, a *tilted* Clemente rounds second during
his spectacular 1971 World Series performance. Baltimore Orioles'
second baseman Dave Johnson looks on.

Clemente, the thinker.

With his weight shifted awkwardly onto his front foot, Roberto collects his 3000th—and final—regular season hit. Clemente achieves the milestone against Jon Matlack of the New York Mets.

Roberto's best friend on the Pirates—Manny Sanguillen.

A moment of poignancy. Roberto holds his youngest son, Enrique.

At the 1973 Hall of Fame Induction Ceremony, Vera (bottom right)
holds Roberto's newly created plaque. Clockwise from the bottom right
are Vera; Mrs. Julia Weiss (daughter of Mickey Welch); George Kelly;
William Evans (grandson of Billy Evans); Warren Spahn; Monte Irvin
(Roberto's boyhood idol); and Commissioner Bowie Kuhn.

"The Great One."

The three Clemente sons—Luis, Enrique and Roberto, Jr.—observe the Hall of Fame Induction Ceremony in front of the Hall's Library.

Vera, her three sons, and Roberto's mother Luisa pose in front of the Clemente plaque.

ROBERTO WALKER CLEMENTE
PITTSBURGH N. L. 1955-1972
MEMBER OF EXCLUSIVE 3,000-HIT CLUB. LED
NATIONAL LEAGUE IN BATTING FOUR TIMES.
HAD FOUR SEASONS WITH 200 OR MORE HITS
WHILE POSTING LIFETIME .317 AVERAGE AND
240 HOME RUNS. WON MOST VALUABLE PLAYER
AWARD 1966. RIFLE-ARMED DEFENSIVE STAR
SET N.L. MARK BY PACING OUTFIELDERS IN
ASSISTS FIVE YEARS. BATTED .362 IN TWO
WORLD SERIES, HITTING IN ALL 14 GAMES.

Hall of Famer Roberto Clemente.

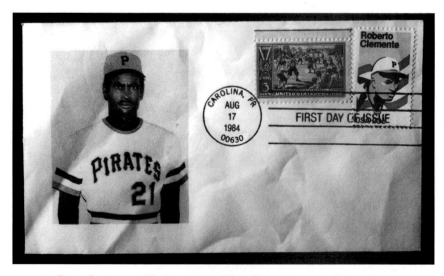

A first-day cancellation issued by the U.S. Postal Service on
August 17, 1984.

A commemorative beer can issued by the Pittsburgh Brewing Company—part of the effort to raise funds for the Roberto Clemente Statue, now located outside of Three Rivers Stadium.

Hall of Fame still life. A replica of Roberto's jersey, along with the last two Clemente cards issued by the Topps Company. The 1972 Topps card is to the left of the No.21; at the bottom is the 1973 card, which was issued after Clemente's death.

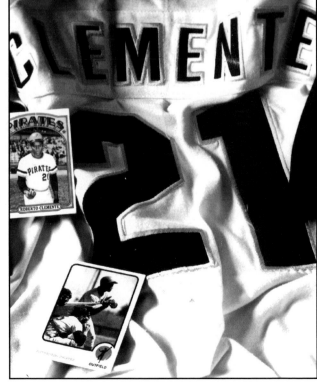

12

The Hat

The new season brought managerial change to the Pirates. Danny Murtaugh had retired after the 1964 regular season, the victim of recurring health problems. In searching for a replacement, Joe Brown offered the job to an unlikely candidate. Former National League star Harry Walker, who hadn't managed in the major leagues since guiding the Cardinals in 1955, accepted Brown's invitation. Nicknamed "The Hat," Walker loved to talk, especially about hitting. He knew more than a little bit about that subject, having won the 1947 batting championship with a .363 average. As an accomplished singles hitter, Walker batted .296 over an 11-year career with the Cardinals, Phillies, Cubs and Reds.

Some of the Pirate beat writers wondered how Clemente would fare in his relationship with Walker, who was known for his healthy ego. One reporter, citing Walker's tendency for non-stop chatting, approached Clemente and predicted that he would not like the new manager. Roberto scoffed at the suggestion. To the contrary, he liked the idea of playing for a manager who enjoyed talking about baseball. After all, Clemente enjoyed talking baseball as much as anyone.

Clemente actually reported to spring training on March 28, eight days after Dr. Buso's initial prediction and four weeks after the opening of Pittsburgh's pre-season camp. By now, Roberto had regained 10 of his lost pounds. In his first batting practice session, Clemente stunned his teammates by hitting an array of searing line drives into the outfield. "If malaria can make a fellow hit like that, then I want some," observed light-hitting shortstop Dick Schofield in an interview with Les Biederman of the *Pittsburgh Press.*

Impressive batting practice exhibitions aside, Clemente still complained of feeling weak and tired. Harry Walker decided to use Clemente for only a few innings at a time. He eventually lengthened Clemente's stints, but Roberto continued to struggle with his strength and stamina.

As he battled a general lack of energy, Clemente also sought to set his financial record straight with the local media. On March 31, three days after reporting to spring training, Clemente finally signed his 1965 Pirate contract. Several writers reported that Clemente had agreed to a one-year deal worth $50,000. About a month later, Clemente disputed the figure. "Do you think I'd sign for only $50,000,?" Clemente asked Les Biederman rhetorically, while pointing out that he had accumulated 10 years of major league service. "I'd rather go home. I have the best [batting] average for the last five years of anybody in the majors."

Clemente then struck up a comparison to another player. It was a comparison that had annoyed him when brought up by others, but he wanted to use it now to illustrate his point. Clemente asked one writer what he thought Willie Mays was making with the Giants. Clemente suggested $100,000, to which the writer agreed. Clemente then reminded the writer of his alleged $50,000 salary, half the amount being paid to Mays. "Do you think Mays is twice as good as I am?" Clemente said, concluding his case.

So what *was* Clemente making? He wouldn't tell the press, leaving certain writers to speculate about the amount. Les Biederman surmised that Clemente's salary neared the $70,000 mark, which included general expenses and a stipend for off-season scouting in Latin America. In this sense, Clemente's contract differed from the deals signed by almost all other major league players. The Pirates had agreed to give him additional money—tax-free no less—for keeping an eye on young talent in Puerto Rico. In other words, Clemente doubled as a team scout.

Once the regular season began, Harry Walker played Clemente in right field every day. Clemente picked up only one hit in first 11 at-bats, and only two hits in his first 16 tries. From April 18-21, Clemente's bat pepped up. He collected two hits in each of four straight games, driving in three runs along the way. Then came another slump: only two hits in his next 18 at-bats. A four-hit game on April 27 seemed to signal the end of the swoon, but Clemente's bat quickly returned to mediocrity.

The poor start at the plate convinced Walker that he should cut back his star's schedule. On May 2, Walker rested Clemente during a Sunday doubleheader against the Cardinals. Since the Cardinals planned to start two right-handers, Walker saw an opportunity to play two left-handed hitters in his starting outfield. "This enabled me to put Jerry Lynch and Willie Stargell in the same outfield and take advantage of the short right field in Busch Stadium," Walker explained to Les Biederman, corresponding for *The Sporting News*. "And I would have the National League batting champion as a pinch-hitter," Walker said, referring to Clemente.

Walker explained to Clemente why he had decided to sit him during the doubleheader. According to Clemente's comments in the January 31, 1971 edition of the *Houston Post*, Walker had told him the following: "I talked to [New York Mets' player-coach] Yogi Berra and he says you're not the same hitter. I'm going to give you a rest, order you some lighter bats, and when you feel better, let me know and I'll put you back in the lineup." The reasoning seemed sound to Clemente, who readily admitted that he still felt weak after his bout with malarial fever.

Clemente appeared as a pinch-hitter in the first game of the doubleheader, and as a reserve in the second game, striking out both times. In the first game, he came to bat with the bases loaded and no one out and failed to make contact. In the nightcap, he looked futile in another clutch situation, fanning with two on and two out. The Pirates ended up losing both games. Walker decided to keep Clemente out of the lineup for the remainder of the road trip.

After being swept four games by the Cardinals, the Pirates moved on to Chicago. The Cubs used a right-handed starter in the first game of the series. Walker continued to use his left-handed platoon, playing both Lynch and Stargell. The strategy paid off, as Lynch and Stargell each hit two home runs into the Wrigley Field bleachers.

Prior to the second game of the series with the Cubs, Les Biederman walked into the Pirate clubhouse. He asked Clemente how he was feeling. Clemente answered that he felt "terrible," and then made a candid announcement. "I want to be traded," Clemente told Biederman. "You trade me." Biederman, of course, had no power to trade a player. "I don't want to play here any more. I'm unhappy."

Clemente wasn't just upset over his removal from the lineup. His outburst had been fueled by a radio interview Walker had conducted with Harry Caray on Sunday, the day that Clemente had been benched for the doubleheader. Clemente hadn't heard the interview himself, but had learned about it second-hand from one of his friends who was visiting Wrigley Field. Clemente replayed the conversation with his friend in a 1971 interview with Joe Heiling of the *Houston Post*. "What is wrong between you and Walker?" the friend asked Clemente, who responded that he had no problems with his manager. "Well," continued the friend, "I heard Walker in a radio interview from St. Louis say that Ted Williams and Stan Musial could play when hurt and he couldn't understand why you couldn't play too when hurt." Based on the conversation with his friend, Clemente felt that his manager had twisted a knife into his back, insinuating that he would not play if he did not feel well. Clemente explained to Biederman that his removal from the lineup had been orchestrated by Walker, not by his own wishes. "I didn't ask to come out of the lineup," Clemente reiterated. "I've been playing all spring and feeling bad. He [Walker] took me out."

Clemente told Biederman that he wanted to talk to Walker, who was meeting with coach Clyde King in the manager's office. Clemente waited for several minutes, but when the discussion between King and Walker didn't stop, he walked out of the clubhouse onto the field.

In the clubhouse, Clemente had spoken loudly enough for several of his teammates to hear him. A few players claimed they heard him say he wouldn't play for Walker, but both Clemente and Biederman denied that such a remark had been made. In the 1971 interview with the *Houston Post*, Clemente tried to clarify what he had said about his manager. "If he [Walker] did say one thing to me and say another thing behind my back [to Harry Caray]—if it was true, I couldn't play for a man like that." Clemente would later find out what Walker had actually said.

Nonetheless, word of the outburst soon spread throughout the clubhouse and eventually made the newspapers the next day. Walker reacted diplomatically to Clemente's invective. "I'm certainly not trying to punish Clemente," Walker insisted in an interview with Biederman. "He just doesn't look like he's swinging the bat like I know he can and I felt a few days rest would help."

Walker went on to praise Clemente's ability. "I haven't given up on him," Walker said. "Clemente is the best hitter in the league and I'd prefer to have a well-rested Clemente than a tired Clemente. This team isn't going anywhere without Clemente and I'd be foolish to put him on the bench deliberately."

To his credit, Walker didn't end his attempts at repair with his public comments to the media. Prior to the final game against the Cubs, Walker invited Clemente to breakfast in his room at Chicago's Knickerbocker Hotel. Walker explained the reasoning behind the benching. Clemente assured Walker that he never said he wouldn't play for the manager. The meeting resulted in a peaceful settlement. "We had breakfast together and we understand each other," Walker told reporters.

Although a truce had been arranged, Clemente didn't return to his perch in right field right away. With the Cubs starting another right-hander, Walker once again used Willie Stargell and Jerry Lynch as his corner outfielders. Stargell hit two more homers, giving him four for the series, while Lynch added a pair of singles. Clemente did make an appearance as a pinch-hitter. He bounced out, but at least managed to put the ball in play.

The Pirates returned home on May 7 to play the Reds. Clemente remained on the bench, what with the Reds throwing another right-hander the Pirates' way. In the seventh, Clemente entered the game as a pinch-hitter, but once again failed to reach base. This time, however, Walker kept Clemente in the game. Roberto came to bat again in the ninth, driving home the game-tying run with a sacrifice fly. Moments later, Manny Mota's single capped off the comeback win. For the first time in a long while, Clemente had contributed to a Pirate victory. Two days later, Clemente returned to the starting lineup with a two-hit game. He picked up five more hits over his next two games.

Another slump soon hit his bat: a four-game hitless streak from May 16-21. Of Clemente's 27 hits, all but two were singles. He had hit no home runs. The frustrations of April and May coincided with the Pirates' abysmal start. With Clemente's average having plummeted to the low .240s, the Pirates had won just nine games while losing 24.

On May 21, Clemente went 0-for-4 but the Pirates throttled Milwaukee, 6-1, behind the pitching of Vern Law and Alvin McBean. The next day, Clemente banged out three hits in five at-bats during a 9-4 bombing of the Braves. Three more hits fell in the next day, followed by a season-high four-hit day. Clemente kept hitting, and the Pirates simultaneously kept winning. A 12-game winning streak brought the Bucs within a few games of the .500 mark. Not so coincidentally, the National League's batting champion had finally returned from the hitter's cemetery.

On June 6, the Pirates hosted the Mets in a doubleheader at steamy Forbes Field. The Pirates won the first game, 5-3, before facing future Hall of Famer Warren Spahn in the nightcap. Spahn handled the Bucs easily over the first four innings, facing the minimum 12 batters. In the fifth, Spahn allowed a pair of scratch runs. With the Pirates leading 2-0, Clemente came to bat with the bases empty in the sixth inning. A proponent of trying to jam Clemente at the plate, Spahn had retired the Pirate right fielder his first time at-bat by throwing pitches at his hands. In the sixth, Spahn continued to brush the Pirate right fielder with inside fastballs. He threw Clemente another fastball, one that rode several inches inside. Clemente dropped his hands in toward his body and smacked the ball, depositing it over the left field wall for his first home run of the season. "The pitch was a foot inside," an exasperated Spahn told Larry Fox of the *New York World Telegram*. Spahn then tried to belittle his opponent by saying that all of the Pirate hitters, including Clemente, were merely guess hitters who were fortunate that baseball rules discouraged knockdown pitches.

Clemente felt Spahn had made a mistake by repeating his pattern, and by leaving the pitch in a poor location. "Sure I knew he was trying to brush me back, but I'm no guess hitter," Clemente told the *World Telegram*. "He brush me back the first time, so I know later he try again and I look for it. But this pitch stay up and I hit it."

Clemente's at-bat exhibited the benefits of the visualization technique that he used throughout much of his career. "A lot of players do this," says Nellie King, "but he was dedicated to it. He was always criticized for being a malingerer and going into the trainer's room and staying on the rubbing table. He'd turn the lights out when he'd go in there. He said to me, 'You know what I do when I go in there? Everybody thinks I am hurting, or there is something wrong with my back again.' He said, 'If [Bob] Gibson is pitching, I will lay down and I will bat against Bob's pitches four times before I play the game. I will see his fastball come inside and I'll see his slider go away and the curveball, and I will poke the ball to left field. Then I will see the curveball outside and I will see another pitch, and I'll hit his fastball to right field. Then I'll see his slider on the outside corner and I'll hit that to center field. I will bat four times [in my mind] and I will get four hits before I go out there, but I have seen every pitch he has. And on a good day, I go out there and see that pitch that I've already hit against [in my mind], so I hit it.'"

King says Clemente religiously followed his visualization practices. "I think there's a lot of guys who do that," King explains. "I think pitchers do that a lot before they pitch, and I see golfers do that. A lot of sports people do it, but he really had it down to a dedicated [science]."

In addition to visualizing that day's pitcher, Clemente also spent time in the trainer's room receiving a rubdown from one of his teammates. "He used to ask me to massage him every day, whether I was pitching or not," Bob Veale tells researcher Andrew O'Toole. "He'd say, 'I got an ache here.' Or, 'I got an ache here.' It was just something he used to trigger him, to get him started. That's what he thrived on."

The extreme heat of the June afternoon at Forbes Field had resulted in Veale, Pittsburgh's second game starter, losing 16 pounds in perspiration. Clemente, still recovering from the effects of malaria, said he felt fine. He had run out two doubles and a triple in the first game, but felt well enough to play in the nightcap. His home run against Spahn had finalized a 3-0 victory and a double-header sweep.

Now a two-time batting champion, Clemente's first-half recovery put him in position to stake claim to a third. As the Pirates neared the All-Star break, Clemente overtook Willie Mays for the National League's batting lead. Then, on the final day before the break, Clemente faced Sandy Koufax of the Dodgers. The overpowering left-hander collared Clemente in four at-bats, pushing him back to second in the batting race. Clemente's batting average rested at .338, only one point behind Mays. Somehow, Clemente had lifted his average nearly 100 points from its mid-May low of .243.

Clemente's grapple with Mays for the batting leadership spurred the recurring comparisons that fans and writers liked to make between the two stars. They both played the outfield phenomenally, they both ran the bases with unprecedented flair, they both hit well above .300. The comparisons ignited the debate. Who was the better player in the 1960s: Mays or Clemente?

National League beat writers frequently asked Clemente about Mays. They wanted to know if he considered himself as great a player as the Giants' center fielder. Or, they asked Clemente if he modeled himself after Mays. "I don't play like Willie Mays," Clemente told a reporter from UPI. "I play like Roberto Clemente."

King remembers hearing that statement again and again. "This was a line he used," says King. "He was trying to say that he has his own individual identity—that he doesn't need to look like somebody else. 'Willie Mays was a good player, but Roberto Clemente was a good player, too. Hank Aaron was a good player, but Roberto Clemente was as good a player.' And I don't think he wanted to be compared, either better or on the same level, with them. He just had his own identity he strongly believed in."

A decade before, the two outfielders had played together in the winter league. As teammates with Santurce, they never became close. In spite of the lack of real friendship, Luis Mayoral believes that Mays had an important effect on Clemente's career. "I think that the presence of Willie Mays in major league baseball—and to me he is the best player ever in the game, including Roberto, as much I love Roberto, to me Mays was the best all-around player—I think that the media trying so many times to compare Clemente with Mays, created in Roberto a desire to be a better ballplayer overall. Because Roberto didn't like to be compared to anyone. Repeatedly during his career, they were saying the 'next Willie Mays' and so forth. So I think that Mays was an invisible force to really get the best out of Clemente, because Clemente didn't want to prove that he was better than Mays. Roberto wanted to prove that he was Roberto Clemente, and that he did not deserve to be compared to any other ballplayers. Just like Juan Gonzalez with the [Texas] Rangers—they say Clemente—and he says, 'Hey man, that's a disrespect to Clemente. He's a Hall of Famer; I'm a young man.' That kind of thing."

The pursuit of Mays provided Clemente with added motivation to raise his batting average. Yet, Clemente's first-half surge did little to impress the fans who had registered votes for the All-Star team. Clemente finished third in the balloting among National League right fielders, behind Milwaukee's Hank Aaron and Chicago's Johnny Callison.

National League All-Star manager Gene Mauch announced that he would pick Clemente as one of his reserve outfielders. The news didn't appease Clemente, who felt snubbed by the fans. "I won't play," Clemente told Les Biederman of the *Pittsburgh Press*. Clemente explained that he wouldn't even make the trip to Minnesota, where the All-Star Game was scheduled to be played at Metropolitan Stadium.

When Pirate manager Harry Walker heard about Clemente's personal boycott, he approached his star. Walker explained to him the importance of representing both himself and the Pirates at the All-Star festivities. Buoyed by the conversation with Walker, Clemente changed his mind and agreed to make the flight to Minnesota. The relationship between the two men had come a long way since their blowup in early May.

Clemente joined two of his teammates at the All-Star Game: outfielder Willie Stargell, who had been elected as a starter, and pitcher Bob Veale, selected by Mauch to help round out the National League staff. A fourth Pirate, hot-hitting first baseman Donn Clendenon, should have made the team but didn't. Clendenon's dangerous right-handed bat had helped motivate Clemente to further hitting excellence, while also offering "The Great One" needed protection in the Pirates' batting order.

Clemente's torrid hitting of late May, June, and early July didn't cease for the rest of the summer. He picked up hits almost every day he played, raising his average to a high-water mark of .345. "Amazing," Pirates first base coach Johnny Pesky told Les Biederman of the *Pittsburgh Press* in response to a query about Clemente's hitting skills. "The only other batter I ever saw who gets good wood on the ball as consistently as Clemente was Ted Williams," raved Pesky, a one-time teammate of the retired Boston Red Sox' star.

Clemente would fade a bit during the final days of September, but still finished the season at .329. The final batting average fell under .350—the minimum level of acceptance suggested by Joe Brown during the winter—but given Clemente's winter bout with malaria and his early season fatigue, Brown had to be pleased. The .329 average was also good enough to earn Clemente his third

National League hitting crown and a sterling silver Louisville Slugger bat, courtesy of the Hillerich and Bradsby Co.

Clemente joined special company, becoming only the fifth player in National League history to claim at least three batting titles. The others? Rogers Hornsby, Stan Musial, Honus Wagner and Paul Waner, all Hall of Famers. Clemente also became the first Pirate player to win back-to-back batting titles since Wagner collected four straight crowns from 1906-09. Meanwhile, in the American League, another Latino star won his second straight batting championship. Minnesota's Tony Oliva, a native of Cuba, defended his title with a .321 average.

Clemente also continued to show speed, hustle and unusual desire in making plays considered well beyond the call of duty. One of Clemente's maneuvers in a 1965 game against the Houston Astros stretched the bounds of defensive credibility. With runners on first and second and no one out, an Astro batter popped up a bunt toward the second base bag. Since Gene Alley had vacated short to cover third base, it appeared the bunt would result in a base hit. Playing shallow in right field, Clemente raced across the outer portion of the infield diamond, dove headfirst and smothered the ball in his glove. From his knees, his face littered with infield dirt, Clemente fired to third base to retire the hesitating lead runner, Walter Bond. The throw beat Bond easily—by five feet. Unlike most outfielders, Clemente had smartly anticipated the bunt by moving closer to the infield, before fully involving himself in the play with his extraordinary athletic skills.

Clemente's brilliant fielding and third batting championship did not impress the voters for the United Press International All-Star team. For the second straight year, UPI snubbed Clemente, picking Oliva, Willie Mays and Hank Aaron to represent the starting outfield. With 11 votes, Aaron surpassed Clemente's vote total by one.

As a teenager, Luis Mayoral had met Pirate scout Howie Haak during a flight from Miami to Puerto Rico. Mayoral also knew another Pirate scout, a man named Frank Coimbre, who had established a friendship with the Mayoral family. Coimbre knew Mayoral's uncle, who broadcast games for the Ponce Leones (Lions) of the Puerto Rican Winter League. Through these contacts, Mayoral came to meet Clemente for the first time. "Mid-sixties, I can't be precise, '64 or '65, but I do recall it was in the month of November," says Mayoral. "Howie asked me to go with him to Roberto's house in

Carolina." When Mayoral arrived at the Clemente residence, he noticed the Pirates superstar performing one of the regular household chores. "We made it out to Roberto's place; I remember he had been doing the lawn of his home. He was wearing gray Bermuda shorts, no shoes, no shirt, and we all went into the house."

Although Mayoral was not yet an adult, he had heard plenty about Clemente while growing up in Panama, where his father served as an officer in the U.S Army. "I mean, I got bit by the baseball bug when I was maybe seven or eight years old," recalls Mayoral. "So when Roberto made it to the Pirates in 1955, even though I was a kid, I knew of his existence. I knew that he was a talented ballplayer because prior to me going to Panama, he had played briefly in our [Puerto Rican] winter baseball league. His name was being heard—over and over—Roberto Clemente."

In spite of significant differences in age and levels of fame, Clemente made Mayoral feel comfortable. "We could have been there maybe three hours," says Mayoral, "but what I do recall is that a guy of his stature paid attention to me—a kid." Surprisingly, the two did not talk about one of their most common interests, but they did discuss other subjects. "We may have spoken 20 to 25 minutes, and I know we didn't talk baseball. I think we talked about the status of Puerto Rico, people on our island, education and so forth."

Although Mayoral may have felt initial intimidation in talking to a baseball star and national celebrity, his concerns quickly passed. "My first impressions of him, after that first meeting, were that he was a really low-key individual, down to earth." Far different than the perception of Clemente held by many of the writers who covered him and the Pirates.

13

A Push For Power

Harry Walker noticed the power totals on his ballclub. Other than Willie Stargell, who had clubbed 27 home runs, no Pirate had hit more than 17 home runs. As the team's starting catcher, Jim Pagliaroni, the Pirates' second leading power hitter, couldn't be counted upon to match that total again. Walker realized that his best player could supply gaudier power numbers; he just needed to be motivated to do so.

In a spring training conversation with Clemente, Walker challenged him to become a more well rounded offensive player. Walker liked Clemente's ability to compete for a batting title, but felt he needed to do more than hit 10 home runs and drive in 65 runs, as he had done the previous season. "He told me he wanted more homers and runs batted in," Clemente revealed to the *Associated Press* after the season. "He even named the figures: 25 homers and 115 RBIs."

Were such numbers realistically attainable? In his best power season, Clemente had hit 23 home runs. That was in 1961. In his most productive year, he had driven in 94 runs. That was in 1960. In order to reach Walker's target number for 1966, Clemente would have to surpass his best RBI season by 21. For a player hitting out of the No. 3 spot in the order—a player who preferred to smack line drives instead of trying to uppercut home runs—that number seemed like an unrealistic goal. Perhaps Walker had set the bar too high.

Walker also asked Clemente to help one of the Pirates' key off-season pickups. Center fielder Matty Alou, acquired from the San Francisco Giants in a winter trade, had hit .231 in 1965. Alou had no power and some speed, but needed to hit for a much higher average to justify his presence in the lineup. Walker wanted him to change his approach to the plate, but realized that Alou, who spoke little English, had trouble understanding his suggestions.

Walker asked Clemente, who was fluent in Spanish, to talk to the left-handed hitting Alou. "I'm trying to get Matty Alou to hit the ball to left field, but I'm having trouble," Walker informed Clemente, recreating a conversation for Arthur Daley of the *New York Times*. "He wants to pull everything to right. The pitchers work the outside corners on him and he becomes an easy mark. I still haven't convinced him that he'll be a better hitter if he slices the ball to left and goes with the pitch." Playing in San Francisco, Alou had tried to take advantage of the wind gusts that regularly blew toward right field. If he possessed some power, a pull-hitting approach might have made some sense. At best, the diminutive Alou figured to hit five to seven home runs a season. He needed to use all sides of the playing field in order to become the .300 hitter that Walker envisioned.

Clemente agreed to Walker's request. Early in spring training, he approached Alou about changing his hitting philosophy. Rather than just talk about hitting, though, Clemente helped Alou apply the changes practically. When Alou stepped to the plate during batting practice, Clemente stationed himself along the third base line. "Punch the ball at me," Clemente yelled repeatedly in Spanish. "Forget about pulling it to right. Hit to left. Hit to left." With Clemente serving as a friendly target, Alou tried consciously to hit the ball down the third base line. After batting practice, Clemente encouraged his new teammate to continue aiming for the left side of the field in exhibition games. Complying with Clemente's instructions, Alou quickly adapted to the new approach. He consistently hit line drives during spring games, raising his batting average to newfound heights.

In addition to helping new teammates, Clemente showed an eager willingness to improve his own game. One day in the spring, Clemente noticed Gene Alley and several other infielders working with Harry Walker and the Pirate coaches on their baserunning and sliding techniques. Rather than continue with his wind sprints, Clemente asked the group if he could participate in the basepath seminar. Clemente was already one of the best baserunners in either league, but he wanted to become better.

After committing baserunning errors in the early stages of his career, Clemente's work on the basepaths had evolved to the point of near flawlessness. "I can't think of many mistakes Roberto made over a period of time," Joe Brown says. "If he went for an extra base, he got it. He was seldom thrown out going for the extra base, and it wasn't because he lacked aggressiveness because he was an aggressive baserunner."

In the early days of spring training, an article by Myron Cope in *Sports Illustrated* once again cast Clemente in the light of a hypochondriac. After referring to him as a "chronic invalid," the article quoted Clemente's personal physician, Dr. Roberto Buso, who described his patient as having little tolerance for pain or discomfort. "If his back hurts, he worries, and then it becomes a vicious cycle, leading to more things," Dr. Buso told Cope. "If he has a little diarrhea, he worries that he has a serious stomach difficulty." A drawing of Clemente accompanied the article, complete with scattered references to his various injuries and ailments, ranging from "tension headaches" to "legs that do not weigh the same."

Dr. Buso did stop short of calling Clemente a hypochondriac. "I wouldn't call him a true hypochondriac, because he doesn't go to the extreme of just sitting down and brooding." Although the *Sports Illustrated* feature went on to acclaim Clemente's greatness as a player—one of the game's underrated talents—the other sections of the article portrayed him as a borderline neurotic, a man who was fearful of nightmares and obsessed with his own insomnia. The tone of those parts of the article infuriated Clemente.

"So many people seem to want to make a big thing out of Roberto being a hypochondriac," says Joe Brown. "Anybody who played as hard as Roberto is bound to come up with bumps and bruises and nicks, and even more serious injuries." Unlike other athletes of that era, Clemente willingly talked about his aches and pains rather than engage in the usual pleasantries." They talk about his being a hypochondriac, but he was an open, frank person,"

Brown says. "When I see someone first thing in the morning, I'll say, 'How are you?' Well, when you asked that of Clemente, he thought you wanted to know how he was. So he'd say, 'Well, I'm fine, but I got a little crick in my neck, or my knee bothers me, or my shoulder.' And I think he was such a magnificent athlete that anything less than 100 percent bothered him. He wanted to be 100 percent all the time."

During his career, Clemente's occasional involvement in controversy usually came about as a result of strained relationships with the press. In early May, an alleged altercation with a fan placed Clemente in the center of a storm. After an 11-inning loss in Philadelphia, Clemente made his way from the clubhouse to the team bus. Several fans crowded around Clemente, who stopped to sign autographs. A 19-year-old fan named Bernard Heller claimed that Clemente suddenly stopped signing and threw out his hand, hitting the youngster in the mouth. The teenager was admitted to a local hospital with three loosened teeth and a possible broken jaw.

Clemente denied throwing an intentional punch. Referring to the incident as a "scuffle," Clemente explained to police detective James Coyle that he was simply trying to make his way past several fans who were pushing and shoving him. In rushing toward the team bus, Roberto said he may have accidentally bumped one of the fans. He didn't know whom he might have hit, or where the point of contact might have occurred.

Heller did not file any criminal charges against Clemente, who returned to his hotel after answering Coyle's questions. The police ended their investigation.

As the Pirates neared the end of June, Harry Walker's preseason power targets for Clemente looked unreachable. In his first 37 games, Clemente hit only three home runs. He drove in only 17 runs, and had only two games in which he had multiple RBIs. If he kept struggling at this rate, Clemente would finish the season with about 12 home runs and 68 RBIs. This was not what Walker had in mind in spring training.

On May 30, the Pirates played a Forbes Field doubleheader against the Cubs. In the first game, Clemente hit a home run, helping the Pirates to a comebacking, 3-2 win. In the nightcap, Clemente made a 375-foot throw from right field, nailing George Altman, who had tried to score from first on a double. In the seventh inning, Clemente faced Cubs rookie Billy Connors. The young right-hander tried to waste a fastball high and away, but Clemente swung and tomahawked the wayward pitch into the right field stands. The two-run homer capped off a three-run rally for the Pirates, who claimed a 5-3 decision.

After a brief road trip to New York, the Pirates returned home for a lengthy homestand. By the time the 11-game party at Forbes Field had ended, Clemente had garnered 28 base hits, including four more home runs. He had also driven in 13 runs.

Two of Clemente's home runs mesmerized watchers at Forbes Field. Both drives carried well over 435 feet to right center field, at a point in between a tall light tower and the monument to former Pirates' owner Barney Dreyfuss. One of the drives landed 60 feet beyond the right field wall, on a baseball diamond where some children were playing. None of the youngsters were hit by the ball, which had traveled an estimated 500 feet. Veteran observers of Forbes Field claimed they had never seen a home run hit that far. For a hitter—especially one who was not considered a home run hitter—to reach such uncharted territory ranked as both unlikely and awe-inspiring.

Yet, Clemente did not consider the right-center field blast his longest home run. "I hit one at Wrigley Field one day that left the park near the left side of the scoreboard," Clemente revealed to Les Biederman, corresponding for *The Sporting News*. "The next day, I measured it and I figured maybe 600 feet."

On June 13, Clemente continued to show his preference for off-field home runs. Greeting Reds' left-hander Billy McCool, who had just entered the game as a reliever, Clemente's clubbed a three-run shot to right field. Clemente's sixth home run in his last 15 games, all flying out of Forbes Field, helped the Pirates to a 5-4 win.

Why had the line drives of Clemente's batting repertoire been replaced by the sudden surge of home runs? Roberto suggested an intriguing theory. "For years, I have been pleading with someone in charge at Forbes Field to put clay instead of sand in the batter's box," Clemente told Les Biederman. "Sand causes your feet to slip. Clay gives you a chance to keep your feet solid." The previous use of sand explained one of Clemente's many habits at the plate. Whenever he stepped into the batter's box, he scraped the ground with his bat and feet to cover up the holes that had been formed by the looseness of the sand. "Suddenly this year, they put clay in the batter's box," revealed a contented Clemente. "Now I have firm footing. Now I can get a toe hold."

In addition to landscaping the batter's box and rolling his neck, Clemente's at-bats involved other rituals. He usually picked up some dirt with his hands, tossed it back on the ground, and then gingerly wiped his hands on the pant legs of his uniform. He also patted the top of his helmet with one hand, as if to make sure that the hat fit securely and would not fall off his head. Clemente then took two chopping practice swings, stepped into the box and eyed the pitcher.

The productive homestand left Clemente happy—at least from a baseball perspective. Unfortunately, the ending of the homestand reminded Clemente of the unpublicized sacrifices made by professional players in the states. Clemente watched as Vera and his 10-month old son, Roberto, Jr., boarded a plane for Puerto Rico. Vera was about to give birth for a second time, necessitating a return trip to their home in Rio Piedras, which bordered Carolina. "When the children were about to be born," Vera explained many years later in an interview with *The Diamond,* "he made sure his three sons were born in Puerto Rico."

The Clementes had endured their first parting in 1965, when Vera had flown to Puerto Rico to give birth to Roberto, Jr. "I didn't feel so sad then," Clemente said of Vera's first absence. "But this time something hit me. When the baby turned around and clapped his hands and my wife waved good-bye, I almost cried." Roberto had experienced similar feelings in 1954, when he had left his mother and father to play ball in Montreal for the first time.

Loneliness aside, Clemente's newfound power stroke helped earn him selection to a National League All-Star berth. He picked up a single and a double in the midsummer exhibition, assisting the NL in a 2-1 win over the American League.

In August, Clemente sounded off on a theme he had first broached at length in 1964. The status of minority players, particularly Latinos, continued to bother the game's greatest Hispanic player. "The Latin American player doesn't get the recognition he deserves," Clemente angrily told a reporter from the Associated Press. "Neither does the Negro player, unless he does something really spectacular, like Willie Mays."

In particular, the lack of off-season publicity and rewards given to successful Latin American players upset Clemente. "We have self-satisfaction," Clemente acknowledged, "but after the season is over, nobody cares about us. Zoilo Versalles was the Most Valuable Player in the American League last year, but how many times has he been asked to make appearances at dinners or meetings during the winter. Juan Marichal is one of the greatest pitchers in the game, but does he get invited to banquets?"

Some writers had suggested that high airfare costs from Latin American countries to the states discouraged teams from inviting Latino stars to winter banquets. Citing economics, Clemente offered a fast rebuttal. "That's a lousy excuse. It costs $90 round trip from Puerto Rico to New York," said Clemente, one of several major leaguers who lived on the island during the off-season. As Clemente pointed out, airfares to California sometimes ran higher than they did to Puerto Rico. And other Latin American stars lived close to the cities in which they played during the season. "Versalles lives in Minnesota," Clemente informed the *AP*. "So does Tony Oliva."

Clemente also resented those who insinuated that he was a foreigner from a strange land. "I am an American citizen," Clemente told the AP. "I live 250 miles from Miami. But some people act like they think I live in the jungle some place. To the people here, we are outsiders, foreigners."

Several decades later, Latin American players continue their search for what they feel is the appropriate level of credit. "We love, particularly in this day and age, the pithy quote, the person who can turn a phrase, and not having that ability, a lot of Latin players, they slip between the news columns. So what they do on the field doesn't resonate as strongly," says Marcos Breton, a Mexican-American writer who specializes in Latino baseball. "Clemente challenged that reality a long—you know we're talking 25, 30 years—a long time ago. And the reason that he still remains so vivid today, in a sense sadly, because no one has stepped forward to take his place. While Robbie Alomar and Rafael Palmeiro and a few others have been quoted as saying that they don't feel that their contributions have gotten the proper attention, there has been no one who has consistently addressed that issue the way that Clemente did."

In September, Clemente continued to pile up home runs and RBIs in his drive to win the Most Valuable Player Award. On September 2, he reached an important milestone when he collected his 2,000th career hit. Unlike some milestones, which occur in meaningless late-season games, Clemente's most recent hit took on added resonance. The hit—a three-run home run to right field—lifted the Pirates to a 7-3 win over Chicago and put them in sole possession of first place in the National League. The three RBIs vaulted his season total to 101—the first time that he had surpassed the century mark. Clemente's milestone blow also came at the expense of a young right-hander named Ferguson Jenkins, himself a future Hall of Famer.

Even as his season-long annihilation of National League pitching—which included hitting streaks of 15 and 17 games—drew near its conclusion, Roberto complained of a recurring affliction. In an interview with Larry Merchant of the *New York Post*, Clemente talked about the problem. "You know, I have such a hard time sleeping," Clemente said, referring to the insomnia that had deserted him in 1964, only to return again. "Nobody but my wife knows how I feel."

Clemente explained to Merchant that he had tried a number of remedies and consulted medical authorities to rid himself of insomnia, but none had worked. "I went to the hospital once," said Clemente. "I try to go to sleep for the doctors. They find nothing. They send me home and say, 'Go to sleep.'" Needless to say, the simple solution offered by the doctors didn't help.

The Pirates lost the pennant race to the Dodgers in the final two weeks, but couldn't blame their star right fielder for the breakdown. In the weeks before the announcement of the National League's MVP, Harry Walker cast his unofficial ballot for Clemente. "I know the votes are already in for Most Valuable Player," Walker told Arthur Daley of the *New York Times*. "I'm convinced that Clemente deserves it. Whether he gets it or not, he's most valuable in my book." Walker pointed to Clemente's work ethic and repeated sacrifices. "No man ever gave more of himself or worked more unselfishly for the good of the team than Roberto."

The manager recalled a specific series of plays during the season, when Clemente's hustle resulted in an extra-inning victory. "One night against the Phillies, he hit a shot to Dick Groat and would have been out by 20 feet," Walker told Les Biederman of the *Pittsburgh Press*. "But he tore down the first base line, Groat fumbled, hurried his throw, and darned if Clemente didn't beat the play. Then he barreled into Groat and broke up a double play as a big run scored." The Pirates tied the game, eventually winning in extra innings.

In contrast to his first few major league seasons, when a few teammates accused him of occasionally failing to run out batted balls, no one questioned Clemente's hustle throughout the 1966 season. Every ball, every pop-up, he ran out. More vocal than in the past, Clemente also offered his teammates encouragement from the bench. As a younger player, he had felt hesitant to talk to other players during the game. Racial tensions, language barriers, and feelings of intimidation created by older teammates discouraged Clemente from becoming a verbal presence in the clubhouse and in the dugout. Now in his early thirties and established as the team's best player, Clemente realized that he was truly credible as an on-field leader.

More assertive and confident in his leadership role, Clemente started to socialize with his teammates more than he had done in the past. The atmosphere surrounding the 1966 Pirates certainly helped. The clubhouse developed a comic looseness. The formation of a group called the "Black Maxes"—where each member dressed up like World War II fighter pilots—epitomized the team's collection of light personalities. Although Clemente did not join the charade, he did not feel excluded from the clubhouse frivolity, as he had in the past.

Clemente finished the season with a .317 average. No longer the batting champion, he settled for a fourth-place tie in the National League hitting race. Yet, Clemente had managed to reach the goals laid down by his manager in the spring. Harry Walker wanted 25 home runs and 115 RBIs from his everyday right fielder. Clemente bettered both marks—reaching career bests with 29 home runs and 119 RBIs. By sacrificing a few points from his batting average, and swinging with more ferocity than in the past, Clemente became the productive power hitter that Walker had envisioned. He also helped the Pirates improve by two games in the won-loss column, while coming within a few lengths of the Dodgers for the National League pennant.

Clemente had done his part, but would the writers acknowledge him? On November 16, the Baseball Writers Association would announce the winner of its Most Valuable Player Award for the National League. Would it be Sandy Koufax, the decade's most dominating pitcher who had been named the winner of the Cy Young only two weeks earlier? Or would it be Clemente, the three-time batting champion coming off the finest all-around season of his career? If Koufax owned an advantage, it was in his team's placement in the standings. The Dodgers had won the pennant with a record of 95-67, while Clemente's Pirates settled for third, three games back.

The results of the balloting showed Koufax with nine first-place votes, one more than Clemente. Yet, the writers based their award on a system of points. A first-place vote earned a player 14 points. A second-place vote carried a worth of nine points, and a third-place vote eight points. The progression continued downward to a tenth-place vote, which was worth one point. Therefore, the MVP was decided on the basis of total points, not the number of first-place votes.

All 20 writers placed Clemente's name on their ballots, ranging from first to third place. One writer, perhaps believing that a pitcher should not win the MVP, didn't include Koufax anywhere on his ballot. As a result, Koufax finished with 208 points, 10 points behind Clemente. Based on the higher point total, Clemente won the National League's most coveted award.

For a man who believed that he should have won the award six seasons earlier—or at least finished higher than eighth—the MVP represented overdue fulfillment. Now that he had finally won it, Clemente offered no false modesty. "It's the highest honor a player can hope for, but I was expecting it," said Clemente, who learned about his selection while working on a farm he had recently bought. "Of course, it could have gone to Sandy Koufax, but I had the best season of my career and I was confident the writers would vote for me," Clemente told the Associated Press. He had not been so confident in 1960, when a Los Angeles writer had told him about the underground campaign for teammate Dick Groat. There was no similar campaign in '66. The award belonged to Clemente.

Clemente's remarks upon winning the MVP reflected the confident pride that drove him to baseball supremacy. "He was a very serious and dedicated individual when it came to anything he did in life. Professional," says Luis Mayoral. "Let me see if I can pick out a name. Maybe a Paul Molitor-type of guy. Quiet, but firm. Dedicated completely. He had a lot of pride in being Roberto Clemente the baseball player, but it was not the type of pride where he thought he had authority to demean other people. He never did that. He was simply proud of the ballplayer that he was."

In addition to individual recognition, the award carried broader significance. For the first time in history, a native of Puerto Rico had won the MVP. The occasion also represented the first time in National League annals that a player from any Latin American country had been named MVP. Only one other Latino player had previously captured the MVP Award; in 1965, Minnesota's Zoilo

Versalles—a native of Cuba—won the American League's top honor.

All in all, 1966 proved a watershed year for Latinos in the major leagues. Four of the top five hitters in the National League hailed from Latin American countries. Felipe Alou, the Braves' Dominican star, led the league in hits, total bases, and runs. Another Dominican, San Francisco's Juan Marichal, won 25 games and led the league in winning percentage. In the American League, Minnesota's Tony Oliva paced all hitters with 191 hits. Yet, Clemente's MVP season was the best of them all.

"I think the bottom line for him," says Luis Mayoral, "was trying to show other Puerto Ricans and other human beings that—regardless of how poor you are, the color of your skin, your main language—if you dedicate yourself to a cause, you can be a winner. That was bottom line for him." At times, Clemente's critics confused his pride with ego. "A lot of people misinterpreted that pride that he had," says Mayoral. "They tried to put it in a category of arrogance—*arrogancia*, in Spanish. But that was not the Roberto I met, no. He was a very down-to-earth individual."

"One thing about him hasn't changed over the years," wrote Bill Mazeroski in the November 1971 edition of *Sport* magazine. "He's the same person to the clubhouse boys that he is to the league president. He doesn't hang around with the big shots, the superstars."

A short story told by Art Howe illustrates Clemente's grounded personality—his willingness to associate with the common people. As a youth, Howe had enjoyed watching Clemente from afar, but didn't actually meet the Pirate star until the mid-1960s. The informal encounter didn't take place at the ballpark, but at a local tavern in Fort Myers, Florida, where the Pirates held spring training. It was an ordinary setting, one that other superstars might have shied away from in favor of posh night clubs or four-star restaurants. "We were at Pirate City, and Roberto stopped by one evening and shot a little pool with some of the kids—some of the Latin kids," says Howe, who was still a fan at the time and not yet a professional player. "When we heard Roberto was there, everybody went into the pool room to gaze at him. He had a nice-looking suit, nice and clean." Clemente may have dressed differently than the average fan, but he still felt a common bond with him, especially the young Latino.

Clemente showed his concerns for young Latinos during the off-season. In November, he received an invitation to address the

San Juan Rotary Club, an organization that had agreed to sponsor Little League baseball in Puerto Rico. Even though one of Clemente's older brothers was gravely ill with cancer of the spine—his condition concerning Roberto throughout the season—he agreed to speak to the club. "I could not say no," Clemente told Rafael Pont-Flores of *The Sporting News*. "I owe so much to baseball that it is only by coming here that I can pay a very small interest on the principal."

As Clemente addressed the members of the rotary club, he reminded them of his own experiences as a youngster trying to play organized baseball. "When I was a kid, they did not have Little League Baseball," Clemente pointed out to the audience. "It was called 'Future Stars.' People from the town would donate uniforms, bats, balls and gloves. Chances are that the donors do not remember what they gave to us. But I haven't forgotten."

During his speech, Clemente discussed how some major league players gave only a half-hearted effort. He emphasized the importance of playing hard at all times, in the context of making contributions to a team effort. In concluding his address, Clemente thanked the members of the rotary club for their involvement in supporting youth baseball. "A major leaguer goes all out, all the time, all the way," said Clemente, prefacing his final point. "Standing here today, talking to you who are sponsors of Little League baseball, I feel that you are all major leaguers." A few days after making the memorable speech, Roberto's brother died.

Clemente's 1966 season not only earned him his first MVP Award, but two other high honors: *The Sporting News'* National League "Player of the Year" and his second "Dapper Dan Award," which recognized Pittsburgh's most significant and influential athlete over the past year. Only two other Pirates, Dick Groat and Ralph Kiner, had won the "Dapper Dan" twice. In voting conducted by the *Pittsburgh Post-Gazette,* Clemente received 59 of 91 tallies. Other members of the Pirate organization earned solid support in the "Dapper Dan" voting. Harry Walker finished second in the balloting, garnering 19 votes. General manager Joe Brown earned four votes, while Pirate players Matty Alou and Gene Alley picked up one ballot apiece. In total, Pirate players and officials monopolized 84 of the 91 votes cast in the "Dapper Dan" balloting.

Alou's placement in the "Dapper Dan" voting testified to his improved play. A poor hitter with the Giants, Alou batted .342 in his first season with the Pirates, as he wrested the league's batting crown away from Clemente. Compared with his 1965 performance, Alou had raised his average by 111 points, an unthinkable improvement. Some of the credit belonged to Harry Walker, who realized that Alou needed to cease his insistence on pulling the ball. Clemente had played a part, too. After being asked by Walker to talk to his teammate about his hitting, Clemente had worked diligently with Alou during the spring. If not for Clemente, Alou might have improved by a much smaller margin.

On January 29, 1967, Clemente officially received the "Dapper Dan Award" at the organization's annual banquet. A sellout crowd of celebrities and members gathered at the Hilton Hotel in Pittsburgh to honor Clemente and recently elected Hall of Famer Lloyd Waner. Another Pirate Hall of Famer, third baseman Pie Traynor, also attended the Dapper Dan dinner, an annual event in Pittsburgh. In spite of the presence of legends like Waner and Traynor, Clemente received the loudest response when Dapper Dan founder Al Abrams introduced him to the crowd. The 2,000 guests who had packed the Hilton ballroom rewarded Clemente with a standing ovation.

Several members of the Pirate family spoke on Clemente's behalf, including newly acquired shortstop Maury Wills, who had never played with Clemente, and manager Harry Walker. A one-line comment attributed to Walker in the May 26, 1967 issue of *Time* magazine epitomized his regard for the 1966 MVP. Clemente "is just the best player in baseball, that's all."

14

The Hat Falls Off

*P*rior to the 1967 season, the Pirates made two
significant off-season deals. General manager Joe Brown sent relief pitcher Wilbur
Wood to the Chicago White Sox for left-hander
Juan Pizarro, another Puerto Rican standout whose
career had been aided by Pedrin Zorrilla. Brown also
acquired veteran shortstop Maury Wills from the Los
Angeles Dodgers, surrendering two young players in
return: infielders Bob Bailey and Gene "The Stick"
Michael. More importantly, the Pirates promoted three
of their most talented prospects—and key contribu-
tors for the future. Catcher Manny Sanguillen, first
baseman Bob Robertson and pitcher Bob Moose
would all make their major league debuts during the
summer of '67.

In January, Clemente traveled to the states for a
series of winter banquets. While in Pittsburgh, Clemente
planned to negotiate his 1967 contract with general
manager Joe Brown. On January 25, a two-hour meeting at the Hilton Hotel produced a milestone contract:
$100,000 for the upcoming season. Clemente became
the first player in the history of the Pirates' franchise to

sign a one-year contract in the six-figure range. Slugging outfielder Ralph Kiner had come close during the 1950s, earning a salary as high as $90,000.

In spite of the large money being doled out by the Pirates, the contract talks went quickly and smoothly. According to Brown, the two men spent most of the two-hour session talking about topics other than the contract. When they finally did begin to negotiate, they agreed to salary within a matter of minutes. The meeting typified the negotiations between Brown and Clemente over the years. "Never had any problems with him, never came close to a holdout," Brown says of his many negotiations with Clemente. "I always felt that I was pretty easy to negotiate with because I always try to be fair. I never had any problems with Roberto." The comments of Clemente supported Brown's contention. "Brown usually says what he has in mind and I sign," Clemente explained to Les Biederman of the *Pittsburgh Press*. "He has always been fair."

Clemente appreciated the staggering amount of money, a far cry from the 45 cents a day his father had earned working on a sugar plantation in the thirties and forties. The salaries Roberto earned with the Pirates allowed him to comfortably support his wife and children with a house in Puerto Rico and an apartment in Pittsburgh, buy a new home for his parents, and offer financial help to a niece and nephew. "Baseball has enabled me to support 11 people and it has given me an education," Roberto said to Les Biederman later in the year. "It has brought me a measure of fame and money. I'm very grateful." He was also generous. Clemente once gave his nephew Pablo the gift of an 18-foot cruiser. On another occasion, he donated half of his banquet fees to teammate Diomedes Olivo, a 40-year-old pitcher who had struggled in the minor leagues for years before making his big league debut. In addition, Clemente regularly gave $20 tips to National League clubhouse men. He treated John Hallahan, the Pirates' equipment manager, in similarly generous fashion. In his native Puerto Rico, Clemente often handed out money to poor children in the streets.

Clemente was also giving in his dealings with the Pirates' rookie players. "[Roberto] reacted more to rookies than to guys who had been around for awhile," wrote Steve Blass in a 1973 edition of *Sport* magazine, "maybe because he would've liked someone to have helped him when he was a rookie." In 1967, a 23-year-old Panamanian catcher made his major league debut. As a young Latin American, Manny Sanguillen endured his share of problems adjust-

ing to major league life. "[Roberto] had known the same problems," wrote Blass, "the new language, getting acclimated to the big
league atmosphere, the way to deal with the media, where to eat
on the road, how to dress." When Sanguillen made rookie mistakes,
Clemente helped him overcome them. "Sangy got picked off twice
in one game," wrote Blass. "Robby came into the clubhouse and got
a big piece of cardboard and put two sticks through it. He told
Sangy to pretend it was a machine; that he would use it to take
control of Sangy when he got on base. We laughed for 20 minutes,
but it made Sangy realize that he didn't have to stick his head in his
locker if he made a costly mistake in a game."

Sanguillen appreciated Clemente's willingness to reach out.
"When I joined the Pirates, he took me with him to best places,
meet everybody," Sanguillen recalled in a 1973 interview with Al
Abrams of the *Pittsburgh Post-Gazette*. "He did this all the time." Thanks
to the efforts and intervention of Clemente, he and Sanguillen soon
became close friends.

Few writers publicized it at the time, but Clemente also acted
as an intermediary between the Latin American players on the Pirates and the team's administration. If a Latin player had a complaint, Clemente tried to resolve the situation by approaching one
of the team's front office officials. In turn, Clemente also provided
counsel to the young Latin player, by sharing the experiences of
the obstacles that he himself had encountered.

In May, Clemente experienced perhaps the finest single day—
and month—of his career. On May 15, he splattered Cincinnati
pitching with four extra base hits. He hit two-run homers in the
first and fifth innings, doubled in the seventh, and added his third
home run in the ninth. The last home run gave the Pirates a 7-5
lead, but Juan Pizarro allowed two runs in the ninth and a single
tally in the 10th to lose the game. The outcome left the team-minded
Clemente disappointed. "It was my biggest game, but not my best
game," Clemente told *The Sporting News*. "My best game is when I
drive in the winning run."

Still, the 8-7 defeat did little to diminish Clemente's four hits,
three runs and seven RBIs, or the impression that he left on several
members of the Reds. "When I play second base," said infielder-
outfielder Pete Rose, "Clemente hits balls harder at me than any
left-handed batter." Reds manager Dave Bristol offered the ultimate
praise. "The best player in the game today," *Ebony* magazine quoted

Bristol in assessing Clemente's value. "I'd have to take him over [Hank] Aaron and all the rest."

The outburst against the Reds highlighted a terrific month of May for Clemente. Over a 27-game span, he collected 44 hits, an average of nearly two per game. He hit nine home runs, the most he had ever hit in one month, and added 29 RBIs. In an anticlimactic vote, writers and broadcasters convincingly selected Clemente as the National League "Player of the Month." Even though San Francisco Giants' right-hander Juan Marichal had won six of seven decisions with a 1.29 ERA over the same duration, Clemente easily won the award, 33-9.

On June 17, the Pirates played the Phillies at Connie Mack Stadium. That afternoon, manager Harry Walker wrote in the following names on his lineup card:

Matty Alou, CF
Maury Wills, 3B
Roberto Clemente, RF
Willie Stargell, 1B
Manny Mota, LF
Jose Pagan, SS
Andre Rodgers, 2B
Jessie Gonder, C
Dennis Ribant, P

The first eight names in the lineup belonged to black and Latino players. Dennis Ribant, the pitcher, represented the Pirates' only white starter. Although complete research has yet to be conducted on this matter, this game may have represented the first time in major league history that all eight of a team's starting position players were black.

Nellie King, who had returned to the organization as a broadcaster by the start of the 1967 season, remembers hearing the reaction of several Pirates to the nearly all-black lineup. "Fellows, they won't be playing the National Anthem today," proclaimed Willie Stargell, the game's starting first baseman. "They're going to play Sweet Georgia Brown." Dock Ellis, one of the team's few black pitchers, chimed in with his own bit of humor. "We got to find a way to get Ribant out of there early," suggested Ellis, "and get Alvin O'Neal McBean in there so we have nine brothers playing."

If taken at face value or out of context, Ellis' remarks might have been misconstrued as mean-spirited. Yet, Ellis was quite clearly kidding, as was Stargell. Their reactions typified the humorous, good-natured way that most Pirates dealt with the unusual racial composition of their team. Pirate players—black, white and Latino—tended to mix with each other, both in the clubhouse and in social settings away from the ballpark. The Pirates' ability to mesh well across racial lines stemmed, at least in part, from the leadership of Clemente.

"It was most visible during the height of the race problems in the late 1960s, when the Pirates had more black and Latin players than any team," says Nellie King. "This openness came from the leadership of veteran players such as Clemente, Mazeroski and Stargell, along with the humorous agitation of Steve Blass, Dock Ellis, Dave Giusti and Dave Ricketts." On the day the Pirates came within one player of fielding the first all-black lineup, racial humor had never been more prevalent.

"Race was never a problem with the Pirates during their successful years," King contends. "It was brought out into the open, instead of, as Sanguillen would say, 'Someone talking on the back of my neck.'" Clemente, it seems, had set the precedent five years earlier when he refused to respond to a reporter's critical remarks about a teammate, Bob Friend. The practice of back-stabbing, be it racial or otherwise, was frowned upon by Clemente and the other leaders of the Pirate clubhouse.

"One of the strengths of the successful Pirate teams was the openness among players in the clubhouse," says King. "There were no cliques; nobody stood higher than anyone else. Although the star of the team and an MVP and batting champion, Clemente was part of the reason for that openness by taking the brunt of humorous agitation." An exchange during spring training in 1967 typified the by-play involving Clemente and other Pirate players. As Clemente talked at length with a reporter, Jose Pagan interrupted the interview. "Every time I see you, you like Cassius Clay, yak, yak, yak," Pagan said, using humorous sarcasm. "Don't you ever stop?" Clemente smiled before responding. "He wouldn't want to talk to you," said Clemente, still smiling. "There'd be nothing to talk about."

For years, National League pitchers had enforced a singular strategy against Clemente: back him off the plate with inside pitches early in the count, then come back with low pitches on the outside corner later in the count. No pitcher believed in the philosophy more than the Dodgers' Don Drysdale. The sidewinding Drysdale liked to pitch most every right-handed batter inside, but especially Clemente. On June 4, Drysdale allowed a home run to Clemente, the first longball he had surrendered on the season. Predictably, Drysdale decided to send Clemente a message during his next at-bat in the seventh inning. A high inside fastball threatened to shatter Clemente's helmet, but Roberto managed to avoid the pitch. In the past, Roberto might have tended to shy away from the plate on the next set of pitches, understandably concerned over his personal safety. This time, an angry Clemente stiffened. He strode into the next pitch, driving it into the stands for his second home run of the game. The three-run shot sealed a 4-1 victory. Clemente had heard Drysdale's message and had decided to return it with his own: don't throw at me again.

Clemente's success as a hitter also sent another subtle message to opposing hurlers: don't repeat your pitching patterns. "Roberto is one of the toughest hitters in the league, the kind you can't pitch to any certain way," Atlanta Braves right-hander Tony Cloninger said in an interview with *Ebony* magazine. "You may get him out on one pitch, but if you throw him the same pitch again, he'll hit it for a bullet."

Two days after Clemente's punishment of Drysdale, the Pirates dropped both ends of a doubleheader against the Mets. Concerned that the two extra-inning losses had damaged the club's morale, Clemente called a team meeting. Clemente did not invite the manager or coaches; he wanted only the players to attend.

Several writers questioned the wisdom of calling players-only meetings, something Clemente had done several times the previous season. They wondered whether Clemente was undermining the authority of his manager. They suggested that several Pirates resented Clemente for calling meetings. Several major league managers, including Baltimore's Hank Bauer, the Cubs' Leo Durocher and Philadelphia's Gene Mauch, said they didn't approve of such a players-only meeting. Clemente tried to defend his motivation in calling the players together. "This is the first time [meeting] this year," Clemente explained to Dick Young of the *New York Daily News*. "We have to talk. We can play better. Sometimes it is not how good you are, it's how hard you try. Some are not doing it."

Young asked Clemente why he had excluded the manager and the coaching staff. "I think sometimes a meeting with just the players is better than with the managers and coaches," Clemente countered. "If a player has something to say, he will say it; get it out in the open." Young asked Walker whether the players' meeting indicated that he had lost control of the ballclub. "That's not so," responded Walker, who expressed no opposition to the players' gathering.

The meeting paid short-term dividends, as the Bucs won their next three games. Unfortunately, the beneficial effects of the meeting lasted only a few days. The Pirates won only eight of their next 21 games to finish the month of June. The team improved only slightly in July, playing mediocre ball over the first half of the month. With the Pirates well out of contention in the pennant race, general manager Joe Brown decided to make a major change. On July 18, he fired Walker, replacing him with old favorite Danny Murtaugh.

Walker's firing raised the issue of the recent players-only meeting called by Clemente and the manager's relationship with his star player. Some writers speculated that Walker and Clemente didn't get along, but the Pirates' right fielder later denied such conjecture. "That is not true," Clemente said in a 1971 interview with Joe Heiling of the *Houston Post*. Clemente explained that misconceptions of a poor relationship with the manager stemmed from the controversial episode of May 1965, when Walker had benched him and then supposedly criticized him for not wanting to play while feeling sick. "This was the only problem we ever had," Clemente told Heiling. "We always got along very good. I have much respect for Harry." Clemente said he enjoyed talking baseball and hitting philosophies with "The Hat." "I got along with Harry so good," said Roberto, "because he thinks baseball the way I think and I'm glad."

Upon winning the 1966 MVP Award, Clemente had praised the work of Walker. "Maybe he is not the best manager there is," Clemente had told the Associated Press, "but to me he is tops." And only a month and a half before Walker's firing, Clemente had once again offered an endorsement of his manager. "I am playing hard because of him," Clemente informed *The Sporting News*. "He treats me like a human being. He makes me feel wanted, makes me feel important. He gives me peace of mind." Those did not sound like the words of a man who disliked his manager.

The decision to fire Walker produced mixed feelings for Joe Brown. He felt the move was best for the good of the team, but also realized that Walker had successfully extracted the most from Clemente's immense talents. Walker had encouraged Clemente to become a more aggressive outfielder by charging ground balls more forcefully. He had also helped Clemente become a more dynamic run producer. "The one player that Harry Walker reached the most, inspired more than anyone else was Roberto Clemente," Brown says. "He convinced Roberto that he didn't have to just single to right field, [but] hit home runs to right field. 'Don't cut down on your power any; don't be content to hit a single.' And you look at the years that Harry managed Roberto and see the statistics for those two years, you will see those are the most productive years that Roberto spent in the major leagues."

In July, a film crew's visit to Shea Stadium coincided with the Pirates' trip to New York. The crew was looking to shoot footage for a baseball scene. One of the producers approached Clemente, asking him if he would be willing to appear in the scene for a $100 payday. Thinking that the producer was actually working on a documentary for children, Roberto accepted the offer.

The night before the scheduled shoot, Clemente learned a few details about the film crew's real work. During a conversation with Matty Alou at the team hotel, Clemente revealed that the filmmakers had agreed to pay him $100. Alou laughed. "He says I am foolish," Clemente told Jerry Lisker of the *New York Daily News*. Alou informed Clemente that this was no children's documentary; the crew was working on a major feature film, *The Odd Couple*.

At $100, Clemente now felt he was being shortchanged. Alou suggested that he receive no less than $1,000. Roberto became even more irritated when he learned that the movie script called for him to hit into a triple play. As a man proud of his playing abilities, Clemente wanted no part of that.

Clemente returned to Shea Stadium the next day. A director saddled up to Clemente and put his arm on his shoulder, acting as if he had just met one of his closest friends. "Hiya, Roberto, how's my old buddy?" the man said to Clemente, whom he had never met. Turned off by the director's inappropriate manner and the film crew's deception, Clemente told him he would not appear in the movie. "I thought that it was something like a documentary for the kids, or something like that," Clemente told Jerry Lisker. "Then I find out that it is a big movie, that they will show it in Latin America. They insult me. One hundred dollars, that's what they want to pay me. Who they think they try and fool? They think Roberto Clemente was born last week?"

The lowball offer and the lack of honesty only added to Clemente's biggest complaint with the filmmakers. "What would fans in Latin America say if they see me hit into triple play? They would not understand." Having lost the services of Clemente, the producer asked Pirates' shortstop Maury Wills to participate. Wills also turned down the offer. The film crew finally hired Bill Mazeroski to hit into the triple play.

A few minutes after his exchange with the director, Clemente stepped into the batting cage and took his pre-game swings. With his final cut, Clemente unleashed a 440-foot drive over the left-center field fence. As the ball soared toward the outer limits of Shea Stadium, Roberto yelled in the direction of a cameraman. "Hey movieman," Roberto exclaimed, "take a picture of that home run and put it in your stinking picture. You can have it for nothing."

As the season-long struggles of the Pirates continued throughout the summer, Clemente, for one of the first times in his career, expressed discontent with the game. "Once upon a time, I never believed I could ever get tired of baseball," Clemente told Les Biederman the day before his 33rd birthday. "I played baseball from morning to night. But today it isn't as it once was. I just never seem to get enough rest. And if I can't play at my best all the time, why play?"

Clemente hinted that he might play only two or three more years before ending his career. He suggested a change of positions as a way of lengthening his career further. "I might finish my career at first base," Clemente told Biederman, "and this would enable me to play a little longer." With power-hitting Donn Clendenon entrenched at first base and Clemente still a Gold Glove-caliber outfielder, a move to the infield didn't seem imminent.

On September 15, Clemente and Willie Stargell filed separate lawsuits against a 20-year-old writer who was the editor and co-publisher of a local sports magazine. The publication, entitled *Pittsburgh Weekly Sports*, had reported a physical confrontation between Clemente and Stargell. The August 4th article maintained that both men had thrown punches at each other in the clubhouse after Clemente had ripped several Pirates for failure to hustle. Both Clemente and Stargell denied that a fight had taken place. Clemente asked for $1 million in damages, while Stargell filed a suit for $750,000. Ironically, the recipient of the lawsuit had moved into Clemente's Pennley Park apartment building just one month earlier. The neighbors were now legal combatants.

As it turned out, the story in *Pittsburgh Weekly Sports* had no merit. The young writer had foolishly relied upon a second hand source, a ballpark usher, who had heard about a clubhouse fight from another person. Although there had actually been a small fight, it had not involved either Clemente or Stargell. The writer settled the case by penning a formal apology to both players, who agreed to drop their lawsuits.

When the season came to an end, Clemente did not win a second consecutive MVP Award. Yet he did lead the National League in hits for the second time in his career. More significantly, Clemente staked claim to his fourth batting title. He became only the seventh player to win as many, joining a gallery of Hall of Fame batting marksmen: Ty Cobb (12 titles), Honus Wagner (8), Rogers Hornsby (7), Stan Musial (7), Ted Williams (6), and Harry Heilmann (4).

Of the quartet of batting championships, all of which Clemente won during the 1960s, this one ranked as the most impressive. A .357 batting average, the best of his career, placed him 18 points higher than the runner-up, Philadelphia's Tony Gonzalez. Clemente achieved the lofty average without sacrificing much power. He still hit 23 home runs and piled up 110 RBIs, the best figures on the Pirates' roster.

Clemente broke many of the fundamental rules of hitting: he swung at too many pitches, bailed out too often, batted off his front foot, and swung too hard. Yet, Clemente was able to incorporate all of these tendencies into a simplified approach to hitting. "You know, it's really funny," says Nellie King, who studied hitters from a pitcher's perspective. "I think good hitters break things down into simple things. I once asked Stan Musial and I asked Clemente—one's a great left-handed hitter, one's a great right-handed hitter. I asked, 'What's your philosophy on hitting?' I asked Stan Musial and he said, 'I never want to hit a ball into center field.' I said, 'Why?' He said, 'It's the biggest part of the park. The best outfielder plays center field. And he's got a guy on his left and a guy on his right. If I hit it down the lines, only one guy can catch it, and generally the guys in the corners aren't the best fielders. They're not as good as the guy in center field.'"

The response sounded simple to King, who was surprised that Musial didn't mention technical aspects of hitting involving the movement of the hands and legs. King later approached Clemente with a similar line of questioning. "I asked him, 'What's your philosophy on hitting?' He said, 'Number one, you must put the ball in play. You must find a spot that you can hit the ball. Number two, you must [swing] hard and then hit the ball on the ground.'

The second part of the answer puzzled King, who asked Clemente why he tried to hit the ball on the ground, as opposed to lifting it in the air. "He said, 'Well, if you hit the ball in the air, eight or nine people can catch the ball. If you hit it on the ground, only two people can catch it. And when they catch it, they have to make a play on it; to make a play they got to throw it. Your percentages of getting hits are a hell of a lot better there than they are hitting the ball in the air.' That's all he wanted to do, to hit the ball on the ground, put the ball in play, hit it hard."

Clemente incorporated other philosophies into a successful hitting style. "I can see now why Clemente was such a great hitter," says Joe Christopher, himself a student of hitting. "He hit the same way that Rogers Hornsby said things should be done: 'Make the outside part of the plate the closest part because all great pitchers pitch you away, they don't pitch you in.' And Clemente hit most of the balls from shortstop to first base.

"The left knee would be his strength. The left knee he would always bring back, and when he'd bring his left knee back, he would cock the bat at the same time. He would never swing the bat at the baseball; he would always throw the bat at the baseball. Sometimes he would say to me in Spanish: 'Joe, look at me, what I'm doing. Always try to drive the ball, don't swing. When you swing the bat, actually your hands tighten up. If you would just cock the bat and throw the head of the bat ahead of you, it would stop your body from lunging forward.' Clemente was a great hitter in that way."

Clemente's defensive play remained top notch, as well. He registered 17 assists, pacing the National League in that category for a fifth season. Clemente had previously topped the league leader boards in 1958, '60, '61 and '66. No other major league outfielder had led his league in assists as many times as "The Great One."

Although Clemente had relinquished the MVP crown to Orlando Cepeda, the award remained in the possession of a Puerto Rican. In the meantime, another Puerto Rican had contributed greatly to his team's surprising pennant success. Right-hander Jose Santiago had forged a record of 12-4 for the Boston Red Sox, giving him the highest winning percentage in the American League. Without Santiago's pitching, the Red Sox would not have fulfilled their "Impossible Dream—that of winning the AL pennant.

In November, Clemente, Cepeda and Santiago received an invitation to visit the residence of Puerto Rican governor Sanchez Vilella. The three major league stars earned praise from the governor. According to an Associated Press report, Vilella predicted that the feats of Clemente, Cepeda and Santiago would "greatly benefit the development and interest of sports in Puerto Rico." In Vilella's estimation, the combined accomplishments of the three Puerto Rican players is "something no other country but the United States can boast of."

After meeting the governor, the three players answered questions from reporters. One writer asked Clemente if he would play winter ball with the San Juan Senators after sitting out the last two Puerto Rican seasons. Clemente offered a noncommittal answer while referring to the owners of the Senators. "They are the ones who will have to decide," Clemente told the *Associated Press* cryptically.

After spending the first month and a half of the off-season making public appearances and conducting youth clinics, Clemente finally reported to the Senators. "The Puerto Ricans have been good to me and I owe it to them to play ball there," Clemente explained to *The Sporting News*. He singled as a pinch-hitter in his first appearance and then went 4-for-4 with a home run in his first start. Clemente also made a leaping catch in right field, preventing what appeared to be a certain home run. Despite not playing competitive baseball for six weeks, Clemente had somehow vaulted himself into immediate mid-season form.

15

A Troubled Summer

On February 2, Clemente signed his 1968 contract with the Pirates. For the second straight year, his salary broached the $100,000 mark. Clemente remained the highest paid player in the history of the franchise. Based on his 1966 and '67 seasons, he had clearly established himself as the Pirates' best player. But was he the best player in the game?

The March 1968 edition of *Sport* magazine posed that very question. Veteran writer Joe Falls polled every major league general manager. Six of the general managers refused to answer, either because they weren't sure or didn't want to offend any of their own players. Of the 18 managers who did respond, six candidates emerged: Atlanta's Hank Aaron, the Tigers' Bill Freehan, St. Louis' Bob Gibson, the Cubs' Ron Santo, the Red Sox' Carl Yastrzemski, and Clemente.

Aaron, Freehan, Gibson and Santo each received one vote. Yastrzemski, the 1967 American League MVP, earned the selection of six general managers. But even after winning the Triple Crown, Yaz could not match the support of Clemente. A total of eight general managers voted for the Pirates' superstar, anointing him unofficial status as the "best player in baseball today."

Joe Brown placed his vote next to Clemente's name. "He can do more things superbly than any athlete I've ever seen," Brown told Joe Falls. "For a good many years, I thought Willie Mays was the best all-around performer I'd ever seen in baseball. Over the past three years, though, Roberto has convinced me he is the best."

Clemente was in Mexico City when he learned that the general mangers had tabbed him as the game's greatest. "That is a great honor," Clemente told *Sport* magazine. A reporter then asked Clemente whom *he* would have selected. "It is a very difficult question," Clemente said in prefacing his remarks. "I think I am the greatest player in the world, but I cannot say such a thing. I say it one time and a newspaperman, he misunderstands me and thinks I am boasting about myself. I am just saying that I have great confidence in myself."

Back at home before the start of spring training, Clemente tried to lift himself up a wall that contained an iron railing. "In Puerto Rico, my home is on a steep hill," Clemente explained several months later in an interview with Sandy Grady of the *Philadelphia Bulletin*. "We have two patios. I was climbing down a wall from one to the other." As Clemente tried to maneuver himself, one of the iron bars collapsed. The four-foot-long, three-inch-wide bar nearly rammed him in the chest, but he managed to hold it off with his hands. Roberto fell to the ground and rolled about 100 feet down the hill, before coming to rest on the back of his neck.

"I'm lucky to be alive. I could have been killed in that fall," Clemente would tell Charley Feeney of the *Pittsburgh Post-Gazette*. The mishap damaged his right shoulder, leaving him subpar only days before the start of spring training. A doctor told him to wear a brace for a few months, but Clemente refused. He told the Pirates nothing of the accident. When he informed Joe Brown that he would have to report to Fort Myers a few days late, he claimed that the delay was caused by the illness of his mother-in-law. After arriving for spring training, he finally told Brown what had really happened. He then staggered through for an 0-for-29 disaster at the plate.

By the end of spring training, Clemente's spring training struggles seemed inconsequential, given the assassination of civil rights leader Martin Luther King, whom Clemente had met four years earlier in Puerto Rico. With 11 black players on the Opening Day roster, no team seemed more emblematic of the work of King than the Pirates, baseball's most integrated team. The Pirates' black players held two team meetings to discuss their response to the tragedy. Maury Wills, the team's player representative, announced that the players preferred not to play Sunday's final exhibition game or the Opening Day game against the Astros on Monday out of respect for the slain activist. When the players learned that King would be buried on Tuesday, and not Monday as originally scheduled, they asked Pirate management to postpone the season's second game, as well.

General manager Joe Brown agreed to cancel the final spring training game against the Yankees, scheduled to be played in Richmond, Virginia, but said he could not postpone the first two regular games against Houston without the permission of Astros' management. Two other teams, the Cincinnati Reds and Washington Senators, quickly announced the postponement of their Opening Day games, but the Astros hesitated.

The Pirates' players did not like the noncommittal response, and once again voted to hold firm on their decision not to play the first two games on Monday and Tuesday. After discussions with Astros' officials, Brown offered a compromise: the team would not have to play on either Monday or Tuesday, but would play on Wednesday, which had originally been scheduled as a travel date. At a clubhouse meeting, the players voted to accept Brown's plan. Roberto Clemente, representing the team's black and Latin players, and Dave Wickersham, one of the team's white players, released a joint statement to the media. "We are doing this because we white and black players respect what Dr. King has done for mankind."

A year later, Clemente expressed disappointment over the indecisive response of some to the King tragedy. "When Martin Luther King died, they come and ask the Negro players if we should play," Clemente told Phil Musick of the *Pittsburgh Press*. "I say, 'If you have to ask Negro players, then we do not have a great country.'"

By 1968, blacks on the Pirates no longer had to travel or dine separately from their white teammates, but Clemente still combated racism in other settings. One day he and his wife went shopping for furniture at a New York City department store. A salesman informed them that the store featured only one section of furniture located on one of the upper floors. He showed Roberto and Vera the furniture, which was not of the same quality as the furniture displayed in the store's showroom.

Clemente recalled his response to the salesman in a 1972 interview with Sam Nover. "I said, 'We would like to see the furniture downstairs that was in the showroom.' And they said, 'Well, you don't have enough money to buy that.' And I said, '*how* do you know that I don't have enough money? I would like to see it because I have the right to see it as a human being, as a person that buy from you.' So finally, they show it to us."

Remembering that he had several thousand dollars in his pocket for an upcoming vacation, Clemente showed the salesman his wallet. "'I have $5,000 in my wallet,'" Clemente told the salesman. "'Do you think [this is enough to] buy it?'" The salesman asked Clemente for his identity. "When they found out who I was, they said, 'We have seven floors full of furniture and we're going to show it to you, and don't worry about it. We thought that you were like a [poor] Puerto Rican.' And right I away I just got mad. I said, 'Look, your business is to sell to anybody. I don't care if I am Puerto Rican, or Jewish, or whatever you want to call me. You see, this is what really get me mad, because I am Puerto Rican, you treat me different from the other people; I have the same American money that you are asking for. I don't want to buy your furniture.' So I walk out."

With Clemente continuing to keep his injury a secret from the media, feelings of optimism supported the Pirates throughout spring training. Joe Brown had supplied the pitching staff with a needed boost—future Hall of Fame right-hander Jim Bunning. Although the former Phillie and Tiger legend had reached his mid-thirties, he had still managed to win 17 games for the fifth-place Phillies, while posting an earned run average of 2.29. The addition of Bunning to a staff that already featured two double-digit winners in Tommie Sisk and Bob Veale, and promising right-handers like Steve Blass, Dock Ellis and Bob Moose, gave the Pirates reason to believe that they would improve on their .500 finish of a year ago.

The optimism put even Clemente in a playful mood, providing him with an opportunity to display his little-known sense of humor. One day in spring training, Nellie King heard Clemente mimicking the team's new manager, Larry Shepard. "Yeah, the new manager this year, he gets to spring training and he says, 'Fellows, we have got a good team here.' He says, 'We do not have to worry about anything. We will just work on the fundamentals. That's what we have to do. So take your time, and get yourself in shape, and we'll work on the fundamentals.'" Anyone who had heard a manager talk about fundamentals, one of baseball's most repeated springtime cliches, could appreciate the humor in Clemente's good-natured imitation.

As spring training continued in Bradenton, Clemente continued his managerial refrain. "You can go play golf," Clemente said mockingly to the other players in the clubhouse, "because you are good. You will just work on the fundamentals. Do not worry about anything. You are good players."

The Pirates opened the regular season by losing to Larry Dierker and the Astros, 5-4. The Bucs won their next three games, but dropped seven of their next 12 to finish April at .500. "They started the season, they didn't get off to such a good start," says King. "So Clemente says, 'Now gentlemen, we've got to start working, keep working on these fundamentals. We are a good team.'"

The Pirates did not play like a good team in May. After their mediocre start, they suffered through several losing streaks, dropping three straight decisions on two occasions and five consecutive games during their poorest stretch. The Pirates won only 10 out of 25 games during the second month of the season. As the team headed toward June, Clemente carried a meager batting average of .222. The culprit? The pre-season injury to his shoulder, resulting from the fall at his home in Puerto Rico. He had aggravated the problem by trying to do pushups during the team's first road trip.

Early in the season, Pirate players called a team meeting, at which Clemente continued the act that he had begun during spring training. "We're working on the fundamentals," Clemente told his teammates, his voice becoming angry. "What are these fundamentals for? Gentlemen, bleep the fundamentals! You stink!" Several of the Pirates started laughing as Clemente culminated his season-long routine, mixing a little bit of anger with a large dose of comedy.

"It was kind of a satire thing," says Nellie King. "[The last routine] lasted for almost 10 minutes and he had the whole place laughing at it. He seldom, you know, was that kind of guy on the bus, or in public." Clemente saved his humor for the privacy of the clubhouse, and for the benefit of his teammates.

"He was the judge of our Kangaroo Court," Bob Veale tells researcher Andrew O'Toole. "He'd put on a wig and everything. He'd bring people up and he'd fine you. Everyone that went before the magistrate [Clemente] had to pay the money. He'd stand on a bucket or something, and start telling jokes, just cutting up the guys. But it just went as far as the clubhouse."

Clemente's humor featured subtlety when he spoke in English, but reached higher levels of comedy in his native language. "I understand that in Spanish he was really funny," says Roy McHugh. "I know that the Spanish players would gather around him when he was talking and there'd be bursts of laughter. He was a pretty good mimic."

He also showed his strong sense of humor with friends— away from the ballpark. "Oh yes, of course he did, man" says Luis Mayoral. "He liked to tell a lot of jokes." Mayoral says Clemente particularly liked to make exaggerations in his humor. "He used to tell me that when he was 10 or 11 years old, he was so strong that he could take with his hands a three-inch long nail, and he was so strong that he could bend it. And no one can bend a nail, even if you're an adult—you don't have that kind of strength."

Clemente's humor contained other features. "He had kind of a sneaky sense of humor," Mayoral explains. "I remember always that whenever he saw me with a shirt he liked—and this happened many times—he used to tell me, 'Luisito, that's a nice shirt. But I'll get you a better shirt when I come back from the states next year because I have a friend who has a factory in California. He makes the best shirts in the world.' So for three years, I waited for the shirts. But they never arrived, you know."

By his own admission, Clemente's outward personality changed in baseball settings. "I'm a completely different person in the ballpark than I am at home," Clemente told the Associated Press in 1971. "You see me scowling, cursing and hollering at different guys in the clubhouse, but that's not really me. I'm just trying to keep this club loose and ready to play heads-up baseball." As serious as Clemente could be at the ballpark, especially around reporters, he could be very carefree in demeanor away from the baseball settings. "He was that kind of a guy," says Mayoral. "He was very light, spiritually speaking, among friends. There was a peaceful Roberto Clemente, a funny Roberto Clemente." Away from the ballpark, Clemente refrained from cursing, rarely raised his voice in anger, and smiled more often.

Unfortunately, most of the writers covering the team saw little of Clemente's lighter side. "Now among friends, he was a clown," Mayoral contends. "He liked to speak so much; you know, he was like a parrot at times, he couldn't stop talking. Among people he trusted. But based on the fact that he was such a great personality, he was obliged to kind of build a wall of protection around him. He would only open a little door in that wall and let the people he knew and trusted come in."

"There was sort of a barrier around Robby after he became a superstar," Steve Blass wrote in a 1973 edition of *Sport* magazine. "I don't know if he built it or it just grew because he was put on a pedestal, but it came down in the privacy of the Pirate clubhouse."

In early May, Roberto had missed a game with shoulder pain, forcing him to publicly disclose his pre-season fall and ensuing shoulder injury. The following month, he contracted the flu, which sapped 11 pounds from his already lean frame. In spite of his weakened throwing and hitting, the Pirates finally started playing better baseball in mid-June, when they won nine straight games against the Giants, Dodgers and Astros. A miserable July, which included a mammoth 10-game losing skid, prevented the Pirates from making a legitimate run at the pennant.

Clemente played so poorly that he failed to make the All-Star Game, not even as a reserve. For the first time since 1960—breaking a string of 11 straight All-Star appearances—Roberto rested during the three-day break. Given the condition of his shoulder, the rest might have been the best remedy. Yet, the problem lingered. Continuing pain caused by the muscle tear in his shoulder led Clemente to question his own future in the game. In early August, Roberto made a stunning announcement to the *Pittsburgh Post-Gazette*. "I won't play next year if the shoulder continues to hurt," Clemente declared. In the interview, Clemente said that he had been told by a member of the organization to keep the injury quiet, as far back as spring training. Clemente hinted that the Pirates had applied pressure on him to play even though they knew the injury was causing him great pain. "I shouldn't have been playing in spring training," Clemente insisted. "After the accident, one doctor in Puerto Rico told me that I should rest for three months."

A Pirate spokesman offered up a different story, claiming that Clemente had reported to spring training with the injured shoulder, but had chosen not to tell the team about it. The spokesman also downplayed the seriousness of Clemente's retirement threat, citing reports from doctors who believed the injury would heal itself by the following spring.

A late-season surge lifted Clemente's final average to .291, but did little to lift his spirits. With his shoulder still bothering him, Clemente opted for an off-season of complete rest. If the shoulder still hurt come February, he would quit the game.

16

Bowie, Boos, and Bandits

Bowie Kuhn became baseball's fifth commissioner in 1969. In March, Kuhn toured spring training sites throughout Florida. The tour provided the setting for Kuhn's first meeting with Roberto Clemente. It was an encounter unlike any others that Kuhn experienced with a major league player. "In that spring, I went around and visited all the teams, though I may have missed a couple," says Kuhn. "I met with Pittsburgh ballplayers, so it would have been in the spring of '69. Probably in Bradenton, where the Pirates had spring training. And yes, I do remember my first impressions. It was the same impression I always had of him, of Clemente. He was a very commanding man, commanding in manner of style and appearance; even in the way he moved, he was commanding. And I was struck immediately with the fact that he had none of the sort of reticence that ballplayers are apt to have when talking to the commissioner—not at all. He spoke to the commissioner and everybody else as equals, that's the way he was. And I don't say that in any sense critically. It was refreshing and it was all done with excellent style."

Kuhn realized almost immediately the effect that Clemente had on his Pirate teammates. "It was his commanding character that I will always remember about him as vividly today, all these years after his death, as it was at the beginning. Commanding of everybody, particularly the ballplayers around him. He was the leader and nobody dared to be performing at less than his best as long as Clemente was looking."

Kuhn met with Clemente several times during his reign as commissioner. Like most of his talks with "The Great One," his first one was short in duration. "When I saw the Pittsburgh team," says Kuhn, "I tended to see Clemente. He was not a man for extended conversations on anything. He was not a loquacious man. His style was very reserved. So I doubt that almost anybody [talked at length with him]; Vera may have had extended conversations with him." When asked if Clemente's lack of familiarity with English may have played a part in keeping their talks brief, Kuhn offers a fast response. "No, no, he could communicate very well," says the former commissioner. "No, I don't think it was that at all. I think it was just— that was his style."

While their conversations may have lacked length and depth, they still created an emotional stir with Kuhn. Unlike most players, Clemente had an unusually regal quality to his character and personality. "Most conversations with him were not memorable in terms of what he said," says Kuhn, "but in terms of Clemente being Clemente. Not in terms of the content. Simply in terms of Clemente—you were having a conversation with the king."

An off-season of rest had helped Clemente's right shoulder. He had wisely accepted the advice to forego his usual ritual of winter ball. "It doesn't hurt now," Clemente told Charley Feeney in March. "But I can't be sure until I play. Only then will I be sure that I can play baseball."

A 400-foot home run in an intra-squad game provided the Pirates with an early answer. Hopeful that he could improve on his poor output of 1968, Clemente embarked on his usual spring training regimen. On March 14, the Pirates played one of their early spring games in Bradenton against the Red Sox. When a Boston hitter dumped a fly ball down the right field line, Clemente gave chase. Even though the exhibition game meant nothing in terms of winning and losing, Clemente ran hard in pursuit of the fly. After crossing the foul line with his sprinter's speed, Clemente dove for the ball, falling on his shoulder. This time, he injured his left shoulder.

Clemente removed himself from the game, and stayed out of the lineup for a few days. Dr. Joseph Finegold, the team physician, prescribed heat treatments and rest for his patient. Dr. Finegold hoped that Clemente could return within a week, but his shoulder remained sore and tight for nine days. Frustrated over the inability of the team's medical staff to improve the shoulder, Clemente decided to take matters into his own hands. On March 25, Clemente returned home to San Juan to have his own personal specialist, Arturo Garcia, examine the injury. In explaining the pain to reporters, Clemente offered up one of his most memorable quotations. "My bad shoulder feels good," said Clemente, "and my good shoulder feels bad." The Pittsburgh writers gleefully printed Clemente's comedic remarks in their respective newspapers.

According to one writer, the Pirates' team physician did not react so humorously to Clemente's latest injury and subsequent departure from spring training. When Dr. Finegold learned that Clemente had left camp to consult Garcia, a man who was not even a full-fledged doctor, he allegedly became furious. "Clemente better not complain to me about his shoulder again," Dr. Finegold reportedly said in front of a local reporter. "He can just go back to that doctor in Puerto Rico. I'm sick and tired of listening to his complaints." Several writers interpreted Dr. Finegold's remarks as an insinuation that Clemente was a malingerer.

Clemente returned to Bradenton after a five-day stay in Puerto Rico. He praised Garcia's work in improving the condition of his sore shoulder. "He is the man who helped make my back better, and is making my shoulder better," Clemente told Dick Young of the *New York Daily News*. "He gave me all kinds of heat treatments. He worked on my shoulder with his hands. It is 100 percent better, but not all healed yet. I will be able to play soon."

When Clemente heard about Dr. Finegold's critical remarks, he continued to defend Garcia, but refrained from criticizing the team doctor. Clemente claimed that reporters had blown the story of a rift between him and Dr. Finegold well out of proportion. One source close to Dr. Finegold claimed the doctor had been kidding when he made his remarks about Clemente.

Whatever the case, Clemente was far more upset by a recent comment from television reporter Dick Stockton, who had reported an anonymous accusation against the Pirate star. The latest criticism? Clemente was not a team player. Clemente believed the charge came from another member of the media, not one of his teammates."You say, maybe I no team player," Clemente said, addressing the media at-large."I win four batting titles. I kill myself in outfield. I play when I hurt. What more do you writers want?"

Clemente took his response a step further, claiming that the writers held a hidden agenda."They are trying to create a bad image for me," Clemente said, as more writers gathered near the first base dugout to hear his amplifying diatribe."You know what they have against me? Because I am black and Puerto Rican." As Clemente had said repeatedly throughout his adult career, he was a double minority, a fact that left him even more susceptible to racism than his African-American contemporaries.

Clemente's outburst against the media reflected his passionate nature. His emotions often ranged perceptibly."He was a mercurial person," says Joe Brown,"because compassionate people very seldom stay on the same keel. They're up and down, things affect them, bad things affect them and make them down, and they're happy when things are going well and people are kind to them, and they're up. He was up and down because he was a passionate, compassionate, loving, caring person."

After venting his frustration with the media, Clemente played five and a half innings before Larry Shepard rested him in favor of Jose Pagan. Still, Clemente felt well enough to continue playing the pre-season schedule. On April 1, Clemente expected to play an exhibition game against the Mets, but a pre-game workout resulted in the stiffening of his shoulder. Hopeful of loosening the shoulder again, Clemente left St. Petersburg to resume his batting practice routine in Bradenton. With one week to go before the start of the regular season, Clemente vowed he would be ready when the games counted."I have been in the lineup Opening Day for 15 years and I expect to be in this one," Clemente told the *New York Daily News*.

Clemente did make the Opening Day lineup, but a few days later he must have questioned his decision to return. On April 13, Clemente struck out in his first at-bat before bouncing into double plays in his next two appearances. For the first time in his long career with the Pirates, Clemente heard boos from the fans at Forbes Field. In the eighth inning, Roberto allowed a single to go through his legs, an embarrassing two-base error. When he came to bat in the bottom half of the inning, he heard another round of boos— this one far louder than the first. As Clemente walked from the dugout to the batter's box, he doffed his cap to the crowd. The collection of boos melted into cheers.

After the game, Clemente tried to explain his gesture. "I wasn't trying to be smart with them," Clemente told Luke Quay of the *McKeesport Daily News*. "I just wanted to show them that if they wanted to boo, it was all right with me." Clemente then offered an intriguing analogy. "If my mother and father punished me when I was a boy, I would never raise my hand against them."

Clemente understood the frustrations of the fans, who didn't realize how badly his shoulder hurt. "I haven't been swinging the bat and they have a right to get down on me. I don't remember it ever happening before, but I guess every ballplayer hears it sooner or later." In his 15th year with the Pirates, Clemente had finally heard the first signs of fan discontent.

Throughout his career, Clemente had consistently made efforts to reach out to his fans. In the clubhouse, he often talked about "owing" the people of Pittsburgh another pennant. "We are here for the purpose to win for the fans," Clemente told Charley Feeney of the *Pittsburgh Post-Gazette* in a 1972 interview. "That is who we work for. Not for Joe Brown. He does not pay our salary. The fans pay our salary." Even though Clemente received more fan mail than any other Pirate, he tried to answer each letter personally. According to one magazine article's estimate, Clemente sent out over 20,000 signature photos in a given year. Unlike other star athletes, Clemente rarely turned down requests for autographs—especially if they came from children. If he had the time, he tried to converse with youngsters who asked for his signature. He reminded them of the importance of all-out effort and the learning of fundamentals. He also cautioned children about their behavior. "Keep out of trouble," *The Sporting News* once quoted him as saying. "Don't do anything your dear ones will be ashamed of."

At the request of Nellie King, Clemente once visited a young fan in the stands at the Houston Astrodome. Roberto did his best to communicate with the 14-year-old boy, who was deaf. Unsure whether the boy had understood his words, Clemente returned to the dugout, picked up a bat, wrote an inscription on it, and then climbed back into the stands to present it to the boy. The message read: "Jamie, you don't have to be able to hear to play baseball and enjoy the game. Best Wishes, Roberto Clemente."

As he struggled with a batting average that fell as low as .226 in late May, Clemente became involved in perhaps the most bizarre incident of his life. In the midst of a West Coast series with the Padres, Clemente went for a walk outside of the Town and Country

Hotel in San Diego. He noticed Willie Stargell carrying a box of take-out fried chicken, and asked the slugger where he had purchased the food. Stargell pointed him in the right direction. As Clemente returned from the restaurant, box of chicken in hand, a car pulled next to him near the sidewalk. As the car window rolled down, a man holding a gun pointed it at Clemente and told him to get in. Roberto obliged, entering the vehicle that carried the four strange men, including the gunman. The bandits drove Clemente to a solitary mountainous area that looked down on Mission Valley, ordered him to strip down to his underwear, and took his wallet, $250 in cash, and his All-Star game ring.

"This is when I figure they are going to shoot me and throw me into the woods," Clemente told Bill Christine of the *Pittsburgh Press* 15 months later. "They already have the pistol inside my mouth." At that point, Clemente pleaded with the men not to kill him. Hoping that the bandits were baseball fans, he told them he was a major league player for the hometown Padres. Roberto pointed to the identification in his wallet and his All-Star Game ring as proof. Perhaps impressed by this discovery, the men returned his wallet and ring, along with his clothes. According to Clemente, one of them said, "Don't forget to put on your tie; we want you to look good."

The bandits drove Clemente to a location within three blocks of the hotel and dropped him off. Clemente started to walk away, but heard the car coming back toward him. He thought the men had changed their mind and had decided to kill him after all. As the car pulled next to him, one of the men called out to him and politely handed him the box of fried chicken.

Shortly after the story of Clemente's abduction appeared, a fan in San Diego threw a rubber chicken at Clemente in right field. When other members of the media heard the details of the incredible story, some reacted with skepticism and outright disbelief. One of Clemente's teammates, Donn Clendenon, didn't believe the part about the bandits returning the money and the chicken. Bill Christine, who had broken the original story, investigated it further by checking the records of the San Diego police department. According to the police report, Clemente had indeed informed authorities of the incident at the time. To this day, Christine believes the story of Clemente's abduction.

In June, Clemente blasted a three-run homer against Cincinnati's Jim Merritt to pass Max Carey and Pie Traynor for third on the Pirates' all-time hit list. The team milestone raised the issue of Clemente eventually achieving the ultimate career milestone—3,000 hits. With a total of 2,417 hits, Clemente needed nearly 600 hits to reach the mark.

In a conversation with Pittsburgh writer Charley Feeney, Clemente spoke honestly about the possibility of reaching 3,000. "Once I thought I'd reach 3,000 hits. Now I don't see how I can make it," Clemente told Feeney, who figured that Roberto would need a decent finish in 1969, followed by three seasons of about 150 hits per year to reach 3,000. "I don't expect to play that long," the 34-year-old Clemente countered. "If I did, I could make it, but I just don't expect to play four more years." Clemente added that he would not accept a role as a part-time player. In other words, once his days as the Pirates' everyday right fielder came to an end, so would his days as a player.

For the third straight summer, Clemente hinted at his impending baseball mortality. "The time has come when I won't play baseball anymore," Clemente told Feeney. "It could come soon." Clemente cited the wear and tear of travel, the slow speed of injury recovery, and family considerations in making him think about early retirement. As usual, family ranked highest on Clemente's list of concerns. "I'd like to be home to see my kids grow up," Clemente said, noting that Vera had recently given birth to their third child, Roberto Enrique.

Clemente's talk of retirement seemed premature given a subsequent hitting tear in July. Clemente batted .402 with 20 RBIs during a 25-game stretch, earning him another National League "Player of the Month" Award. Clemente played so well that the 60-man panel of writers and broadcasters picked him over St. Louis' sensational left-hander, Steve Carlton, who won four games, lost none, and posted a 1.56 ERA during the month.

In early August, Clemente responded to recurrent media criticism that had referred to his alleged hypochondria, while also questioning his leadership skills and his desire to play in spite of injuries. "I kill myself for this club," said an angry Clemente, directly addressing his critics. "They make sarcastic remarks on TV, say I'm not hurt, that I should play when I have injury—that I'm not a team player."

Clemente's complaints were reminiscent of remarks he had made to *Sport* magazine two years earlier. "I've been hurt too many times in the past by the writers," Clemente had told sportswriter

Lou Prato in 1967. "They've called me a hypochondriac, a gold-brick, a troublemaker and worse. They do not understand me and it makes me mad."

Dave Cash made his major league debut during the 1969 season, quickly taking note of the contentious relationship between Clemente and some reporters. "Sometimes, he rubbed the media the wrong way a little bit, but Robby was the type of guy that really didn't want to be involved with the media while the game was getting ready to take place," says Cash. "He used to prepare for the games and he wanted that peace of mind. And he was a very popular guy and a great ballplayer; guys wanted to interview him all the time, and a lot of times he wasn't ready to do an interview. Some of the media just didn't understand that."

At times, sportswriters felt intimidated when approaching Clemente. "That came out of ignorance from the writers," says Luis Mayoral, who now helps Latino players on the Texas Rangers foster their relationships with the media. "The tendency there was to categorize: 'He's Latino, Puerto Rican and black, so he's inferior.' It was so difficult for them, so they were so ignorant, when all they could have done, little by little—they could have become his friends and tried to understand the fact that he was like one man alone in this country. When I say 'one man alone,' he hadn't mastered the language, it was another culture, completely different. Many, many writers then didn't have the mentality that they have now. They didn't have the knowledge; there was no one to bridge the gap like I do here in Texas."

Without a media relations bridge, Clemente wondered about the motivation of certain critical writers and broadcasters. "Why they do this?" Clemente asked aloud. "I'm going to stop this one way or the other." Clemente did not explain how he intended to stop the Pittsburgh media from continuing to aim criticism his way. A few days later, a batting display would provide at least part of the explanation.

On August 13, Clemente experienced one of his best single-game performances as a major leaguer. With his neck bothering him, he collected four hits in five at-bats against Giants' pitching, matching his career high with three home runs. Incredibly, Clemente used different bats during each of his five at-bats. "I do that a lot," Clemente explained to Murray Chass of the *New York Times*. "I have five different bats which I switch around to, depending on how I feel." The unconventional offensive splurge lifted the Pirates to a 10-5 win, while vaulting Clemente's league-leading batting average from .351 to .357. There would be no critics on this day.

Clemente continued to hit well—and play spectacularly afield. On September 20, Bob Moose came to appreciate Clemente's artistry in right field more than most. Through the first five and two-thirds innings, Moose held the Mets hitless at Shea Stadium. With two outs in the sixth, the left-handed hitting Wayne Garrett powered a fly ball to the depths of right field. Clemente raced to the warning track and speared the ball with his glove hand. Having watched Clemente's great catch eradicate the Mets' most threatening drive of the day, Moose pitched three more sterling innings to preserve his first career no-hitter.

Clemente's dramatic catch momentarily overshadowed his most recent hitting spree, which lifted his batting average into the .330s. He even challenged the Reds' Pete Rose and the Mets' Cleon Jones for the batting title. From September 25 to October 1, Clemente batted a scathing .500, rapping out 11 hits in 22 at-bats. The surge put him within six points of Rose heading into the final day of the season.

Clemente continued to apply the pressure to Rose with a 3-for-4 explosion against the Expos. In the meantime, Rose went hitless in his first three at-bats against the Braves. In the eighth inning, Rose came to bat with two outs and runners on first and second. Pulling a surprise, Rose laid down a bunt to the left of the pitcher's mound, perfectly placed for a single. The last at-bat maneuver sealed the batting championship for Rose. Some observers criticized Rose for bunting in such a situation, but the Reds outfielder offered no apologies. Whatever the case, Clemente finished three points short of Rose's league-leading .348 mark. Considering his early-season shoulder injury, Clemente's .345 batting average seemed even more remarkable.

The Pirates finished the season a respectable 88-74, which would have put them in serious contention if they played in the National League West. Unfortunately the Pirates played in the East, where the Mets won 100 games on their way to a world championship. Although the Bucs finished a dozen games back, the season had been successful. They had improved eight games over their 1968 finish and achieved their best record since 1966.

The 1969 Pirates improved in other ways. The clubhouse atmosphere continued to evolve into a setting of racial harmony. Good-natured racial kidding became more prevalent, even as more black and Latino players joined the team. Most of the cliques of the past had begun to dissolve. More than ever before, the Pirates had grown into a close-knit team.

17

The Irishman
Returns

During the off-season, the results of the "Player of the Decade" voting were announced. Pirate followers expected Clemente to receive heavy consideration for the award. They were wrong. Sandy Koufax finished first in the voting, followed by Mickey Mantle, Willie Mays and Hank Aaron. Clemente didn't even finish in the top five, settling for a distant ninth in the balloting. Once again, Clemente wondered what he must do to impress the people who did the voting.

After a 1969 season split between two managers, Joe Brown decided the Pirates needed another dose of the managerial elixir provided by Danny Murtaugh. The news brought favorable reaction from the Pittsburgh media, but grudging acceptance from the team's most prominent player. In spite of his general popularity, Murtaugh had repeatedly struggled in his relationship with Clemente. In previous years, Murtaugh had both directly and publicly questioned the severity of some of Clemente's many injuries, calling into doubt the toughness of "The Great One." On one occasion, Murtaugh had accused Clemente of "faking" an injury when he begged out of the lineup with one of his ailments.The lack of support from his manager tore at the proud Clemente, who expressed an open dislike for Murtaugh during his earlier managerial terms.

In the spring of 1970, the two men did not become instant friends, but they learned to co-exist. As Charley Feeney wrote in the April 11 edition of *The Sporting News,* "The big surprise of spring in the Pirates' camp is the happy relationship between Roberto Clemente and manager Danny Murtaugh." Murtaugh had come to realize how important Clemente was to the Pirates, how he helped unify the black, Latin and white segments of the team. Like few other players, Clemente served as a role model for all of his teammates, regardless of their ethnicity. With that in mind, Murtaugh began confiding in Clemente. Murtaugh knew that he could learn about his players, and communicate important messages to them, just by seeking out Roberto. In turn, Clemente's respect for Murtaugh as a manager grew considerably. "He's got a good knowledge of the game," Clemente would tell the Associated Press in August.

Longtime Pirates' public relations director Bill Guilfoile first met Clemente during the spring of 1970. Guilfoile, who had left his job as the Yankees' assistant public relations director, had just reported to Bradenton for the start of spring training with the Bucs. Upon arriving at McKechnie Field for the first time, Guilfoile encountered a camera crew from a Pittsburgh television station."The sports director there inquired about the possibilities of interviewing Roberto Clemente," Guilfoile recounts."I explained to him that this was my first day on the job, really; I had never even met Clemente. [But] I would certainly be happy to go in the clubhouse and inquire as to his availability. So I went in the clubhouse and I looked around and I found Roberto, and I went over and introduced myself to him as the new Pirates' public relations director.

"Then I mentioned to him that there was a camera crew outside, and mentioned the person's name and the [name of the] station. I was wondering if Roberto would be agreeable to doing an interviewer with this particular sports director. And at that," Guilfoile recalls with a smile, "Roberto unleashed a barrage of English and Spanish and I don't know what all, in which he was obviously indicating his displeasure with this particular individual. Unknown to me, they had had some problems over the years. I just happened to be in the wrong place at the wrong time."

At this point, Guilfoile must have wondered whether Clemente might be on the verge of suffering a heart attack! Guilfoile might have also questioned the wisdom of taking his new position with the Pirates. Fortunately, Clemente's mood shifted. "After this outburst," Guilfoile recalls, "Roberto sort of settled down and he looked at me and said, 'Would it help you if I would do this interview?' I said, 'Well, yes, I guess it would. This is my first day on the job. I don't know you and I don't know him [the sports director] and I'm trying to get off on the right foot.' And Roberto said, 'OK, for you, I will do it.' And he got dressed and went out and talked to this individual for the first time, apparently, in several years."

Guilfoile appreciated Clemente's willingness to suspend his feud with the television station's sports director. "He did it as a favor to me," Guilfoile says, "someone he had only met a few moments before. I just never forgot that. I don't think you would find many athletes who would have been so solicitous and so understanding, and go out of their way as he did to accommodate me that day. We went on to become very good friends, but I never forgot that gesture on his part. It was just an indication of the type of person that he was."

Guilfoile also remembers Clemente for his play on the field, in particular a kind of defensive play that he made routinely during his later years. "Clemente perfected that sliding catch," Guilfoile says. "I don't know how many times he would be at full speed in pursuit of a foul ball that looked like it might drop into the stands. He would approach the wall at a tremendous rate of speed. Then, when he hit the warning track, he would slide and catch that ball a couple of feet in front of the wall, and avoid colliding with the wall by virtue of his slide. He was so good at that; I saw him make a number of catches using that technique."

Clemente also made his feet-first slide in fair territory, gliding across the outfield on his rear end while snatching a fly ball one-handed. He often used the sliding technique on artificial turf, sometimes as a means of cutting off drives into the gap. As Clemente slid with his legs extended, he grabbed the ball with his glove, and then almost immediately jumped to his feet and flung the ball toward the infield. By executing this genuinely athletic play, Clemente often prevented runners from stretching base hits into doubles or triples.

Of the many lasting images he retains of "The Great One," Guilfoile says that he remembers one aspect of Clemente's on-field performance more than any other. "I used to love to see him go from first to third," Guilfoile says with special fondness. "His arms and legs seemed to be going in all directions, but he could really move. He would slide into a base, and in one move he would be on his feet, looking for the ball to see if there was a chance of advancing another base. I guess that's what I probably remember most about him."

Clemente's unique running style—a kind of wild gallop—drew the attention of teammates, as well. "When he turned first base," wrote Steve Blass in a 1973 edition of *Sport* magazine, "it looked like part of him was heading for the pitcher's mound and the other part toward right field." Even in 1970, Clemente had retained the same baserunning speed that he had displayed as a younger player. Only in the outfield had Clemente lost a step, maybe a half step. "It's in the outfield where I feel I have slowed up a little," Clemente told Al Abrams of the *Pittsburgh Post-Gazette*. "[But] not running bases."

Although he ran as fast as almost any player in the National League, Clemente did not attempt to steal many bases. He would finish his career with only 83 stolen bases, with a seasonal high of 12 in 1963. Why didn't Clemente try to test opposing pitchers and catchers more often? Clemente never publicly discussed the issue, but his place in the batting order may have provided a partial explanation. Clemente usually batted third, just ahead of cleanup man Willie Stargell. Third-place hitters don't usually take the chance of stealing many bases, not when a left-handed slugger can drive them in with a double or a home run. Clemente's tendency to become injured probably factored into his reasoning, as well. If he had tried to steal more bases, he might have strained his leg muscles while running, or aggravated his back condition while sliding. Since he already played the game so hard and hell-bent in the field and on the basepaths, why run the risk of further injury trying to steal bases that the team really didn't need in the first place?

By 1970, Clemente had achieved such stature with the Pirates that he carried influence with general manager Joe Brown. As Brown pondered an off-season trade for veteran pitcher Dave Giusti of the Cardinals, he sought the opinion of Clemente. "Very seldom did I talk to any of the players [about whom] I might acquire," Brown relates. "I wasn't too sure about Giusti; I hadn't seen him that much. He hadn't pitched against us much in Pittsburgh and I guess I'd seen him maybe two or three times in the couple of years he was with Houston."

In 1969, Giusti had struggled to a 3-7 record, numbers that left Brown unimpressed but wanting to know more about the palmballing right-hander. Brown figured that an astute hitter like Clemente could provide some insight. "All I asked him was, 'What kind of pitcher was Giusti? Should we get him? Is he a good pitcher?' And Clemente said, 'Yes, yes, I think he's a better pitcher than he's pitched.' He found him tough at times to hit and he told me why and so forth."

Clemente's scouting report convinced Brown to finalize the trade for the veteran right-hander, who featured a deceiving palmball and a sound knowledge of pitching. "Knowing that [Clemente] respected his abilities certainly cemented in my mind that we ought to get him," Brown says. With Clemente providing a seal of approval, Brown sent catcher-outfielder Carl Taylor and a minor leaguer to St. Louis in exchange for Giusti. The deal would prove to be one of Brown's best.

Brown would call on Clemente for more advice during the season. On June 8, the Pirates played an in-season exhibition game against the Kansas City Royals, one of the American League's recent expansion teams. Prior to the game, former major league reliever Orlando Peña pitched batting practice for the Royals.

The 36-year-old Peña hadn't pitched in the majors since 1967, when he split the season between the Tigers and the Indians. As an out-of-work journeyman, Peña was hoping to convince the Royals, or some other major league team, to give him a look. With the Pirates needing some help in long relief, Joe Brown watched Peña closely during batting practice.

After watching Peña, Brown approached Clemente to ask him his opinion of the aging right-handed reliever. As he did with Giusti, Clemente nodded his approval, telling Brown that he liked the movement on Peña's pitches. He told Brown what he remembered about his encounters with Peña, a pitcher he had once batted against in the late 1950s. After the game, the Pirates announced that they had signed Peña to a contract. "He told the Pirates they ought to pick me up, so they did," a grateful Peña told Roy Blount, Jr. of *Sports Illustrated*.

Peña would pitch in 23 games for Pittsburgh before drawing his release. Although his earned run average of 4.74 seemed unimpressive on the surface, he pitched well in several important games for the Pirates. At a time when the organization lacked depth in middle relief, Peña provided a boost. For that, the Pirates could thank Joe Brown—and Clemente.

Others sought Clemente's endorsement. A television company asked him to film a short instructional film warning children about the evils of drug abuse. Roberto agreed to participate in the project, but only if the producers agreed to tape their message in both English and Spanish. When the producers explained that they had no budget for hiring a Spanish scriptwriter, Clemente offered to personally translate the script. He laboriously converted the English language version into acceptably readable Spanish.

The Pirates played poorly over the first two and a half months of the 1970 season, partly because of Clemente's own health problems. Clemente had tried to overcome a heel injury, which he had suffered when he stepped hard on the first base bag after running full throttle on an infield grounder. After losing the first game of a doubleheader to the Cardinals on June 22, the Bucs' record dropped two games below break-even. In the nightcap, unheralded rookie pitcher Jim Nelson blanked the Cardinals, 1-0. The unexpected shutout served as a springboard to a week-long winning streak.

At the tail end of the seven-game ride, the Pirates played their final games at Forbes Field. The June 28 doubleheader against the Cubs marked the end of the venerable ballpark, which had run its course after 61 years. Clemente played in the first game of the twinbill but sat out the second, as he often did in the later years of his career.

In between games, Nellie King interviewed Clemente for the Pirates' flagship radio station, KDKA. Clemente talked about the old ballpark, which meant a great deal to him, along with the people who worked there. "I remember our last game at Forbes Field," says Sally O'Leary, who worked for the Pirates in the public relations department. "[Roberto] autographed a baseball for each front office person, personalized to each person with his best wishes, which I think was a very class act. It was something that nobody else thought of. And I know I was completely floored when it was delivered to me. It's one of my prized possessions."

After the Forbes Field finale, the Pirates began a mammoth 14-game road trip. Two opening losses to the Mets didn't prevent the Bucs from coming together on their longest road swing of the year. The Pirates won 10 of 14 games from the Mets, Cubs, Phillies and Cardinals. On July 11, the second to last day of the trip, the Pirates beat the Cardinals to move into first place in the National League East.

Given the Pirates' exceptional play, capped off by a four-game sweep of St. Louis, the three-day All-Star break arrived at an inappropriate time. After three days of rest, the Pirates christened their new ballpark. July 16 marked the opening of Three Rivers Stadium. Eight days later, the Pirates honored their most storied player by holding "Roberto Clemente Night" at the new stadium, or "The House That Clemente Built," as some referred to it.

As Clemente walked from the dugout to the field for the pre-game ceremonies, the fans bathed him with a standing ovation. His parents, his wife, and his three small children joined him on the field. With friends from Puerto Rico in attendance and the rest of the island watching the event via satellite, Clemente delivered an address in Spanish. Each of Clemente's Latin American teammates walked up to him and saluted him. Clemente tried to fight off tears. "There are things in life that mean the most to me, my family—and the fans in Pittsburgh and Puerto Rico," said Clemente, now speaking in English. Across the field, in the dugout of the visiting Astros, Houston manager Harry Walker stood and applauded.

"I don't know if I cried," Clemente told Roy McHugh of the _Pittsburgh Press_ afterward, "but I am not ashamed to cry. A man never cries from pain or disappointment, but we are a sentimental people. I don't have the words to say how I felt when I stepped on that field."

During the moving ceremonies, Roberto received over 100 plaques, trophies, and gifts, including a television set, a new car and a life-size wax figure. Clemente's teammates gave him a silver tray and a set of silver mugs, complete with autographs from all of the players, the coaching staff and manager Danny Murtaugh. A group of Puerto Rican soldiers—veterans of the Vietnam War—presented Clemente with a commemorative plaque. Perhaps the most meaningful gift came from the families of John Galbreath and Tom Johnson, the owners of the Pirates. The Galbreaths and Johnsons provided Clemente's three sons with a special trust fund, which would pay the tuition for their college education.

The ceremony also included a presentation of a check to Pittsburgh's Children's Hospital. With the help of a local sports organization, Roberto had asked all fans to make donations to a fund in his name. "I want the money to help poor kids," said Clemente, who made sure that all $5,500 in donations were designated for crippled children whose parents could not afford medical costs.

Such actions typified Clemente's charitable nature—especially toward youngsters. "One of the things that he really liked to do was go to Children's Hospital in Pittsburgh and visit kids," recalls Joe Christopher. "That's something that many people don't write about. That's where his real passion was—making other people feel important." As Joe Brown says, "I don't think Clemente turned down many people who wanted his help—if anybody."

Several children from underprivileged homes in Puerto Rico won contests to travel to Pittsburgh for Clemente's special night. The group, which included a blind child and a deaf youngster, gathered to sing songs in Spanish. Their favorite song? "Viva Clemente."

Playing in front of a crowd of 43,290 fans, Clemente collected a walk and two hits to raise his average to .356, while making a pair of sliding catches on the artificial turf that covered the ground of the new stadium. His running grab of Denis Menke's seventh-inning drive into the right field corner prompted another set of loud cheers. Clemente cut his leg on the play, resulting in his removal from the game in the middle of the eighth inning. As Clemente jogged off the field, the fans gave him his fifth standing ovation of the night.

After the game, an 11-0 Pirates rout, Clemente thanked the fans during a half-hour press conference. "We are on the field doing what we love to do," Clemente told a reporter from the Associated Press. "[The fans] have to work in the mill or other places eight hours a day and work much harder than us and they pay their way in."

Pittsburgh remained at the top of the Eastern Division standings for nearly the rest of the month, until yielding first place on July 31. Two days later, after scoring 30 runs in back-to-back bombardments of the Braves, the Pirates returned to first place.

The Pirates continued to play well through the middle of August, even with Clemente missing games early in the month due to injury. When he returned to the lineup, he continued to feel uncomfortable. With his back bothering him, Roberto sought some unconventional treatment from trainer Tony Bartirome prior to the second game of a series at Dodger Stadium. "Tony rubbed him down with goat's milk," says Richie Hebner, recalling the odd scene in the Pirate clubhouse. "And he went 5-for-5 [actually 5-for-7]." Clemente also scored the game-winning run in the top of the 16th inning, ending a four-hour and 21-minute marathon.

His back and his hitting woes cured, Clemente instructed Bartirome to continue the goat milk treatment before the next game. "And he had to rub him down the next night and he got five hits [again]," says Hebner. "He went 10-for-10 [actually 10-for-13] at Dodger Stadium. You know, Dodger Stadium is a tough park to hit in, mainly because they had good pitching. It was the biggest laugh around the clubhouse. After the first night, Clemente would say to Bartirome, 'You got the goat milk, didn't you?' And Tony would be rubbing him with goat milk. And I'd look at them and say 'What the hell is going on here?'"

Clemente's 10-hit spree, assisted by the use of goat milk, had set a modern day National League record for the most hits in two consecutive games. The outburst, which included his 14th home run, a double and three singles in the latter game, pushed him ahead of the Braves' Rico Carty for the league batting lead and helped the Pirates to two consecutive wins on the West Coast. And as it did often, Clemente's health provided a source of good-natured humor for his Pirate teammates.

In the past, Clemente had vented anger whenever someone reacted humorously to one of his injuries. In 1970, he began to treat such situations more lightly, adding his own dose of comedy to descriptions of his injuries. Clemente also became more encouraging to those backup outfielders who replaced him when he sat out with ailments.

Goat milk cures aside, Clemente's performance against the vaunted Dodger pitching staff stirred conversations filled with praise among his teammates. Infielder Dave Cash and relief pitcher Dave Giusti chatted about the latest Clemente heroics. "Clemente is a super player, not a super star," Cash said to Giusti in an effort to categorize his teammate. He continued to search for the proper description of the All-Star right fielder, but couldn't find the right words. "Clemente is a super something," the rookie second baseman said with admiration. "Maybe he belongs in the stars."

Despite losing the last six games of their western swing, the Bucs remained in first place. In early September, they lost Clemente to another injury. He had actually injured his back a week earlier in a game against the Giants, but had continued to play. In the September 4 game against the Phillies, he aggravated the injury reaching for a fly ball. When he came to bat in the first inning, he could hardly walk, much less swing the bat. After a futile at-bat against Rick Wise, Clemente left the game. He once again sought the advice of Arturo Garcia. Two days after hurting his back, he entered Presbyterian Hospital for a two-day stay, which included traction, the application of hot towels, and several shots of novocaine. The Mets felt their chances of catching the Pirates had gotten that much better.

On September 9, a 6-4 loss to the Cardinals, teamed with the Mets' 3-1 win over the Phillies, put Pittsburgh and New York into a first-place tie. Two days later, the idle Pirates moved back into first place when the Mets' Tom Seaver lost a 5-2 decision to the Cardinals' Bob Gibson. On September 13, the Pirates lost to Chicago, 3-2, with the Cubs scoring one of their runs on Don Kessinger's short single to right field. Clemente told reporters that if he had been playing right field, he would have positioned himself shallower against Kessinger and would have thrown out pinch-runner Ken Rudolph. No one doubted him.

Unfortunately, Clemente started to harbor doubts about his playing future. On September 13, he said that continuing pain might keep him out of action for the rest of the season. Without Clemente, the Pirates did their best in not relinquishing the lead. On September 18, they opened a four-game series at Shea Stadium, with Clemente still unavailable. Managing a 3-2 win in the opener, the Pirates expanded their lead over the Mets to two and a half games, but saw the Cubs move within a game and a half after a double-header sweep.

Clemente finally returned to the lineup for the second game against the Mets. He doubled home one run and scored another, accounting for both runs in a 2-1 victory. On Sunday, the two teams wrapped up the series with a doubleheader. Clemente went hitless in four first-game at-bats, as the Pirates lost, 4-1. Danny Murtaugh rested Clemente in game two, but the Pirates scored four runs in the tenth inning to cap off a 9-5 win. With three wins in four games, the Pirates had increased their lead to three and a half games. The Cubs, losers to Montreal, slipped two games out of first.

One week later, the Pirates held a two and a half game lead over both rivals as they prepared to open a three-game set against the Mets at Three Rivers Stadium. Clemente went hitless in three at-bats, but Willie Stargell threw out a runner at home plate in the eighth inning to preserve a 4-3 win. The Cubs lost their game with the Phillies, dropping them three and a half games back.

Playing a day game on Saturday after the Friday night win, Danny Murtaugh again rested Clemente. The absence of the right fielder didn't hurt. Recent acquisition Jim "Mudcat" Grant earned a 4-3 victory with a scoreless relief stint, helping the Pirates clinch a tie for the National League East crown.

On Sunday, a record Pittsburgh crowd of 50,469 fans packed Three Rivers Stadium in the hopes of witnessing the outright clinching of the division title. Clemente returned to the Pirate lineup, batting third against Mets right-hander Jim McAndrew. The Mets took a 1-0 lead early, but Clemente's double—one of his two hits on the day—set up the tying run in the third. Dave Cash's sacrifice fly the following inning gave the Pirates their second run—and the winning margin in a 2-1 victory. The National League East belonged to the Pirates. For the first time in a decade, the Pirates had played well enough to qualify for the post-season.

The Pirates' half-pennant had come in spite of frequent absences by Clemente, who had missed a solid two weeks during a critical stretch in early September. For the season, Clemente sat out a career-high 58 game starts. In four of those games, he appeared only as a pinch-hitter. Never had Clemente been so inactive since first arriving in the major leagues in 1955.

When Clemente did play, he played exceptionally well. Despite his chronic back ailment, Clemente had still prospered as a hitter; his .352 mark in 1970 represented the second-best batting average of his career, and gave him a .300 average or better in 11 of the last 12 seasons. The .352 average would have placed him second to Atlanta's Rico Carty in the batting race had he accumulated the requisite number of plate appearances. Clemente needed a minimum of 502 appearances to qualify for inclusion in the top five batting leaders, but his repeated back problems limited him to 455 appearances. As the Pirates finished out the season with a meaningless series in St. Louis, Clemente remained in Pittsburgh to receive treatment from a McKees Rocks chiropractor.

With the opening of the National League Championship Series—now in its second year of existence—just a few days away, the Pirates hoped that Clemente would be able to play. The day before the opener against the Western Division's Cincinnati Reds, Clemente took batting practice. Danny Murtaugh and a local chiropractor named Charles W. Murray, whom Clemente had met only nine days earlier, watched with particular interest. Clemente swung the bat freely, his lower back muscle causing him no pain. After batting practice, Clemente walked away from the cage. He knew that he would be able to play. Even though Clemente didn't need it, Dr. Murray nodded his approval.

Clemente's health and the playoff games themselves seemed lost amidst the controversy created by a sudden umpire walkout. In an effort to gain increased pay for the playoffs and World Series, the six regular umpires picketed outside of Three Rivers Stadium. Having received $2,500 for the Championship Series and $6,500 for the World Series per umpire in 1970, the regular umpires wanted raises to $5,000 for the playoffs and $10,000 for the World Series. The owners said no, instead hiring a quartet of minor league umpires to work the first game.

Neither of the starting pitches seemed affected by the calls of home plate umpire John Grimsley, who had worked most recently in the American Association. Dock Ellis and Gary Nolan pitched remarkably in the first game, holding each of the powerful lineups scoreless through the regulation nine innings. In the 10th, Reds manager Sparky Anderson lifted Nolan, his scheduled leadoff batter, for pinch-hitter Ty Cline. The left-handed hitting outfielder smashed one of Ellis' sliders into right-center field, a line drive that skidded beyond Clemente's reach. Clemente retrieved the ball off the wall quickly, convincing Reds' third base coach Alex Grammas to signal Cline to stop at second. Cline never saw the sign, however, and chugged into third with a triple.

Ellis remained in the game as Danny Murtaugh instructed his infield to move in. Pete Rose followed with a broken-bat single past Al Oliver at first, bringing home the game's first run. Four batters later, Lee May doubled home two additional runs. In the bottom of the 10th, Reds relief ace Clay Carroll held the Pirates hitless, sealing a 3-0 win.

After the game, Rose hinted that a few wet spots in the outfield turf had caused Cline's drive to skip past Clemente, handcuffing the Gold Glove outfielder. When one reporter relayed Rose's comment to him, Clemente respectfully disagreed. "That was a hard hit ball over second base," Clemente told Roy McHugh of the *Pittsburgh Press.* "How can it skip by me? The only way I could play the ball is the way I try." Clemente also refuted the theory of slick artificial turf. "Wet field?" Clemente asked rhetorically. "The field was dry. I have my shoes to prove it."

The loss was especially frustrating for the Pirates, who felt they would be able to score plenty of runs against Cincinnati's questionable pitching staff. Clemente epitomized Pittsburgh's exasperation, posting an 0-for-5 clip with three strikeouts. Clemente twice fell victim to called strikeouts, but didn't protest either of

Grimsley's calls. To his credit, Clemente refused to place the blame on the replacement umpire, who had called a "perfect game" in the words of Reds' catcher Johnny Bench. Earlier in the season, Clemente had drawn praise from veteran umpires Nick Colosi and Mel Steiner, who credited Roberto with helping to end a nasty brawl with the Cubs. Clemente had successfully calmed down an angry Dock Ellis, telling him to stop yelling at Chicago's players and assume his place in the batter's box. Both Colosi and Steiner appreciated Clemente's defusing of the situation. Ironically, Colosi was now one of the umpires on strike.

In the final hour of preparation before Game Two, the regular umpires came to an agreement with major league officials on postseason wages. The replacement quartet of Grimsley, Fred Blandford, George Grygiel and Hank Morgenweck gave way to the playoffs' scheduled six-man crew. While the umpiring situation returned to normalcy, the Pittsburgh bats did not. The Pirates managed only one run against left-hander Jim Merritt, who had posted six wins in six starts against Pittsburgh over the past two seasons. They did their only offensive damage in the sixth, when Clemente picked up his first hit of the series, driving in Dave Cash. Clemente's hit highlighted a 1-for-4 performance, but only four other Pirates matched him with hits of their own. Reds center fielder Bobby Tolan picked up three hits against Luke Walker and Dave Giusti, and scored all of Cincinnati's runs in a 3-1 victory.

Unlike the first game, when he had expressed no objection to the work of replacement arbiter John Grimsley, Clemente argued vehemently with home plate umpire Stan Landes, who had returned after the one-day strike. The veteran Landes, a National League umpire since 1955, irritated Clemente with several of his called strikes. Clemente wasn't alone in voicing his displeasure; Landes' work also angered teammate Jose Pagan and Cincinnati's Johnny Bench. After the game, Clemente sarcastically suggested that Landes and the other umpires were tired—from too much early morning picketing.

Yet, Clemente didn't blame the loss on the returning umpires; he placed that responsibility on the Pirates' hitters and their insistence on trying to hit home runs. He also hinted that the Pirates may have lacked the needed respect for Merritt's ability. "When I was at the All-Star game, there were hitters laughing at Merritt," Clemente told the *Pittsburgh Press.* "They said they would like to make a living batting against him all the time. I told them not to bet on it."

After a regular season filled with conquests of rivals Chicago and New York, the Pirates had fallen short in their first two post-season games. Left with no margin for defeat, one more loss would eliminate the Pirates from the Championship Series. In order for the Pirates to make the World Series, they would have to win the next three games, a feat made more difficult due to the shift in venue from Three Rivers to Cincinnati's Riverfront Stadium.

The Pirates scored a run in the first inning, reaching Reds' starter Tony Cloninger. Unfortunately, Bob Moose could not prevent Cincinnati from matching and exceeding the score when he gave up consecutive home runs to Tony Perez and Johnny Bench in the bottom half of the first. The Pirates repeatedly mounted threats against Cloninger, but could not tie the score until pushing across a single run in the fifth.

Moose recovered from the rockiness of the first inning to pitch shutout ball over the next six frames. In the bottom of the eighth, with the game still tied, Moose retired the first two Reds' batters. He had now set down 13 straight Reds batters. Sparky Anderson then pinch-hit for Milt Wilcox, the 20-year-old reliever who had hurled three scoreless innings after Cloninger's departure. Ty Cline, one of the hitting heroes of Game One, drew a walk. Pete Rose followed with a single, putting runners on first and second. With the dangerous Bobby Tolan coming up next, Danny Murtaugh decided to lift Moose, replacing him with veteran southpaw Joe Gibbon. Tolan smashed a hard single to left, which Willie Stargell played urgently. As Cline raced for home, Stargell unfurled a strong throw to the plate. Manny Sanguillen applied the tag, just after Cline's feet scraped home plate. The Reds led, 3-2.

In the top of the ninth, sidewinding Wayne Granger easily retired the first two Pirates, pinch-hitter Bob Robertson and the lefty-swinging Matty Alou. Granger now faced Clemente. Not bothered by the sidearming swipes of the Reds' right-hander, Clemente singled to sustain the Pirates' season. With Willie Stargell coming up next, Sparky Anderson called on hard-throwing left-hander Don Gullett to replace Granger.

Stargell's two-out single put runners on first and third. Gullett faced another left-handed hitter, Al Oliver. Swinging at the first pitch, Oliver hit a routine grounder to Tommy Helms at second base. The Championship Series—and the Pirates' season—was over.

With two hits and a run scored in the finale, Clemente had put forth his best game of the playoffs, but it hadn't mattered in the final outcome. For the most part, Clemente had struggled during the brief series. He managed only three hits in 14 at-bats—a measly success rate of .214. He drove in only one run and scored only once. In fairness, though, Clemente was not alone in enduring failure. Manny Sanguillen and Dave Cash fared even worse, both batting well under .200. In fact, only two Pirate regulars had good offensive series: Richie Hebner, who collected four hits in six at-bats, and Willie Stargell, who batted an even .500. It was hard to find many standouts on a team that had scored three runs in three games, hit no home runs, and left 29 runners on the bases.

The season's sudden ending had disappointed Clemente; his improved relationship with Danny Murtaugh had not. "I hope he manages again," Clemente told the *Pittsburgh Press* when asked if Murtaugh would return in '71. "All of the fellows on the team like him. He has brought us together and you like to play ball for a man like this." One could hardly have imagined Clemente making such a statement during any of Murtaugh's previous tenures in Pittsburgh.

After the abrupt playoff loss to the Reds, Clemente readied for his next baseball assignment, ironically his own managing job with the San Juan Senators of the Puerto Rican Winter League. Did Clemente want to manage in the major leagues somewhere down the line? "I'd only manage one team in the major leagues. The Pirates," Clemente had told Charley Feeney of the *Pittsburgh Post-Gazette* in mid-August. "I think I could manage. It would be something I would like to try. But I wouldn't want to manage any other ball club."

Knowing that Clemente had agreed to his second managerial stint (he had managed San Juan on an interim basis in 1964-65), Pirate general manager Joe Brown arranged for several of his best young players and prospects to sign contracts with San Juan. The group included Dave Cash, Al Oliver and Manny Sanguillen and minor leaguer Fred Cambria. When Cambria injured his arm pitching for San Juan, Pirates shortstop Freddie Patek replaced him. Clemente's roster also included Mike Cuellar, one of the Orioles' pitching stalwarts, and Ken Singleton, one of the Mets' top outfield prospects.

Clemente joined another major league star-turned-skipper, the Orioles' Frank Robinson, who was returning to manage the Santurce Crabbers for a third season. On opening night, scheduled for October 22, Clemente's Senators hosted Robinson's Crabbers at Hiram Bithorn Stadium. Anticipating Clemente's first game as a full-time manager, a paid crowd of 19,979 jammed into Bithorn Stadium in time to see the first pitch. Unexpectedly, a bank of outfield lights went out, the result of a power failure. The outage caused a two-hour delay in starting the game.

By the time play began, the crowd had swelled to over 26,000, well above the stadium's capacity. According to one report, about 6,000 fans had entered the stadium without paying. In the meantime, Clemente's Senators protected a 2-0 lead, thanks to the dominant pitching of Ken Brett. In the bottom of the seventh, Clemente removed Brett for a pinch-hitter, eventually replacing him on the mound with Jim Colborn. The move backfired, as Colborn allowed three runs in the top of the eighth. The Senators failed to score in the bottom half of the inning.

Thanks to the power outage delay, winter league curfew rules now came into play. According to league rules, no inning could start after 12:15 a.m.. Since it was past that hour, the umpires awarded a 3-2 victory to Santurce. Clemente came out to argue the decision. Robinson soon joined in the discussion. The two managers engaged in a long discussion with the umpires near home plate. The umpires' ruling stood until the next day, when league president Rodrigo Otero Suro announced that the game would be completed before the regularly scheduled contest of November 3. Clemente's first game as manager had been more than memorable.

Clemente's no-nonsense style of managing impressed some observers. He showed no inclination for preferential treatment, regardless of a player's status. On one occasion, an American League star decided to challenge Clemente's authority by showing up late before a game. Clemente confronted the star player immediately, informing him that he would receive no special privileges. As a result of Clemente's talk, the American League star did not challenge him again. "A manager has to be tough with the players," Clemente explained in a 1971 interview with Milton Richman of United Press International.

On November 27, Mike Cuellar made his first winter league start for San Juan after pitching in the World Series for the Orioles. The veteran left-hander pitched three shutout innings before collapsing in the fourth and fifth. Cuellar surrendered two home runs to Reggie Jackson and another longball to Ellie Hendricks, prompting the hook from Clemente. Cuellar didn't like being removed after five innings.

A week later, Clemente walked to the mound and lifted Cuellar during the third inning of a 6-2 loss to Santurce. The two men reportedly exchanged heated words. After the game, Cuellar explained that his arm was tight after pitching in the World Series against the Reds. Clemente recommended Cuellar work out his problems in the bullpen, a suggestion that the veteran left-hander did not like. "I'm in no condition to pitch the way Clemente wants me to," Cuellar complained to Miguel Frau of *The Sporting News*. "I prefer to hang up my glove for the remainder of the season." With that, Cuellar left the Senators, replaced by Boston Red Sox' veteran Jim Lonborg.

Although Clemente believed that local newspapers in Puerto Rico exaggerated the severity of the dispute, he felt that Cuellar's conditioning left something to be desired. "He wasn't in shape," Clemente would tell Roy McHugh of the *Pittsburgh Press* one year later. "His screwball did not break. He just threw a blooper all the time. I told him, 'Mike, you can't pitch that way.'" As an accomplished veteran, Cuellar did not appreciate being told how to pitch.

Clemente also showed a temper during his managerial stint. During a December 19 game against Santurce, home plate umpire John Ross ejected San Juan third baseman Max Oliveras. Clemente ran out of the dugout to support his player and protest the ejection. As Clemente became more and more upset, he bumped Ross slightly. The umpire, who felt the contact was intentional, reported the incident to the league president. Four days later, the league announced a seven-game suspension for Clemente.

A few long-time observers of the Puerto Rican Winter League felt Clemente should have been suspended for much longer. Only two years earlier, Arecibo manager Vic Power had been suspended for an entire season after a similar incident. Ironically, Power now served as the secretary for the Puerto Rican Players Association.

The week-long ban did delay Clemente's playing debut. With his back problems cleared up, Clemente had been activated to play on December 22. A day later, the suspension came down from the league office. Clemente didn't play his first game until January 3, when he scored the winning run as a pinch-runner in the ninth inning.

Under Clemente's guidance, San Juan finished with a record of 37-30, second only to Caguas in the league standings. In the playoffs, Clemente contributed to one of San Juan's victories with a ninth inning pinch-hit single that delivered two runs. Yet, the Senators went on to lose their best-of-seven playoff series to Santurce. Much like the Championship Series against the Reds, a first-round playoff ouster in winter ball had ended another season too quickly for Clemente's liking.

18

Integration's Team

In 1971, the Pirates gave trials to three of their most heralded prospects: infielder Rennie Stennett, outfielder Richie Zisk and pitcher Bruce Kison. More significantly, Joe Brown made two crucial trades prior to the season. First, the Pirates added hard-throwing right-hander Bob Johnson and slick-fielding shortstop Jackie Hernandez from the Kansas City Royals in exchange for catcher Jerry May, shortstop Freddie Patek and pitcher Bruce Dal Canton. In the second deal, the Pirates acquired left-handed hitting outfielder Vic Davalillo and injury-plagued pitcher Nelson "Nellie" Briles from the St. Louis Cardinals for Matty Alou and reliever George Brunet. The pair of trades, followed by the in-season acquisition of veteran pitcher Bob Miller, stamped Joe Brown as one of the game's shrewdest general managers and helped make the Pirates contenders once again.*

Prior to the 1971 season, Clemente made a stirring impression at the annual Houston baseball writers' dinner, where he received the "Tris Speaker Award" for his contributions to the game. Rather than deliver a typical, clichéd speech focusing on the game of baseball, Clemente spoke sincerely about his own philosophical views, including his hopes for improved race relations. This issue had mattered greatly to Clemente, especially during a major league career that had been filled with numerous instances of racism. "We must all live together and work together, no matter what race or nationality," Clemente told the crowd of 800 guests at the Astroworld Hotel's main ballroom.

During his talk, Clemente urged the members of the audience to become active in improving their communities. "Any time you have the opportunity to accomplish something for somebody who comes behind you and you don't do it," said Clemente, "you are wasting your time on this Earth." Those words became arguably the most famous uttered by Clemente during his life.

At the end of his speech, the crowd of over 800 baseball writers and dignitaries showered Clemente with a standing ovation. According to *The Sporting News*, one writer called it "the best talk any baseball player ever made." Even though Clemente often felt embarrassment while making speeches, he had succeeded in stirring the assembled baseball writers, a group known for cynicism and skepticism. The speech was even more impressive considering that Clemente spoke in English—his second language. Clemente had always felt more comfortable speaking in his native Spanish.

Clemente not only left an imprint on sportswriters, but on his teammates and the club's front office, as well. After the 1970 season, Joe Brown asked Clemente for his opinion on a veteran pitcher whom he was considering in a possible trade. "I asked him about Nellie Briles, whom we got from the Cardinals," Brown says. As with the earlier acquisitions of Dave Giusti and Orlando Peña, Clemente's advice provided Brown with some impetus in pulling the trigger on a trade. Shortly thereafter, Brown sent Matty Alou and George Brunet to St. Louis for Briles and backup outfielder Vic Davalillo, the National League's most prolific pinch-hitter in 1970. Clemente once again played a role in a trade that would yield substantial benefits for the Pirates.

In a related matter, Clemente proved especially influential to one of the team's best young players, Al Oliver. Most comfortable as a first baseman, Oliver was trying to establish himself as an everyday player in 1971, while making the difficult transition to center field. The off-season trade that sent Alou to the Cardinals had opened up an opportunity for Oliver to play regularly in center field, a position that he had hardly played in the past.

Oliver had played 151 games in 1970, but had split his time between first base, his best position, and left and right field, where he was less certain about his abilities. Joe Brown reasoned that with Clemente and Willie Stargell entrenched in right and left field respectively, and with the up-and-coming Bob Robertson providing power at first base, it was time to get the 24-year-old Oliver into the lineup—somewhere. Furthermore, the constant shifting from position to position had affected Oliver's hitting ability. In order to achieve his potential, the Pirates would need to find a stable place for Oliver in the lineup.

Brown felt that center field might be the best available position for Oliver to make his breakthrough, but he needed more input before making a decision. He consulted the opinion of Pirates' coach Bill Virdon, who had been a fine defensive outfielder and had played center field on the Pirates' 1960 championship team. Virdon agreed with the rest of the free world that Clemente was Pittsburgh's No. 1 defensive outfielder, but he regarded Oliver as second best on the team.

During the off-season, Oliver played center field for the San Juan Senators, the winter league team managed—not so coincidentally—by Clemente. The perennial Gold Glove right fielder offered a favorable opinion of Oliver's defensive play. "He plays too shallow with men on base. [But] it is a fault that will be corrected the more he plays the position," Clemente told Charley Feeney of the *Pittsburgh Post-Gazette.*

Clemente's words could hardly be interpreted as a ringing endorsement, but coupled with the opinions of Virdon, they were enough to convince Brown to deal Alou and make room for Oliver. Once Oliver arrived in Bradenton for spring training, he felt comfort when he saw Clemente next to him in the Pirate outfield. "Number one, he was definitely a security blanket," Oliver says. "Number two, like I've said so many times before, just like my father led me as a human being, Roberto Clemente led Al Oliver as a major leaguer. What I mean by that is he hustled, he ran out ground balls. When he took the field, there was no shucking and jiving. He wanted to win, and he wanted to perform at his best, day in and day out, in every game in which he played. I think that that's the thing that really made him our leader. He was able to do those things on the field. He didn't do a lot of talking because he didn't have to, because he was a great player. Usually great leaders do not talk a lot; they lead by example, which he did. But when something had to be said in the clubhouse or to the team on the bench, he never hesitated. Everyone respected him, and they all listened to him when those things came about."

The Pirates won their first four exhibition games of the spring, even though Clemente had yet to play an inning. Clemente wasn't hurt; Danny Murtaugh had merely decided to give his best player a few days off. Clemente finally made his spring training debut on March 9, when the Pirates traveled to St. Petersburg to face one of the National League East's contenders, the Mets. Clemente went 0-for-2 in a 3-0 loss, the first pre-season defeat for the Pirates.

Although there was nothing physically wrong with Clemente, Murtaugh had wisely chosen a cautious approach in playing his star right fielder sparingly in the spring. During the offseason, Clemente had undergone treatment on his chronically bad back, a condition that dated all the way back to his 1954 car accident. In 1970, Clemente's back had acted up more than ever, limiting the 36-year-old outfielder to 108 games.   In late November, doctors had given Clemente's back a thorough examination. The check-up, followed by Clemente's rehabilitation, gave the Bucs every indication that he would be healthy in 1971.

Although Clemente's batting skills remained sharp, he had reached the stage of his career where he might not be able to play 130 or more regular season games. Murtaugh had no intention of extending him in the spring, especially in games that had no bearing on the regular season standings. After all, Clemente was still one of the most important figures on the team. As much as anyone, Clemente's presence was critical to the spiritual health of the Pirate clubhouse, a fact that was duly noted by one of the newest Pirates. "Roberto Clemente was kind of an introvert as far as the public was concerned, but was a 'player's player' when I played there in '71 and '72," says Nellie Briles.

Upon his arrival in Bradenton, Clemente made sure to help Briles feel comfortable with his new surroundings. "When I came over he sat down [next to me]," says Briles, "and as I mentioned, he was kind of a 'player's player.' And so when I came over, he wanted to make me feel welcome." Mimicking the right fielder's Spanish accent, Briles remembers well the first conversation he had with Clemente. "He sat down in front of my locker, and he said, 'Nelson, you win many, many games with the Pirates. The only thing that I ask you, if you want the great Roberto to help you, you got to keep the ball in the ballpark. I cannot catch the ball that leaves the ballpark,'" Briles says, laughing loudly. "He just laughed and went back to his locker. But it was a very nice gesture on his part, to keep it very light, to welcome me, and to just say, 'Hey, just go ahead and pitch and I'll help.' He sure did that. Unfortunately," Briles says with a modest chuckle, "he didn't catch enough of my mistakes."

Once the regular season began, some of the Pirates' best hitters struggled, most notably Clemente. He stranded more than a dozen baserunners over the first two weeks and piled up only two RBIs. Richie Hebner, suffering through an 0-for-20 stretch, failed to hit with runners on base, or with the bases empty. Only Willie Stargell, Dave Cash and newcomer Jackie Hernandez seemed to be hitting up to—or above—their capabilities.

The offensive frustration reached its apex during a three-game series against the Giants. Willie Stargell missed the first two games of the set with a virus. In the first game, rookie right-hander Steve Stone posted his first major league win by blanking the Pirates, 2-0. The Bucs fared no better the next day. Unproven left-hander Ron Bryant, pitching only because of an injury to scheduled starter Frank Reberger, limited the Pirates to three hits in a 2-0 Giants' win that was delayed for half an hour by a light failure. For the second straight game, the Bucs had allowed a young pitcher to earn his first major league shutout. Without Stargell in the lineup, the Bucs lacked the intimidating middle-of-the-order presence needed to support line-drive hitters like Clemente and Manny Sanguillen. The Pirates, the team with arguably the best nine-man lineup in the National League, had been held scoreless for 20 consecutive innings. In fact, in their first 17 games of the season, the Pirates had already been blanked four times.

Clemente's bat did show signs of life during the series against the Giants, helping him reach another milestone. Roberto banged out four hits in 10 at-bats against San Francisco pitching, surpassing Hall of Famer Lou Gehrig on baseball's all-time hit list.

Unfortunately, Clemente's hitting spree against the Giants stood alone among his early season highlights. As productive as Willie Stargell had been, Clemente had struggled in almost equal proportions. The veteran right fielder had entered the season with a lifetime batting average of .316 and four batting titles to his credit. In April, Clemente's average hovered around the .250 mark, but his failure to drive in runs was an even more glaring concern. During a 16-game period in April, Clemente stranded 25 men on base, a simply unheard-of rate of failure for a superstar known as an exceptional clutch hitter. Some Pirate observers pointed to Clemente's birth certificate; he was 36 years of age and perhaps on the inevitable downhill slide of a Hall of Fame career.

Clemente, however, placed the blame on his winter employment. "My biggest mistake was managing in Puerto Rico this past winter," Clemente told *The Sporting News*. "I had more responsibilities and did not get my rest. The long bus trips out of town, I have to make them because I am the manager. They take something out of me." Since travel by bus in the Puerto Rican Winter League was not as relaxing or as comfortable as airplane travel in the United States, it was more likely to put strain on his chronically fragile back.

As a result of those physically demanding bus trips, Clemente's back pain had resurfaced once again. "My doctor, he tell me not to play, to give my muscles in my back a rest," Clemente confessed to *The Sporting News*. The prospect of Clemente missing games, despite the depth provided by Vic Davalillo and Gene Clines, did not bode well for the Pirates. As well as Stargell had been hitting, the Bucs required a healthy and productive Clemente in their effort to win the National League East.

The criticism of Clemente early in 1971 typified the reactions of the media during the times that he struggled, either with injuries, or through slumps, or both. If Clemente's injuries harmed his performance or prevented him from playing at all, some writers criticized him as weak or fragile. Yet, Clemente was victimized by the media's double-edged sword. If Clemente complained of sickness or injury, and played well, some writers comically poked fun at him. As a writer once quoted Clemente as saying: "I feel better when I am sick." Did Clemente actually make such a nonsensical statement? According to Roy McHugh, he did. "They made him look like Yogi Berra simply by quoting him accurately," says McHugh. "Just by quoting him, they sort of turned him into a comedian, and he was anything but." Although Clemente may have made such illogical remarks, it's likely that his limitations with the English language twisted what he actually meant.

In citing Clemente's frequent complaints about his physical condition, some writers seemed to be minimizing his sincerity. Although Clemente had once suffered from a serious disease like malaria and had developed bone chips in his elbow—with the validity of each ailment supported by the testimony of doctors—it was as if many writers did not believe that he was sick, or hurt.

"Clemente is a hypochondriac," or, "Clemente is always whining about his injuries," were two of the most common refrains heard from members of both the Pittsburgh and national media. Even some of the most positive of articles made a point of mentioning Clemente's frequent injuries and his supposed unwillingness to play with pain. The persistent criticism, especially the questions regarding Clemente's intensity and effort, rankled many of his teammates, including Dave Giusti. "Before I came over to this ballclub," Giusti told Milton Richman of UPI, "I heard how Clemente is always ailing and wanting to sit out games, but everything I heard was strictly bull. He goes full blast all the time."

Yet, some writers continued to assault Clemente with the labels of "whiner" and "chronic complainer." According to Dave Cash, those reactions did not represent the sentiments of Pirate players. "Oh, there's no doubt the love and respect that the guys that played with him had for him," Cash says. "They [the media] talk about him whining and not wanting to play, but if you look back at his statistics, anybody that gets 3,000 hits over the career that he had, did a lot of playing."

Contrary to much of the criticism, Clemente was a fairly durable player—one who played through many of his injuries. In 1960 and '61, Clemente averaged 145 games a season, or only nine games fewer than the 154-game regular season schedule that was used at the time. From 1962 to '67—a span of six years—Clemente averaged just over 150 games per season, or a dozen games fewer than the expanded 162-game season. Throughout his career, he also participated in 15 winter league campaigns with Santurce, Caguas and San Juan, adding to his workload of games. It was only beginning in 1968, when Clemente turned 34 years of age, that he began to miss significant chunks of time due to injuries. Even so, it should not have been considered unusual for a player in his mid-30s to begin breaking down so often. And over the course of his entire career, Clemente averaged more games per season than two other Pittsburgh legends, Bill Mazeroski and Willie Stargell, neither of whom drew criticism for games they missed. Not bad for a hypochondriac.

In the midst of a season-long power drought, Clemente's home run swing returned during the latter stages of a West Coast road trip. In the first game of a series at San Diego, Clemente managed his first longball of the season. Incredibly, the calendar read May 11 by the time that Clemente connected for the first time. Clemente's two-hit game helped the Pirates coast to a 10-4 win over the Padres. Clemente had actually exhibited hopeful signs throughout the West Coast trip. He had exploded for four hits in one game against the Dodgers and collected two hits in another game against LA, before reaching the seats against San Diego. Perhaps the warm weather of California had acted as a tonic for Clemente's tender back and sore swing.

Although Clemente's bat livened in California, he continued to hit poorly in pressurized situations. That would change during a series against the Expos. On May 17, Clemente smashed an eighth-inning home run to help bring the Pirates within one run of Montreal. The Bucs still trailed by one in the ninth inning, when Clemente faced Expo relief ace Mike Marshall. With two out and two men on base, Clemente responded by smacking a two-run triple off the center field wall, scoring Gene Alley and Dave Cash with the game-tying and game-winning scores.

Clemente later credited Pirates trainer and close friend Tony Bartirome with giving him some helpful advice prior to the game-winning at-bat. "I don't feel right at the plate," Clemente told United Press International. "I move in, move back, sometimes I move out. [Tony] tell me just to try to pull or hit through the middle."

Earlier in the game, Clemente had experienced a rare chorus of boos from the Pirate fans, who usually conducted a love affair with their favorite son in right field. In fact, the game against the Expos marked only the second time that Clemente had heard such booing from his hometown fans. The first time had occurred during a game against the Phillies in 1969. On that occasion, Clemente had defended the fans' right to boo him.

In contrast to the 1969 incident, the latest reaction of the fans clearly upset Roberto. In the Pirates' clubhouse after the game, a reporter from UPI asked Clemente about the boo-birds. "They pay for their ticket, let them do what they want to do," Clemente answered, before letting loose with a few paragraphs of frustration. "I get mad. One of these days, I'll leave my uniform on the field and keep on walking."

Clemente continued his outpouring of emotion. "If I don't hustle, or something like that, I'd say that it would be good for me to get booed." Clemente was hustling; he just wasn't hitting, partly due to a pre-season injury. "This season start, I hurt my finger the last weekend of spring training. I couldn't grip the bat right and I was pulling everything. The fans would look for you to start every year from the beginning, right on top, boom, boom, boom. Now I start a season a little bit slowly, so they boo."

Clemente also broached the subject of retirement, which had been suggested to him by some critics during his early season doldrums. "They always say, 'Retire when you're on top.' I'll quit when I should quit," Clemente said defiantly. "No one will tell me when to quit." There was no reason to quit. Clemente had lifted his batting average to .295, which coupled with his still-marvelous defensive skills, made him an all-around asset to the Pirates.

The next night, the Pirates again beat Mike Marshall with a ninth-inning run before heading to Cincinnati for a rematch of the previous fall's National League Championship Series. The first game at Riverfront Stadium offered another glimpse of vintage Clemente. Playing his best game of the season to date, Clemente rapped out four hits, including a triple and an inside-the-park home run, a rather stunning accomplishment for a man with 36-year-old legs. "When I'm not hitting, the pitchers throw the ball by me, boom-boom. When I'm hitting, the pitchers don't do that," Clemente told Charley Feeney, in providing rather simplistic analysis for his batting fortunes. Clemente's hitting spearheaded a 6-1 win over the Red Legs, which coupled with the Mets' loss to the Phillies, allowed the Pirates to move into first place.

During the 1971 season, reporters from other National League cities asked two of the most prominent Pirates if they had interest in becoming the game's first black manager. Several writers asked Clemente the question under the assumption that he would be retiring within the next two or three years. "It's difficult right now to say what I want to do when I stop playing," Clemente told *The Sporting News*. "There are times I think of managing, and there are times I don't. I guess I haven't made up my mind because I still am playing baseball." Clemente had decided not to return to managing in the Puerto Rican Winter League, citing the stress on his back and overall fatigue caused by the many uncomfortable bus rides. Pirates coach and interim manager Bill Virdon would take over the reigns of the San Juan Senators during the winter.

While Clemente was noncommittal about his managerial future, Willie Stargell provided a more direct response to the writers' questions. "I do not want to be a manager," Stargell told the *Newark Star Ledger*. Yet, he hoped that the baseball establishment would soon appoint a minority manager, perhaps selecting one of his own teammates. "We haven't had a black manager yet," Stargell told *Black*

Sports, "and nobody can tell me that Frank Robinson, Maury Wills, Junior Gilliam, Roberto Clemente, Hank Aaron and Willie Mays aren't qualified." While Stargell had tried to rule himself out, he had championed the cause for the respected Clemente.

Although many observers have credited Clemente as the sole leader of the 1971 Pirates, the leadership role was actually divided among three players, each of whom contributed in different ways. Through hustle and determination, Clemente supplied his teammates with an appropriate example of behavior. Bill Mazeroski exuded a quiet professionalism and a guiding hand to younger players like Dave Cash, who would replace him at second base. And Stargell, through his outgoing, charismatic personality, provided the team with a proper social setting. Such a relaxed, enjoyable atmosphere enabled Pirate players to make further strides in bonding, strides that would not have been possible solely in the confines of a ballpark clubhouse.

"You had a Latino player in Clemente, a black guy [in] Willie Stargell and you got a white guy in Bill Mazeroski, who was still on the ballclub," Steve Blass says. "We had the whole program covered. They were leaders. All three of them, and by that time in 1971, almost in terms of equal status. Stargell got us to the World Series in '71, in certain respects, and had a big year in home runs and RBIs. And Maz was a quiet leader; neither one of them hollered a whole lot. Most of the hollering came from us young guys like Robertson, Hebner, Dock Ellis, Giusti and myself. But those three guys—Clemente, Stargell and Mazeroski—were very much the [leaders] of that team."

Nellie Briles says the 1971 Pirates featured a number of leaders, but he agrees that the three veterans stood out. "Bill Mazeroski, even though he wasn't playing on an everyday basis, was still there. Bill was always a guy who was very professional, went about his job, worked everyday, did the things to always be prepared . . . [Clemente was] a guy who could carry the team offensively and defensively, and was a real steadying force as far as our Latino players were concerned, and really could lead by example on the field, which was very important. And I think 1971 [saw] the emergence of Willie Stargell as a leader. Of course, he put together a phenomenal year in 1971. But I think that also established Willie as the beginning of the era of 'Pops.'"

Al Oliver says that Clemente and Stargell differed in the ways they provided leadership. "The one thing about our '71 team that was very unique," Oliver says, "was that we all were leaders within ourselves, but we also needed that veteran leadership by example. We've already spoken about how Roberto led. Well, Starg was the type of guy that would have team parties. You know, that's how Will would lead us. He would lead us in a social manner. If we might lose three or four games in a row, which was kind of uncharacteristic of our ballclub, if he thought something wasn't going right, well, he would call a team party. He would have one and it always worked out right. I would say that Will [Stargell] led more off the field, and Roberto led more on the field."

Some Pirate observers had feared that Stargell, who frequently played in pain, might show outward resentment toward the fragile Clemente, who often missed games with back and neck woes. To his credit, Stargell did not publicly question Clemente's periodic absences from the lineup. Stargell seemed to understand that a proud player like Clemente didn't like to play at less than 100 per cent, out of the fear that he might embarrass himself on the field.

Contrary to the predictions of a potential rift between the two players, Clemente and Stargell enjoyed a solid relationship. On at least one occasion, a caring Clemente helped Stargell recover from his own back problems. "He stayed with me for a good hour, what he actually did was he took ice—a block of ice—in his bare hand and he massaged my back for a solid hour. And you know it's difficult to hold ice in your hand for five or 10 minutes, at the very most. But he was so intense in terms of doing something to make me feel better. I felt great, and the next night I played."

Few teammates showed their caring side the way that Clemente did in painfully applying the ice. "He didn't have to do that," says Stargell. "But he did. And he wanted to do it in such a way that very few people, if any, knew about it, other than the two of us. That was just one of many things he did. And it's those kind of things that separate him from most people."

Although the flu would force Clemente to the sidelines for a couple of days in early June, the Pirates' resident superstar had enjoyed recent rejuvenation at the plate. He needed such a hot streak, especially after Pirate observers had questioned the staying power of the 36-year-old Clemente in April and May. Criticism had been leveled in several areas. *Clemente could no longer handle the fastball. Clemente was standing too far away from home plate, leaving himself vulnerable to outside breaking pitches. An aging Clemente had lost enough of his ability to render himself a mere mortal among major league players.* Clemente offered a simple response to the criticism. "I heard a lot of reasons why I was not hitting," Clemente told *The Sporting News* in June. "I know I was standing away from the plate, but I always was ready for the outside pitch. It just was a case that I wasn't hitting. That's all it was."

In May, Clemente had been batting in the .260 range, a simply unacceptable batting mark for a player who didn't draw walks and was not considered a true power hitter. For only the second time in his career, Clemente had heard boos from the home fans. Unlike some players with thicker skins, the verbal catcalls had wounded the sensitive Clemente. He felt betrayed by the fans, many of whom had overlooked his continuing effort and determination. It was as if they had forgotten about the special relationship between themselves and Clemente.

By the middle of June, Clemente had erased all concerns about the talents that he still possessed as a hitter. On June 10, his batting average stood at a robust .313, and he had lifted his power numbers to six home runs and 31 RBIs. Even in the best times of his career, Clemente had failed to employ sound fundamentals in his hitting style, which had left him susceptible to occasional periods of ineptitude at the plate. In the past, these were referred to as slumps, but with Clemente approaching his 37th birthday, they had caused some critics to claim the end of his greatness.

Despite the media and fan prophecies, Clemente still possessed sufficient bat speed. In fact, Clemente needed *incredible* bat speed to counteract his unorthodox tendencies at the plate. Although an impatient hitter, Clemente almost never swung at the first pitch, even when it was thrown right down the middle. After taking the first pitch, Clemente transformed into the most aggressive of hitters, often swinging at pitches that were several inches outside and just off the ground, or a good foot above the strike zone. "He's the only wild swinger who hits .300 every year," Felipe Alou had told *Ebony* magazine in 1967. Ted Williams, a student of the strike zone and perhaps the most patient great hitter in the history of the game, must have shuddered when he watched Clemente hack at pitches that clearly would have been called balls.

Furthermore, Clemente's hitting technique was as unusual as his pitch selection. Unlike most hitters of the day, he preferred a thick-handled bat, one that accommodated his large hands. Clemente's bat had no knob at the end, an uncommon feature for players of that era. His bat also had an unusually large barrel, making it look more like a club than the thinner, whippet-like bats used by most hitters in the 1990s. In fact, a Clemente bat looked more like a bat from the 19th century than one from modern day baseball.

Clemente's bats usually weighed in the range of 40 to 42 ounces. As a point of comparison, all-time home run king Hank Aaron generally used a bat that weighed only 32 to 34 ounces. Frank Robinson preferred a 35-ounce bat. Willie Mays opted for bats that weighed 33 to 34 ounces. Mickey Mantle used bats of similar weights to Aaron and Mays. Stan Musial's bats typically weighed no more than 32 to 33 ounces.

Why did Clemente use such a heavy bat, which seemed incongruous with his relatively lean five-foot, 11-inch, 175-pound frame? Clemente explained his reasoning to Nellie King. "Branch Rickey always said the worst thing about hitters are guys who overstride or get out front," says King, who played for the Pirates when "The Mahatma" was the team's general manager. "When you get out front, you can't do anything. And Clemente seldom pulled the ball foul down the left field line. He hit for power, probably center field, left-center, or right-center. He always waited on the pitch, instead of trying to whip the bat. He kept from getting out front by using a heavy bat; he couldn't get out front, you know. And if the ball was inside, he'd just fight it off and hit it to right field. But when he got it flush, he would hit it. I think he hit a ball in Wrigley Field halfway up the scoreboard in center field. I think that's the longest ball he said he hit."

Clemente stood especially deep in the batter's box, far away from home plate, while holding his hands near his waist. As he fired the bat at the ball, he usually found himself off-balance, with his weight shifted awkwardly onto his front foot. When he finished his ferocious, all-out swing, he sometimes ended up facing the third base dugout. Often when he swung and missed, he spun around completely in the batter's box and grasped for his helmet, trying to prevent the embarrassment of it from falling off his head. Somehow, in spite of all this spitting in the face of fundamentals, Clemente could hit.

Clemente often dazzled teammates with his ability to seemingly steer line drives in certain directions, especially during pregame batting practice. One of those teammates was Bob Robertson. "Clemente, the way he used to do some things at the batting cage," Robertson says with awe. "He used to tell us, 'Well, I'm gonna hit one to right-center now, I'm gonna hit one to center field, I'm gonna drive one into left-center. Well, I'm gonna hit this one out.' And it was amazing how we would stand around in the cage, and he would say things like this and back 'em up. That was such fun..."

One year in spring training, Clemente's skill in pinpointing his line drives taught Willie Stargell a lesson about paying attention on every pitch. "We were taking extra hitting," says Stargell. "I was throwing to him, and he was throwing to me. So the time I was throwing to him, he said, 'Look, this round, I'm gonna hit everything back up the middle, so be alive.' Maybe three out of 10 pitches a guy could do that, hit the ball right at the pitcher. The first pitch I threw, as soon as I threw it, a bullet went right by my ear. Phew. I said, 'Whoa!' The next one, phew, by this ear. The next one was coming directly toward me, and I had to duck. That's three out of three. And then I got the message. I'm gonna be alive 10 out of 10."

As a youngster, Art Howe had watched Clemente play at Forbes Field throughout the late 1950s and early 1960s. By the late sixties, Howe had met Clemente informally during spring training. By 1971, Howe fulfilled a dream by signing a minor league contract with the team that played in his hometown—Pittsburgh. Late in the season, the Pirates afforded Howe a chance to watch Clemente during one of his trademark batting practice sessions. "It was my first year in the Pirate organization, I signed with them in '71," Howe recalls. "I lived in Pittsburgh, so when our [minor league] season was over, the Pirates let me come out for batting practice and take ground balls [at Three Rivers Stadium]. So I take BP with those guys. Just to watch [Clemente] take batting practice was something that youngsters should watch and learn. Because with his first round, he would just inside-out the ball and hit everything to right field. Then the next round, he'd move the ball around and start hitting the ball up the middle a little bit. And then in his last few rounds, he'd just start turning on the ball and stinging the ball. He used such a big bat, I recall, a big, long, heavy bat. He was so strong with his hands; the ball just jumped off the bat. When him and Stargell hit—when they were in the cage—you actually didn't even have to be around the cage to know that one of those two were in the cage hitting. The ball had a different sound coming off their bats. It was like a rifle shot. When the rest of us would be in there hitting, it didn't sound quite like that."

Even during his early season batting skid in 1971, no one had questioned Clemente's speed on the basepaths, or in particular, his defense in right field. His throwing arm remained unparalleled and his glovework impeccable. Perhaps best remembered for making his below-the-waist, against-all-fundamentals "basket catch" on routine fly balls, Clemente would make his most difficult and demanding catch during the summer of '71.

On June 15, Clemente positioned himself in right field during the eighth inning at the Houston Astrodome. With two outs and the Pirates holding a one-run lead, the Astros' Joe Morgan led off first base. Bob Watson, a powerful right-handed batter, stroked a hard line drive that sliced severely toward the right field corner. Clemente, in full gallop, raced toward the ball and neared the outfield wall. The placement of Watson's drive would not allow Clemente to show off his stylish basket catch on this occasion.

Nellie King watched the play develop from his position in the visiting broadcast booth at the Astrodome. "Blass is pitching, got a 1-0 lead in the eighth inning," says King, setting the scene. "There's a runner at first base, two outs, and Watson's a right-handed batter. Hits a shot down the right field line and it's slicing away from Clemente as he goes to the line. It's right at the wall, and it [looks like] a home run."

Only a few feet from the wall, Clemente made a jolting leap. With his body fully extended off the ground and his back to home plate, Clemente attempted a backhanded snare of the ball, just as it was about to clear a 10-foot-high yellow line painted onto the Astrodome wall. If the ball were to hit above the yellow line, the umpires would have to credit Watson with a home run, as dictated by Astrodome ground rules. "He reaches up and gets there at the same time as the ball does," says King, continuing his recollection of Clemente's play. "He reaches above the line, catches the ball, hits the concrete wall headfirst—face first—and falls down."

The remarkable play was not yet complete, since Clemente needed to retain possession of the ball upon impact. Clemente crashed into the wall violently, resulting in a badly bruised left ankle, a gashed left knee and a swollen left elbow as he dropped to the warning track. "He holds onto the ball," says King, "third out of the inning." Somehow Clemente held on, even after colliding with the wall and slumping to the ground. When he lifted himself up—the ball securely in his glove—the 16,000 plus fans in attendance at the Astrodome rewarded him with a standing ovation. Clemente had just deprived Watson and the Astros of a tie-breaking two-run homer, but the Astros faithful, fully realizing the greatness of the acrobatic play, had seen fit to give Clemente a round of rousing applause.

Astros' manager Harry Walker, who had managed Clemente in the mid-sixties, tabbed it the finest play he'd witnessed in his 34-year baseball career. "It was the best I'd ever seen," Walker told *Sports Illustrated*. "The Hat" had seen many of Clemente's finest plays in person—during his prime seasons of 1966 and '67—but none ranked as impressive as this one. "He took it full flight and hit the wall wide open," Walker told UPI, admiring Clemente's courage. "He never slowed up. I don't see how he could keep the ball in his glove." Bill Mazeroski compared it to a play Clemente had made at Forbes Field in 1960 against the Giants, when he had robbed Willie Mays of an extra-base hit and smashed into the right field wall. On that play, Clemente had sustained a seven-stitch cut to his chin and minor abrasions to his knees and buttocks.

Clemente's catch against the Astros preserved a 1-0 lead for the Pirates, who went on to win the game, 3-0, behind the pitching of Steve Blass. Afterwards, the right-hander declined to take credit for his fourth shutout of the season. "That shutout belongs to Clemente," Blass told John Wilson of the *Houston Chronicle*.

On the ride back from the Astrodome, Nellie King sat next to Clemente, who had soaked his knee, ankle and elbow in ice packs. "I'm sitting with him on the bus going back to the hotel, and I said, 'Roberto, I've seen a lot of good catches, but that's the greatest I've ever seen you make.' And he said, 'Nellie, I want to tell you something. If the ball is in the park and the game is on the line, I will catch the bleeping ball.' That's what he said."

The greatest defensive right fielder in the history of the game, a man who would accumulate a dozen Gold Gloves during his career, had made arguably the greatest catch of his life—and perhaps in the history of the game. Unfortunately, the remarkable play had taken place in a regular season game, not in the post-season, and was not preserved on film or videotape. It would be maintained only in the minds of those who had seen it first-hand: Nellie King, Harry Walker, Bill Mazeroski, Steve Blass and 16,000 observers at the Astrodome. Later in the season, Clemente would duplicate his defensive prowess for a much larger audience—and a televised one at that.

The following night, Roberto Clemente's bat—and not his glove—gave the Bucs another lift. Clemente picked up two hits and three RBIs in the Pirates' 6-4 win at the Astrodome. Clemente's seventh home run of the season, a two-run shot, broke a 4-4 dead-lock in the seventh. Thanks to another game-winning hit by the resurgent Clemente, Dock Ellis earned his 10th win of the season.

As July hovered around the bend, the Pirates continued to lead the National League East. Their record now approached that of the Giants, who owned the highest winning percentage in the entire league. Surprisingly, Pirate attendance, while up 147,000 fans from a year ago, continued to lag at a mediocre pace. Nine National League teams owned better attendance figures than the Bucs. That fact partially explained why only one Pirate—Manny Sanguillen—rated among the top two vote-getters for any position for the National League All-Star team. Slugging outfielder Willie Stargell, perhaps the leading contender in the league's Most Valuable Player sweepstakes, ranked only third in the outfield voting, behind Willie Mays and Hank Aaron, the game's two most legendary active players. Even Clemente, the most well known of all the Pirates, ranked no better than sixth among National League outfielders.

On June 21, Willie Stargell hit his 25th home run in a 6-0 shutout of the Mets, the second place residents in the National League East. Just when it seemed the Pirates might start to pull away from the Mets in the divisional race, they succumbed in their next game, a disheartening 3-2 loss at Three Rivers.

The loss turned out to be only a temporary setback, as the Bucs claimed the series finale. Clemente chipped in with a four-hit night. Stargell clubbed his 26th home run—and with four runs driven in—raised his league-leading total to 72 ribbies. Luke Walker and Mudcat Grant combined to pitch two-run baseball.

The Bucs started a road trip in Philadelphia, and took three out of four from the lowly Phils. The series featured two-homer games from Richie Hebner and Jackie Hernandez—the lightest hitter on the team—the 27th and 28th home runs of the season for Stargell, and Clemente's 1,200th career RBI, which came on a game-winning pinch-hit home run.

Clemente's revitalized hitting overshadowed his more subtle contributions, such as his influence on outfield partner Al Oliver. Along with the teaching of coach Bill Virdon, the defensive presence of Clemente had helped motivate Oliver in smoothing his transition from first base to center field. "No question about it, because one thing you didn't want to do was go out there in that outfield and embarrass yourself," Oliver says with a laugh. "When you have possibly the greatest right fielder to ever play the game, and then you had in my opinion, a great left fielder, with a great arm, in Willie Stargell, you definitely had to go out there and do a more-than-adequate job. There's no question that that was some serious motivation for Al Oliver." Heading into the season, some scouts had considered Oliver the next Pirate star, the man who would succeed Roberto Clemente as the club's best all-around player. Clemente was trying to help Oliver do just that.

With continued poor support in the fan voting, Clemente did not merit a starting position for the National League in the 1971 All-Star Game, but was selected as a reserve by Cincinnati Reds' manager Sparky Anderson. Clemente joined Manny Sanguillen, Willie Stargell and Dock Ellis—the latter two earning starting nods—as Pirate representatives in Detroit. Anderson chose Stargell to play his regular position of left field and gave Ellis the honor of starting the game against Vida Blue of the Oakland A's. As the game's two hottest starting pitchers, Ellis and Vida Blue prepared to square off in the national spotlight, marking the first time that black pitchers had started against each other since the All-Star Game's inception in 1933.

In the bottom of the third, with the Nationals leading 3-0, Ellis faced Boston Red Sox' shortstop Luis Aparicio, the inning's leadoff man. Aparicio, who was batting only .209 in regular season play, singled up the middle. American League manager Earl Weaver called upon Oakland slugger Reggie Jackson to pinch-hit for Vida Blue. Jackson, a last-minute All-Star Game replacement for the injured Tony Oliva, drove a mediocre Ellis fastball deep toward right center field. The ball, seemingly still on the rise hundreds of feet away from home plate, caromed off the light tower that perched above the right field section of the Tiger Stadium roof.

Observers estimated that Jackson's home run had traveled 520 feet. Reggie claimed he had never hit a ball harder. All-Stars Luis Aparicio, Al Kaline and Carl Yastrzemski said that Jackson's blast was the *hardest* they had ever seen. Norm Cash said the home run was the *longest* he had seen. And Ellis, despite his brilliant first-half pitching, would now be remembered more vividly for giving up an embarrassingly gargantuan home run on national television.

In the eighth, with the American League having extended its lead to 6-3, Clemente strode to the plate to face Tigers' left-hander Mickey Lolich. Although most of the 53,559 fans at Tiger Stadium were focusing their concentration on their hometown pitcher, their collective attention would soon shift to the batter's box. Clemente, making his 14th and final All-Star Game appearance, was about to produce one of the game's most memorable batting sequences.

Lolich, it seemed, wanted no part of pitching to Clemente. Even though Lolich enjoyed a three-run lead, he threw two offerings that sailed well out of the strike zone. Clemente, visibly upset, stepped back from his accustomed position deep in the batter's box and flipped his bat in the air, letting it fall to the ground (The dropping of the bat was something that he did from time to time to express his displeasure with a particular pitch. Now he was doing it in front of a national television audience.)

Clemente gestured toward Lolich, as if to say, "Pitch to me!" Later in the at bat, Lolich delivered another pitch, one that appeared to be sailing high and away from Clemente, again out of the strike zone. Surprisingly, Clemente swung at the rising fastball. At first glance, it appeared that Clemente would be able to do nothing more than pop the pitch, which wasn't close to being a strike, weakly to the second baseman. Clemente flicked his wrists, and launched the ball deep toward right-center field. The ball carried—and carried some more—and finally landed in the upper deck of the center field bleachers.

It was as if Clemente had challenged Lolich to throw him a strike, and when he refused, he simply expanded his strike zone, determined to deliver a hard-hit ball. Clemente wanted no part of drawing a walk in baseball's most exalted exhibition game. In a showcase like the All-Star Game, Clemente wanted desperately to show the fans of Detroit, and the nationwide fan base watching on television, that he could hit.

Clemente's home run was the sixth by an All-Star that night in Detroit, joining Johnny Bench, Hank Aaron, Reggie Jackson, Frank Robinson and Harmon Killebrew in the long ball parade. While Clemente's home run against Lolich failed to prevent the National League from losing the game, and was overshadowed by the monstrous home run hit by Jackson—perhaps the most famous longball in All-Star Game lore—it remains one of the most stunning examples of his intriguing confrontations with pitchers. And an example of his desire, athleticism and power. While a reputation as a line drive hitter followed him throughout his career, Clemente's launch into the center field seats showed that he could hit with power when he wanted to.

After the All-Star break, Pittsburgh welcomed the San Diego Padres to town. In one of the most thrilling games of the season, the lowly Padres forced the Pirates to a 17-inning limit, marking the longest game on the National League schedule to date. The Pirates trailed the Padres, 1-0, heading to the bottom of the ninth, but a walk, a single and a sac fly by Gene Alley tied the score at 1-1. In the top of the 13th, San Diego slugger Ivan Murrell hit his sixth home run of the season, giving the Padres the lead. Willie Stargell matched the home run with his 31st in the bottom of the inning. San Diego again assumed the lead in the 16th inning, but Richie Hebner's 14th home run tied the score in the bottom half. Then in the 17th inning, Clemente stepped to the plate, nagged by an 0-for-7 collar on the night. Facing right-handed reliever Danny Coombs, Clemente cleared the Three Rivers Stadium wall with a one-out blast—his ninth home run of the season. Somehow, after three desperation comebacks in the bottom of the ninth, 13th and 16th innings, the Pirates had managed to win again.

Dramatic victories like that fostered one of the major leagues' loosest clubhouses, which in turn acted as a catalyst to the Pirates' winning ways. The atmosphere also reflected the team's upbeat personalities, especially Dock Ellis, Manny Sanguillen and Willie Stargell. Before one game, Ellis stood in the locker-room, listening to some of his favorite music, which he had pumped in at a high volume. Suddenly, one of the players turned down the level of the music, apparently in response to the entrance of Clemente. "Did you notice how the room went silent?" bellowed Ellis, before stepping into a mock imitation of Clemente. Ellis began twitching his neck in Clemente-like style, just as Roberto often did to loosen his back muscles during at-bats. Ellis then spoke in a feigned Latino accent, "Oh, I not like I used to be. I a little bit of an old man."

In his earliest major league days, few players would have dared to kid or mock Clemente in such a way. At a younger age, the sensitive Clemente might have reacted with a display of temper, especially in a clubhouse that was not as friendly toward Latino ballplayers. In the late sixties and early seventies, such good-natured ribbing of the Pirate superstar was now considered acceptable behavior by the Pittsburgh players—and by Clemente.

Throughout the '71 season, Pirate players enjoyed playing jokes on one another—and on members of the off-field staff. One practical joke indirectly involved Clemente, some local artwork, and the gullibility of the Pirates' team doctor. "There was a sculptor in Pittsburgh," says former Pirates' executive and Hall of Fame vice-president Bill Guilfoile, "who sculpted two life-size wax figures of Clemente. One was to go in the Pittsburgh Hall of Fame, which was located in Three Rivers Stadium. The other one was then to be sent to Cooperstown.

"While it was being stored, awaiting shipment to Cooperstown, it was in one of the storerooms under the stands at Three Rivers Stadium. And it was a tremendously good likeness of Clemente, with the uniform and cap and everything; it was really quite life-like. This particular night, Tony Bartirome, who was the trainer for the Pirates, and a couple of others got the key to this storeroom. During batting practice, they went in there and very gingerly removed the wax figure and carried it down the hallway. They brought it in the Pirate clubhouse and laid it out on the trainers table. Then they dimmed the lights and summoned the team doctor, Joe Finegold. The batboy was sent out to tell him that Clemente had passed out! The batboy promptly told the physician that Clemente needed immediate attention in the clubhouse.

"So, Joe Finegold came running with his little black bag," Guilfoile says, "and, of course, the players were all hidden around the clubhouse waiting for him to show up. He burst into the trainers' room, and, of course, he tried to get a pulse out of this wax figure without any success. He was getting panicky when there was no pulse at all." As Sally O'Leary remembers, Dr. Finegold let out a loud shriek: "My God, he's cold!"

The Pirate players burst out laughing, as Dr. Finegold massaged what he believed to be the actual wrist of Clemente. Afterward, even Dr. Finegold seemed to appreciate the humor of the incident. Clemente himself learned about the practical joke later on. What was Roberto's reaction to his teammates' perpetration of humor, considering his dislike of the hypochondriac label that others had pinned on him? "When Clemente heard about it, he laughed himself," O'Leary says. "He didn't take it the wrong way. He enjoyed it."

By the early 1970s, Clemente even enjoyed poking fun at himself in his dealings with writers. "Toward the end of his career, he mellowed and he began to be able to smile at himself," recalls Roy McHugh of the *Pittsburgh Press*. When McHugh inquired about how he was feeling, Clemente no longer detailed his ailments, as he might have done in his earlier years. Instead, he offered a light-hearted response. "He would say, 'Oh, I am perfect,'" McHugh recalls. "'If I say I am not perfect, you won't print it anyway.' And then he'd sort of smile and the writers would smile, too."

The Pirates continued to pace the National League East through mid-summer. In late July, the Bucs opened up a 14-game road trip by scoring back-to-back wins against the Padres. Without warning, the Pirates' bats then fell silent in a doubleheader at San Diego Stadium. Clemente went 2-for-4 in the first game against left-hander Fred Norman, but only three other Pirates managed hits in a frustrating 2-1 loss. In the nightcap, Danny Murtaugh rested Clemente, using him only as a late-inning pinch-hitter for Charlie Sands. The offense fared even worse in game two, collecting only three hits and no runs in a 2-0 loss to Steve Arlin, who had entered the game with a record of 4-13.

Two days later, perhaps still stung by the doubleheader defeats at the hands of San Diego, the Pirates fell to the Dodgers at Chavez Ravine. After a strong six innings, Dock Ellis weakened in the seventh, giving up run-scoring singles to Tom Haller and Maury Wills. Murtaugh replaced Ellis with Mudcat Grant, who served up a grand slam to young outfielder Billy Buckner. A six-run seventh inning gave the Dodgers an 8-5 win and saddled Ellis with a loss, finally ending his winning streak at 15 games.

After the loss to the Dodgers, Pirates' broadcaster Nellie King witnessed an unusual scene in the team's clubhouse. None of the Pirates were arguing with each other or pointing the finger to account for a difficult loss. Rather, King observed a poignant exchange involving the game's losing pitcher and one of the team's leaders. "Grant was depressed," says King. "He was still in uniform after everybody had showered and left. He was all alone, or so he thought. Someone then pulled up a chair. It was Clemente." As King told Pittsburgh writer Phil Musick, Clemente offered Grant a form of a pep talk. "He kept telling him, 'You can pitch! You can still get people out. Forget this game! It is gone!'"

On most teams, few players would have taken the time to talk to a veteran pitcher after such a loss. Clemente was different, however. He had sensed that Grant was particularly down on himself after such a brutal performance, especially one that had cost a fellow pitcher a chance at a victory. Clemente felt the situation mandated sincere encouragement—one veteran to another. "Clemente emotionally held his hand for 20 minutes," King recalls. "That was the only time anyone did that for [Grant]. [Roberto] was a star. He didn't have to care, but he did." Perhaps encouraged by

Clemente, Grant pitched better in his next outing, a two-inning stint against the hard-hitting Giants.

As July slipped into August, Pittsburgh began to show its first signs of team wreckage. The Pirates dropped all four games to the Giants, who embarrassed their Eastern Division rivals in a slaughterhouse of a series. On the final day of a weekend series against the Phillies, the Pirates managed a split of a twinbill, as Bob Johnson pitched his first National League shutout in the nightcap. The 4-0 win averted an embarrassing doubleheader sweep at the hands of the league's worst team. Yet, the Pirates had still lost three out of four games to a club that had played awful baseball most of the season. That scenario was hardly satisfactory for a team that had advertised itself as a pennant contender. The Pirates, for the first time in 1971, were trapped in a major free fall.

During their worst stretch of the season, the Bucs had lost 11 out of 16, including four straight losses to the Giants, the team the Pirates would likely have to face in the National League playoffs— if they even made the playoffs. The Giants had dominated the Pirates in the regular season, winning nine out of 12 overall, including five straight at Candlestick Park. As the losses mounted, Danny Murtaugh tried to inject some humor into a funereal atmosphere. "If I were a drinking man," Murtaugh told *Sports Illustrated*, "I'd have one." In reality, Murtaugh didn't drink, and the Pirates weren't winning games.

Why had the Bucs turned sour so suddenly? At one juncture, the Pirates' bullpen sported a post-All-Star break ERA of 7.26, and had surrendered 67 hits in 53 and a third innings, including nine home runs and three grand slams. Left-hander Bob Veale had somehow managed to go 7-0 while accumulating an ERA of 7.50. Set-up man Mudcat Grant, so effective in the first half, had begun to hang too many pitches, as had closer Dave Giusti. The ineffectiveness of Veale and Grant had caused Murtaugh to summon Giusti earlier— and more frequently. With his bullpen now struggling, Murtaugh tended to stay too long with his starters, who were becoming increasingly ineffective. Wherever Murtaugh turned, he found new cracks and leaks on his pitching staff.

On August 10, Joe Brown engineered a pair of related player moves aimed at repairing the team's pitching damage. First, Brown sold Grant to the Oakland A's, the same team that had traded him to the Pirates the previous summer. Having cleared a spot on his 25-man roster, Brown acquired journeyman reliever Bob "Monk" Miller and a sum of cash from the Padres for a pair of minor leaguers, pitcher Ed Acosta and outfielder John Jeter. After a mid-season release by the Cubs, Miller had justified the Padres' faith in him by forging an impressive record of 7-3 with the tiniest of ERAs—1.41. The deal, while hardly a headline-maker, would turn out to be another Brown stroke of mastery.

A two-game split with the Cubs maintained Pittsburgh's seven-game lead on Chicago. The Pirates owned an eight-game bulge on the Cardinals, who were coming to town for a critical four-game series. In the opening game, the Pirates faced the unenviable prospect of meeting red-hot left-hander Steve Carlton, who had already won 15 games. In the first inning, a two-run double by Clemente gave the Pirates an early boost. But with Clemente on second and no one out, Carlton bore down and left "The Great One" stranded by retiring Willie Stargell, Manny Sanguillen and Bob Robertson in succession. With the Pirates leading just 2-0 heading to the top of the third, a defensive miscue opened the floodgates. Gene Alley bobbled Dal Maxvil's leadoff grounder, bringing Carlton to the plate. Cards' skipper Red Schoendienst decided to forego the bunt and watched Carlton deliver a line single. After retiring Lou Brock, Luke Walker surrendered a run-scoring double to Ted Sizemore and an RBI grounder to former Pirate Matty Alou. With two outs and Sizemore at second base, the Cards' best hitter, Joe Torre, delivered a clutch single that scored Sizemore. Torre's RBI proved to be the game-winner, as the Cards held the Pirates scoreless over the final six innings.

Cardinal pitching continued to dominate the Bucs. On August 13, Jerry Reuss held the Bucs to four hits and earned his 11th win. Another error by Alley in the second inning led to an unearned run against Steve Blass. The miscue supplied the Cards with all the offense they would need in a 2-0 victory.

With the lead now down to six, the Cardinals readied for the kill. In an apparent overwhelming mismatch, right-hander Bob Gibson faced the inconsistent Bob Johnson. On a Saturday afternoon in August in Pittsburgh, against one of the best lineups in baseball, Gibson readied himself for one of the Cardinals' most important games of the season. Gibby proceeded to strike out 10 Bucs, including Willie Stargell on three occasions. One of the strikeout victims, Milt May, reached base when Ted Simmons failed to corral a wild pitch third strike. Three other Bucs made it to first base via walks. But none of the baserunners would get as far as second base, and no Pirate would manage a hit against the future Hall of Famer.

The masterpiece marked the first no-hitter of Gibson's career. Gibson had considered the possibility of throwing one remote because of his pitching style. "I never thought I'd throw a no-hitter," Gibson explained to *Sports Illustrated,* "because I'm a high-ball pitcher. There are many more high-ball hitters than low-ball hitters."

In a curious decision, Danny Murtaugh had decided to bench Clemente, one of his best "high ball" hitters. Murtaugh had also sat down Sanguillen, another hitter who prospered against pitches up in the strike zone. Opting to load the middle of his lineup with four left-handed bats, Murtaugh had banked on the percentages of platoon baseball. The strategy didn't work. The Cardinals had now crept to within five games of the Pirates.

What else could go wrong for the Bucs? Well, plenty. In the series finale on Sunday afternoon, before a crowd of nearly 50,000, the Pirates endured another indignity. In the eighth inning, the bullpen failed to preserve a 4-1 lead. Instead of summoning an overworked Dave Giusti, Murtaugh chose the well-rested Bob Miller, making just his second appearance with the Bucs. After allowing a two-run single, Miller faced Matty Alou, who had already picked up three base hits against Pittsburgh pitching. Hardly known for his power, Alou clubbed a three-run home run against Miller, providing the winning margin in a 6-4 decision. Alou had done more than haunt his former mates; he had taken possession of their souls. Alou finished the afternoon 4-for-5, with three RBIs and a run scored. Despite two more home runs by Willie Stargell, the Pirates' divisional lead had dwindled to four games. Ouch.

On Monday, August 16, the Pirates continued their homestand against the Astros. With their season on the brink and Clemente held out for rest, the Pirates responded with one of their most encouraging efforts of the season. The superhuman Stargell rapped out four hits and four RBIs, bringing his season total to a career best 108. Vic Davalillo, playing right field for Clemente, piled up two triples, a double and two RBIs. Bob Robertson plated two more runs with clutch sacrifice flies. Dock Ellis earned his 17th victory by working the first seven innings. The Pirates also received good news from Cincinnati, where the Reds, with a 6-5 win, ended the Cardinals' winning streak at three. The Bucs' lead was now back up to five games in the East.

Clemente returned to action the following night, but the Pirates stumbled by coughing up a 4-1 lead in the top of the seventh inning. Relievers Bob Miller and Bob Veale failed to retire a single batter, as the Astros rallied for five runs. Jesus Alou delivered the game-winning blow against Miller, marking the second time in three days that a member of the Alou family had victimized the Pirate journeyman. (Thankfully, brother Felipe was playing for the New York Yankees in the American League.) The fateful seventh inning marred a terrific game for Clemente, who returned to the lineup with four base hits, including his 12th home run.

In late August, Clemente missed a few games with a minor injury. He returned on August 25, in time to play the series finale against the Braves. Prior to the game, backup catcher Milt May took his wedding vows. That evening, the Pirate offense celebrated the occasion by accumulating a season-high 21 hits, including eight singles during a six-run first inning. Clemente went 5-for-6 and scored three times.

On September 1, Clemente became part of an unusual piece of baseball history. That afternoon at Three Rivers Stadium, manager Danny Murtaugh made out the following lineup card as the Bucs prepared to face Phillies' left-hander Woodie Fryman.

Rennie Stennett, 2B
Gene Clines, CF
Roberto Clemente, RF
Willie Stargell, LF
Manny Sanguillen, C
Dave Cash, 3B
Al Oliver, 1B
Jackie Hernandez, SS
Dock Ellis, P

With usual starters Bob Robertson and Richie Hebner ailing, Oliver and Cash took their places on the infield corners. As a result, Murtaugh filled out what baseball historians determined to be the first all-black lineup in the history of major league baseball.

The offense provided by the all-black lineup accounted for nine runs in the first three innings, enabling the Bucs to hold an early three-run lead. Clemente, Clines, Oliver, Sanguillen, Stargell and Stennett each rapped out a pair of base hits. Although the Phillies knocked out Dock Ellis in the second inning, he was aided—

somewhat ironically—by the relief pitching of Luke Walker, a white Texan who hurled six brilliant innings. Walker's pitching capped off an impressive 10-7 victory for the Pirates and their all-black lineup.

In an April 25th interview with Milton Richman of United Press International, Clemente had recalled joining the Pirates as a rookie in 1955, when the team had very few minority players. At the time, most players, black or white, resisted the temptation to speak out against what they considered unjust treatment. Players did not want to anger management, which held most of the leverage in contract negotiations. Clemente, however, represented one of the exceptions. "Anytime I feel something is wrong, I'm gonna say something," Clemente explained to Richman. "Baseball has changed in many ways since I first came to the big leagues. Ballplayers feel they can speak up much more now than they did then. I spoke up even then."

Clemente took pride in his own role in helping to improve perceptions about minorities who happened to be baseball players. "My greatest satisfaction comes from helping to erase the old opinion about Latin American and black ballplayers," Clemente said. "People had the wrong opinion. They never questioned our ability, but they considered us inferior in our station of life. Simply because many of us were poor we were thought to be low class. Even our integrity was questioned. I don't blame the fans for that. I blame the writers. They made it look like we were something different from the white players. We're not. We're the same."

Although racial relations between Pirate players had improved considerably since the mid-1950s, Clemente was not completely satisfied with the ways that black and white major leaguers, especially on other teams, related to each other. "Baseball has come a long way in this regard," Clemente acknowledged in his interview with Richman, "but there is still room for improvement. When I came here you very seldom saw a black player get together with a white player and go someplace together after a ballgame. Now it is more common. Yes, there has been some improvement but some things still remain the way they were. I cannot, for example, go up to a white player and say to him 'Are you for real?' or, 'Are you concerned with me at all?' But now, once in a while they will ask you about it. They don't turn their backs on you like they used to."

With the Pirates of the early seventies featuring such ethnic diversity in their clubhouse, the atmosphere seemed ripe for racial tension between the players. Yet, such problems rarely occurred. Players like Clemente, Steve Blass, Gene Clines and Dave Giusti, along with coach Dave Ricketts, helped create a clubhouse of racial harmony. They instigated friendly bouts of ribbing and joking, often basing their humor on race. Clemente and Giusti sometimes needled each other to the point of hilarity, drawing roars of laughter from other Pirate players. "The by-play between him and Dave Giusti became almost a ritual for us," Steve Blass wrote in a 1973 edition of *Sport* magazine. "Any subject and suddenly they'd be hollering and insulting each other. Robby was our player rep before Dave and when something would come up, he'd say, 'When I was the player rep, we never had these kinds of problems, but you give an Italian a little responsibility and look what happens.'" On other teams, such racial kidding and jousting might have led to outright warfare in the clubhouse, but that was not the case with the Pirates. Players generally doled out ethnic humor good-naturedly, and did not take such banter personally.

Why did such clubhouse by-play work for the Pirates, whereas it might have damaged the atmosphere on other teams? Two players deserved much of the credit for promoting and maintaining clubhouse unity. "The reason why we did get along so well is because of the leadership that we had with a Clemente and a Stargell—mainly," Giusti explains. "It was just understood that there was instant respect for those two, and also respect for anybody else. You know, Clemente was outstanding in that area. I can recall a number of times when people were having problems, and he would sit people down, including myself, and just go over things, that baseball is not everything, it's your family and how you get along with people that are more important." Giusti says Clemente offered such advice without self-promotion. "Nobody would know about it, because it would be after a ballgame was over, or in the hotel," says Giusti. "And Stargell was the same way. We had that kind of leadership that presented itself. And I think that, more than anything else, was the answer to why we got along so well with each other."

The Cardinals, in spite of their August push, drew no closer than four games to the Pirates in the standings. A two-game set between the Pirates and Cardinals in mid-September offered the Redbirds a last-chance gasp to close in on the Bucs. Trailing by seven and a half games in the National League East, the Cardinals needed both wins to maintain faint hopes of matching the Pirates. For the first game, Danny Murtaugh turned to staff ace Dock Ellis, who had missed his last few starts with a sore elbow. The Cards countered with 18-game winner Steve Carlton, their best pitcher in 1971, and a constant nemesis of the Pirates.

The Pirates' offense set the tone early in the first game by displaying immediate speed and aggressiveness. In the first inning, Gene Clines led off with a single. With one out and Clemente at the plate, Clines broke for second on a hit-and-run play. Clemente roped a single, and Clines, never breaking stride, scored all the way from first. In executing such a play, the Pirates had exhibited that they themselves could play the aggressive style of game preferred by the Redbirds.

Ellis performed as well as he had done in the season's first half, shackling the Cards on six hits and one run through seven plus innings. Recently recalled left-hander Ramon Hernandez (like Clemente, a native of Carolina, Puerto Rico) finished off a 4-1 win with two sparkling innings of relief, as the Pirates increased their separation from the Cardinals to eight and a half games.

In the second and final game of the miniseries with the Cards, the Pirates applied the full swing of their hammers in pounding the Cardinals into a pennant afterthought. Clemente played a small, but important role in kick-starting Pittsburgh's offense. With the game scoreless in the bottom of the third, walks by Rennie Stennett and Richie Hebner, a single by Gene Clines, a Clemente sacrifice fly and an RBI single off the bat of Manny Sanguillen spearheaded the Bucs to an early 2-0 lead. The Pirates plated two more in the fourth, when Cardinals' center fielder Jose Cruz misplayed a Jackie Hernandez single, allowing the ball to roll past him into deep center field. The four early runs would prove to be more than enough for starter Luke Walker. Ramon Hernandez posted his second consecutive save with two and two-thirds innings of scoreless relief.

With the calendar reading September 17 and the Pirates now up by nine and a half games, the pennant race had practically ceased to exist. Four days later, the magic number for clinching the division shrank to one. Fittingly, the Pirates and Cardinals began a three-game series. The Cardinals staved off elimination by beating Dock Ellis in the first game, 6-4. In the second game, Bob Gibson took the mound for St. Louis against Pittsburgh's inconsistent Luke Walker. Gibson had pitched a no-hitter against the Pirates only six weeks earlier, but on this day he was not nearly as effective—or as fortunate. The Cardinals' defense failed to support Gibson, who was betrayed by a passed ball and an error in the first inning. The early mistakes contributed to a Pirate run. A fourth-inning RBI single by Manny Sanguillen plated a more legitimate run, giving the Bucs a 2-1 lead. In the top of the eighth inning, the Cardinals' defense again undermined Gibson. A throwing error by reserve shortstop Ted Kubiak accounted for three unearned runs.

Dave Giusti, who had entered the game in the bottom of the seventh inning, needed just six more outs to ensure the playoff berth. With a rested Giusti on the mound, and a four-run lead in hand, the Pirates prepped for a victory celebration. The Pirates' palmball specialist, who had struggled through a horrid mid-season pitching slump, dusted off the Cards for his 29th, and most important save of the season.

Giusti's brilliant pennant-clinching relief stint might not have happened without the intervention of Clemente. "It was about the middle of the season," Giusti recalls. "I seemed to have problems at one time or another for about a two-week stint, maybe even longer. Boy, I wasn't getting anybody out. After this particular game that I had given up the winning run, the game's over, and I'm over in my locker, pouting and all. And here comes Clemente. He sat down and we talked about how important it was for you to take care of the family. Family was very, very important to him. He depicted that by talking to people like myself. That gave me a helluva boost. Here's the superstar coming over without having anybody ask him to, on his own, and making those kind of comments to me. That was really helpful."

As he had done earlier in the season with the since-departed Mudcat Grant, Clemente once again boosted the spirits of a slumping teammate. He repeatedly reminded other players to maintain the correct perspective and the proper hierarchy of priorities. There were things, such as family, far more important than winning or losing a ballgame.

Shortly after in the Pirate clubhouse, key role players like Vic Davalillo and Nellie Briles—who had been acquired after a recommendation from Clemente—took turns dousing manager Danny Murtaugh with the obligatory supply of champagne, which had been put into storage four days earlier. In the meantime, Clemente celebrated the way he preferred—quietly, and in the background.

With the Pirates having clinched a playoff berth, Clemente could truly savor the special honor bestowed upon him by a pair of Latin American politicians. On September 24, prior to a game against the Mets at Shea Stadium, New York congressman Herman

Badillo and Puerto Rican Senate president Rafael Hernandez Colon formally acknowledged Clemente's contributions to baseball and the Latino community.

Shea Stadium, and its crowd of 35,936 fans, served as a reunion ground for the Clemente clan. A large group of Clemente's neighbors and friends flew in from his hometown of Carolina to see the superstar right fielder. Even the mayor of Carolina, Heriberto Nieves, made the trip to New York. Danny Murtaugh spoke about the privilege of guiding a star like Clemente. "It's been a real pleasure through the years to manage a great player like him," Murtaugh told the *New York Times*. "He's the type of player you're proud to have on your side."

During the ceremony, Badillo and Hernandez Colon presented Clemente with a new Cadillac. At first, Clemente expressed reluctance to accept the gift. "If I want a car, I can buy it myself," a proud Clemente told Thomas Rogers of the *New York Times*, before softening his stance. "But this is not something you can refuse. I know the Puerto Rican people had to go through hell to give me this honor."

Later on, Clemente tried to clarify his remarks, explaining that he was upset only because he felt the money used to buy the Cadillac could have been better spent on charitable causes. In addition to the gift of the Cadillac, Clemente did receive promises of funding for two of his favored charities: one for retarded children, and another for youngsters with physical handicaps.

The staging of the ceremony in New York was fitting on two counts. First, Badillo and Colon had made the presentation to Clemente on behalf of the large Puerto Rican population in the New York metropolitan region. As Spanish language broadcaster Buck Canel told the *New York Times* about Clemente: "He is very conscious of race, very proud, somewhat old fashioned. He feels he does not get the recognition around the league that he does in Pittsburgh. There are close to two million Spanish-speaking persons in the three-state Metropolitan area, and almost half are Puerto Rican."

Second, the hometown Mets had become one of the first major league organizations to institute a program to teach their Latin American minor league players to speak better English. The Mets had recently signed a wave of Latino prospects, and soon realized that some of them spoke the language so poorly that they could not even order meals in restaurants. Some players had not eaten a full meal for several days. Furthermore, most other players and members of the media did not speak Spanish, making every-day conversations virtually nonexistent. In the spring of 1971, the Mets had hired English professor Albert Miner, who had set a goal for each player to learn approximately 750 words in English. Miner designed the language sessions to help the players order meals and engage in other basic and necessary conversations. Miner worked with the young Latino players for six hours a day at the Mets' spring training site in St. Petersburg, Florida.

A player like Clemente appreciated the struggles of young Latino players trying to learn a new language in a strange country. As Bill Mazeroski wrote in an article that appeared in the November 1971 issue of *Sport* magazine, Clemente had struggled to over-come the language barrier during the early years of his career. "He went through some years when he didn't trust writers, and I don't blame him. Some of them put words in your mouth. They tried to make him look like an ass by getting him to say controversial things," wrote Mazeroski. "He was just learning to handle the language and he couldn't express what he felt or thought and it frustrated him. Writers who couldn't speak three words of Spanish tried to make him look silly, but he's an intelligent man who knows people and knows the game."

"There were only certain writers he would talk to because he didn't want to be misquoted," Roberto Clemente, Jr. told *USA Today* in 1997. "It was very difficult to make himself understood and, because of that, a lot of people took him the wrong way." Early in his career, Clemente had frequently felt misused by those writers who insisted on phonetically writing out his spoken quotes. While this tendency gradually diminished as Roberto became more accomplished with the English language, it did not completely disappear. Even in 1971, some writers continued this unfortunate practice, as seen in the following excerpt:

"When we have a meeting een thee clubhouse, when Harry Walker ees thee manager, thee writers say that Clemente he ees is taking the team away from Walker," Clemente was quoted by Dick Young of the *New York Daily News*. "Thee press crucify me, but they do not know what ees all about... Eet ees not too much that you geev one hunert per cent. That ees thee only theeng that make me mad, when a player don' ron."

Although Clemente continued to speak English with a heavy Latino accent—even in 1971—Young's article clearly exaggerated his dialect. "I know I don't speak as bad as they say," Clemente told Myron Cope of *Sports Illustrated* in 1966. "I know that I don't have the good English pronunciation because my tongue belongs to Spanish, but I know where the verb, the article, the pronoun go. I never in a life start a sentence with 'me,' but if I start it with 'I,' the sportswriters say 'me.'" Clemente felt that by exaggerating his grammatical mistakes and placing such an overemphasis on his Spanish accent, writers were continuing their attempts to make him—and other Latino players—sound foolish.

"It makes him sound like he's dumb," Nellie King says of some of the written quotations attributed to Clemente. "And you know he was a very intelligent man. When you start doing everything phonetically, it's like he didn't take time to speak the language, you know. But they didn't take time to understand him or appreciate the culture he came from. I don't know why the media did that. It sure made him seem less than intelligent. I mean, how would you like to go to Puerto Rico and have guys quote you the way you sound?"

While Clemente never spoke English smoothly, he was by no means unintelligible. "He spoke very broken English," King admits. "Even to the end, he wasn't that articulate in English, but he was certainly understandable and did a very good job with it. Much better than Americans going to the Latin American countries would do in speaking Spanish, certainly."

Clemente had also *played* better than some of the early-season skeptics might have predicted. After a poor April, Clemente had clearly maintained his status as the Pirates' best all-around player. He finished the season with a .341 batting average, only 11 points off his pace of 1970. In spite of an early season power drought, he finished with 13 home runs, only one fewer than the previous season's total. Clemente also drove in 86 runs, an improvement of 26 RBIs. While some of the fans and media had questioned Clemente in April and May, his teammates had maintained a belief in his playing, character, and leadership abilities all along.

19

Slaying the Giants

The National League Championship Series opened up on October 2 in San Francisco, where the Pirates had lost five straight games during the regular season. A less-than-capacity crowd of 40,977 showed up at Candlestick Park to watch Steve Blass battle San Francisco's staff ace, Gaylord Perry.

In the fifth inning, with the Pirates leading 2-1, Blass ran into major difficulties. Chris Speier reached on a leadoff single, before Blass retired both Perry and Ken Henderson. With Willie Mays and Willie McCovey waiting on deck, Blass realized the urgency of retiring Tito Fuentes. The singles-hitting second baseman had drawn a mere total of 18 walks and managed only four home runs during the season. Blass threw Fuentes a slider below the knees—out of the strike zone. Fuentes muscled up on the stray slider, lifting a fly ball over the outstretched leap of Clemente, and over the screen fence in right field. Disconcerted by the unlikely home run, Blass proceeded to walk Mays on four pitches, and then served up another two-run homer to McCovey.

The Pirates, now trailing by three runs, would draw closer in the top of the seventh. A two-run single by Al Oliver made it a one-run deficit. But Gaylord Perry would allow the Pirates no more. Exhibiting pinpoint control, Perry went to a three-ball count only once during the Giants' 5-4 victory.

Having lost six straight games at Candlestick Park, some of the Pirates began questioning their ability to beat the Giants. That group did not include Clemente. "We'll win this and the World Series," Clemente confidently told Al Abrams of the *Pittsburgh Post-Gazette.* "You just wait and see."

The loss in Game One did apply more pressure to Game Two starter Dock Ellis, who had placed himself in the midst of controversy by criticizing Pirate management for providing players with poor accommodations at San Francisco's Jack Tar Hotel. Ellis opposed southpaw John Cumberland, who found an immediate nemesis in slugging first baseman Bob Robertson. In his first at-bat, Robertson delivered a double. In his second at-bat, Robertson sliced a Cumberland delivery down the right field line. Dave Kingman raced to the foul line, leapt for the ball, and appeared to make an impressive circus catch. But as Kingman crashed into the foul pole, the impact of the collision knocked the ball out of his glove and over the fence in *fair* territory. Robertson's unconventional solo blast tied the game at 2-2.

In the sixth inning, with the Pirates now leading 4-2, the Giants loaded the bases with one out. Bob Miller, who relieved Dock Ellis on the mound, struck out Tito Fuentes. With two outs, the dangerous Willie Mays stepped to the plate. Mays lashed a line drive into right-center field. At first glance, the ball appeared ready to split the gap, potentially clearing the bases. Suddenly, Clemente caught up with the ball, spearing it with his glove hand.

Clemente would not have made the play, if not for his last-second decision to move five steps to his right. "It's a good thing he did, because if he had to go five yards more, he wouldn't have made the play," an appreciative Danny Murtaugh told Bill Christine of the *Pittsburgh Press.* "The great ones have that instinct about where to play."

As Bill Mazeroski would say of Clemente in a 1972 interview with Phil Musick: "He is a thinking outfielder. Some guys go to a particular spot for a particular hitter and stay there. Clemente doesn't. He adjusts to the situation each time a guy comes to the plate and then readjusts with the count."

In the seventh inning, with the Bucs still owning a 4-2 lead, Bob Robertson faced left-hander Ron Bryant. With two runners aboard, Robertson launched a high drive over the left field fence. The three-run clout blew the game open, giving the Pirates a 7-2 advantage. Robertson came to bat a final time in the ninth inning. With the Bucs leading 8-2, Robertson smacked a slider from Steve Hamilton, yet another left-hander, over the wall in left-center field. Robertson's unforeseen power barrage—three home runs and five RBIs—had suddenly launched him into national prominence and tied the series at a game apiece.

After a day off for travel, the Pirates and Giants resumed the best-of-five series at Three Rivers Stadium. Giants' skipper Charlie Fox turned to longtime ace Juan Marichal, who had forged a record of 25-10 vs. the Pirates during his brilliant career. Danny Murtaugh decided to counter with Nellie Briles, who had pitched impressively as a starter down the stretch. Unfortunately, Briles re-aggravated his hamstring while warming up just before the scheduled start of the game. The veteran right-hander reluctantly informed Murtaugh that he could not pitch.

As a result of Briles' honest admission, Murtaugh was forced to dip further into his bullpen for a starter. The Irishman quickly decided on hard-throwing right-hander Bob Johnson. For the first time in the short history of the Championship Series, the umpires delayed the start of a game to allow a pitcher to throw extra warm-up tosses in the bullpen.

Working on short notice, Johnson pitched brilliantly. The right-hander overcame several rough spots, including a key situation early in the game. Willie McCovey and Bobby Bonds started the second inning by reaching on back-to-back singles. Johnson responded by striking out Dick Dietz, retiring Alan Gallagher on a groundout, and fanning Chris Speier.

The Pirates dented Marichal for an early run when Bob Robertson continued his longball deluge with a solo home run. The 1-0 lead stood up until the sixth inning, when Johnson and the Pirates' defense began to falter. Ken Henderson led off with a single and headed for second when Tito Fuentes dropped a bunt down the third base line. On the play, Richie Hebner tried to lead Dave Cash with the throw to first base, but ended up tossing the ball down the right field line. Henderson raced home on the overthrow, scoring the tying run. Fuentes moved up to second base. With no one out, Johnson now prepared to face the middle of the

Giants' order: Willie Mays, Willie McCovey and Bobby Bonds. Mays, the No. 3 hitter in the lineup, opted for some unconventional strategy when he attempted to lay down a sacrifice bunt. Mays punched the ball a few feet in front of home plate, where Pirate catcher Manny Sanguillen nabbed the ball quickly, held Fuentes at second base, and threw to Bob Robertson at first to nail Mays. With one out, Murtaugh ordered Johnson to intentionally walk McCovey. Johnson then struck out Bonds for the inning's second out. After a walk to Dick Dietz, Johnson retired Alan Gallagher on a routine grounder to Jackie Hernandez at shortstop.

In the bottom of the eighth inning, Marichal retired Vic Davalillo—the pinch-hitter for Johnson—and leadoff man Dave Cash. With two outs and no one aboard, Richie Hebner stepped to the plate. The lefty-hitting Hebner reached out for a Marichal pitch and lifted it toward the right field stands. Bobby Bonds raced to the warning track and set himself to make a leaping grab. Bonds jumped, but the ball eluded his outstretched glove by a scant six inches and sailed into the bleachers. Hebner's home run gave the Pirates a 2-1 lead—and eventually their second win of the series. The Pirates were now within one victory of their first World Series appearance since the magical summer of 1960.

After the game, reporters questioned Willie Mays about the sacrifice bunt he had attempted to lay down in the sixth inning. Mays defended the strategy. "If it's anybody but Juan [Marichal] or [Gaylord] Perry pitching, I hit," Mays explained to the *New York Daily News*. "But the way Juan is pitching, I didn't think they'd get many runs off him." When a reporter asked Clemente about the wisdom of bunting in such a situation, he defended Mays' unusual decision as sound strategy.

The fourth game of the National League Championship Series, set for October 6, offered up a rematch of Game One starters: Steve Blass and Gaylord Perry. Blass, who had struggled in the first game, continued to pitch poorly in Game Four. He surrendered a run on three singles and an error in the first inning. Clemente helped Blass in the bottom half of the inning, driving home Dave Cash and Richie Hebner to put the Pirates ahead by a run.

Unable to sustain the momentum established by Clemente, Blass served up a home run to Chris Speier and a one-out single to Ken Henderson. Tito Fuentes then lofted a catchable fly ball to left-center field. Willie Stargell and Al Oliver mis-communicated, allowing the ball to drop in, while putting runners on first and second.

Blass then retired Willie Mays on a pop-up. With two outs, Blass faced his nemesis, Willie McCovey. The Giants' first baseman rocked a fastball deep into the right field stands. The three-run homer gave the Giants a 5-2 lead.

With Blass having failed, the Pirates' offense responded with championship resiliency in the bottom half of the second. After a single by Manny Sanguillen and a fielder's choice, Danny Murtaugh decided to pinch-hit for Blass. Nineteen-sixty World Series hero Bill Mazeroski responded with a first-pitch single, putting runners on first and second. Richie Hebner followed with his second post-season home run, a three-run shot, which knotted the game.

With the game tied at 5-5, Bruce Kison emerged from the Pirate bullpen. The 21-year-old right-hander, making his first post-season appearance ever, turned in a brilliant performance. Kison hurled four and two-thirds innings of shutout relief, keeping the game even until the bottom of the sixth. In the meantime, Gaylord Perry recovered to match Kison with three straight scoreless innings.

In the bottom of the sixth, Clemente broke the deadlock with his third RBI of the day, a solid single that scored leadoff man Dave Cash. Giants' manager Charlie Fox lifted Perry, summoning right-hander Jerry Johnson. After a passed ball allowed Clemente to advance to second, Fox ordered Johnson to intentionally walk Willie Stargell and pitch to another left-handed batter, Al Oliver. The Pirates center fielder drove a Johnson offering on a line toward the right field stands, pushing Bobby Bonds to the fence. Bonds watched helplessly as the ball sailed into the bleachers. The Pirates now enjoyed a 9-5 lead.

Kison remained in the game to start the seventh, but soon gave way to Dave Giusti. Two and a third innings later, Giusti closed out a 9-5 win over the National League West champions. The Pirates—and Clemente—were headed back to the World Series for the first time in 11 seasons.

The hitting of Clemente, coupled with the slugging of Bob Robertson and tablesetting of Dave Cash, had compensated for the Championship Series struggles of Willie Stargell. The Giants had pitched carefully to the Pirates' leading power hitter throughout the series, as evidenced by two intentional walks and a hit-by-pitch. Stargell had gone 0-for-14 against Giant pitching and had failed to drive in a single run.

Clemente batted .333 in the four-game playoff, driving in four runs. In Game Four, Clemente had enjoyed his finest offensive game of the series, picking up two singles and three RBIs in the clinching victory. While Clemente was glad that he had contributed to the pennant, he bemoaned his physical condition. "I am happy, very happy, but I am not myself," Roberto told Harold Kaese of the *Boston Globe*. "I am not swinging [well], because my back is hurt. How many times do you see me strike out three times in a game?" The performance left Clemente, ever the perfectionist, unsatisfied.

Clemente also made some intriguing remarks about Giants' star Willie Mays, who had batted a mediocre .267 during the play-off series. "The man is the best player I ever saw in my whole life," Clemente told sportswriter Jack Chevalier, "but he is 40 and has had his days. Sure I like for him to do good, but you know he is tired." Clemente went on to discuss the comparisons that fans and writers had made between him and Mays during their long National League careers. One reporter asked Clemente why Mays had always received a higher level of recognition. "Willie Mays is an American," Clemente said pointedly. "I am an American, but I am [also] a Puerto Rican. That is the difference. A Puerto Rican player will never be the idol that an American player is."

For much of their careers, fans and writers debated who was the better player, Mays or Clemente. A survey of objective baseball observers—if there is such a thing—would likely yield a vote heavily in favor of Mays. Although Clemente possessed the speed to play center field, and could have stolen more bases had he desired, the fact remains that Mays *did* do both. Mays played center field, the most demanding of the outfield positions, and stole far more bases— 338 for Mays, compared with Clemente's total of 83. Mays hit with far more power, drove in more runs, and drew more walks—all by large margins over Clemente.

The perception, however, that Mays was a *far* better player than Clemente may be exaggerated. Clemente's baserunning matched the daring standards set by Mays. Clemente was a better hitter for average (.317 to .302), and possessed a superior throwing arm—perhaps the best in history. While Mays played on two more pennant winners, Clemente contributed to more divisional champions and World Series winning teams. Mays played in two Championship Series and on one world championship club, while Clemente visited the playoffs three times and earned two World Series rings. Clemente may have also forged a stronger clubhouse presence, as evidenced by the considerable influence he held on teammates during the latter stages of his career.

After the playoff win, Pirate owner John Galbreath approached Clemente in the clubhouse and personally thanked him for his playoff contribution. While most of the other Pirate players openly celebrated by dousing each other with champagne, Clemente elected not to take part in that post-series tradition. A reporter asked him why? "That's OK for some of the younger fellows," the elder statesman of the Pirates told Milton Richman of UPI. Dave Giusti, who frequently targeted Clemente with friendly agitation, prepared to spray him with a beer. The right fielder called him off. "No, no, I got bad eye," said Clemente, who decided to apply the needle to his friend and teammate. "Get out, Italian," Clemente shouted to Giusti. "You know I don't like Italian people." Even a serious professional like Clemente could hand out good-natured racial humor at the appropriate time. A few moments later, the strapping Bob Veale lifted Clemente onto his shoulders and carried him into the showers. Giusti clapped his hands in approval.

In 1960, Clemente had drawn widespread criticism when he elected not to participate in the clubhouse celebration after the seventh game of the World Series. Eleven years after leaving his teammates during their post-Series party, Clemente remained quiet and reflective, but now felt comfortable showing his lighter side to teammates. Yet, his reserved behavior continued to prevent him from being acknowledged as one of the game's great all-round players—either by the media or by fans outside of the Pittsburgh area. Clemente would soon alter national recognition of his stardom— not by the spoken word, but through three things that meant much more to him: the bat, the glove and the arm.

20

Clemente's Showcase

Based on the consensus of the writers, the four-game Championship Series win over the Giants represented the high point of the Pirates' season. After all, Pittsburgh's World Series opposition would be provided by the Baltimore Orioles, the defending world champions. The Birds had fashioned the best record in either league during the regular season, compiling a mark of 101-57. The O's had won the American League East and the Championship Series in a runaway.

The Orioles featured an incredible array of four 20-game winners, who had combined for 81 wins against only 31 losses. How could the Pirates possibly beat a balanced pitching staff that featured right-handers Jim Palmer and Pat Dobson, and left-handers Mike Cuellar and Dave McNally? Conversely, how could the Pirates' pitching staff handle a Baltimore offense that showcased the powerful bats of Boog Powell, Frank and Brooks Robinson, Merv Rettenmund and Dave Johnson? Lastly, the Orioles' defense, anchored by the left side infield combination of Brooks Robinson and Mark Belanger, provided opposing offenses with few "second-chance" opportunities to score runs.

Las Vegas oddsmakers, at seven to five, made the Orioles considerable favorites to win the Series. One particularly sarcastic scribe predicted Baltimore would win in *three* games, an obvious impossibility. In addition to their overwhelming edge in talent on paper, the Orioles enjoyed the advantage of momentum. The O's had won their last 11 consecutive regular season games, and had swept aside the Oakland A's three games to none in the American League Championship Series. These were the same A's who featured two 20-game winners in Catfish Hunter and American League MVP Vida Blue, two terrific relief pitchers in Rollie Fingers and Mudcat Grant, and an everyday lineup that included the talents of Sal Bando, Campy Campaneris and Reggie Jackson.

The oddsmakers might have made the Orioles even stronger favorites had they known about the physical condition of Roberto Clemente. After the World Series, Clemente would inform reporters that he had eaten some bad shellfish in Baltimore the night before Game One. "I never got so sick in my life," Clemente told Milton Richman of UPI. "I told my wife, 'I'm dizzy, my chest is sore, and I feel terrible. Call the doctor.'" As Roberto and Vera waited for the doctor to arrive, Clemente became nauseous and began throwing up. "I kept vomiting and I never did that before in my life," Clemente told Richman. "When the doctor came, I told him I didn't want anybody to know I was sick. I knew what everybody would say. 'Same old Clemente. Complaining again.' The doctor examined me. He said it was food poisoning." As a result of Clemente's bout with the disagreeable seafood, he would play the first game of the Series with a queasy stomach and a persistent feeling of nausea.

Regardless of his health, Clemente felt as if he would have to carry more of the offensive load for the Pirates during the World Series. The night before the World Series, Clemente and Willie Stargell rode the hotel elevator to their rooms. Nellie King, having also boarded the elevator car, listened in as the team's two stars chatted. One sentence, in particular, caught King's attention. "I will carry the team," Clemente calmly said to Stargell.

Concerned that Stargell, the team's best home run hitter, had fallen into a slump at just the wrong time, Clemente felt a heightened sense of urgency. He also realized that Stargell was playing in his first Fall Classic—a nerve-wracking experience—something that Clemente had done 11 seasons earlier against the Yankees. "I'm going to have to sacrifice myself to hit the long ball," Clemente confided to Manny Sanguillen, his best friend on the Pirates. Clemente usually approached his at-bats by trying to bang line drives to all fields, especially the gaps in left and right-center field. Clemente was now willing to expand his game to include the consistent threat of the home run—a testament to his greatness as a player.

Clemente knew he would have to play supremely to help the Pirates beat a talented team like the Orioles, but he tired of hearing stories of Baltimore's superiority. "You don't see the Baltimore players popping off," Clemente complained to several writers near the batting cage. "It's the writers that put that stuff in the paper. You read that Baltimore's better this way, better that way—in other words, we shouldn't be here."

Even the citizens of Baltimore subjected Clemente to tales of Oriole dominance. "I remember going to the park in a cab before the Series began," Clemente told Charley Feeney of the *Pittsburgh Post-Gazette*. "The cab driver—he drive me crazy. He kept saying how great the Orioles were. He got me so mad that I started arguing with him. I know he didn't know what he was talking about, but I argue with him anyway."

The boastful cab driver dropped Clemente off at Baltimore's Memorial Stadium, where the World Series would open on a Saturday afternoon. The Orioles' home field possessed a particular quirk that figured to bother at least a few of the Pirate hitters, who had not played in the pitcher-friendly ballpark. In the daytime, a white frame house located beyond the center field fence provided an unsuitable hitting background, the white baseball dissolving into the similar shading of the house. The backdrop figured to be especially troublesome whenever tall right-hander Jim Palmer, who released the ball from the top of an overhand motion that seemingly merged with the white house, made an appearance in the Series.

One obstacle after another loomed for the Pirates. The impending matchup seemed so one-sided that Baltimore may have been tempted to relax—except for one reason. The Orioles' brass had major concerns about pitching to Clemente. "Roberto Clemente's weakness, whatever little he has, is so close to his strength that you are always in danger," Baltimore superscout Jim Russo warned the Orioles' pitchers in his pre-Series briefing. "There's only one way to pitch to him, and that's low and away, but he's going to make you throw strikes on that part of the plate. If you make a mistake, he's going to hit it out of sight to right field."

Dave McNally would become the first Oriole pitcher to concern himself with Clemente. Baltimore skipper Earl Weaver selected the left-hander to pitch Game One, surprising some observers who had considered Jim Palmer the more logical selection. McNally did lead the staff with 21 wins, despite spending 38 days on the disabled list with a strained elbow. Yet, second-guessers deemed him a curious choice to pitch the first game of the Series given that Palmer, the staff ace and team leader in ERA among starters, had not pitched since Game One of the American League playoffs and was well-rested. In the meantime, Danny Murtaugh called upon his most talented pitcher, the oft-ailing Dock Ellis.

Early in Game One, McNally struggled with his control. In the top of the second inning, Bob Robertson led off with a walk and advanced to second on a wild pitch that skidded past Baltimore catcher Elrod Hendricks. Manny Sanguillen followed by hitting a ground ball to Mark Belanger at shortstop. When Robertson foolishly tried to advance to third, Belanger fired in the direction of Brooks Robinson. Fortunately for the Pirates, Belanger's throw struck Robertson in the helmet and caromed into the Orioles' dugout. The errant throw enabled Robertson to score the first run of the Series, and allowed Sanguillen to move up to second base. After Jose Pagan's slow roller advanced Sanguillen to third base, Jackie Hernandez laid down an attempted squeeze bunt. McNally fielded the ball quickly but his throw eluded Hendricks, who claimed he never saw the ball. McNally then retired Dock Ellis, but surrendered a run-scoring single to Dave Cash. Thanks to unusually porous infield play by the Orioles, the Pirates enjoyed a charitable 3-0 lead.

The Orioles managed to cut the lead in the bottom of the second inning, when Frank Robinson reached Ellis for a leadoff home run. Yet, the Orioles' major concern continued to be McNally's mystifying and sudden lack of control. At the start of the third inning, McNally allowed a leadoff single to Clemente and committed the mistake of walking the lefty-swinging Stargell. That brought the dangerous right-handed bat of Bob Robertson to the plate. Earl Weaver seemed to be considering a switch to his bullpen, but stayed with his struggling left-hander. McNally justified his manager's faith by fanning Robertson, striking out Sanguillen, and inducing Jose Pagan into an inning-ending fly ball to Don Buford in left.

McNally's sudden change in fortune seemed to ignite the Orioles' offense. In the bottom half of the inning, Mark Belanger and Don Buford sandwiched singles around a McNally strikeout, bringing Merv Rettenmund to the plate. Dock Ellis tried to paint the outside corner with a breaking ball, but left the pitch too far inside. Rettenmund jumped on the mistake and powered the ball over the fence in left-center field for a three-run home run, giving the Orioles an instant 4-3 lead. Concerned by Ellis' inability to command his breaking pitches, Danny Murtaugh walked to the mound and signaled for the bullpen. The Orioles later added an insurance tally in the bottom of the fifth inning, giving the resurgent McNally a two-run advantage.

From the third through the ninth innings, McNally dominated the Pirates, retiring 19 consecutive batters. A throwing error by Mark Belanger ended the string, but McNally recovered to retire Jose Pagan on a fly ball and pinch-hitter Al Oliver on a game-ending strikeout. The heavily favored Orioles, after trailing by three runs, had taken the first game of the World Series, 5-3.

Game Two of the Series was scheduled for Sunday, October 10, but was postponed because of a rainstorm that dropped two-and-a-half inches of precipitation on Baltimore. The inclement weather produced the first rainout of a World Series game since 1962. After some debate, the Orioles and Pirates agreed to reschedule the second game for the following afternoon.

The weather turned sunny and breezy in Baltimore on Monday, with temperatures hovering near the 60-degree mark. The rain left the Memorial Stadium playing surface soggy in certain spots, especially in the outfield.

Danny Murtaugh's made a surprising choice for Game Two, calling upon Bob Johnson to start over a rested Steve Blass. Johnson, who had pitched so well as an emergency starter for Nellie Briles in the playoffs, retired the Orioles in order in the first inning. In the second, a Frank Robinson single, an Elrod Hendricks walk and a Brooks Robinson single produced the Orioles' first run. In the fourth inning, Johnson unraveled completely. He surrendered a single to Frank Robinson, hit Hendricks on the ankle with a pitch, walked Brooks Robinson and yielded a two-run single to Dave Johnson.

With his Pirates down 3-0, Murtaugh summoned 21-year-old Bruce Kison from the bullpen. Kison proceeded to walk both the weak-hitting Mark Belanger and the pitcher, Jim Palmer, before retiring Don Buford on a fly-out. The Pirates now trailed the Orioles, 4-0.

In the fifth inning, Murtaugh turned to Bob Moose, and watched the move produce disastrous results. Six singles, two walks and a Pirate fielding error contributed to six more runs and a runaway lead of 10-0. The outburst, the prelude to an 11-3 final, confirmed the Pirates' worst fears about their own pitching staff and the sheer dominance of the Orioles in all aspects of the game.

Even the playing field at Baltimore had posed problems for the Pirates, especially Clemente. In Game Two, Clemente had struggled to find Mark Belanger's fly ball, which caromed off his glove and then his knee. After the defeat in the second game, Clemente cited the poor lighting of Baltimore's Memorial Stadium. "You cannot see the ball in the outfield. You can't see where it's going when they hit it in the air," Clemente told Charley Feeney of the *Pittsburgh Post-Gazette.* Clemente also criticized the condition of the outfield grass. "When they hit it on the ground, you cannot charge it. You have to watch the ditches." Considering both the lighting and the outfield surface subpar, Clemente called Memorial Stadium the "worst field I've played on in the major leagues." In fact, Clemente regarded it as no better than a minor league facility. "This is not a big league ballpark," said a frustrated Clemente.

A rainy summer in Baltimore, coupled with a series of exhibition and regular season NFL games at Memorial Stadium, had left the playing surface in less than ideal condition for the World Series. Although Clemente insisted that he was not blaming the Pirate losses on the playing surface, the timing of his remarks created that distinct impression. At least some of the Orioles thought so. Yet, in fairness to Clemente, he had also criticized Memorial Stadium prior to the start of the Series. "Go out there and see how bad the field is," Clemente had told a group of writers during pre-Series batting practice.

The Pirates, however, could hardly blame their two-game Series deficit on Clemente. At the plate, Clemente had rapped out four base hits in nine at-bats. He had collected a single and a double in the first game, matching the production with another single and double in Game Two.

Clemente's fielding ranked as no less impressive. Despite his problems with the Memorial Stadium turf, Roberto had made one of the greatest throws in baseball history during Game Two. With no one out in the fifth inning and speedy Merv Rettenmund on second base, Frank Robinson had lofted a fly ball down the right field line. Even if caught, the fly ball seemed like it would easily advance Rettenmund to third. Clemente raced to the line and snared the ball in full motion, with his momentum pushing him completely away from the direction of second base. Once Clemente gloved the ball, he stopped immediately, spun himself around completely, planted his right foot, and fired the ball on one hop toward third base. Running hard from the moment of the catch, the fleet-footed Rettenmund slid into third base, just as Richie Hebner applied a sweeping tag. Third base umpire Jim Odom ruled Rettenmund safe—the proper call—but Clemente had somehow made it a close play.

Given the context of the game, the play was meaningless. The Orioles would score six runs in the inning, on their way to an embarrassingly one-sided victory. Clemente hadn't even thrown out Rettenmund at third base. Yet, Clemente's throw was so startling that Orioles' catcher Andy Etchebarren felt moved enough to call it "the greatest throw I ever saw by an outfielder." Having seen opposing right fielders like Detroit's Al Kaline and Cleveland's Rocky Colavito, men who possessed howitzer right arms, Etchebarren had witnessed a collection of fine throws over the course of his career. Yet, none had left such an impression as the off-balance, foul line-to-third base heave by "The Great One."

The throw stunned Rettenmund, too. "At that time, I could really run—I was one of the fastest guys on our team," Rettenmund told *Inside Sports* in 1997. "I was running hard and I shouldn't have even had to slide." As Rettenmund approached third base, he saw base coach Billy Hunter signaling him to "get down" on the play. "That's not supposed to happen," Rettenmund explained. "It's a play that, as you see it developing, you usually just tag and go to third. I was safe, barely. I remember saying, 'Wow! How did he do that?'"

Clemente's throw involved unusual torque and athleticism, considering the momentum of his body driving him toward the right field line. Yet, Clemente claimed the throw could have been better—if not for a sore shoulder that had been bothering him since July. "If I have my good arm," Clemente told Dick Young of the *New York Daily News,* "the ball gets there a little quicker than he [Rettenmund] gets there." A scary thought.

Clemente claimed repeatedly that he played much of the later stages of his career with an arm that was not nearly as strong as it had been during his first few seasons. Injuries—such as bone chips in his elbow and recurrent shoulder soreness—had taken their toll.

For that reason, Clemente did his best to preserve his throwing arm. Unlike most other outfielders, he did not take warm-up tosses prior to games. And after making catches with no one on base, he usually threw the ball with a lazy underhand motion, softly looping the ball back toward the infield. He put as little stress on his arm whenever possible, unleashing powerful throws only in important game situations. When he did make meaningful throws, he sometimes used such force that he ended up hurtling himself to the ground face-first after releasing the ball.

As stunning as the throw against Rettenmund was, it was probably not Clemente's best. Once, while playing in old Forbes Field, Clemente had made a throw from the iron gate in right field to home plate on a fly. Estimated distance? Four hundred and twenty feet. Other Pirate witnesses pointed to a play against the Cardinals, which ironically involved an error by Clemente. He had allowed a ground single by Tim McCarver to go through his legs, enabling Orlando Cepeda to advance from first to third. With his back turned to the infield, Clemente retrieved the ball on the warning track in deep right-center field, spun, and fired the ball on the fly to Jerry May at home plate. May applied the tag to a stunned Cepeda.

Other than cloning Clemente, what plan did Pirate manager Danny Murtaugh have to engineer a turnaround for his team, which was suddenly on the brink of World Series extinction? When pressed on the issue, Murtaugh offered a philosophical and typically humble response. "The leader of any team in professional sports has to play an important part in its success," Murtaugh told a reporter from *Sports Illustrated*. "Every manager must realize what his ball club needs. We are all equal in this knowledge. [But] We all make about the same moves. Eventually it is a question of strength."

Game Three offered the solace of Three Rivers Stadium, where the artificial turf ensured a minimum of bad hops for Clemente in right field. More importantly, the faster surface aided the slashing, line-driving hitting style of the Pirates, and played counter to the slower, plodding attack of the Orioles. Home field also enabled the Pirates to resurrect one of the greats from their past. Hall of Fame third baseman Pie Traynor threw out the ceremonial first pitch to the ring of a discernibly loud standing ovation. The crowd of better than 50,000 appeared ready to provide the Bucs with some much needed emotional support against the seemingly unbeatable Orioles.

In reality, the Pirates' hopes rested not so much on the crowd, but on skinny right-hander Steve Blass, who had followed up an impressive regular season with two subpar pitching lines in the playoffs. Blass held the Orioles hitless until the fifth inning, when Brooks Robinson looped a single to left field. More importantly, Blass kept the O's scoreless until the seventh, when he hung a slider to Frank Robinson, who homered into the second tier of the left field stands.

The Pirates, however, had already done some significant offensive damage. In the first inning, Dave Cash doubled down the left field line and moved to third on Al Oliver's ground ball to Boog Powell. On the play, the burly first baseman tried to toss to Mike Cuellar covering at first, but his throw sailed wide, allowing Oliver to reach safely. With the Orioles' infield playing back, Clemente bounced a routine grounder to Dave Johnson, the apparent beginnings of a double play. Johnson threw to Mark Belanger for the force at second, erasing Oliver as Cash crossed the plate. Belanger relayed to first—too late to nab the hustling Clemente, whose RBI gave the Pirates a 1-0 lead. "I don't care if you have one leg, somehow you run," Clemente told Roy McHugh of the *Pittsburgh Press*. "When you play in the World Series, nothing bother you."

In the seventh, with the Pirates now leading 2-1 on a Jose Pagan RBI single, Clemente once again displayed how great baserunning can be achieved through sheer hustle. Leading off the inning, Clemente tapped a routine comebacker toward Cuellar. While many batters would have conceded the out, Clemente ran hard from the outset. After initially bobbling the grounder, Cuellar fielded the ball slightly off balance in front of the mound. Noticing Clemente's full sprint toward first base, Cuellar hurried his throw to Boog Powell. Cuellar's hasty reaction resulted in a slightly errant toss, which pulled Powell off the bag. Shockingly, Clemente was safe at first base. A routine pitcher-to-first-putout had become an error on Cuellar—and had resulted in the leadoff batter reaching first base.

"I remember him hitting a routine ground ball back to the pitcher at some stage in the Series, and it should have been the most routine of outs," says Bowie Kuhn, who was watching the game at Three Rivers Stadium. "But there was something about Clemente, his enormous hustle and dash that caused the pitcher to rush the throw, and he made a bad throw and Clemente reached first base. It was pure dynamism on his part to have accomplished that. And I'm not certain that any other player wouldn't have been thrown out routinely, as he should have been. I remember sitting in my box; we all said, 'Only Clemente would have gotten on base with that.'" For those adult Pirate fans with capable memories, the play was strangely reminiscent of Clemente's eighth inning infield single in Game Seven of the 1960 World Series against the Yankees.

Perhaps shaken by his fielding miscue, Cuellar walked Willie Stargell, putting Pirate runners at first and second with no one out. Cuellar now prepared to face Robertson, and ran the count to one-and-one. Danny Murtaugh, noticing that Brooks Robinson was playing deep at third, signaled to Frank Oceak, his third base coach. At first, Oceak couldn't believe the sign, which called for the hulking Robertson to lay down a sacrifice bunt. "I wanted to see how the Baltimore defense was playing," Murtaugh explained to the *New York Daily News.* "When they kept Brooks back after Cuellar got a ball and a strike, I gave the sign."

Leading off second base, a surprised and uncertain Clemente waved his arms frantically in an attempt to call time. He wanted to confirm that Oceak had indeed signaled for Robertson, who almost never bunted, to lay down the sacrifice. Or maybe, Clemente thought to himself, Oceak had called for the hit-and-run. To Clemente's frustration, home plate umpire Jim Odom failed to grant the time-out, as Cuellar delivered one of his trademark screwballs to the plate. Strangely, Robertson did not square his body into bunting position. Instead, Robertson unleashed a full uppercut swing at the Cuellar offering. Robertson drove the ball deep toward the opposite field. Several seconds later, the ball landed in a section of stands over the 385-foot sign in right-center field.

Robertson greeted both Stargell and Clemente at home plate, ready to celebrate his three-run homer. At that point, Stargell whispered to Robertson, "That's the way to bunt the ball." For the first time, Robertson realized that he had missed the bunt sign. The first baseman jogged back to the dugout and turned to Murtaugh, saying sheepishly, "I guess I fouled it up, huh?" Murtaugh responded in classic deadpan. "Possibly," said the ever-calm manager. "But under the circumstances, there will be no fine." The bunt-turned-home run had given Blass and the Bucs a comfortable 5-1 lead in the late innings. Blass would finish off the Orioles with scoreless work in the eighth and ninth.

After the game, Robertson chided himself for missing the sign from third base coach Frank Oceak. "I should've been fined,"

Robertson told Murray Chass of the *New York Times.* "Being in this situation, the World Series, you're not supposed to miss signs." Robertson's mistake had translated into an unexpected benefit for the Pirates. "The way things turned out, I'm glad I did miss it."

Robertson says that Cuellar may have been distracted by the presence of Clemente, an aggressive and daring runner, on the basepaths. "I stepped in there and Cuellar, he was checking the runner at second, which was Clemente," Robertson recalls. "And his first pitch he threw me a screwball and I hit it out to right-center a long ways. I was going around the bases and I touched home plate and I shook Clemente's hand."

Robertson's home run ensured the Pirate victory, which ended a 16-game winning streak for the Orioles, dating back to the final month of the regular season. Although Robertson was clearly and deservedly the hero of Game Three, Clemente's subtle play against Cuellar had set up the big inning for the Pirates. "It all began with Clemente hustling to first," said National League MVP Joe Torre, who watched the game from a box seat at Three Rivers Stadium. Although he played for one of the Pirates' rivals—the Cardinals—Torre appreciated the virtues of Clemente's consistent all-out effort.

Clemente's hard dash to first base typified the style of play that had been noted by a clinical psychologist three years earlier. "No one drives himself like Clemente," Dr. Thomas Tutko had told David Wolf of *Life* magazine after working with the Pirates in spring training of 1968. "I've never seen a more intense player. If Clemente were a football player, he'd make Ray Nitschke look like a pussycat."

In addition to setting the tone for the rest of the inning and eventually scoring on Robertson's home run, Clemente had also banged out a hit and driven in a run of his own. *New York Daily News* sports columnist Dick Young raved about Clemente's play in the first three games of the Series. "The best damn ballplayer in the World Series, maybe in the whole world, is Roberto Clemente," Young wrote. "As far as I'm concerned they can give him the automobile right now [for winning the World Series MVP award]. Maybe some guys hit the ball farther, and some throw it harder, and one or two run faster, although I doubt that, but nobody puts it all together like Roberto."

As they prepared for Game Four, the Pirates faced another critical match-up. Apart from being an essential game for the Bucs, the fourth game also represented a groundbreaking piece of baseball history—the first night game in World Series play. Prior to Game Four, all 397 World Series games had been played in the daytime, dating back to the first Series in 1903. The decision to make Game Four a nighttime affair was largely motivated by NBC-TV. The network felt it could attract a larger viewing audience by experimenting with a weeknight telecast, as opposed to a mid-afternoon broadcast, when most adults were preoccupied with work and children were in school. With an expanded television audience, more people would have a chance to watch Clemente play in what was becoming a brilliant Series.

A Pittsburgh-record crowd of 51,378 turned up at Three Rivers to witness baseball's break with one of its longest-standing traditions. Gametime conditions—72-degree temperatures and calm winds—provided an ideal backdrop for the first World Series night game. Even the forecast, which called for a 30 percent chance of rain, did little to harm the festive atmosphere at Three Rivers. Hall of Famer Stan Musial, a native of nearby Donora, Pennsylvania, threw out the ceremonial first pitch. Commissioner Bowie Kuhn and famed entertainer Bing Crosby, a part-owner of the Pirates, gathered around the former Cardinal standout, as baseball prepared to show off its best teams in a national, prime-time spotlight.

The history-making nature of the game overshadowed Danny Murtaugh's pitching choice. Murtaugh announced that enigmatic left-hander Luke Walker would pitch Game Four. Dock Ellis seemed like the most logical selection, but Murtaugh bypassed the controversial right-hander, whose elbow pain had contributed to his weak performance in Game One.

Walker pitched poorly—and briefly—in Game Four. The young left-hander made only 22 pitches and failed to escape a disastrous first-inning jam. Walker allowed a leadoff single to center fielder Paul Blair, and then endured back-to-back infield hits by Mark Belanger and Merv Rettenmund. A passed ball by the usually sure-handed Manny Sanguillen allowed Blair to score from third, while the other runners moved into scoring position. After Walker issued a free pass to Frank Robinson, Brooks Robinson and Boog Powell delivered sacrifice flies to give the Orioles a 3-0 lead. Having seen enough from Walker, Murtaugh brought in side-arming right-hander Bruce Kison to face Dave Johnson. The Orioles' second baseman pounded a routine grounder to Richie Hebner, ending the uprising, but the Pirates already faced a three-run hole. The Bucs seemed well on their way to a deficit of three games to one in the Series.

Pittsburgh's offense prepared to face right-hander Pat Dobson, who, like Walker, had not pitched in the post-season. Because Dobson had not worked in a game since September 28, the Pirates hoped that the 20-game winner had lost his sharp control. Smartly, leadoff man Dave Cash patiently worked out a walk, but remained at first base when Dobson retired Hebner and Clemente. With two outs, Willie Stargell drove a ringing double into right-center field, scoring Cash from first base for the Pirates' first run. Al Oliver then blooped a fly ball into short center field. Paul Blair raced in quickly and attempted a diving catch. Although an excellent defensive center fielder, Blair missed the ball, which bounced over his head for a double. Stargell scored easily from second to give the Pirates their second run.

In the top of the second inning, Kison retired Andy Etchebarren on a grounder to Dave Cash at second, and then struck out his pitching counterpart, Dobson. With two outs, Paul Blair looped a double into right-center field, beyond the reach of Clemente. Unbelievably, Blair's extra-base blooper would represent the Orioles' last hit of the game.

The Pirates continued their comeback in the bottom half of the third inning, but not before a controversial call that went against them. With one out, Richie Hebner grounded a single up the middle. Clemente then lined the first pitch from Dobson down the right field line. The slicing liner caromed off the wall and back into the field of play. Believing that the ball was fair, Pirate players climbed to the top step of the first base dugout and jumped in the air. Then, to their surprise, right field umpire John Rice ruled that the ball had gone foul. Clemente and first base coach Don Leppert ran toward Rice and argued that the ball had hit the wall in fair territory. "Fair ball," Leppert screamed over and over. "It hit the right hand corner of the foul line."

Many hitters might have allowed the frustration of a lost double to damage their concentration at the plate. Brimming with anger, they might have discarded the at-bat as a lost cause. Not Clemente, who returned to home plate with his usual determination. Moments later, Clemente lined another ball to right field—this one clearly fair—in front of Frank Robinson. The base hit advanced Hebner to second base. Al Oliver then delivered the game-tying run with another line-drive single to right field. Ultimately, the questionable call had not hurt the Pirates, largely due to the persistence of the focused Clemente.

In the fifth inning, Clemente once again flashed his daring baserunning skills. With one out, he lashed a ground single up the middle. Stargell followed with another grounder that eluded Dobson and headed toward center field. Never hesitating, Clemente decided to challenge Paul Blair, the owner of a strong throwing arm and a player whom Earl Weaver considered the game's finest defensive center fielder. Clemente rounded second sharply, pushing for third. Perhaps surprised by Clemente's aggressiveness, Blair threw wildly, over the head of Brooks Robinson. As a result, Stargell moved up to second base. Thanks to Clemente's hell-bent running, the Pirates had placed two runners in scoring position.

Kison continued to retire Oriole batters in easy succession, while Dobson persisted in his struggle. In the fourth inning, the Pirates placed two runners on base via a hit and a walk, but left the runners stranded. In the fifth, the Pirates loaded the bases with one out, but Bob Robertson popped up and Manny Sanguillen grounded into a forceout.

In the sixth inning, light-hitting Jackie Hernandez stroked a ground single into left field. With one out, Hernandez stole second. Dave Cash lined a comebacker to the mound that caromed off of Dobson's glove, pushing Hernandez to third. With the lefty-swinging Hebner scheduled to bat, Earl Weaver summoned southpaw Grant Jackson from his bullpen. Murtaugh decided to forego the pinch-hitting option of Jose Pagan, and left Hebner in to face Jackson. Hebner, going with the pitch smartly, smacked a line drive to the left side of the infield. At first glance, it appeared that Hebner's smash would land in short left field and easily score Hernandez from third. But Brooks Robinson dove to his right and snared the ball on the fly before it could leave the infield. With two outs, Jackson walked Clemente to load the bases, bringing another left-handed hitter, Willie Stargell, to the plate. Stargell mustered a weak ground ball to Dave Johnson for the inning's final out. For the third straight inning, the Pirates had placed at least two runners on base but had failed to produce the tie-breaking run.

In the top of the seventh, Kison yielded only his second baserunner when, with one out, he hit Andy Etchebarren with a one-out pitched ball. In the process, the side-arming Kison had set a new World Series record by hitting his third Oriole batter of the night. (Wildness was nothing new for Kison, who at one time in the minor leagues had thrown six wild pitches while warming up in the bullpen.) Kison recovered from his erratic tendencies to retire pinch-hitter Tom Shopay, batting for Grant Jackson, on a forceout. When Paul Blair's deep fly ball to left field landed safely in the glove of Willie Stargell, Kison breathed another sigh of relief.

Even though the game was still tied, Weaver elected to bring in his ace reliever, right-hander Eddie Watt, to pitch the seventh inning. Watt struck out Al Oliver, who rarely fanned against right-handed pitching. Watt then faced Bob Robertson, whose comebacker eluded the pitcher into center field for a base hit. Manny Sanguillen lined another single to center field, putting runners on first and second with one out. At this point, with Jackie Hernandez scheduled to bat, Murtaugh looked to his bench. The Pirates skipper called upon his top left-handed pinch-hitter, Vic Davalillo, who sprayed a fly ball into left-center field. The speedy Blair, who was shading Davalillo toward left field, raced over and positioned himself to make the catch. Incredibly, Blair dropped the ball, allowing both runners to move up; Bob Robertson advanced to third and Sanguillen sprinted for second. But the Pirate catcher committed an uncharacteristic base-running mistake. After reaching second base, Sanguillen rounded the bag too aggressively. Shortstop Mark Belanger fired to Dave Johnson, who applied a quick tag to a diving Sanguillen.

Instead of enjoying a bases-loaded, one-out situation, the Pirates now had runners on first and third, with two outs. Either way, Murtaugh realized he needed to pinch-hit for the ultra-effective Kison, who had hurled six and a third innings of unblemished relief. Murtaugh had already burned his best pinch-hitting option, Vic Davalillo. Murtaugh now called upon the untested bat of the youthful Milt May, who had batted only 126 times during the regular season.

May decided to take an aggressive approach, figuring that Watt would try to jump ahead of him with a fastball early in the count. As he held his bat high above his head, May awaited Watt's first delivery. Watt did indeed throw a first-pitch fastball, over the outer half of the plate. May lowered his bat from its high perch and swung, lifting a semi-looping, half-hearted line drive into right-center field. The ball eluded the reach of Paul Blair and Frank Robinson, dropping in for a run-scoring single.

The Pirates now possessed a 4-3 advantage. Murtaugh turned the lead over to relief ace Dave Giusti. After working a perfect eighth inning, Giusti prepared himself to collect the final three outs. Pitching aggressively, Giusti retired Brooks Robinson on a leadoff grounder to Gene Alley at short. Giusti now had the option of pitching carefully to Boog Powell, the Orioles' second leading home run hitter, who had been hampered by a sore right wrist throughout the World Series. Giusti ran up a three-ball count to Powell. When Giusti fired his next, a palmball, over the plate, Powell elected to swing. The mammoth slugger swung under the pitch, lofting a weak pop-up that Richie Hebner corralled near home plate. Giusti now went after Dave Johnson, who had belted 18 home runs during the season. Johnson stroked a grounder to the left side of the infield. Alley moved in from his position at shortstop, scooped up the ball, and fired to Bob Robertson at first, well ahead of Johnson's arrival. In spite of leaving 13 runners on base, the Pirates had won the game. Suddenly, a World Series that once appeared on the verge of a blowout had undergone a major change in momentum. The Series was now a best two-out-of three.

Baseball could not have selected a more dramatic matchup than Game Four for the showcase of the first night game in World Series history. Television ratings for a World Series day game would not have approached the record number of fans—estimated at 61 million—who watched the game on NBC and saw Roberto Clemente pick up three hits in four at-bats.

For the second straight game, Danny Murtaugh called upon an unlikely starter: 28-year-old right-hander Nellie Briles, who had started only 14 games during the regular season and had missed his scheduled start in the playoffs with a pulled leg muscle. Now, Murtaugh was asking him to pitch the most important game of his life, Game Five of a deadlocked World Series.

Although his excitably restless children had difficulty staying quiet in their beds, Briles slept well the night before the fifth game at Three Rivers. Briles opened Game Five by retiring Don Buford, Paul Blair and Boog Powell in order. In the second, Briles handled Frank Robinson and Elrod Hendricks with ease before Brooks Robinson reached first base on a line-drive single. No one realized it at the time, but Robinson would represent the first of only two Oriole batters who would manage to break through against Briles.

In the meantime, the Pirates went to work against Dave McNally. Bob Robertson led off the top of the second by smashing McNally's first pitch 410 feet to center field. The solo home run gave the Pirates a 1-0 lead. Manny Sanguillen followed up Robby's shot with a line-drive single, and later stole second base. McNally now prepared to face the lower half of the Pirates' order. McNally regrouped, striking out both Jose Pagan and Jackie Hernandez. McNally appeared on the verge of ending the rally, as his counterpart, Nellie Briles, stepped to the plate. The left-hander picked up two immediate strikes on Briles, but then missed with his next three pitches, filling the count. McNally and catcher Ellie Hendricks decided to throw Briles a breaking ball, specifically a slider. The pitch hung high in the strike zone, and Briles swung. Nellie vaulted the ball on a line into center field. The clean single scored Sanguillen from second base, giving the Pirates a 2-0 lead.

In the third, the Pirates added to their margin when Gene Clines walked, moved to second base on a Clemente grounder, and advanced to third on an error by Brooks Robinson. Clines came home on a wild pitch, giving the Bucs a three-run advantage. In the fifth, the Pirates tallied again, sending McNally to the clubhouse in favor of relief pitcher Dave Leonhard.

The Pirates had supported Briles with three runs, which would prove to be more than sufficient on this day. The veteran right-hander brilliantly spotted his pitches and exhibited remarkable control, considering his recent lack of work. Briles surrendered only two hits and two walks and extended the Orioles' run-scoring drought to 17 innings. In addition to his standout pitching, Briles had also accounted for one of the Pirates' insurance runs with his two-out single in the second inning. In the bottom of the eighth inning, Briles came to bat and received a thunderous standing ovation from the fans at Three Rivers Stadium, who appreciated his pitching—and his hitting.

In the top of the ninth, an emotionally drained Briles retired the first two Oriole batters. Briles then staggered, walking Don Buford on four pitches. Since Briles was noted for his control, the sudden fit of wildness prompted a visit from pitching coach Don Osborn, and some warm-up action in the bullpen, where Dave Giusti and Luke Walker stirred. Ultimately, neither reliever would be needed. Briles recovered by throwing two consecutive strikes to Paul Blair before retiring the Orioles' center fielder on a force play. With three straight wins in Pittsburgh, the Pirates had moved within one game of the world championship.

After the Pirates' win in Game Five, Orioles right fielder Frank Robinson responded to Clemente's recent complaints about the playing surface at Memorial Stadium. After Game Two, Clemente had criticized the condition of the outfield grass in Baltimore. "I don't know why he's knocking ballparks," Robinson told Jerome

Holtzman of the *Chicago Sun-Times*. "Until they moved into this place [Three Rivers Stadium], he'd been playing in a coal hole [Forbes Field]."

Robinson also responded to Clemente's criticism that the Memorial Stadium outfield forced him to play deeper than usual, in contrast to the shallow positioning he preferred in right field. "Close?" Robinson said sarcastically. "Every time I've seen him here in Pittsburgh, he's been near the warning track." Like most good flychasers, Robinson considered it a poor practice to play deep in the outfield. Completing his diatribe, Robinson then told reporters to pass along a message to his right field counterpart. "If he's all that great an outfielder," Robinson told Roy McHugh of the *Pittsburgh Press*, "he should be able to adjust. If he can't adjust, tell him to watch the way I play right field—or buy a ticket and sit in the stands."

Wow. Based on the severity of the remarks, Robinson had willingly seized the opportunity to savagely criticize the Pirate legend. Perhaps Robinson had long felt deep resentment toward Clemente. Or perhaps Clemente's recent complaints had simply struck a raw nerve with Robinson. Whatever Robinson's rationale, Clemente did not let the remarks of the Orioles' right fielder pass without a quick response. "Well, Frank Robinson is a better ballplayer than I am," Clemente said sarcastically to Jerome Holtzman of the *Chicago Sun-Times*. "He's an American fellow and I'm from Puerto Rico. That makes him the best." And one more thing. "In Puerto Rico, when I am a boy, I play without shoes. I am a professional. I can play anywhere." Robinson, a future Hall of Famer, had publicly challenged another superstar on the national stage of baseball's most visible showcase. Clemente had defended himself with sarcasm and pride. In the process, Robinson and Clemente had hatched the first major controversy of the World Series.

Clemente wasn't done with his feelings of anger. Prior to Game Six, Clemente stomped around the batting cage, taking his batting practice swings with an extra measure of ferocity. Clemente was not upset about Robinson's attack of words, at least not at the moment. The words of another man, a sportswriter, had stirred Clemente's ire. After the fifth game, a Baltimore scribe had written that Clemente could no longer pull the ball. According to the writer, Clemente had lost just enough bat speed to render him an opposite-field hitter. Given his standout play through the first five games of the Series, Clemente—and others—couldn't believe the latest criticism.

With the Orioles facing a must-win situation for the first time, Earl Weaver chose Jim Palmer, the winner in the second game of the Series, to pitch Game Six in Baltimore. In bypassing Steve Blass, who would have been pitching on three days rest, Danny Murtaugh countered with yet another surprising and controversial choice— swingman Bob Moose. The right-hander would become the sixth different Pirate starter in the six-game series, matching a record achieved by the Brooklyn Dodgers in 1955.

In the first inning of Game Six, Clemente came to bat to face Palmer, who was heavily favored in the matchup against Moose. The Baltimore fans greeted Roberto with a round of loud boos, perhaps in retaliation for Clemente's critical remarks of Memorial Stadium and his recent response to Frank Robinson. Clemente would respond to the fans—with his bat—later in the game.

The Pirates jumped ahead early against Palmer, the winner in Game Two. In the second inning, an Al Oliver double and an RBI single by Bob Robertson produced the Pirates' first run. In the third inning, Clemente added to the scoring with a long home run, making it 2-0. Even though the home run was *merely* an opposite field shot, a fact most likely noted by that critical Baltimore sportswriter, it still counted.

In the meantime, Bob Moose surprisingly mowed down the Orioles through the first five innings, allowing only two base hits and no runs. In the bottom of the sixth, Moose prepared to face the leadoff batter, the switch-hitting Don Buford. Moose unleashed a belt-high fastball to the diminutive, but powerfully built left fielder. The stocky Buford swung hard, pulling the ball deep toward right field. With no chance to make a play on the ball, Clemente watched it carry over the wall. Buford's first home run of the Series brought the Orioles within one. Dave Johnson followed by hitting a high hopper to Richie Hebner, who dropped the ball, enabling Johnson to reach first base. A single by Boog Powell put Oriole runners on first and third with no out, forcing Moose to the clubhouse.

Murtaugh brought in hard-throwing right-hander Bob Johnson to face Frank Robinson, Merv Rettenmund and Brooks Robinson. Johnson overpowered F. Robby with a high fastball, popping him up to shortstop Jackie Hernandez. Johnson struck out Rettenmund looking. He then retired Brooks Robinson on a grounder to third.

In the bottom of the seventh, Mark Belanger reached on a one-out single to right field. Johnson struck out Jim Palmer, but Belanger stole second base, putting himself in scoring position. With the game on the line, Murtaugh walked to the mound and signaled for his fireman, Dave Giusti. Murtaugh hoped that his most reliable reliever could register the final seven outs of the game—and end the Series.

Giusti decided to pitch carefully to Don Buford, who had homered in his previous at-bat against Bob Moose. As a result, Giusti walked the Orioles' left fielder, putting runners on first and second. The right-handed hitting Dave Johnson came to the plate. Johnson worked the count to two balls and two strikes. Giusti opted for his best pitch, the palm ball. Johnson, using a one-handed swing, looped the ball into short left field. The ball dropped in front of Willie Stargell, scoring Belanger with the tying run.

The game remained tied through the bottom of the ninth. After striking out Ellie Hendricks, Giusti walked Mark Belanger. Earl Weaver then lifted Jim Palmer for pinch-hitter Tom Shopay, who flied out to Al Oliver in center field. With two outs, the dangerous Buford stepped to the plate. Buford drove one of Giusti's deliveries into the right field corner, out of the reach of Clemente. Without question, Buford would be able to make second base with a double, but would Belanger be able to score all the way from first? An above-average runner, Belanger raced for third, intent on making the turn and trying to score. Clemente quickly scooped the ball off the wall, turned his body and made a 309-foot throw from the darkness of the right field corner to Manny Sanguillen at the plate—on one short, nearly perfect bounce. Baltimore third base coach Billy Hunter threw up his hands, halting Belanger, who had made a sharp turn at third base. The Orioles were not about to test the best right field throwing arm in the game's history.

Against any other right fielder, Belanger might have tried to score, and likely would have reached home plate ahead of the throw. But not against Clemente. Although the wisdom of Belanger and Hunter prevented an Oriole from being thrown out on the play, Clemente's throw was no less impressive, and perhaps as incredible as his heave in Game Two.

"A throwing arm virtually second to none," says longtime Baltimore sportswriter John Steadman, who watched the game from the press box. "If it was second to anyone, it would have been Rocky Colavito for sheer power. But Clemente's arm for accuracy and throwing with authority from right field absolutely would change the outcome of a game. Not very often does the arm of an outfielder change the outcome of the game. But with Clemente, it did."

With Clemente having granted him a game-saving reprieve, Giusti faced Dave Johnson. The hard-hitting second baseman bounded a sharp grounder to Jackie Hernandez at shortstop. Usually sure-handed, Hernandez bobbled the ball momentarily before recovering and throwing to Bob Robertson at first base. Johnson was out—on a very close play.

Earl Weaver brought in one of his starters, Pat Dobson, to work the tenth. Vic Davalillo, pinch-hitting for Giusti, hit a line drive directly at Dave Johnson. Dave Cash rapped a one-out single to right field and stole second base as Richie Hebner fanned. With the go-ahead run on second base, and Clemente at the plate, Weaver decided to bypass "The Great One." Since Clemente had already powered a home run and triple, Weaver had no interest in providing him with another chance to victimize the Oriole pitching staff. Weaver ordered Dobson to intentionally walk Clemente, and then brought in another one of his starting pitchers, left-hander Dave McNally, to face Willie Stargell.

McNally became the third Oriole starter to make an appearance in Game Six. Pitching from the stretch, McNally proceeded to walk Stargell, who was batting only .200 in the Series. The unintentional walk loaded the bases and brought another left-handed batter, Al Oliver, to the plate.

Danny Murtaugh had three quality right-handed pinch-hitters available: Gene Clines, Jose Pagan and Bill Mazeroski. Murtaugh realized, however, that if he put up a right-handed pinch-hitter, Weaver would counter with a tough right-handed pitcher like Eddie Watt or Dick Hall.

Murtaugh stayed with Oliver, who had struck out against McNally to end the first game of the Series. Oliver lifted a lazy fly ball to center fielder Merv Rettenmund, ending the Pirate threat. To make matters worse, the Bucs had also lost the services of their best relief pitcher, Dave Giusti, who had been removed for a pinch-hitter.

As the Orioles prepared to bat in the bottom half of the tenth inning, Murtaugh executed a double switch. He kept Davalillo in the game in center field—replacing Oliver—and called upon journeyman Bob Miller to take the mound. Miller retired the first batter, Boog Powell, on a bouncer to second. Miller now faced the dangerous Frank Robinson. Pitching carefully, Miller walked the Orioles' most feared hitter on a three-and-two pitch.

Merv Rettenmund followed umpire John Kibler's questionable call by hitting a dribbler up the middle, past Miller. Although Rettenmund hit the ball slowly, neither Dave Cash nor Jackie Hernandez could knock it down. Robinson, one of the best and most aggressive runners in the American League, decided to make a hard run for third base, despite an injured Achilles tendon. Robinson realized that Davalillo, the center fielder, possessed a weaker throwing arm than the man he had replaced, Al Oliver. Davalillo charged the ball hard and made a surprisingly strong line-drive peg to Richie Hebner, who caught the throw on the fly. Sliding headfirst to the right of third base, Robinson eluded the swipe tag of Hebner. In the process of making such a hard run, Robinson pulled his thigh muscle. But the tradeoff of an injury for an extra base in a critical situation was well worth it for Robinson, who realized that the Orioles *had* to have the game.

With runners on first and third and only one out, the Pirates moved their infielders and outfielders in against the power-hitting Brooks Robinson. Miller jumped ahead of Robinson, running the count to one ball and two strikes. An intelligent hitter, Robinson understood that he now had to shorten his swing to protect against the strikeout. On the next pitch, Robinson lofted a fly ball to medium-depth center field. At first glance, the ball did not seem to have the distance to score a hobbling Frank Robinson from third base.

With the bottom of the order coming up, and Davalillo possessing a subpar arm in center field, F. Robby realized that the short fly ball represented the Orioles' best chance to score. Even with a weakened thigh muscle, Robinson knew that he had to gamble, and tagged up at third base. Davalillo caught the ball in medium center field and quickly released the ball, firing in the direction of catcher Manny Sanguillen. The ball sailed to the left of home plate, several feet off line. The ball bounced once, and then hopped high on the second bounce. Sanguillen vaulted himself in the air, sustained a graceful vertical leap, and cleanly grabbed the ball. Still in mid air, Robinson slid between and under Sanguillen's suspended legs. As Sanguillen returned to the ground with a swipe tag, Robby's feet scraped home plate. Umpire John Kibler signaled "safe." Robinson's mad dash around the bases—from first to third, and third to home—had given the Orioles a 3-2, extra-inning victory. It was the most dramatic win for either team in the Series.

21

Game Seven

Very few people knew about it at the time, but Roberto Clemente made a stunning revelation to Pirate scout Howie Haak before Game Seven. "Howie, you have been a good friend of mine over the years," Clemente said privately. "I want you to be one of the first to know something. If we win today's game, I'm going to quit baseball." Clemente told no one else about his plans, except for his wife, Vera. The story would not be made public until after the World Series, when Charley Feeney revealed it exclusively in the *Pittsburgh Post-Gazette*.

In another development, one that *was* made public, Danny Murtaugh talked to reporters about the possibility of retirement—his own retirement. "I'm going home to play golf and relax and talk to my family. And I'll decide on the basis of what's best for me and my family," Murtaugh told *The Sporting News*. Murtaugh said the outcome of Game Seven would have no bearing on his decision to return for the 1972 season. As they headed to the seventh game, the Pirates faced the real, but unknown possibility of playing their final game with both Murtaugh and Clemente.

On a more immediate front, Murtaugh decided to alter his lineup against Orioles' left-hander Mike

Cuellar. Murtaugh dropped a struggling Willie Stargell from the cleanup spot to the No. 6 position, and advanced Bob Robertson and Manny Sanguillen to the fourth and fifth spots, respectively. Clemente, of course, remained anchored to the No. 3 position in the order.

Murtaugh also had a decision to make with regard to his starting pitcher. The Irishman opted for Steve Blass, who had pitched so well in the third game. As Blass took batting practice prior to Game Seven, he tried to hide his nervousness by comically imitating the mannerisms of Clemente during one of his typical at-bats. Blass playfully twitched his shoulders and rolled his neck, drawing snickers of laughter from the assembled media.

Given the suspense and drama of Game Six, it seemed that Game Seven might be destined to provide baseball fans with a letdown. How could the Orioles and Pirates possibly put on a show matching the spirit and intensity of a memorable affair like Game Six, or even Game Four, for that matter? More pointedly, what could Clemente do to better his invigorating performances throughout the first six games of the Series? "He just seemed at that time to be playing at a higher level than the other players were," says writer Marcos Breton, who grew up as an Orioles' fan in the early seventies. "The way he ran, the way he fielded, the way he hit; he didn't seem like the other players, he had a rhythm to him that really stood him apart from the other players. He almost seemed dangerous jumping off at the television screen. It almost seemed like to someone who was rooting against the Pirates at that time, it almost seemed like it wasn't fair, like he had some sort of inner thing propelling him that made him above and beyond the other players. You know, when you're a child you don't appreciate that kind of talent. But as I recall my memories from that time, and then fast forward so many years now, he was a special player, and he just sort of jumped off the television screen."

Large, dark clouds appeared over Memorial Stadium only minutes before the start of Game Seven. Umpires ordered the field lights to be turned on, and pondered weather reports that called for a 20 percent chance of rain showers during the afternoon. The backdrop of storm clouds and overcast skies on this "slate gray day"—in the words of NBC's Curt Gowdy—produced a surreal setting for the Pirates and Orioles, whose players were about to play the most important game of their major league careers.

The ominous weather may have partially accounted for the 5,917 empty seats at Memorial Stadium, but did not disturb the concentration of either pitcher. Steve Blass and Mike Cuellar displayed effective brilliance in the early innings. Cuellar set down the first 11 batters he faced, and allowed only two balls to reach the outfield. Bob Robertson and Jackie Hernandez hit the hardest drives against Cuellar: one a line shot to Brooks Robinson at third, the other a line smash to Frank Robinson in right field.

In contrast, Blass labored substantially more than Cuellar while working against the Orioles' vaunted lineup. Blass walked the lead-off batter, Don Buford, in the first inning. Then, in a maneuver that contradicted manager Earl Weaver's preference for big innings, Dave Johnson tried to lay down a bunt. An unskilled bunter, Johnson popped the ball up to the mound, where Blass cradled the ball with a waist-level catch. Blass then faced Boog Powell, who pulled a hanging fastball into the farthest reaches of Memorial Stadium's upper deck—albeit hundreds of feet foul. With the count one-and-two on Powell, Weaver stormed out of the Orioles' dugout to protest that Blass wasn't keeping his right foot in contact with the rubber, a violation of the rules.

Weaver's argument with Nestor Chylak caused a delay of several minutes, and rattled Blass, albeit temporarily. Blass threw two straight balls, but recovered to strike out Powell and retire Frank Robinson on a first-pitch fly ball to Clemente in deep right.

In the top of the fourth inning, Cuellar breezed through the first two Pirate batters. Dave Cash lined softly to Dave Johnson, who made a nifty on-the-run grab. Gene Clines dropped down a bunt, which Cuellar fielded barehanded and fired to first, where Powell neatly scooped up a low throw. Having now retired 11 consecutive Pirates to start the game, Cuellar faced Roberto Clemente. With two outs and no one on, the tricky left-hander didn't have to pitch aggressively to Clemente. Hoping to throw Clemente off balance, Cuellar threw "The Great One" a curve ball over the outer half of the plate. Cuellar's desired pitch location was consistent with the Orioles' scouting report against Clemente: throw him breaking pitches away, but keep the ball down, as Baltimore scout Jim Russo had warned prior to the Series.

Unfortunately for Cuellar, this curve hung high. Clemente unleashed his typically long, exaggerated swing and powered the ball into left-center field. Don Buford and Merv Rettenmund raced to the wall, thinking they would be able to make the catch. At the least, they figured they would be able to field the carom off the wall. Instead, Buford and Rettenmund watched the ball sail into the empty Memorial Stadium bleachers, just to the right of the 390-foot sign. Even the Pirate players were surprised that the ball had traveled as far as it did. "We saw the ball heading for the fence," Dave Cash told *The Sporting News.* "All of us in the dugout had a sense of disbelief. We saw Rettenmund go back and we didn't think the ball would go out. You know, the ball doesn't carry too well in this park." This time it did. Someone might have reminded that critical Baltimore sportswriter that Clemente had *pulled* the pitch for a home run.

It was strangely ironic that Clemente and Cuellar crossed paths in Game Seven. One year earlier, Cuellar had clashed with Clemente, his manager in the Puerto Rican Winter League. As Orioles' outfielder Merv Rettenmund explained to Dick Young of the *New York Daily News:* "You wouldn't exactly want Cuellar pitching for you in winter ball. He wants to pitch once a month, at home, and pick his team. Right here, though, I want Mike pitching for me anytime." Although a young and relatively inexperienced manager, Clemente believed in discipline, consistently applied. Any rules established by the manager would be enforced for everyone—at all times—whether it was in the winter league or the World Series.

Reporters had asked Cuellar and Clemente to discus the run-in earlier in the Series, but both players insisted that they harbored no resentments from their winter league encounter. "Nothing happened between us that was ugly," Clemente explained to Roy McHugh. "In fact, he has been a guest in my house. We're professionals."

As Clemente raced to his position to start the bottom of the fourth, hundreds of Pirate fans in the right field stands—who had made the drive from Pittsburgh—massaged him with a standing ovation. Meanwhile, without the benefit of applause, Blass went back to work. Although the Pirates had taken a 1-0 lead on the Clemente home run, Blass did not feel overly confident about the Pirates' chances of winning. Blass recalls his mindset after watching Clemente's blast from the dugout. "I'm locked in," Blass says. "I'm happy to have the lead, but my focus at that point was simply on getting everybody out. I wasn't paying too much attention to the score. I can't control the score. I can control what I do out on the mound. The home run did not change my philosophy or approach. You can't get real comfortable with one run."

Through seven innings, Cuellar would allow only one other base hit, a line drive single by Manny Sanguillen in the fifth. Yet, the Clemente home run had done important damage. It had given the Pirates a small degree of momentum and provided Blass with a slight surge of optimism. In his first five innings, Blass had struggled with his pitching rhythm, as he fought off the nerves created by a seventh game, winner-take-all situation. At times, he had labored in efforts to throw his curveball for strikes. From the sixth inning on, Blass began to mix in his darting slider more frequently and continued to turn back the swaggering Orioles' attack.

The Pirates continued to lead, 1-0, heading to the top of the eighth inning. Willie Stargell led off against Cuellar and delivered a ground single just to the left of Mark Belanger's failed backhand attempt. With the right-hand hitting Jose Pagan scheduled to bat, Weaver might have considered bringing in a right-hander reliever like Dick Hall or Eddie Watt, or even one of his starters, Pat Dobson.

But Weaver stayed with Cuellar. And why not? Cuellar, who was pitching brilliantly—one of the best games of his career—did not appear tired. Danny Murtaugh flashed the hit-and-run sign to third base coach Frank Oceak, who relayed the message to Pagan. Unlike Bob Robertson in Game Three, Pagan did not miss the sign. The slow-footed Stargell broke from the first base bag, and Pagan swung, banging a fly ball toward the left-center field fence. Pagan was supposed to hit the ball to right field on the hit-and-run, with the idea of pushing Stargell to third base. But with Stargell running and the ball neatly placed between Merv Rettenmund and Don Buford, Stargell made it to third anyway, with ease. As he neared third base, Stargell stopped for a moment to watch the ball, which had caromed off the wall in deep left-center. With no one out, Stargell should have been satisfied to hold at third. Instead, Rettenmund's momentary bobbling of the ball in left-center field prompted an unwise decision. Big Willie rounded third and headed for home. First baseman Boog Powell made a questionable decision of his own, cutting the relay off between the mound and the third base line. (Although replays of the play are inconclusive, it appears that the Orioles might have had Stargell at the plate had Powell let the ball go through.) Stargell crossed the plate with the Pirates' second and all-important insurance run.

Up till now, Pagan had helped the Pirates in the Series—but only with his glove. He had played a brilliant defensive third base in Game Five, and had added two more fine plays to his fielding resumé in the seventh game. Now, the onetime winter league team-mate of Roberto Clemente had contributed with the biggest hit of his long career.

Afterwards, Pagan explained that he had altered his original strategy—and his bat selection—against the soft-tossing Cuellar. "The first two times up I used a 38-ounce bat and I was swinging in front of everything," Pagan told the *New York Times*. "Knowing the way he was pitching to me—he was throwing me breaking stuff, screw balls—I knew I had to use a heavier bat. So when I came up to bat in the eighth, I switched to a 40-ounce bat." The heavier bat produced greater distance, enough to elude Rettenmund and Buford in left-center field and enough to score the lead-footed Stargell from first base.

With Pagan at second base and the Bucs now threatening to ice the game, Cuellar toughened. The screwballing left-hander re-tired Jackie Hernandez on a fly to deep right field, with Pagan hold-ing his ground at second, not wanting to test the arm of Frank Robinson. Cuellar then put away Steve Blass on a tapped comebacker, and induced an inning-ending grounder off the bat of Dave Cash.

In the bottom of the eighth inning, Blass faced his first major crisis of the game. Elrod Hendricks led off with a grounder just a few feet to the left side of second base, where the shortstop, Jackie Hernandez, would normally have been stationed. But with the Pi-rates overshifting and Hernandez playing to the *right* of second base, Hendricks' routine grounder turned into a leadoff single. With the O's now down by two, Belanger swung away and looped a limp single to center field. Suddenly, the Orioles had placed the tying runs on first and second, with no one out.

Earl Weaver summoned Tom Shopay to pinch-hit for Cuellar. Shopay took the first two pitches, one a ball, the other a strike. Then came a curious move by Weaver, who called upon the lefty-swinging outfielder to attempt a sacrifice bunt. If Weaver had wanted to bunt, why hadn't he left in Cuellar—who had bunted many times in his career—to lay down the sacrifice himself? Un-der that scenario, the Orioles would have moved both runners up without burning a pinch-hitter. At the same time, Weaver would have retained the services of Cuellar; except for hanging two pitches to Roberto Clemente and Jose Pagan, he was still pitching very well for the Orioles.

Whatever Weaver's thinking, Shopay skillfully executed the sacrifice, moving Hendricks to third and Belanger to second. On the play, Blass threw to first for the sure out, but only after ignoring Sanguillen, who had directed him to throw to third base.

With runners on second and third base, and the switch-hitting Don Buford scheduled to bat, Danny Murtaugh faced a tough decision. The Irishman elected to stay with a still-effective, though obviously tiring Blass. Drained but still determined, the skinny right-hander prepared to face the top of the Orioles' order: Buford and Dave Johnson.

Buford slapped a hard grounder down the first base line. Bob Robertson backed up a few steps and fielded the high-hopping grounder before running to the bag for the second out of the inning. Still, Hendricks scored the Orioles' first run of the game on the play, and Belanger, the potential tying run, moved up to third.

Blass was now left with no margin for error. If he were to throw a breaking pitch, it might bounce in the dirt past Sanguillen and allow the fleet-footed Belanger to score. At the same time, Blass needed to pitch aggressively to Dave Johnson, what with Boog Powell waiting in the on-deck circle. Blass simply *had* to retire Johnson, or face the American League's most intimidating left-handed power hitter this side of Reggie Jackson.

Johnson hit a Blass slider into the hole between short and third. As soon as Johnson laid bat on ball, Blass thought he had surrendered a run-scoring single to left field. Jackie Hernandez, blessed with good range and adept feet at shortstop, moved quickly to his right, and fielded the ball on a long hop, deep in the hole. Hernandez set himself, and from the back of the infield dirt, unleashed a strong, accurate throw. Bob Robertson corralled the chest-high toss in his racket-sized first baseman's glove, two steps ahead of Johnson's arrival at first base. Thanks to the fine play by Pittsburgh's oft-criticized shortstop, the Pirates had escaped the eighth inning with a one-run lead.

The Pirates threatened to expand their lead in the ninth, but Dave McNally ended a two-out rally by retiring Willie Stargell on a grounder to second. Game Seven moved to the bottom of the ninth. As the sun forced its way through the cache of clouds for the first time in the afternoon, Blass faced Boog Powell. The slugging first baseman bounded a high-hopping ground ball to Dave Cash at second base. One out. Now Blass prepared to meet Frank Robinson, the Orioles' fiery leader and outspoken critic of Clemente. Blass badly hung a slider, but in his words, Robinson "missed the pitch," and popped up meekly to Jackie Hernandez in short left field. Two outs. Next up came Merv Rettenmund, a solid .300 hitter with enough power to reach the seats at Memorial Stadium.

On Blass' eighth pitch of the inning, at exactly 4:10 p.m., Rettenmund swung and grounded a Blass pitch up the middle. The solidly hit ball caromed off the mound, bounding toward the right side of second base. Jackie Hernandez, who was shading Rettenmund toward second base after initially playing him to pull, raced over to a point a few feet beyond the bag, fielded the ball on the run near the lip of the outfield grass, and fired against his body to Bob Robertson at first base. Much like he had done to end the eighth inning, Robertson squeezed the ball securely in his glove.

This time, the end result was far more climactic for the Pirates. The Pittsburgh Pirates, for the first time in over a decade, thanks to the gutsy pitching of Steve Blass, the deft fielding of Jackie Hernandez and the clutch hitting of one Roberto Clemente, had won Game Seven of the World Series.

In the Pirates' clubhouse, Clemente, Steve Blass, Danny Murtaugh and longtime broadcaster Bob Prince stood on a podium as Commissioner Bowie Kuhn presented the Bucs with the World Championship trophy. Prince congratulated Clemente, who responded by delivering a personal message in Spanish to his parents. "En el dia mas grande de mi vida, les pido sus bendiciones," Clemente said to the television cameras. In English, Clemente's words translated as follows: "On this, the proudest day of my life, I ask for your blessing." For Clemente, his personal list of heroes began with his parents. "Roberto admired them like he admired God," says Luis Mayoral.

Clemente's decision to make a post-game address in Spanish also made an impression on at least one youngster who was watching on television. "I recall when the Series was over," says Marcos Breton, "and they were filming the locker room celebration and interviewing Clemente, him speaking in Spanish and addressing the people of Puerto Rico. At the time, I didn't really appreciate how significant that was—you know this was in the early seventies—and I think that you can make the argument that Latino culture is just now sort of coming into its own. You're going back a quarter century; here was this really proud man, the star of the showcase World Series, and he was addressing his people in Spanish on national television. The significance of that was sort of lost in the event."

The emotional scene also included a moment of personal awkwardness for Steve Blass. "I was so fired up," says Blass. "Prince was up there and Roberto, and he congratulated Roberto, and Roberto said, 'Bob, before I respond, I would like to say something in Spanish to my parents,' and Roberto acknowledged his parents, his mom and dad in Puerto Rico, in Spanish. And then I, with my big mouth, said, 'We love him, too, Mr. And Mrs. Clemente.' I remember that exchange. That probably wasn't necessary. He said what he had needed to say to his parents. I probably should have shut up for awhile, but I was just so fired up that I couldn't help but respond. But being up there with Bob Prince and Roberto Clemente, what a great visual memory that is."

Later on, Blass shared an even more poignant moment with Clemente, in a far more sedate atmosphere. "My wife, Karen, and I were on the plane [heading back to Pittsburgh]," Blass told Milton Richman in 1973. "And Roberto suddenly came over and embraced me. That was a very personal thing with me. I could feel the true warmth of the man."

In the clubhouse, Clemente felt especially good when he noticed two of his teammates together. "I saw [Jackie] Hernandez and [Willie] Stargell come into the clubhouse with their arms around each other and they were crying," Clemente observed. "To me, that I could bring together a black Latin and a black American was my joy." Hernandez' involvement in the storybook Series victory—including two excellent defensive plays in Game Seven—underscored the unity that Clemente had helped develop among the Pirate players. Back in September, after the Pirates had clinched the division title, poor fielding by Hernandez had cost Dock Ellis a shot at his 20th win. After that game, Hernandez sat at his locker, moping over the error he had committed and two other balls he had misplayed. Then, as Jackie slowly walked toward the showers, Clemente followed him. As Hernandez stood under the running water, Clemente reminded him that this was only one game; much more important games would follow in October. Clemente then bought Hernandez dinner. Bolstered by the counsel of a supportive Clemente, Hernandez played the best shortstop of his career during the balance of the regular season and the World Series before recording the final out of the Pirates' championship season.

For over an hour, Clemente remained trapped on the NBC-TV platform, unable to move because of the mass of players, reporters and officials that had packed into the Pirates' visiting clubhouse. While on stage, Clemente conducted a host of interviews and expressed optimism that his World Series effort had changed people's opinions of him. Clemente received some reinforcement when Orioles' owner Jerry Hoffberger searched him out among the masses, congratulating the Pirate superstar on his World Series performance. "You're the best of all," Hoffberger said to Clemente, shaking his hand in the ultimate gesture of sportsmanship. Sentiment continued to flow in Clemente's direction when *Sport* magazine named him the outstanding player in the Series. "Now people in the whole world know the way I play," Clemente told Joe Heiling of the *Houston Post*. Clemente continued to hold court with the assembled reporters, reminding some of them that they had been negligent in recognizing his talent. This was Clemente's grand opportunity to say, "I told you so."

As Clemente boasted—rightfully so—his best friend on the team watched from a stool in the corner of the clubhouse, one of the few quiet areas in the clubhouse. "He's going pretty good, eh?" noted a smiling Manny Sanguillen, without a trace of jealousy. "Everything he is saying is true, you know. He is a great one, maybe the greatest."

Aside from the satisfaction derived from winning the World Championship, the single-most significant by-product of the Series was the emergence of Clemente on the game's national stage. For many years, Clemente had been respected by baseball insiders and the Pittsburgh media as one of the game's great players, but the Pirates' status as a small-market franchise had caused Clemente to be overlooked by fans and media nationwide. Clemente's Series accomplishments included hits in all seven games—matching his 1960 Series performance—12 hits in 29 at-bats for a .414 batting average, two home runs, four RBIs, aggressive and intelligent baserunning, and a series of spectacular plays and throws from right field. He had played so well, in fact, that the organist at Three Rivers Stadium, Vince Lascheid, had taken to playing the song, "Jesus Christ Superstar," when Clemente came to bat.

As Dick Young wrote in his *New York Daily News* column immediately after the World Series, "Roberto Clemente is discovered every 10 or 11 years, when the Bucs make it to the World Series. That is when he gets the ink he should have been getting the rest of the time. This annoys him. It's not the dinero [money]. He's getting that. He gets about $125,000 in salary, and you can live pretty well on that with your family in Rio Piedras, Puerto Rico.

What annoys him is that the people are so dumb that they don't appreciate Roberto Clemente the rest of the time." Unfortunately, Young's assessment was an accurate one. Prior to the 1971 Series, many fans and media types had failed to recognize the swath of Clemente's greatness. Here was a man who had begun his major league career 16 years earlier, and had been a star since 1960.

Clemente's all-around performance on national television transformed the public's perception of him as a very good player into an awareness of his true greatness—a major league superstar. In 1971, there was no widespread cable television—and therefore no superstations—to provide out-of-town fans in New York, Chicago or Los Angeles with the chance to watch a player like Clemente on a regular basis. There was no national daily publication like *USA Today*, with circulation in all major markets, to provide coverage of a star like Clemente. Local newspapers tended to focus coverage on the hometown team, while only spotlighting opposition players when they came to that particular city for a short series.

"I was just so happy in retrospect," says Bill Guilfoile of Clemente's performance in the World Series and the recognition that came with it. "When you play in Pittsburgh, or in other cities of that size where you don't have that media exposure, a lot of people really never had a chance to appreciate how good Clemente really was. Most of those people, certainly in Baltimore, had never seen him play before. The Pittsburgh fans had, of course. Even on television, your exposure is limited when you're playing for a team like Pittsburgh. We who were with the team—who were in Pittsburgh—knew the talent that Clemente had. But it was one of the best-kept secrets because it really wasn't made visible to the whole world, as was done during the television [coverage] of that World Series. I was just so happy that he finally got the attention and acclaim and respect that was due him. He'd been playing that way, really, all his career."

Clemente's lack of true home run power, especially when compared to contemporaries like Hank Aaron and Willie Mays, also contributed to his status as an underrated player. As Richie Hebner points out, "He was in the era of Mays and Aaron, and those guys hit home runs. Everybody likes to talk about home run hitters." In 1971, Danny Murtaugh made an intriguing remark about Clemente's power hitting. "If Clemente were a selfish player," Murtaugh told the Associated Press, "he could hit 25 to 40 home runs a season. But he's always been content to set up the other hitters."

Longtime Pirate scout Howie Haak seconded Murtaugh's contention. "The only thing you ever hear about Clemente is that he doesn't hit enough home runs," Haak said. "The criticism is ridiculous, because he could hit 40 a year if he wanted to. He has the greatest physical ability of anybody I have ever seen in a long time. He's got as much power as anyone on this ballclub. Only [Bob] Robertson may have a little more."

Early in his career, Clemente had made a conscious decision to forego the long ball for a line-drive hitting approach, especially to the opposite field. The reason? Forbes Field ranked as the major leagues' most difficult ballpark for home run hitters. "He was too smart to try and pull the ball at Forbes Field, where the left field foul pole was 365 feet away and you had to hit the ball over a 40-foot scoreboard," Bill Mazeroski wrote in *Sport* magazine in 1971. "What Roberto always spoke to me about," recalls Luis Mayoral, "was the fact that the day he went to Forbes Field—when he saw Forbes Field for the first time—that field was so spacious. And it took him maybe a year or two to understand that to be successful hitting in Forbes Field, he had to become a contact, all-fields hitter."

The overwhelming dimensions of Forbes Field, which contained a reach of 457 feet to its deepest point in left-center field, created a roadblock for batters who preferred to crank up their bats a notch and take aim on the outfield bleachers. "Roberto hit only 240 homers lifetime," says Mayoral, "but he always stated that if he played the majority of his years elsewhere he would have been much more recognized because he would have hit a lot more home runs." As it was, Clemente played 15 and a half of his 18 seasons at Forbes Field, compared to only two and a half seasons at Three Rivers Stadium.

In a 1992 interview with *USA Today,* Willie Stargell tried to estimate the impact of Forbes Field on the Pirates' home run hitters. "Each of us lost about 20 home runs a year there," said the Hall of Fame slugger. While that number is most likely an exaggeration, it is probably safe to say that from 1955 to 1969, Clemente hit about five to eight "home run" balls a year that either fell in for triples or doubles, or were caught on the warning track. If we were to multiply the 15 years he played at Forbes Field by a relatively conservative estimate of six home runs, Clemente might have hit an additional 90 home runs during the course of his career. Instead of finishing with 240 home runs, Roberto might very well have broached the 300-home run milestone.

The general lack of coverage and respect given to Clemente prior to the '71 World Series was also caused by other factors. The list of reasons included racism. As Wells Twombly wrote in his column in the November 6th edition of *The Sporting News,* "Roberto was overlooked and he felt it was an ethnic thing. With only one or two exceptions, the writers were white. But they were willing to throw kisses at black athletes as long as they were fellow Americans. So how could an Hispanic black get any recognition? At age 37, Roberto found a way. They couldn't keep him off the bases with a flame-thrower. He had 12 hits and a .414 batting average."

Even the opposition Orioles, disappointed in their failure to defeat the supposedly overmatched Pirates, acknowledged the worth of Clemente. Brooks Robinson, one of the game's most respected and well-liked gentlemen, went so far as to hail Clemente as major league baseball's best player during the 1971 season. "If you talked to 10 players," Brooksie said in 1972, "they would all say he was the best in the game and I have to go along with them, just on what he's done. In ability, he was the best all-around player in either league last season." As for his performance in the World Series? "I knew he was good," Robinson told *Sports Illustrated,* "but I didn't know he was this good."

Clemente's seven-game effort against the Orioles made a lasting impression on Pirate officials like Bill Guilfoile, who had seen players like Mickey Mantle and Roger Maris perform in the World Series during his days as the Yankees' assistant public relations director. "I've never seen a player dominate a Series in all aspects of the game as he did," Guilfoile says of Clemente's 1971 World Series. "I've seen some players have a great Series; Brooks Robinson had a tremendous World Series in 1970. Others have done well... But here was a player [Clemente] who excelled in all aspects of the game: at bat, in the field, on the basepaths. He just played that entire Series the way the game is supposed to be played, using his many talents."

Bowie Kuhn has special recollections of Clemente's performance in the World Series, which he rates among his 10 greatest thrills in baseball. "It was just how one man could dominate a Series," says Kuhn, who watched the World Series games in person. "In two consecutive Series, one player had so dominated the Series: Robinson in '70 and Clemente in '71. And what was memorable was that he didn't necessarily do it by hitting home runs or [doing] something dramatic, but it was the way he would run out grounders." His hustling play in Game Three, where he had some-how managed to reach first base on a ragtag ground ball to the pitcher, took as large a place in Kuhn's memory as any of Roberto's World Series accomplishments.

"Clemente won it with everything," says Kuhn. "The way he ran bases, the way he made throws—of course, he was famous for his throws as well as the way he hit—but it was everything. One sensed that the Pirates were not going to lose that Series, even though they fell behind [two games to none], because of Clemente. He wasn't going to let them. They didn't dare lose it."

Taken a step further, how great was Clemente over the course of his career? It might be stretching credibility to anoint him as the greatest player of his time, not when players like Hank Aaron and Willie Mays simultaneously performed in the primes of their ca-reers. But Clemente does tend to be overlooked, especially given the overemphasis of the home run. In 1971, Clemente's all-around play had surpassed that of a declining Mays (.271, 18 HRs, 61 RBIs) but still lagged behind the amazing Aaron (.327, 47 HRs, 118 RBIs), who, at 37, was actually a year older than Clemente. Yet, there's little doubt that Clemente ranked as the best player that most of the Pirates would have as a teammate during their careers. Even a player like Dave Cash, who would go on to play with the likes of Hall of Famer Mike Schmidt, offered little hesitation when asked to name his greatest playing teammate. "The best player I've ever played with," Cash says, "was Roberto Clemente—without a doubt. Clemente could do it all. He could hit with power, he could run, he could throw. And at any time, he was a great clutch hitter."

Prior to Game Seven, Clemente had told Howie Haak that he would retire from baseball—if the Pirates were to win. Now that the Pirates had won the Series, the timing seemed right for Clemente to make an official announcement to the press about retirement. But no announcement was forthcoming. Why not? Apparently, Clemente had changed his mind. In an article by Pirates' beat writer Charley Feeney, Clemente explained the reasons behind the change to Haak. "When I ran off the field after the last World Series game, I saw my wife, Vera, crying," Clemente told Haak. "She said to me: 'Roberto, don't quit baseball now. Please don't quit now. It's your life.'" Vera's tears—and words—were enough to convince Roberto to keep playing the game he loved so much. "He always explained everything to me before he made a decision, including business," Vera told Douglas McDaniel of *The Diamond* in a 1993 interview. "He always wanted to know my opinion." Thanks to the pleas of his wife, and his willingness to listen, the baseball world would have the opportunity to witness the splendor of Clemente for at least one more season.

After the World Series, Clemente traveled to New York City to officially receive the *Sport* Magazine MVP award, given to the outstanding World Series player. Clemente seized the opportunity to speak out on several issues that topped his agenda. First, Roberto claimed that his World Series performance had given him much needed peace of mind about his place in the game. "I believe I'm the best player in baseball today," Clemente said proudly. "I'm glad I was able to show it against Baltimore in the Series."

Clemente also expressed support for Curt Flood in his continuing battle against the reserve clause. In 1969, Flood had been traded by the Cardinals to the Phillies, but had refused to report to his new team. Flood subsequently took baseball to court over the reserve clause, which tied a player to his team year after year in perpetuity. Like Flood, Clemente opposed the principal of the reserve clause. Clemente, who was actually the first black player representative to sit on the executive board of the Players' Association, also sympathized with a player being traded against his wishes. Flood, who had enjoyed playing for a successful and racially harmonious team like the Cardinals, did not want to play in Philadelphia. "If I were ever traded, I would quit baseball," Clemente told Maury Allen of the *New York Post.* "I have felt that way for 10 years."

On another front, Clemente criticized the baseball establishment for its failure to hire any black managers at the major league level. "If a black player wants to become a manager," Clemente told Maury Allen, "the owners tell him he has to go to the minors to get experience. But a white player does not. And sometimes the white player has not even made it to the major leagues. I think that is a double standard."

Clemente said that he was not interested in managing a major league team, even though he had managed successfully in the Puerto Rican Winter League after the 1970 season. Clemente recognized that his relationship with other players would become more adversarial if he were to become a manager. "I notice on a lot of clubs the players don't want to talk with the manager," Clemente told Milton Richman. "I get along with the players very good. I enjoy the relationship. I want people to like me, and the way I talk with the players now, I can't do that as a manager."

Clemente did make a point of endorsing two other noted black stars as managerial candidates. He felt that Ernie Banks and Frank Robinson would make excellent managers at the major league level.To his credit, Clemente made sure to endorse Robinson, even after the Orioles' star had blistered him with criticism during the World Series.

After receiving a 1971 Dodge Magnum from *Sport* magazine, Clemente announced plans to build a "sports city" for youngsters in Puerto Rico. It was an idea that he had first conceived in 1959. Clemente felt that such a sports city would provide children with an opportunity to receive practical instruction in baseball, swimming, tennis and other recreational sports. It would also allow the youth of Puerto Rico to learn more about personal sacrifice and teamwork.The construction of three baseball fields, a pool, basketball courts and tennis courts would cost about $2.5 million in federal funding. Clemente visited the governor's mansion in San Juan in an effort to obtain funding."If I get the money to start this, if they tell me they'll give us the money this year," Clemente said, "I'll quit right now." Clemente's two greatest passions, other than his family, were baseball and children. A sports city would bring the two together.

Clemente felt that his performance in the World Series might increase the chances of obtaining the necessary money. "This World Series is the greatest thing that ever happened to me in baseball," Clemente told the *New York Times.* "It gives me a chance to talk to writers more than before. I don't want anything for myself, but through me I can help lots of people."

The drama of the '71 World Series had not only lifted Clemente's credibility and recognition; it had helped elevate baseball's overall popularity, at least temporarily. As Dick Young wrote in the *Daily News,* "The 1971 World Series renewed for most people the assurance that baseball is indeed an exciting game, something, for some reason, they had been brainwashed into doubting." Likable and charismatic players like Clemente, Steve Blass and Manny Sanguillen had forced their way into the national spotlight. Through their ample on-field abilities and identifiable personalities, they had helped promote the appeal of baseball and its players.

Unfortunately, the impending strike of 1972 would negate much of the progress that had been achieved from such an exciting, ebb-and-flow, seven-game World Series. The walkout by the

Players Association would delay the start of the 1972 season, cutting down on the number of games played, and would drive some embittered fans away from major league ballparks. As a result, attendance fell from over 29 million in 1971 to below 27 million in 1972. The performance of the '71 Pirates, and their classic World Series against the Orioles, could not, however, be blamed for baseball's sagging fortunes at the gate. Clemente, Blass and the Robinsons had done their part. Especially Clemente.

22

The March to 3,000

As the Pirates celebrated their world championship with a victory party aboard the Gateway Clipper on the Monongahela River, Clemente showed his preference for calmer surroundings. Roberto and Vera spent a quiet night at the Hilton Hotel. "I was lucky to make it to the hotel," Clemente told Charley Feeney. "That mob—it was something." Over 100,000 fans had welcomed the Pirates back to Pittsburgh.

Thousands more greeted Roberto on October 22, when he returned to Puerto Rico for the winter. The massive welcoming party at San Juan International Airport included family, friends and government officials. As Roberto and Vera rode back to Rio Piedras, a convoy of cars followed behind.

After his celebrated display in the World Series, Clemente collected a host of trophies and awards, including the Babe Ruth World Series MVP. "It was the high point, the high point," Clemente told the Associated Press in describing his performance in the Fall Classic. "I was pleased because of my age. What I was doing in the World Series was something you would expect from a young fellow." Clemente also received appreciation for his regular season performance, including his 11th Gold Glove Award for fielding excellence, and a place on *The Sporting News* All-Star fielding team.

By the time that Clemente reported for spring training in February of 1972, the off-season demands of a World Series celebrity had clearly taken their toll. "I had a rough winter," Clemente informed Joe Durso of the *New York Times*. "For a month and a half, my wife and I couldn't sleep. Our house was like a museum—people flocking down the street, ringing our bell day and night, walking through our room." Clemente elected not to play winter ball in Puerto Rico, but was bothered by the illness of his 92-year-old father, which cut short a planned vacation to South America, and by off-season stomach trouble. Clemente revealed that doctors had taken X-rays of his stomach and had found a series of spasms, most likely caused by stress. As a result, Clemente had lost 10 pounds over the winter and now weighed only 176 pounds, his lightest weight in years.

The spring of '72 brought more anxiety to Clemente. Although he believed strongly in the mission of the Players Association and had been an active union member since the late 1960s, the decision to strike did not please him. "I remember the first baseball strike," says Sally O'Leary, who assisted Bill Guilfoile in the Pirates public relations department. "Roberto was always in the office talking to people, and when the first strike happened, he was quite upset, because he didn't want a strike. So the day the strike was over, he came back into the [Pirate] offices. I could see him peeking around my office door. He asked, 'Are we still welcome around here?' I could see he was concerned how that strike was going to affect relationships with the front office people."

The strike would also eliminate seven games at the start of the Pirates' season. Clemente needed 118 hits to reach the 3,000 mark. Although no one gave it much thought at the time, those lost games would imperil Clemente's chance of achieving the milestone during the 1972 season.

On May 11, the rival Mets completed a much-rumored trade with the Giants. New York sent minor league pitcher Charlie Williams and cash to San Francisco for the player Clemente had been compared to so often—Willie Mays. Although the deal fostered headlines in the New York City newspapers, trumpeting the return of the former New York Giants' star to the "Big Apple," it didn't figure to affect the balance of the power in the National League

East. Now 41 years old and no longer an everyday player, Mays was hitting a mere .184 with no home runs and three RBIs. Mays seemed to be nearing the end of his legendary career.

While the trade didn't pose much of a threat to the Pirates' supremacy in the division, it did upset Clemente—for an entirely different reason. Clemente explained his disgust with the trade to one of the team's broadcasters. "Trading Willie Mays, just like that, for as long as he's been in the game, [Roberto felt] it was trading him like a piece of cattle," recalls Nellie King. "Roberto said to me, 'I told Joe Brown, do not ever try to do that to me.' And Joe Brown said, 'Do what?' Roberto said, 'Trade me to another team.' He said, 'I'll tell you what, I want to play for the Pirates for the rest of my life, but if you want to trade me, I will go to another team only if you give me 80 percent of the sale price. I will give you 20 percent, but I want 80 percent. You gave me a chance to play, but the talent that I have is my talent and you cannot sell that to another team without giving me part of that.' And he thought the Giants did that to Mays. I don't know what the Giants got out of it, but he thought that was so unfair that a player that talented could be sent to another team for somebody to make money, and the player gets nothing out of it. He felt so strongly about that. 'Don't ever try to do that to make money by selling me to another team. I want 80 percent, or I will not go.'" For the record, the Giants received $50,000 in cash, in addition to Charlie Williams. Under Clemente's supposed suggestion, he would have asked for 80 percent of the money, or $40,000.

Joe Brown, disagreeing with King's version of the story, says Clemente never asked for any percentage of a potential sale price. "No," says Brown, "what Roberto had told me and told [owner] John Galbreath, was that he would never play for anybody else. He said, 'I love the Galbreaths, I love Pittsburgh, I love the Pirates, I will not play anyplace else.' He said, 'When my career is over, it will be here in Pittsburgh.' But no, he never asked for 80 percent of his sale price.

After the 1971 World Series, Clemente had written a touching note to the Galbreath family. "Whenever you don't think I can contribute to our team's success," Roberto inscribed in the letter, "I will retire. You and the Pirates' organization have been good to me and I thank you. I will never play for any other team." John Galbreath, for his part, held Clemente in such high regard that he once named one of his prized thoroughbreds "Roberto." The horse went on to win England's prestigious Epsom Derby.

In 1972, Clemente would play in only 102 games because of two rheumatic heels, tendonitis in his ankles, inflammation near both Achilles tendons, and repeated bouts with a viral infection. Roberto saw his weight drop to 170 pounds, down from his normal playing weight of 185. At one point, Clemente did not start in 39 of 40 games. When he did not play, he acted almost like a coach, positioning the Pirate outfielders according to hitter and situation. When he did play, he performed like an athlete in his prime, like someone who was 10 or 15 years younger. He would finish the season at .312, make no errors in right field, and claim his 12th consecutive Gold Glove Award. On and off the field, Clemente's contributions would help Pittsburgh clinch a third consecutive National League East title.

During the 1972 season, Pirate broadcaster Nellie King learned about a diary that Clemente had kept throughout his career. "He told me that every year he would keep a log of any injury he had to his body from the time he started playing baseball," King says. "He said, 'If I had an injury to my leg I would mark it down in the diary, how I hurt it, when it was hurt.' He'd get that book out every year and he would exercise and strengthen that part of his body because it was weak. He did that for 17, 18 consecutive years."

While some players and writers might have looked upon Clemente's diary as strange, King did not share their view. "I look on him as being an artist," says the former Pirate broadcaster. "Artistic people, they see things differently. They feel things and hear things differently. They have a different aura about them. We think they're odd, you know, like there's something wrong with that guy, he's not normal. In that respect, Clemente wasn't normal with his body." At times, Clemente refused to play with injuries that others might have ignored. "Like an artist, he wasn't going to paint a bad picture and sign his name to it when he went out on the ballfield," King says. "In his way of expressing himself, his body was a paintbrush. That's the way he painted a picture. And he was not going to paint a bad picture."

As a member of the Pirates' farm system in 1972, Art Howe visited Three Rivers Stadium and caught a glimpse of Clemente's physique in the Pirate clubhouse. "I remember seeing him in the clubhouse," says Howe. "He was 38 years old when I got to come in there. He had a washboard stomach. He had the body of a 21-year-old." Clemente maintained his body better than most aging players because of a healthy lifestyle. He did not smoke, and very rarely consumed alcohol.

Clemente also liked to drink a health milkshake or punch, one of the conditioning secrets that Luis Mayoral had observed a year earlier. "I'll never forget in spring training of 1971," says Mayoral, "I went to Pirate City and spent a few days with him in his room. I remember that he'd get up after taking a quick nap after the workout, and he'd fix me a punch. He'd take grape juice, and then he'd put like 12 eggs in there, and beat it. He always told me, 'This is what keeps me strong.' And between you and me, that tasted like [bleep]. Man, that tasted bad, but I drank a glass or two." Sometimes Clemente created even more exotic concoctions, mixing milk, orange juice, fruit, egg yolks and banana ice cream. As with everything else, Clemente took his health punch seriously. "He even took pride in fixing that punch," Mayoral says.

In King's mind, two of Clemente's attributes stood out above all others. "Pride and dedication," King says. "Nobody can dedicate themselves to a game or sport any more than he had at 38. He was still playing the best baseball [of his career]. He was somewhat like Michael Jordan. Those guys don't come along very often. You know, some guys will lay on their laurels, they'll take an easy year sometimes. But I never saw Clemente [do that]. He still had that great dedication in '72, and I think that's the way Jordan plays basketball today. Even in a pick-up game, he'll play that way. I think Clemente played that same way. His pride and dedication were special."

In spite of his continued excellence on the field, critics continued to cite the increasing number of games he missed due to injury and illness. "And at age 38," says King, "the people who were questioning him—from the standpoint of not knowing the pride he had in what he was doing—those guys to a man today will tell you that nobody at age 38 played baseball like Roberto Clemente did. And the reason he did was because of the dedication he had to the game and his body, in particular."

The 1972 season marked several milestones for the veteran right fielder. On June 19, Clemente slammed a two-run home run in the eighth inning to cap off a three-RBI night and help the Pirates defeat the Dodgers. The three RBIs gave him 1,275 for his career, the most in the history of the Pirates' franchise. Clemente moved ahead of Hall of Fame third baseman Pie Traynor, who had died earlier in the year. When a reporter asked him why he had not acknowledged the Three Rivers Stadium fans who had given him a standing ovation, Clemente tried to explain himself. "The man whose record I broke was a great ballplayer, a great fellow. And he just died here a few months ago. That's why I didn't even tip my cap. You know what I mean..." Clemente hoped the writers and fans understood.

On September 2, Clemente surpassed another Hall of Famer. The 2,971st hit of his career—a double—pushed him past Honus Wagner as the Pirates' all-time hit leader. All the while, Clemente continued his quest for his 3,000th hit. As the Pirates headed toward the latter stages of the 1972 season, with the division title all but wrapped up, Clemente continued to play. He publicly downplayed the significance of reaching 3,000 career hits, but the pursuit of the milestone clearly drove him, as did his relentless pride.

A story told by Nellie King illustrates Clemente's ceaseless effort. "I don't mean just in big games," King says. "I mean in meaningless games. I remember 1972 we were playing the Phillies—Steve Carlton had a helluva year but they were still in last place—and we had already won the pennant by about eight games. The only reason Clemente was playing late in September was to get his 3,000th hit. The Phillies were up at bat in the eighth inning of the game, they were leading, with a runner at second base. [Larry] Bowa hits a shot into right-center field—a line drive—and Clemente cuts it off and holds it to a single. But the guy scored. We end up losing the game. (The Pirates actually won, 5-1.) After the game, I go into the press room, and Rex Bowen, who was scouting for Cincinnati and had been with the Pirate organization, came up [to me]. He says to me, 'What do you think was the key play in that game?'

"I said, 'I can't remember any key plays in that game. What do you think it was?'

"[Bowen] says, 'You remember Bowa's hit in the eighth inning?'

"'Yeah, I remember that,'" King responded.

Bowen continued his point. "'Remember Clemente cutting that ball off and holding it to a single? I tell you what, next week, when the playoffs begin, every right fielder in baseball will make that play. But on September 26, in the eighth inning of a meaningless game in Philadelphia, Roberto Clemente is the only right fielder in baseball who would make that play.'

"That's a pretty good tribute," says King. "He would never shortchange the fans. Somebody said he owed the fans everything. He said, 'Bull— I owe the fans a good game.'"

At times, Clemente playfully mimicked the fans. "Roberto, we love you," Clemente once said to King, while imitating the voice of a typical fan. "You do not have to go out and play the second game of a doubleheader. You can pull a chair out there and you can sit on the chair and we will not holler at you." Clemente then returned to his normal voice. "Bull— they will not holler at me," Clemente told King. "They want [me] to play well. That's what I owe them and I have to give them that."

In the final game of the series with the Phillies, Clemente collected hit No. 2,999, a single against Phillies' ace Steve Carlton. With the division title already clinched, manager Bill Virdon removed Clemente from the game, in order to preserve the possibility of his reaching hit No. 3,000 at home. The next night, the Pirates began their final homestand of the season. Facing the Mets' hard-throwing Tom Seaver, Clemente tapped a bouncer up the middle that caromed off the glove of Mets' second baseman Ken Boswell. The message on the scoreboard immediately indicated a hit—No. 3,000. The crowd of 24,193 erupted, some of the fans throwing streamers onto the field. Second base umpire Frank Pulli tossed the ball to first base umpire John Kibler, who in turn handed it off to Clemente. First base coach Don Leppert patted Clemente on the rear as he threw the ball toward the Pirates' dugout. Then, a large "E" flashed on the scoreboard, signaling that the play had been deemed an error. The fans booed loudly. The official scorer had apparently ruled an error on the sure-handed Boswell from the outset, but the scoreboard operator had not heard his ruling properly. "I worked in the scoreboard operations room at the time and we had the message ready to flash up on the board for No. 3,000," says Sally O'Leary. "The Friday night in September, he hit this ball and it was questionable, but we thought that we heard the people in the press box announce 'hit,' so we immediately flashed that up on the board."

The staffers in the scoreboard operations room found agreement from Clemente himself. "It was a hit all the way," said Clemente, who felt that he would have beaten the throw to first base even if Boswell had managed to handle the grounder cleanly. "But this is nothing new. Official scorers have been robbing me of hits like this for 18 years." On this occasion, Clemente thought that the official scorer was Charley Feeney of the *Pittsburgh Post-Gazette*.

A few moments later, one of Clemente's best friends in the media shouted out to him. "I made the call," said Luke Quay of the

McKeesport Daily News. It was he, and not Feeney, who had served as official scorer for the game. Although Clemente was still upset that he had been denied his 3,000th hit, he did not allow the perceived injustice to affect his sense of humor—or his strong friendship with the official scorer. Quay was one of the few writers who consistently defended Roberto against charges of hypochondria, calling them unfair, even mythical. After the game, Clemente delivered the ball to Quay, with a signed inscription. "It was a **Hit**," Clemente wrote on the first line, before continuing the message. "No, it was an **error**. No, it was superman Luke Quay. To my friend Luke with best wishes—Roberto Clemente." Even in the context of disappointment and anger, Clemente tried to keep perspective—and a sense of humor.

After two other fruitless at-bats, Clemente had sliced a liner toward the right field corner in his final at-bat. Playing Clemente within 10 feet of the line, instead of the way that most outfielders positioned him toward the gap, right fielder Rusty Staub made the catch with ease. Clemente had been denied once again.

The hitless game, followed by a sleepless night filled with early morning phone calls, set up a Saturday afternoon matchup against New York's impressive young left-hander, Jon Matlack. In the first inning, Matlack struck out Clemente, thwarting another bid at No. 3,000. Clemente would probably not get his next chance until the fourth inning, barring a long rally for the Pirate lineup. The possibility of a milestone hit affected the dynamics of the Pirates' broadcasting crew, which featured Bob Prince and Nellie King. Prince and Clemente had developed a special relationship, which King fully realized. "He used the term 'Great One,'" King says of Prince, who had given Clemente the nickname that showed him such respect.

In the Saturday afternoon game against the Mets, Prince did play-by-play for the first three innings, including Clemente's strikeout. King was scheduled to do play-by-play during the game's middle innings. "I was gonna do the fourth inning of the game," recalls King. "[Prince] did the first three and I'd do the middle innings. I did the top of the fourth and then we went off the air and I said, 'Bob, I think Clemente's coming up, I think you'd better do this.'"

Coming to bat for the second time, Clemente led off the bottom of the fourth against Matlack. As Bob Prince accepted the play-by-play microphone from Nellie King, Luis Mayoral announced

Clemente's at-bat for Puerto Rican radio. "That was September 30, it was something like 3:07 in the afternoon," recalls Mayoral, who broadcast the game that day for Puerto Rican radio. "A little bit over 13,000 fans were in the stands. Fourth inning, Jon Matlack was pitching. Yes, I saw that."

Mayoral and Prince would witness and broadcast an important piece of baseball—and Latin American—history. With the count 0-and-1, Matlack threw a curve ball, which Clemente smacked toward the gap in left-center field. The long drive reached the fence on one hop. Center fielder Dave Schneck retrieved the ball and threw it to the infield, as Clemente steamed into second base with a double. Only the 11th major leaguer in history to collect 3,000 hits, Clemente had also become the first Latino ballplayer to reach the milestone.

This time, there would be no reversal from the press box. Unlike the play the previous night, this was a clean, no-questions-asked base hit. Retrieving the ball from shortstop Jim Fregosi, second base umpire Doug Harvey handed the memento over to Clemente and shook his hand. In turn, Clemente gave it to Don Leppert, who stored the ball in his back pocket. Clemente stood atop second base, lifted his helmet with his right hand, and sheepishly raised it to the cheers of the 13,117 fans in attendance at Three Rivers. As the umpires delayed the game, the fans continued their applause for several minutes. Not knowing what to do next, Clemente placed his hands on his hips and rolled his neck, as he often did at the plate. "I feel bashful when I get a big ovation," Clemente told Milton Richman afterwards. "I am really shy. I never was a big shot and I never will be a big shot."

When the applause finally died down, play resumed. Clemente eventually came around to score, his hit having ignited a three-run rally. As he ran to his position in right field to start the fifth inning, the fans thanked him with another standing ovation. Clemente removed his cap, tipping it to his loyal fans. Upon returning to the dugout at the end of the half inning, Clemente received special acknowledgment from one of his opponents. Another future Hall of Famer, playing out his final seasons in a backup role with the Mets, walked across the diamond to the Pirates' dugout. "I clearly remember seeing Willie Mays of the Mets come over from the third base dugout and embrace Roberto after the 3,000th hit," says Luis Mayoral. Even though Mays and Clemente had never felt particularly close to one another, even during their one season as winter league teammates, the former Giants' superstar felt it important to congratulate his rival in person. The gesture showed Mays' respect for one of the few players the media dared to mention in association with the greatness of the "Say Hey Kid."

Clemente left the game when Bill Virdon sent up Bill Mazeroski as a pinch-hitter. It was a fitting choice, given that Mazeroski had been Clemente's teammate longer than anyone. After the game, Clemente took a moment to recognize another important person from his baseball past. "I dedicated the hit to the Pittsburgh fans and to the people in Puerto Rico, and to one man in particular," Clemente said, referring to Roberto Marin, his first coach in softball, the man who had spotted him playing baseball with guava tree limbs and crushed spaghetti cans. At a time when Roberto had accomplished one of the game's most significant individual milestones, he had felt it important to acknowledge the people who had paved the way for his major league stardom.

For Mayoral, the opportunity to witness Clemente's milestone hit would represent his most meaningful thrill in baseball. "Yes, it was," Mayoral says. "I think of all the years I've been as an adult in baseball, that was the highlight right there." Little did Mayoral or anyone else at Three Rivers Stadium know that Clemente's double against Matlack would be his final regular season base hit.

Upset by the small number of writers assigned to cover his chase of the milestone, Clemente had been critical of the lack of media coverage. He pointed out that many more writers had followed Hank Aaron and Willie Mays during their pursuits of 3,000 base hits. Although Clemente did not discuss the size of the crowd publicly, the small gathering probably disappointed him, as well. Richie Hebner remembers with some sadness that overcast day at Three Rivers Stadium. "I don't think there was 12,000 people in the stands," Hebner says of the game that was actually attended by barely over 13,000 fans. "[Here was] a guy who had played 18 years. Sometimes I didn't understand [why the fans didn't support the team better], but Pittsburgh was a hard-working city, and we didn't draw people like we should have." Mayoral shared in the disappointment of the poor turnout. "I thought, yes, personally, that they'd have a full house because we have to go back to the Waners; no one in Pittsburgh had reached 3,000 hits [since then]. When you come to think of it, yes, I think it was disappointing then."

Some defenders of the small turnout have pointed out that the September 30th game against the Mets meant nothing within the context of the pennant race. The Pirates had already clinched the National League East, eliminating the Mets and the rest of the division from post-season contention. According to this line of reasoning, a large crowd should not have been expected. In light of the attention given to players who subsequently chased 3,000 hits, like George Brett, Pete Rose and Carl Yastrzemski, such an argument seems inadequate. Whatever the specific reason for the sparse crowd, the low turnout was not a fitting reward for a player who had done so much for the fans of Pittsburgh for nearly two decades.

In late October, Clemente received belated recognition of his milestone hit in the form of a congratulatory letter. "With the excitement of the playoffs and the World Series, I had neglected to tell you how delighted I was to learn of your 3000th hit in major league ball," said the letter, which was addressed to Clemente's home in Rio Piedras. "This new milestone is further confirmation—if any were needed—of the standards of excellence you have shown on the playing field. Heartiest congratulations and kindest good wishes for many more seasons."

The author of the letter? U.S. President Richard M. Nixon.

The day after the 3,000th hit, Luis Mayoral paid special tribute to Clemente, who received a standing ovation from the 30,031 fans in attendance at Three Rivers. "I had started a movement, maybe two weeks before, to give him a special award that day," Mayoral recalls. "I finally came up with an idea, which a lot of people didn't understand then. And it was to get a little clod of earth from the little ballpark in barrio San Anton, where he started playing baseball as a child. And the ballpark was still there, but really run down. So we went out there one afternoon prior to me going to Pittsburgh, and with a shovel, we dug out maybe a square foot clod of earth, and I put it at the base of the award. I have a picture of that. That's my favorite picture; I have it in my office here. That's what I presented to Roberto."

Although the award received very little attention from the media, and was not recognized by the major leagues, it meant a great deal to Mayoral on a personal level. "That was simply an award, Luis Mayoral loving what [Clemente] had done and admiring him as a human being—as a Puerto Rican and as a brother. It had no official connotation. It was simply Luis, the young baseball man, doing something to honor his friend, the greatest player we've had in Puerto Rico, maybe in all of Latin America."

With the milestone in hand, Clemente planned to rest the final three games in preparation for the playoffs. Three days after collecting his 3,000th hit, Clemente unwittingly reached another significant milestone—with some help from the team's public relations director. "The [second to] last game of the season had no significance as far as the standings were concerned," says Bill Guilfoile, beginning a little-known story. "When I got to the clubhouse and looked at the starting lineup, Clemente was not in the starting lineup. He needed to play one more game to be the all-time leader among the Pirates in games played." Honus Wagner had played in 2,432 games, the same number as Clemente. Guilfoile approached Clemente, mentioned the milestone, and asked "The Great One" if he was planning to play in the game that night against the Cardinals. "He was having some trouble with his back," Guilfoile says, recalling Clemente's response to his question. "Since the game really didn't have any significance, he had told [Bill] Virdon that he didn't feel he wanted to play. So, I reminded him that he only needed one more game to be the all-time Pirate leader in games played. He said, 'So what? Opening Day next year I will have the record. Why should I worry about that?'

"I don't know why, but instead of just dropping it at that," Guilfoile says, "I went to Virdon, who was managing, and I told Bill about this. He said to me, 'Don't worry, I'll get him in the game.' So, late in the game, it was about the seventh or eighth inning, all of a sudden Bill made a substitution and sent Clemente out to right field, where he finished the game. As a result of that, he now is in the record books as being the all-time leading Pirate in games played. It was just sort of strange in retrospect how that all happened. At the time, it didn't seem like a big deal, but for some reason or other, I made an issue of it, and for some reason or other, Virdon went along with it. Now, we're both very happy that we did." If not for the intervention of Bill Guilfoile, Clemente would not have broken the record.

23

A Rematch With the Machine

In 1970, the Cincinnati Reds had beaten the Pirates convincingly in the National League Championship Series. Now the defending world champions, the Pirates seemed better prepared to handle Cincinnati's powerful offense and deep bullpen in a playoff rematch.

In Game One, Steve Blass ran into trouble after retiring the game's leadoff batter, Pete Rose. Throwing what he called an above average fastball, Blass watched Joe Morgan launch a 360-foot home run into the bleachers at Three Rivers Stadium. Although the Pirates' thoughts must have wandered to their 1970 playoff embarrassment, Blass quickly righted himself. The Pirates' offense helped, too, scoring three runs in the bottom of the first on the way to a 5-1 victory.

The Reds rebounded in Game Two, scoring four early runs against Pirate starter Bob Moose. The Bucs rallied for single runs in each of the middle innings, but fell short, 5-3. Clemente went 0-for-3 against Jack Billingham and Tom Hall, each time stranding runners on base. The second game futility left him hitless after seven playoff at-bats. "When you are hitting like I am," Clemente lamented to Dan Donovan of the *Pittsburgh*

Press, "they just throw anything past you. I'm like a fighter who doesn't have a punch."

After the second game of the playoffs against the Reds, WIIC-TV in Pittsburgh aired an extended interview featuring Clemente and the station's sports director, Sam Nover. For one of the few times in his career, Clemente talked in-depth about a wide range of off-the-field topics, including his three young sons. "I want them to enjoy life the way I enjoy life," Clemente told Nover. "I love people, and I love the minority people. I love people that they are not big shots; I like common people, I like workers, I like people that suffer. Because these people, they have a different approach of life [from] the people that really have everything in life, that sometimes they get bored—because they have everything and they don't know what suffering is in life. So I want my kids to suffer. I want them to have what they're supposed to have, but I don't want them to be rich."

Clemente's comments about his children brought to mind a short poem he had written during one of the Pirates' Father's Day games at Three Rivers Stadium. The poem, entitled "Quien Soy?" or "Who Am I?" read as follows:

> *I am a small point in the eye of the full moon.*
> *I only need one ray of the sun to warm my face.*
> *I only need one breeze from the Alisios to refresh my soul.*
> *What else can I ask if I know that my sons really love me?*

Having discussed many issues that mattered to him during his interview with Nover, Clemente returned to the business of the Championship Series. With the setting shifting to Cincinnati, Clemente picked up his first post-season hit, a double. Manny Sanguillen, Clemente's closest friend on the team, drove home a pair of runs—including a home run—to help the Pirates rally from a 2-0 deficit and post a 3-2 win.

Needing one more win to take the pennant, Clemente put forth his best playoff performance in Game Four. In four at-bats, he picked up two hits, including a home run. Unfortunately, most of the other Pirates played their worst games. Other than Clemente, no batter managed a hit, while Pittsburgh pitchers gave up 11 hits and seven runs. Reds' baserunners ran wild on Manny Sanguillen, rumored to have a sore arm. Even Clemente could not prevent a 7-1 loss and a deadlock in the series.

On Wednesday, October 11, the Pirates and Reds played the fifth and deciding game of the Championship Series at Riverfront Stadium. Clemente took the field, not knowing if he would be able to reach a third World Series. The early developments of the game favored the Pirates, who forged a 3-2 lead. Dave Giusti came on in the bottom of the ninth, trying to seal the pennant. He jumped ahead of the first batter, Johnny Bench, one ball and two strikes. Bench sent the next pitch deep to right, driving Clemente to the limits of the fences. Clemente looked up as the ball landed in the right field seats. Tie game, 3-3. Tony Perez and Denis Menke followed with singles. Cesar Geronimo, facing reliever Bob Moose, lofted a fly ball to right field, too deep for Clemente to prevent pinch-runner George Foster from advancing to third base. Moose then retired Darrel Chaney on a pop-up for the inning's second out.

Moose now faced Hal McRae, pinch-hitting for pitcher Clay Carroll. Clemente and the rest of the Pirates watched helplessly as Moose bounced a wild slider past Manny Sanguillen, allowing Foster to score the game-winning run. The Reds had rallied for two runs to win the game and capture the series, suddenly ending the season for the Pirates. Clemente walked off the field—for the last time.

Pirate players streamed slowly into a clubhouse locked in silence. Suddenly, Clemente walked into the middle of the room and spoke up—loudly. "Don't worry about it," Clemente shouted, targeting all of his teammates with his impromptu address. "What we need is a sense of humor." Clemente then noticed a discouraged Dave Giusti, one of the relievers who had failed in the ninth inning, staring at the ground. "Giusti, damn you, Giusti," Clemente yelled. "Look straight ahead. Pick up your head. We don't quit now. We go home and come back in February."

"We lost the game on the wild pitch," says Nellie King, who had broadcast the heartbreaking fifth game back to the fans in Pittsburgh. "Dave Giusti told me that they were going into the clubhouse, and [Roberto] said, 'Do not hang your heads. Do not go into the trainer's room and hide from the media. You stay out here and talk to them. Be proud to be a Pirate.'"

Clemente's words sounded like those contained within a high school speech, but they registered with his teammates. "'Be proud to be a Pirate,'" King says, continuing his imitation of Clemente. "'We are still the world champions until somebody wins. You stand up and talk to them.' And the media was really impressed that the guys stayed there." Listening to Clemente's words, the Pirate players stopped moping. Instead, amidst the heartbreak of a fifth game loss, they patiently answered reporters' questions as they packed up their belongings for the long winter.

One of the Pirates, pitcher Bob Johnson, invited all of the players to his house for a post-game party. Clemente seized the invitation to lighten the clubhouse mood. "Where you live at?" Clemente asked Johnson before drawing Bob Miller into the conversation. "Miller, get me a map. Let me write it [the address] down. [Johnson] might back out."

First encouragement, then humor. Clemente wasn't done with his ladling of emotions, however. He still needed to display some anger. Once all of the media had departed the clubhouse, Clemente approached one of the team's most disappointing performers in 1972. "After it was all over," King says, relaying a little-known story told to him by one of the Pirate players, "he went over to Bob Robertson, who had a hell of a year in '71 and was a complete flop in '72. He walked over to Robertson and said, 'You quit on us this year. You quit. I watched you. You're not hitting. You should be out there at 2:00 in the afternoon taking batting practice. At 4:00, you can find some batting practice again. And then again at 6:00. During the game, you're sitting on the bench and you should be watching the pitchers to see how they pitch everybody, how they work the batters. But I watch you. You don't do that. You go around and drink your beer and chase the girls. I watch you doing that.'"

After King learned about the verbal thrashing of Robertson, he approached Clemente during a meeting in Puerto Rico in November. "I saw him later," King says. "I asked him, 'Is that true? Why did you do that?' He said, 'You know, Nellie, it is really funny when you watch young players. They work so hard to get from the [low] minor leagues into the high minor leagues. They work hard to finally get to the big leagues, and then they really work hard to become an established player. And then they suddenly think, Oh boy, I can finally take it easy now. I am a star and don't have to work anymore.' He said, 'Hell, the better you are in this game, the more you have to work.'"

Clemente used an intriguing analogy to illustrate his point to King. "He said, 'It's like a monkey going up a pole. If they're trying to shoot him, the farther he goes up the pole, the more they see of his rear end, and they shoot him. That's the way it is when you're a good player.'" By confronting Robertson, Clemente hoped that he would motivate the young slugger into resuming the work ethic that he had used to make the major leagues in the first place." 'That's what I was trying to say,'" Clemente explained to King. "'I bet you any money that Bob Robertson is up in Cumberland [Maryland], running in the mountains, getting ready for next year. That's why I did that.'"

At first, Clemente's words upset Robertson. Given the harshness of Clemente's tone, and the disappointment of a playoff defeat, Robertson's initial anger with Clemente was understandable. "Robertson didn't have too many kind things to say about Clemente; I guess it was because of this [exchange in the clubhouse]," says King. "But now, he has a great affection for Clemente. I think he finally understood what Roberto was saying."

In the Pirates' clubhouse, players bid farewell to each other. One of Clemente's closest friends on the team, Dave Cash, approached Roberto and said good-bye for the winter. "I remember leaving the clubhouse, and we shook hands and hugged each other," says Cash. "We just wished each other well and hoped that we could come back and put things together and get back on a winning track again." Cash anticipated that he would see "The Great One" again in February, when the Pirates would gather for spring training in Bradenton. "A lot of us didn't get a chance to see him after the [1972] season," Cash remembers. "I didn't get a chance to talk to him again after he left Pittsburgh." Clemente, who had gone 1-for-3 and had played no special role in that final, frustrating game against the Reds, would never make it to Bradenton.

24

The Fates of Winter

The playoff loss to the Reds notwithstanding, Clemente's 18th season in the major leagues had been a productive one. Although he played a career-low 102 games, he still batted .312, hit 10 home runs, drove in 60, scored 68, and won his 12th Gold Glove Award. Bill Mazeroski's 17th season had not been so fruitful. In 34 games, Mazeroski batted a career-worst .188, with only three RBIs in 64 at-bats. With Dave Cash and Rennie Stennett ahead of him on the second base depth chart, Maz had struggled to find a role with the team.

Yet, Clemente was not ready to give up on Mazeroski. As Nellie King tells the story, Clemente invited Maz to join him in Puerto Rico, where he would play a four-week stint in the winter league. Mazeroski thought about the invitation, but turned it down. Instead, the former Gold Glove second baseman decided to retire. "Maz said he couldn't do it [anymore] due to family genetics," King reveals. Mazeroski's continuing battle with his weight proved discouraging. "Maz said, 'I can't fight that battle anymore. I've done it for 17 years, but not anymore.'"

Like Clemente, Maz shared a sense of artistic pride in his work. "Maz was likewise proud," says King. "He would not continue unless he could play well." Unlike Clemente, Maz no longer had the body that would allow him to continue playing. "At age 38, Clemente was still the best hitter, runner, and thrower on the team." At age 36, Mazeroski's body had simply given out.

The relationship between Clemente and Mazeroski has come under scrutiny in the years since their departures from the game. In their early years, there seemed to be a polite distance between the two players. As with most of his teammates—especially the established white players—Clemente didn't socialize with Maz away from the ballpark. They talked occasionally, but rarely joked with each other. In later years, the separation between the two men gave way to feelings of commonality. "We've always been friendly—in 16 years we've never spoken a cross word—but as we got older, we got closer," Mazeroski wrote in the November 1971 edition of *Sport* magazine. "It's just been the last four or five years that we've really been close friends, close enough to agitate each other." Like others who knew Clemente, Mazeroski appreciated his comical side, his ability to make others laugh.

After the season, Clemente decided to honor one of his best friends in baseball, one of the few members of the media with whom he had achieved a special relationship. Longtime broadcaster Bob Prince, who was celebrating his 25th year in broadcasting and had called the majority of Clemente's games in a Pirate uniform, received an invitation to fly to San Juan. Clemente also invited a large group of children with mental disabilities to the event, knowing that they represented one of the favorite causes of the likable announcer. "[Roberto] had a big day for him in Puerto Rico in '72," recalls Nellie King. "Gave him the silver bat, I think the most treasured thing that he'd won. He didn't wear the ring from the '60 World Series. [Roberto once] said, 'The thing that I treasured most was the first batting championship bat.'" Clemente had received the silver bat after winning the 1961 National League hitting title, the first of his four individual batting crowns.

In addition to Prince, Clemente enjoyed a close relationship with Luke Quay, the sports editor for the *McKeesport Daily News,* who would die from a heart attack in 1976. For the most part, Prince and Quay succeeded with Clemente where many other members of the media had failed. "It's not easy. I can understand the writers' point of view," says Luis Mayoral. "The game's over and [the writer's] got 45 minutes to wire the story in, so he needs a quote or two. But unless you befriend the guy, and you feel comfortable and not intimidated by him because he comes from another culture [you won't have a good relationship]. If you did your homework, then he would give you a quote or two."

For most of his career, Clemente had settled for few endorsement opportunities. His Latin American heritage, skin color and difficulties with the language had all discouraged potential advertisers. Pittsburgh's status as a small market team hadn't helped his marketability either. In 1971, Clemente made only $500 in endorsements, a paltry sum compared with the $30,000 earned by Willie Stargell. "I've had a couple of endorsements but they never came to nothing," Clemente told C.R. Ways of the *New York Times* in the spring of 1972. "I don't need them. If the people who give them out don't think Latins are good enough, I don't think THEY are good enough. The hell with them. I make endorsements in Spanish countries, and give the money to charity." Clemente's teammates sympathized with his plight. "The first time I even saw Clemente on TV, outside baseball," Stargell had told *Black Sports* in 1971, "was on the Mike Douglas show, a year ago. For one of baseball's time-honored superstars, that's a shame." By the fall of 1972, endorsement obstacles started to crumble. Corporations like Eastern Airlines and Marriott Hotels expressed some interest in Clemente, who held discussions with an advertising agency.

Pirates' broadcaster Nellie King talked to one of the representatives of the ad agency, telling him that Clemente wouldn't settle for being a figurehead; he would want to become actively involved in any company to whom he attached his name.

Clemente attended a luncheon with the agency representative, who gave Roberto certain assurances about his involvement with the company. Clemente told King about their conversation "He said to me, 'Funny, after luncheon he handed me an envelope. I asked what it was. He said it was partial payment for our agreement.' Roberto pushed it aside. He told him, 'I do not want it until you do all the things you said you will do today.'"

Although Clemente had legitimate interest in signing an endorsement contract, he wanted to do it his way—the right way. As King recalls Clemente telling him, "'When you put the envelope in your pocket, they got you, Nellie.'"

During the off-season, Clemente enjoyed pursuing his diverse interests: making ceramic figurines and lamps, sculpting driftwood, listening to classical music, writing poetry, and playing musical instruments. In addition, he usually played or managed in the Puerto Rican Winter League. Continuing back problems and the realities of a 38-year-old body dictated that Clemente take the winter off from the rigors of the winter league schedule. Instead, Roberto made arrangements with a local telephone company to sponsor a series of baseball clinics that he would hold for over 10,000 Puerto Rican youngsters. He also continued fundraising efforts for his sports city. On another front, Clemente planned to open a chiropractor clinic that would employ several American doctors.

Roberto also took some time to manage a team of Puerto Rican all-stars in a worldwide amateur tournament. "He had spent almost the whole month of November in Nicaragua," says Luis Mayoral, "managing our top amateur team in the [Amateur Baseball] World Series that was won by the USA, a team managed by Ron Fraser." Although Clemente spent a relatively short time in that Latin American country, he struck up a friendship with the Nicaraguan people. He found the fans and the citizens of Nicaragua to be warm and receptive, even to a man from another country.

By December, Clemente had returned to Puerto Rico to spend time with his family. Unexpected events would interrupt the routine of Clemente's winter. On December 23, a massive earthquake devastated the Nicaraguan capitol of Managua. The earthquake killed over 7,000 people, while injuring several thousand. Damage to residential homes and office buildings mounted, leaving over 250,000 people homeless.

At the suggestion of two acquaintances, Clemente decided to head up a special Puerto Rican committee to collect relief supplies. "Roberto was the leader of the whole mission," recalls Luis Mayoral. "And this came to be maybe a day or two before I last saw him, when the earthquakes really hit. Two television personalities, Luis Vigoreaux—he was a show host in Puerto Rico—and Ruth Fernandez—she's one of the greatest singers ever on the island— they convinced Clemente to go on TV and address the people in Puerto Rico to get together and help send relief supplies for the people damned by the earthquake. That's when Roberto took over unofficially as the leader of that whole movement."

Why would Clemente—or anyone for that matter—undertake such a massive project, especially at a time of year when most people would have been excused for showing a preference to stay with their families? Clemente could have donated money, like most other celebrities, and left the organization of the relief effort to politicians or charitable organizations. So why did Clemente forsake all of his winter plans for the citizens of another country? For one reason, Clemente was not like most other people. He believed in hands-on participation, rather than mere gestures of good will. For another, Clemente had developed a special relationship with Nicaraguan fans during his managerial tour in November. "That's where he kind of fell in love with the people in Nicaragua," maintains Luis Mayoral. "We lost some very good friends in the earthquake," Vera Clemente told Douglas McDaniel of *The Diamond* in 1993. "We met some very nice people there, made friends." In particular, Roberto had become attached to a 14-year-old Nicaraguan orphan who had lost both of his legs. Clemente worried about the fate of the young boy, whom he had arranged to be supplied with artificial limbs.

As the honorary chairman of the earthquake committee, Clemente appeared on local radio and television stations to appeal for food, clothing and other supplies. Putting in 14-hour days, Clemente worked on Christmas Eve, all day on Christmas Day, and then again on the 26th. He committed himself so fully to the effort that he regularly refused meals, barely slept, and never opened the Christmas presents that he had received. He even visited houses in the wealthier sections of San Juan—literally going door to door—asking homeowners to make donations. Spearheaded by Clemente, the committee raised over $150,000 in funds. The relief team also gathered 26 tons of food, clothing and medicine—some of which were donated by the carload—storing them temporarily at Hiram Bithorn Stadium in Santurce.

Clemente also made arrangements to obtain a plane from a company in Miami. The company agreed to lease the plane, for three trips, at a cost of $11,000. In addition to coordinating three successful flights to Nicaragua, the committee organized the voyage of a large shipping vessel filled with goods. Clemente talked of boarding one of the flights personally, but Luis Vigoreaux and Ruth Fernandez discouraged him, citing the uncertain conditions of small cargo planes.

Clemente then received a desperate request from Managua for additional loads of sugar and medical supplies. Clemente agreed to lease another plane, an aging propeller-driven DC-7, for $4,000. When Clemente heard reports that goods targeted for the people of Managua had been intercepted by the Nicaraguan army, he became infuriated. "The Great One" elected to personally accompany the delivery of supplies to Managua.

A few days prior to the scheduled trip to Nicaragua, Mayoral drove to Santurce to drop off some goods for the relief mission. Upon delivery, Mayoral met with Clemente. "I saw him at Hi Bithorn Stadium. They had a little area in the hall—in the main hall—where he was storing goods, you know food and clothing, youth clothing and so forth. And I remember he was dressed in brown; brown slacks, brown boots—he loved boots, not cowboy boots, but [boots] up to the ankle—and a brown shirt. And when I saw him, he was bending over, picking up a ball. So I just went over and slapped his butt like they do when they hit a homer and they come around third base, and he jumped up, you know, surprised. He saw I was leaving and started laughing. So I left a bundle of things there, and that was the last time I saw him."

Mayoral believes that he himself might have accompanied Clemente on that flight, if not for a series of unusual circumstances. "I met with Roberto; it could have been four or five days prior to the trip [to Managua]. I remember I was taking a few days off, and I do recall that something happened, something funny happened. On or about the 15th, 16th or 17th of December, I got a call from a man who ran the scoreboard at Hi Bithorn Stadium. This man lived in old San Juan. And a friend of his family—a grown-up lady—had a grandson in Miami who was going to go through some kind of surgery. The grandson had called his grandmother in Puerto Rico, asking her to get something signed by Clemente. Since she was a friend of the guy who did the scoreboard at Bithorn Stadium, he called me. So I called Roberto between the 15th and the 17th, and I told him that the kid was sick and was going to have surgery in Miami."

As Mayoral describes, Clemente reacted to the request in typical fashion. "So he said, 'Come on over anytime. And I won't only give you a picture, we'll get a ball or something.' So three different times I started to go to Roberto's place. We lived maybe six miles apart. Two times, someone rammed my car from the back. And then, like four days later, I had a new car." Mayoral tried once again to drive to Clemente's house. "Going to Roberto's place, I had a flat tire. When I went to get the spare, it was also flat in the new car. So I was unable to get out. And then I tried [another] time, but something happened and I wasn't able to go out there. I bring this up because today I feel that had I been involved with him those days [during the relief effort], I could well have been on that plane, too."

Clemente had invited Manny Sanguillen, who was playing winter ball with the San Juan Senators, to accompany him aboard the relief mission from San Juan to Nicaragua. On December 29, Clemente and Sanguillen spoke face-to-face. Sanguillen thought about going on the flight, scheduled for the following day. After playing in a winter league game, Sanguillen readied himself for the drive to the airport. When the engine of his car blew up, Sanguillen couldn't make the flight. As it turned out, Clemente's relief committee had already decided to postpone their departure because of problems with the plane and difficulties in finding a crew.

The committee rescheduled the flight for the following day, December 31. Sanguillen decided to drive to San Juan to talk to Clemente about the trip. As Sanguillen prepared to leave his apartment for San Juan International Airport that evening, he and his wife searched frantically for the keys to their car. At seven o'clock, Sanguillen finally found the keys, which were located on a high shelf in the apartment. But it was now too late to reach the airport on time. "I do know that Manny and Roberto were perhaps the two closest ballplayers ever, as to friendship," comments Luis Mayoral. "I don't doubt [that] Manny was supposed to be on that flight. I don't know [for sure] because Manny was playing winter ball."

Clemente and four other men boarded the plane on New Year's Eve. The group included Arturo Rivera—the president of the company that owned the plane—pilot Jerry Hill, flight engineer Francisco Matias, and a man named Rafael Lozano, a friend of Clemente. Several people, including Vera Clemente's and teammate Jose Pagan, had expressed concerns about the old plane, which seemed dangerously overloaded. The eight tons of relief supplies were also unevenly distributed, creating a perilous imbalance once the plane left the ground. "Don't do it," said Pagan, one of the Pirates whom Clemente often confided in. "You know everything about baseball, but very little about airplanes." Rivera claimed the aircraft was safe and declared that he would co-pilot the flight to Managua. Influenced by Rivera, Clemente insisted on boarding the plane.

Knowing that she would not return home until the late hours, Vera had dropped her three sons off at her mother's house, where they would stay overnight. Earlier in the day, seven-year-old Roberto, Jr., the oldest of the three boys, had begged his father not to make the trip. The young boy predicted that the plane would not make it to Managua. That evening, in the hours before the flight departed,

Roberto, Jr. repeated the premonition to his grandmother. "Grandma, grandma, Daddy is leaving for Nicaragua, and he's not coming back," the young boy cried out. "The plane is going to crash. He's not coming back anymore. I know it. Call mama and don't let him go." Roberto's father, Melchor, had endured a similar nightmare a few nights earlier. In November, Roberto himself had envisioned his own funeral in a dream. "He was always saying that he was going to die young, very young," Vera said.

Vera's mother thought about calling the airport, but given the lateness of the hour, decided against it. The flight was originally scheduled to leave at four o'clock in the morning, but troubles with the plane delayed the departure until five o'clock in the afternoon. Assuming that the flight was finally about to depart, Vera kissed Roberto goodbye, and drove to an airline terminal to meet some friends who had flown in from the states. From there, Vera returned to Rio Piedras, thinking that Roberto's plane had taken off.

As the plane taxied down the runway, however, more mechanical problems were found. The delay continued for hours. Finally, at 9:20 p.m., the DC-7 took off under normal weather conditions from San Juan International Airport. As the plane lifted off, an airport employee heard one of the plane's four engines vibrating "excessively." Shortly after takeoff, pilot Jerry Hill sensed trouble with one of the engines, which had caught fire. Hill tried to return to the airport, attempting an abrupt left-hand turn. Watching from the ground, a man named Jose Antonio Paris heard an explosion as the plane neared the water's edge. "There were three more explosions after that," Paris said, offering a rare eyewitness description. After the second explosion, co-pilot Arturo Rivera mistakenly retracted the plane's flaps instead of the landing gear. At 9:23 p.m., another explosion occurred as the plane plunged nose-first into the Atlantic Ocean, about a mile and a half from the shore. Within five minutes, the plane had completely submerged. In the meantime, Vera Clemente, unaware of what was transpiring, continued her work at the earthquake committee's headquarters.

Initial media reports said only that Roberto Clemente and the other passengers were "missing." Within hours, such cautious optimism gave way to somber reality. Two and a half hours before the start of the New Year, Roberto Clemente Walker was dead—at the age of 38. The four other men on board had also lost their lives.

At 12:30 a.m., Vera received a telephone call from her niece, who said that she had heard a report on the radio about the crash. Thinking that Roberto's plane had left seven and a half hours earlier, Vera didn't believe the news. "I kept saying, 'No, no, that's not possible. They should be arriving in Nicaragua by now.'"

Bowie Kuhn, in the midst of his tenure as baseball's commissioner, received a telephone call from a wire service shortly after the crash. "Well, I remember being stunned by the news," Kuhn says. "I mean, it just seemed so impossible. Clemente was immortal. He wasn't going to die in an airplane crash. I was shocked. I think my remarks at that time revealed my honest respect for—I don't know of any ballplayer I ever had more respect for than Clemente."

At the time, Kuhn issued perhaps the most memorable statement ever made about Clemente. "He had about him the touch of royalty," the commissioner told reporters, many of whom used the quotation in their stories. "It was given fairly wide circulation at the time," Kuhn says in retrospect. "I mean, he had a touch of royalty. If I did anything, I understated that. He was royalty."

Pirates' public relations director Bill Guilfoile was at home when he heard the news of the plane crash. "I was asleep. I guess I got a phone call, it must have been one-thirty, two o' clock in the morning, from Byron Yake, who was the sports editor of the *AP* [Associated Press] in Pittsburgh. He told me the sad news. The first thing I did was call Joe Brown. And Joe was so upset, and understandably so, that he didn't hang up his telephone, which meant that I couldn't use my phone because I didn't break the connection."

Guilfoile still needed to contact several members of the Pittsburgh media, in order to assist them with their stories on Clemente's death. The resourceful, hard-working Guilfoile devised a backup plan to contact the media. "I knew that I had a lot of people I had to call at that hour of the morning. Here, I couldn't use my telephone, and it was a very wintry night in Pittsburgh. So, I got dressed and I emptied out all of our children's piggy banks, and loaded down with all the change I could find. I went down to a convenience store about a half a mile away from where I lived to use their pay phone. I spent the next hour and a half calling all the media people and other people that needed to know." Many other front office officials might have given up efforts to contact reporters and broadcasters, but Guilfoile had found a way to fulfill the requirements of his job, as hard as they might be on a tragic night. Without question, it was the most difficult responsibility that he had ever performed as public relations director for the Pirates.

"That was devastating to me," Joe Brown says of the news that Guilfoile delivered to him that night. "Not because I was the general manager of the team, but more because of what he was— a friend and someone that I admired and respected and loved as a person. You name the good qualities in a person. He was loyal as could be, loyal to his family and his country, to his team, to baseball." Even to people that he had just recently met, like the people of Nicaragua.

Brown and his wife left their bedroom and made their way to the kitchen. "My wife and I got up and she made a pot of coffee. I don't [normally] drink coffee, but I had a pot anyhow. And we were sitting there talking about things that we remembered when the door bell rang."

Steve Blass and Dave Giusti had attended a New Year's Eve party earlier in the evening. Sometime after midnight, they received a phone call from Pirates' trainer Tony Bartirome, who informed them of the news. Blass and Giusti tried to contact the rest of their teammates by telephone, informing them of Clemente's death. Some of the Pirates, including Al Oliver and Willie Stargell, had been at a different party. At 5:00 a.m., Oliver received a telephone call from Stargell, who told him what he had heard. One hour later, Blass and Giusti, not knowing what to do next, drove to the house of their general manager.

"I went to the door," Joe Brown recalls, "and there was Steve Blass and Dave Giusti." They said they had been at a New Year's Eve party, which ran to the early hours of the morning, and driving home they heard this report. And they didn't know where to go; they wanted to be with somebody that they knew cared about Roberto as much as they did. So they came in and we sat and talked, had more coffee, and I guess we must have talked for an hour or so."

The events of the night left Brown with a mix of feelings. "It was a memorable evening because of the loss, but still memorable because there was a recognition on the part of two very fine players and two very good people that the general manager could care, too."

Although Giusti often ribbed Clemente, he did so playfully, the way a caring friend does. Giusti noticed how Clemente treated all of his teammates equally well, regardless of their stature. "I've been around other superstars," Giusti told the *Pittsburgh Post-Gazette.* "I never saw any of them have as much compassion for his teammates like Clemente did. He would treat a rookie like he was Willie Stargell."

Clemente made efforts to make all players feel a part of the clubhouse experience. "A lot of the big-name players are approachable," wrote Steve Blass in a 1973 edition of *Sport* magazine, "but where Robby was different was that he would come to you."

Shortly after news of his death spread, tributes to Clemente poured in from all levels of the Pirate organization. John Galbreath, the Pirates' chairman of the board, praised Clemente for his selflessness. "If you have to die," Galbreath told the *New York Times,* "how better could your death be exemplified than by being on a mission of mercy. It was so typical of the man." Manager Bill Virdon, recently named as successor to the retiring Danny Murtaugh, offered a stunned reaction. "I don't know how you can think of baseball in Pittsburgh without Roberto Clemente," Virdon told the *Los Angeles Herald Examiner.* Teammate Willie Stargell also spoke reverently of Clemente's charitable nature. "Pittsburgh lost a heck of a man," Stargell said tearfully. "Clemente's work with the relief effort was typical. Roberto was always trying to help someone."

In retrospect, Stargell says Clemente's personal sacrifices become even more noteworthy given the timing of his planned relief mission to Nicaragua. "Just the way he lost his life, leaving home on the 31st of December," says Stargell. "It's one of the most sacred days in Puerto Rico; it's a very religious day. It's when families traditionally are together. He somewhat broke that tradition because he felt the need to go to Nicaragua to help out those families who were victims of the earthquake. As a result of that, he gave his life trying to do something, at a very special time, when so many people tried to talk him out of going. But he had that determination."

The news of Clemente's death affected all of the Pirate players, including Dave Cash. The young second baseman had played for "The Great One" after the 1970 season, when Clemente managed San Juan in the Puerto Rican Winter League. During the regular season, Cash had spent many hours with Clemente, both at the ballpark and away from it. "As a matter of fact, I lived in the same complex as Robby," recalls Cash. "We used to ride to the ballpark together. Robby was a very good friend."

Cash remembers being at home when he heard the tragic news of the plane crash. "We were all getting ready for Christmas and New Year's and it was a festive time, so to speak. And to get that kind of news at that period of time, when you're getting ready to celebrate on the holidays and you get some tragic news like that, it really kind of turns your stomach," Cash says. "We were shocked to hear of his death, but not shocked at what he was doing."

Luis Mayoral had thought he might see Clemente on New Year's Eve. During their last encounter, Clemente had invited him to an informal get-together. "I do remember him telling me, 'Hey, go by my place on the 31st.' The 31st, they'd have a gathering of friends and family at his house. That day, the 31st, I called from my parents' house in the outskirts of San Juan during the afternoon, maybe two or three or four times. And there was no answer [at the Clemente house]. So I just decided against going." Hours later, Mayoral tuned his car radio and heard a news report about the plane crash. "When I'm going home, maybe at two in the morning from my parents' house to my apartment, I found out by way of the radio. My former wife told me that she had also heard that his plane went down. I couldn't believe it because I thought he'd be back from Nicaragua by then."

Still in disbelief, Mayoral went to sleep, hoping that the news report was not entirely accurate, or that he had heard the story wrong. "I went to bed about two, got up at about 8:30 or 9:00, went to the corner drug store to see if there were any stateside newspapers. And that's where the guy selling me the paper confirmed the fact that the plane went down."

Mayoral had lost his good friend, a man he had known well since the mid-1960s. "Right there I went into shock; it was a peaceful shock," Mayoral says. "For the next month, my life was like a big labyrinth." The night after the plane crash, Mayoral and a group of friends searched the nearby beaches with flashlights, hoping to find a trace of Roberto.

By chance, three of Clemente's teammates were playing winter ball in Puerto Rico: Manny Sanguillen, infielder Rennie Stennett and pitcher Bob Johnson. They had been attending a party at Johnson's apartment when Stennett noticed a fire burning atop the ocean's surface. Stennett didn't realize it at the time, but the fire may have been emanating from the crash of Clemente's plane.

Luis Mayoral picked the players up at their apartment and drove them to Clemente's house, where a large contingent of friends and family had begun to gather. "That whole month of January, people came to the house," Vera said in a 1993 interview with

Douglas McDaniel. "They came from everywhere. The whole island was there and they had to close the street where we lived. It was something that really hurt."

Clemente's best friend in Pittsburgh, Phil Dorsey, joined the gathering in Rio Piedras in an effort to console Vera and their three young children, ages seven, five and four. "You know, Roberto was always doing things for people that nobody ever heard of," a shaken Dorsey told the Associated Press. "But he liked it that way. He said he didn't like when things were put in the paper."

On January 1, hundreds of fans called the sports and news departments of the *Pittsburgh Press* and the *Pittsburgh Post-Gazette*. They also called the offices of the Pirates at Three Rivers Stadium. "The next day I went into the office," says Sally O'Leary, recalling the day after the crash. "We got so many calls from fans who just felt they had to call and express their sympathy to someone. The phones went to everybody at that point. They got overloaded, so everybody was answering phones. And they brought in extra people—extra people that stayed for weeks answering phones and answering mail. It didn't end in just a couple of days. It went on and on. The fans, they really had lost a dear friend, a member of their family."

O'Leary had joined the Pirates' front office in 1964, quickly becoming an integral part of the team's public relations department. As he did with most people, Clemente made an immediate impression on O'Leary. "He was always around the office. I noticed how well-dressed he always was. Very, very neat in appearance. Very classy and flashy," says O'Leary, who noticed that Clemente's behavior belied his appearance. "I saw him as a very gentle person. I took him as a very sincere person, a genuine person. Very friendly. Just a very nice man."

The National Transportation Safety Board launched a full investigation of the plane crash, eventually finding no one culpable. In the meantime, the U.S. Coast Guard and U.S. Navy, ignoring bad weather reports, instituted a surface and air search for the bodies of the passengers and the wreckage in the 125-foot-deep waters. The murkiness of the ocean, coupled with six-foot waves, made the search particularly tedious. A Coast Guard cutter located a wheel, several pieces of metal, a suitcase, and a few life jackets that had floated to the surface, but no signs of bodies. The Coast Guard also spotted the fuselage of the plane, some 800 feet from the point of the crash. One search mission produced a pair of glasses. Another produced a briefcase, containing a lone sock inside. The glasses belonged to the pilot; the briefcase and sock belonged to Clemente.

Civilian deep sea divers tried to find remains of the bodies, while dodging the many sharks that patrolled that treacherous section of the Atlantic Ocean. When the civilians found nothing, the Navy organized its own crew of volunteer deep sea divers, at the request of Vera Clemente. As the rescue missions persisted for several days, Vera and Roberto's closest friend on the Pirates, Manny Sanguillen, watched from nearby Piñones Beach, which happened to be Clemente's favorite beach in Puerto Rico. "I was really hurt for his wife," Sanguillen told *Sports Illustrated* later that year. "I know how much one and the other used to love, and be together. She went down to the beach every day, too, to pray or see what she could do."

Sanguillen spent much of the next several days trying to recover Roberto's body. In full scuba diver's gear, Sanguillen searched the general area of the Atlantic Ocean where the plane had crashed, some two miles off the coast of Puerto Rico. "It was like my own brother die," Sanguillen told *The Sporting News*. "So many things he help me. He go to my room, talk about every different hitter." Pirate general manager Joe Brown tried to talk Sanguillen out of making the dives on his own, citing the dangers of the endeavor. Even though Sanguillen saw many sharks beneath the surface, he continued to make the dives from a boat. Manny dove for several days from "dawn till midnight," according to Steve Blass. So determined to find his friend's remains, Sanguillen missed the January 4th memorial service that was attended by the rest of the Pirate players.

In the days to come, authorities would find only one body—that of the plane's pilot, Jerry Hill—which had floated to the surface of the Atlantic Ocean. In the words of Sanguillen, Hill's body was "completely destroyed." The retired Air Force pilot left behind a wife and three sons, just like Clemente.

What happened to the bodies of Clemente, Rivera, and the two other men on board? No one knows for sure, but their remains may have been consumed by the sharks that patrol the waters near the San Juan Airport. According to another theory, the bodies may still be trapped in the wreckage of the plane, most of which remains on the ocean floor. In 1993, a group of businessmen announced plans to raise the sunken remains of the Clemente plane. Vera and two of her sons, Roberto, Jr. and Luis, met with the businessmen, expressing their opposition to the idea. As a result of the family's wishes, the businessmen called off the project. To this day, Clemente's body remains unrecovered.

Throughout Puerto Rico, many radio stations canceled their regular programming and played soft, somber music as a tribute to Clemente. Friends and acquaintances of Clemente throughout Latin American planned special memorial services. Thousands of Puerto Ricans tied black ribbons to the front doors of their houses and to their car antennas. Others took small boats out to the ocean and dropped flowers on the surface of the water. In the meantime, government officials canceled all public celebrations that had been originally scheduled as part of the inauguration of Governor-Elect Rafael Hernandez Colon. The government also announced that three days of national mourning would take place in Clemente's honor.

Nellie King believes that feelings of intense pride indirectly played a part in Clemente's death. "I thought he was a very proud person," says King, "almost to a fault. I think that's why he got killed in that plane [crash]. He got on board a very bad plane, but he wanted to make sure that things were done right. He got the word that they were not getting the supplies, that Somoza was stealing them. He had played baseball over there [in November], and he told me that he had just been over there and he saw what was going on there. He saw the poverty and he wanted to make sure that things went well."

Even with the reports of stolen supplies, Clemente might not have boarded the plane if he had known of Rivera's history of unsafe flying. In 1970, the Federal Aviation Administration had attempted to permanently revoke Rivera's pilot's license, citing 66 unsafe and improperly licensed flights. In January of 1971, the National Transportation Safety Board supported the charges of the FAA, but reduced the punishment to a 180-day suspension when Rivera argued that a permanent revocation would affect his livelihood. As a result, Rivera regained his license on July 21, 1972, only six months prior to the flight on New Year's Eve.

There were other problems, too. Matias, the flight engineer, had no cockpit training. In addition, the propeller-driven DC-7 was 4,000 pounds overweight and had been involved in a recent mishap, having overshot the runway and settled in a mud-filled ditch during a landing attempt. The incident had damaged two propellers to the plane, which also featured a faulty hydraulic system. In spite of the problems, no test flights were made.

Although Jose Pagan, Manny Sanguillen and Vera Clemente had expressed their concerns about the plane carrying Clemente prior to the flight, others close to the Pirate superstar did not learn about the safety issue until after his death. "I think 99 percent of all Puerto Ricans became aware of [safety problems] after the accident," says Luis Mayoral.

At least one myth has evolved in the aftermath of Clemente's death. A number of published stories, perhaps trying to overdramatize the philanthropy of Clemente, claimed that the Pirate right fielder had made two relief mission flights to Nicaragua prior to the doomed flight of the 31st. "No, that's not true," says Mayoral. "That's not true." Clemente had helped organize earlier flights carrying goods to Managua, but he had not boarded them. Similarly, Clemente had coordinated the departure of a large ship containing relief supplies, but he had not actually accompanied the voyage. The confusion over the number of relief missions Clemente actually made may have stemmed from his trip to Nicaragua in November, when he had managed Puerto Rico's amateur all-star team.

On January 4, dozens of members of the Pirate organization boarded a plane to attend a special mass at Carolina's San Fernando Catholic Church, the same church where Roberto and Vera had wed. The event marked the first time in history that so many members from one organization had gathered during the off-season to honor a fallen player. The mourners included three of Clemente's most recent managers—Bill Virdon, Danny Murtaugh and Harry Walker—who joined Joe Brown, Dan Galbreath, numerous Pirate players, Commissioner Bowie Kuhn, and Players Association chief Marvin Miller, all part of a massive 70-person American contingent in Puerto Rico. The 45-minute mass included a eulogy by Steve Blass, one of Clemente's friends on the Pirates.

Blass read a poem that had been given to him by Bill Guilfoile, the Pirates' public relations director. Guilfoile had sought permission to adapt the words of the tribute, which had been previously used to eulogize Hall of Famer Lou Gehrig, to make them appropriate for Clemente:

We've been to the wars together
We took our foes as they came;
And always you were the leader,
And ever you played the game.

Idol of cheering millions;
Records are yours by sheaves
Iron of frame they hailed you;
Decked you with laurel leaves.

But higher than that we hold you;
We who have known you best,
Knowing the way you came through
Every human test.
Let this be a silent token
Of lasting friendships gleam.
And all that we've left unspoken—
Your friends on the Pirate team.

Bowie Kuhn, who also spoke that day, has many memories of the memorial service. The most prominent remains the sight of Roberto's widow, Vera. "My best recollection of her is that day, the day of his funeral. I was at his funeral in Carolina; that's a very full recollection. I could see the throngs of people in the street, and it was as if a king of Puerto Rico had died, and in a sense, he had. Probably the most respected person on the island and it showed in everything that happened, throngs everywhere, people weeping in the streets. And Vera sort of behind it all." After the service, many of the mourners visited Clemente's home. They paid their final respects and offered their support to Vera.

Kuhn has seen Vera Clemente occasionally since Roberto's death. "She is beautiful," says Kuhn. "She's very outgoing, very warm. She has a beautiful smile. She has wonderful children. I can remember the kids when they were small. I was impressed with her as a mother. She gave the appearance of being a wonderful mother."

Conversations with Vera have provided some insight into Roberto's work with the youth of Puerto Rico and his other charitable efforts, much of which received little publicity while he was still alive. "I used to talk to Vera about it over the years," Kuhn says. "She was the eloquent one, see. You could talk to Vera at length. I don't think I ever talked to him about it." While Roberto had always hoped to receive greater recognition for his play on the field, he wanted no attention for himself when it came to helping others.

On January 14, Hiram Bithorn Stadium in San Juan hosted a special requiem mass for Clemente. Yet, tributes to Clemente were not restricted to his native Puerto Rico. In New York City, with its strong base of Puerto Rican and Hispanic residents, several Latin American groups asked for a special mass to be held in Clemente's honor. City officials responded by organizing a "mass of the resurrection" at St. Patrick's Cathedral, the famed New York City church. Meanwhile, in Pittsburgh, Mayor Peter Flaherty declared the observance of "Roberto Clemente Memorial Week." A picture of Clemente was hung in the hall of the city offices, and religious services were held in the First Spanish Assembly Church and the Trinity Episcopalian Cathedral. Over 1300 admirers filled the cathedral, resulting in an overflow of spectators who watched from the aisles and the front steps of the Gothic structure.

As a testament to Clemente's stature in the United States, President Richard Nixon felt moved to issue an immediate public statement paying tribute to the fallen star. President Nixon, an avid baseball fan, praised Clemente "for his splendid qualities as a generous and kind human being" and called for Americans to "contribute generously for the relief of those he was trying to help—the earthquake victims in Nicaragua." President Nixon made a $1,000 contribution to a national earthquake fund, one of four funds immediately established in Clemente's name.

In the direct aftermath of Clemente's death, the *Cleveland Plain Dealer* became one of the first media outlets to champion the cause of a special Hall of Fame election for the deceased superstar. "It would mean breaking a rule or two," the newspaper's editor wrote in its January 2 edition, "but under the circumstances, the baseball writers might want to consider immediate enshrinement in the Hall of Fame." Jack Lang, the secretary-treasurer of the Baseball Writers' Association of America, announced that his organization would explore the possibility of holding a special ballot. The president of the Baseball Writers, Joe Heiling, supported the idea. "He would have been elected and inducted in his first year eligible," said Heiling, comparing Clemente to first-ballot Hall of Famers like Sandy Koufax and Stan Musial. "So why wait?" Commissioner Bowie Kuhn, having been contacted by the Baseball Writers, added his support to the movement for a special election.

At the time, the writers were in the midst of holding their regular election, and about 30 writers had already returned ballots with Clemente's name written in, even though no decision had been made on his eligibility. The write-in votes for Clemente indicated the growing support for his election by the writers.

Under the existing Hall of Fame election rules, players had to wait five years after the end of their playing careers before they could become eligible. Yet, Lang cited a precedent involving New York Yankees' great Lou Gehrig. In 1939, the writers had waived the traditional waiting period so that Gehrig, who was dying from Amyotrophic Lateral Sclerosis, could enter the Hall of Fame before his passing.

On January 3, the Hall of Fame's Board of Directors announced that it had amended its eligibility rules in the case of Clemente, and would allow the baseball writers to hold a special election. On March 20, the Baseball Writers Association announced the results of the balloting. Clemente received 393 out of 424 votes—good for 93 percent of the vote—which put him well over the 75 percent required for election. Only six previous Hall of Famers had received a higher percentage of the vote: Ty Cobb, Babe Ruth, Honus Wagner, Bob Feller, Ted Williams and Stan Musial. Of the 31 "no" votes cast in the Clemente election, about half of the writers attached explanatory notes stating that they were not actually voting *against* Clemente, but against the decision to waive the five-year waiting period. (Six years after Clemente's election, the tragic death of Yankee star Thurman Munson once again raised the possibility of the Hall of Fame waiving its waiting period. The Hall chose not to cancel the five-year wait for Munson, who also died in a plane crash and ironically was Clemente's teammate with the San Juan Senators during the 1969-70 winter league season.)

The election of Clemente brought to mind an eerie story told by Al Abrams of the *Pittsburgh Post-Gazette*. In July of 1968, Clemente and the rest of the Pirates had visited Cooperstown to play in the annual Hall of Fame Game. During the morning of July 22, Clemente visited the Hall's Museum, snapping pictures of several plaques depicting Hall of Famers. A fan approached Clemente in the Hall's Gallery. "This is where you belong. Someday they will be taking pictures of your shrine," the fan said. "Thank you," Roberto responded in kind. "I guess a fellow like me has to die to get voted in by the writers."

On August 6, 1973, fans, baseball dignitaries and Pirate officials gathered in Cooperstown, New York to witness the induction of the late Clemente into the game's shrine. Clemente's Pirate teammates also attended the ceremony. (As a tribute to Clemente, the

Hall of Fame and the National League had agreed to substitute the Pirates for the Phillies in the annual Hall of Fame Game scheduled for later in the day.) Ironically, Clemente's induction coincided with that of Monte Irvin, his boyhood hero. Standing at the podium in front of thousands of onlookers, Commissioner Bowie Kuhn read from Clemente's newly created Hall of Fame plaque:

Roberto Walker Clemente, Pittsburgh National League 1955-1972. Member of the exclusive 3,000-hit club. He led the National League in batting four times. He had four seasons with 200 or more hits while posting a lifetime average of .317. He hit 240 home runs. He won the Most Valuable Player award in 1966. Rifle-armed defensive star set the National League mark by pacing outfielders in assists five years. He batted .362 in two World Series, hitting safely in all 14 games.

After paraphrasing the words on the plaque, Kuhn continued his address. "The directors of the Hall of Fame unanimously elected to waive the five-year waiting rule in the case of this very remarkable man. So very great was he as a player, so very great was he as a leader, so very great was he as a humanitarian in the cause of his fellow men, so very great was he as an inspiration to the young and to all of us in baseball and throughout the world of sports, and so very great was his devotion to young people everywhere and particularly to the young people of his native island of Puerto Rico. Having said all those words, they are very inadequate to describe the real greatness of Roberto Walker Clemente. We are very deeply honored to have his wife, Vera Clemente, with us here today."

The voice of Commissioner Kuhn, normally a stoic and reserved public speaker, wavered slightly throughout his address to those who had gathered in Cooper Park. "Well, I'm not surprised that you heard that; that's the way I felt," Kuhn admits readily. "The ceremonies brought back the death and the poignancy of the death of Clemente—too soon and tragically. And I think that's what you were hearing. To me, we in baseball had simply lost one of the greatest players that we've had, one of the greatest personalities that we had, and the tragedy of it was still, I think, in my mind. It no doubt manifested itself in what I had to say and the way I said it. I'm quite clear that that would be an accurate description of how I felt."

After a brief exchange with Kuhn, Vera stepped to the podium. "I want to thank the commissioner of baseball, the members of the Hall of Fame, the baseball writers, the Pittsburgh Pirates' organization and all the people who made this event possible, especially Roberto's fans who were the inspiration of his baseball career," Vera said softly. "This is a momentous last triumph, and if he were here, he would dedicate it to our people of Puerto Rico, our people in Pittsburgh, and to all his fans throughout the United States. Thank you."

With his election and induction now complete, Clemente became the first Latin American to gain enshrinement in the Hall of Fame. He would be joined in later years by Cuban Negro League star Martin Dihigo, Dominican pitcher Juan Marichal, Venezuelan shortstop Luis Aparicio and Panamanian infielder Rod Carew. After the ceremony, Vera tried to offer a further reaction to her husband's history-making induction. "I have difficulty expressing the way I really feel," Vera told reporters. "It's not just for me and my children. It's a goal for all Latin American children, too."

Moments before the conclusion of the program, Kuhn acknowledged several other members of the Clemente family who were in attendance on the steps of the Hall of Fame's Library. "I'd like you to meet Luisa Walker," Kuhn pointed out, "who is the mother of Roberto Clemente. Mrs. Walker." The gathering of fans applauded. "And we're also very honored to have Roberto's three fine sons here with us today. Boys, I want you to stand up, one by one if you would." Kuhn introduced each of the three youngsters, who would represent the next generation of the Clemente legacy. First came Roberto, Jr., then Roberto Enrique (known as Enrique), and finally, Luis Roberto. "Three ballplayers, I know," Kuhn concluded.

Two of Clemente's sons—Roberto, Jr. and Luis—*would* become professional ballplayers. In 1984, Roberto, Jr. signed a contract with the Philadelphia Phillies' organization, only to have his minor league career cut short by four knee operations. Four years later, back problems stalled a comeback attempt with the Baltimore Orioles' organization. Luis, after turning down a college scholarship, signed a minor league contract with the Pirates. His career lasted only two seasons, short-circuited by tendinitis in his shoulder.

Roberto, Jr. now works as a broadcaster for the Madison Square Garden Network, announcing Yankee games on Spanish language television. Luis assists his mother as the auxiliary executive director of the "Roberto Clemente Sports City." Enrique, who never played professional baseball but most closely resembles his father physically, also works at the Sports City.

All the while, the three brothers continue to share a common bond: they have lived most of their lives without their father. It has not been easy. Roberto, Jr. began to struggle with alcohol problems during his teenage years. Having completed a rehabilitation program, he often speaks to students about the dangers of drugs. In 1994, he formed the Roberto Clemente Foundation for inner-city children in Pittsburgh. Roberto, Jr. recently married for a second time, wedding a woman that he had lost contact with after she had entered a witness protection program. Luis, who is married with three boys of his own, has also publicly discussed the difficulties of growing up without a father figure. Still, the Clemente sons, through their work in baseball, youth assistance, drug education and the Sports City, continue to carry on much of the work initiated by their late father.

25

Aftershocks

Not surprisingly, the sudden and unexpected death of an active superstar resulted in a rush of media coverage by radio and television stations, newspapers, and magazines. *The Sporting News* devoted several pages to the story, including a full-length obituary. *Sport* magazine ran an extended feature on Clemente's career, delivered from the perspective of Pirate pitcher Steve Blass. An exception to the in-depth coverage was *Sports Illustrated*, which inexplicably deemed the Clemente tragedy worthy of only four paragraphs in its January 15, 1973 issue. The lack of space given to the Clemente story resulted in several angry letters to the editor, complaining about the paltry coverage. Curiously, the magazine had never featured Clemente on its cover during his 18-year career, even during his hallmark performance in the 1971 World Series.

Once the initial reactions of reflection and admiration had passed, some of the Pirate rivals coldly forecast a period of gloom for an organization that had lost its most important player. In a highly publicized article headlined, "BENCH SAYS PIRATES

WON'T BE SAME WITHOUT CLEMENTE," Reds' star Johnny Bench predicted the loss of Clemente would greatly weaken the Pirates' spirit while affecting the aggressiveness of their hitters. An annoyed Willie Stargell downplayed the significance of Bench's suggestion. "That's his opinion," Stargell told *Sports Illustrated* matter-of-factly. "Opinions are like 'behinds.' Everybody's got one."

As much as Stargell tried to prevent it, the death of Clemente would have a devastating effect on the Pirates' success as a team. "It really hurt our ballclub," says Dave Cash. "It hurt the morale of the club. We were stunned when it happened."

In addition to the emotional wrenching created by Clemente's loss, the tragedy would have a tangibly profound effect on Pittsburgh's lineup—and the decision-making of Pirate manager Bill Virdon. Without Clemente, the Pirates featured a gaping hole in their outfield as they prepared for the 1973 season. Virdon considered several candidates for the right field vacancy: bench standouts Gene Clines and Vic Davalillo, first baseman Bob Robertson, and catcher Manny Sanguillen.

Ironically, during their final conversation on December 29, Sanguillen had informed Clemente that he had played 20 of 21 winter ball games in right field. In turn, Clemente ribbed Sanguillen about his abilities as a right fielder. "Roberto has this little grin around the mouth when he is kidding," Sanguillen told Al Abrams of the *Pittsburgh Post-Gazette*. "He say, 'Sangy, you play left field or go back to catching. You have no chance to take my job.'"

After weighing his many options, Virdon decided to experiment with Sanguillen in right field during spring training. Against his wishes, Sanguillen opened the regular season in Clemente's old stomping grounds. "I feel bad being here," Sanguillen told *The Sporting News*. "I know I don't belong. I know I'm here because 'Great One's' gone and I want the best for the ballclub. Only I wish there was somebody in right field to talk to."

It soon became obvious that Sanguillen did not belong in the outfield, as he committed six errors in the team's first 34 games. Virdon wisely decided to move Sanguillen back to his regular position behind the plate. The idea had proved to be a miserable failure, weakening the Pirates at catcher, where Milt May struggled to fulfill his promise, and in right field, where Sanguillen did not feel comfortable defensively.

In retrospect, some critics have roasted Virdon for making the switch of Sanguillen to right field in the first place. Didn't he realize the pressure he was putting on Sanguillen, asking him to play a new position while replacing the Pirates' best player? Such criticism may be unfair. First of all, anyone playing right field for the Pirates in 1973 would have faced inordinate pressure. While no one would have reasonably expected Clemente's successor to match the abilities of "The Great One," whispers would have inevitably begun the first time a runner took an extra base or a catchable fly ball dropped untouched in right field. No one on the Pirates could have lived up to Clemente's standards, not Gene Clines, not Vic Davalillo, and not Sanguillen. As Steve Blass told *Sports Illustrated* in 1973: "Sometime this year, somebody is going to go from first to third against us on a single to right. And I'm going to be shocked. It's never happened before, in all the time I've been in the big leagues, because Clemente has always been there."

Secondly, Sanguillen *did* have experience playing right field, having played there during the most recent winter league season. In fact, the Pirates had ordered him to play the outfield in winter ball as far back as 1970, out of concern that he would wear himself out if he continued to catch. During some spring training and pre-game workouts, Clemente himself had coached Sanguillen on the subtleties of playing the outfield. Several members of the Pirate organization, including Clemente, believed that Sanguillen had the footspeed, agility and arm strength to become a competent major league outfielder.

A third reason—a closer examination of the Pirates' other right field options—offers further support of Virdon's initial reasoning. If Virdon hadn't picked Sanguillen to play the outfield, he might have chosen either Gene Clines or Vic Davalillo, or a combination of the two. Both players could hit for high averages; Clines had hit .334 in 311 at-bats in 1972, while Davalillo had batted .318 in a semi-regular role. Both could run, having combined for 26 stolen bases in 1972. Yet, both Clines and Davalillo had the same flaws: neither could throw well, nor hit with power. Davalillo's arm, once strong and accurate, had become ragged and weak in recent years, rendering him a liability, even in left field. Clines, although gifted with great speed and range, had experienced difficulty throwing out runners from center field. In right field, opposing teams figured to run regularly on his subpar arm. In addition, Clines and Davalillo had combined to hit four home runs in 679 at-bats, compared to Clemente's 10 homers in 378 at-bats.

Rather than receiving criticism for his decision, perhaps Virdon deserves credit for realizing that the move of Sanguillen to right field was not working. Instead of stubbornly trying to make the experiment succeed, and make himself look good in the long run, Virdon quickly cut his losses. He restored Sanguillen to his catching position and began platooning Clines and Davalillo in right field.

Even with the mid-season return of Sanguillen to catcher, the Pirates could not keep pace with the top teams in the National League East. Without the hitting, baserunning and defensive skills of Clemente, the 1973 Pirates lacked the resources to make the playoffs that fall. Future star Dave Parker, Clemente's eventual successor in right field, was still two years away from becoming a full-time major league outfielder. The Pirates would finish the '73 season a mediocre 80-82, two-and-a-half games out of first place.

Clemente's loss also may have affected the fortunes of one of the Pirates' pitchers. In 1972, which happened to be Clemente's final season, Steve Blass enjoyed his best year in the major leagues. The skinny right-hander finished with a career-best 19 wins, an earned run average of 2.49 and 11 complete games. Then, in 1973, without warning, Blass endured excruciating difficulty throwing strikes and posted the following horrifying numbers: a 9.85 earned run average, 84 walks in 88 and two-thirds innings, and a won-loss mark of 3-9.

The situation worsened for Blass in 1974. After a disastrous performance against the Cubs, the Pirates demoted Blass to their Triple-A affiliate in Charleston. Blass continued to struggle, even against minor league hitters, walking an incredible total of 93 batters in 56 and two-thirds innings.

In spring training of 1975, Blass worked only six and two-thirds innings, surrendering 13 runs and 17 walks. In his last appearance in a major league uniform, Blass lasted three sad innings against the Chicago White Sox, giving up 10 runs and 11 walks. In his final inning of work, Blass surrendered *eight* bases on balls and forced in six runs.

On March 27, 1975, the Pirates requested waivers on Blass for the purpose of giving him his unconditional release. Baseball people have offered countless theories in trying to explain Blass' downfall, which ended his career prematurely at the age of 33. Some theorists claimed that Blass did not know how to handle his sudden success of 1971 and '72. Others believed that Blass was masking a sore arm, or hiding personal problems that he may have been experiencing.

In perhaps the most intriguing theory put forth, some Pirate observers claimed that Blass was emotionally devastated by the loss of Clemente, one of his good friends on the team. Some theorized that Clemente's death made Blass more aware of human mortality; perhaps Blass feared that he would hit an opposing batter with a stray fastball, doing him severe bodily harm, while simultaneously creating guilt and anxiety for himself. Such theories were impossible to prove, but without Clemente as a teammate, this much is certain: Blass enjoyed no success as a member of the Pirates. With Clemente, Blass' record was 100-67; without him, Blass won only three games, lost nine and posted an earned run average of nearly 10.00 runs per game.

While the cause and effect relationship between Clemente's death and Blass' pitching remains an inevitable mystery, the fortunes of other players were clearly and tangibly affected. Al Oliver assumed Clemente's No. 3 position in the batting order. Oliver benefited from the upward move in the lineup, reaching a career-high with 99 RBIs. Oliver also took on a greater leadership role with the Bucs. After another fine season in 1974, Oliver received the "Roberto Clemente Award," given to the Pirate player who "best exemplifies the standards of excellence" established by the former Pirate great.

Clemente's absence also expedited the arrival of the Pirates' top prospect, a player who happened to occupy the same position as "The Great One." Dave Parker played 54 games as a rookie in 1973, and made 49 appearances in the outfield the following summer. By 1975, Parker had assumed a starting outfield job, becoming the first long-term right fielder for the Pirates after the death of Clemente.

Although Parker's major league career failed to overlap the 18-season career of his Hall of Fame predecessor, the young, strong-armed outfielder did meet Clemente during spring training. As a minor leaguer hoping to impress the team's front office, Parker learned greatly from Clemente during the springs of '71 and '72. "I was signed as a catcher and I short-armed the ball," Parker told Dennis Tuttle of *Inside Sports* in 1997, recalling his first days in the Pirates' organization. A switch to the outfield forced Parker to change his throwing philosophy, an adjustment that Clemente instructed him to make. "He taught me to reach back and throw it," Parker said. "He had a huge influence on me."

On July 10, 1974, a 27-year-old infielder named Art Howe finally made his major league debut. Appearing as a pinch-hitter for veteran pitcher Daryl Patterson, Howe singled during the Pirates' 10-5 loss to the Atlanta Braves. Howe's debut took place at Three Rivers Stadium, in the city that he had called home since his birth in 1946.

After years of watching games, years of hoping that a professional team would give him a chance, and years of proving himself at the minor league level, Howe had fulfilled a lifelong aspiration—one that had begun at Forbes Field in the late 1950s. As the youthful Howe watched Clemente play, so grew his own passion to become a major league player. "I think the way he played the game gave me the desire," says Howe. "He went all-out. That's one thing I was always proud to say, that he was my idol. I never once saw him not hustle to first base. No matter how hard or how easy he hit the ball, he gave everything going down the line. That was the way he played the game. He was not only a great player, he was a performer."

While Howe had hoped to make the major leagues with any team, he especially wanted to make it with the Pirates. They were Clemente's team, playing in the city that Howe had been born and raised. "That was my dream," says Howe. "My dream was just to get a chance to play pro ball, but to play in Pittsburgh was unbelievable. There I was. In '74, when I got called to the big leagues, I was in awe of the thoughts of sitting in the same clubhouse with guys, who a couple of years before, I was watching on TV and coming to the park and watching them play. It took me awhile to realize I belonged there."

Howe played 29 games with the Pirates in his rookie season. He stayed with the team long enough to assess the lingering affects of Clemente's death, which had occurred only two years earlier. "I think, to a degree," says Howe, "that it started to wear off somewhat." Yet, remnants and reminders of the Pirates' loss remained visible. "I think the whole organization was devastated for several years after he died. He was a big part of that organization. He was a team leader, and quite a few of the players were very close to him. It took awhile before the other guys took over the leadership role. I think that's when Stargell basically grabbed the reins and took the leadership role. I'll tell you, he was a tremendous leader—Stargell was."

With Bill Mazeroski having retired, most writers had assumed that Stargell would replace Clemente as the Bucs' point man. The quiet veteran had already provided ample leadership throughout

1971 and '72, but had been overshadowed by the aura of Clemente. General manager Joe Brown hinted that Stargell possessed the necessary qualities to steer the Pirates. "I think there are other people on this team who will take on an added dimension now that Roberto will not be around," Brown told the Associated Press. "A fellow like Willie Stargell, who plays when he's hurt and gives everything he has."

Stargell himself tried to downplay talk of "succeeding" Clemente as the Pirates' leader. "No one can do the job that Clemente was doing on or off the field," Stargell maintained. "And for me to be an individual, other than what I've been in the last 10 years, I can't change. I have nothing to sell. I'm not trying to impress anyone." While Stargell insisted that he could not replace Clemente, he did promise to counsel any teammates who asked for help. "I know what it's like to be on a winner," Stargell said. "So if anyone asks my advice, or wants to be evaluated on different things, then I'm in a position to talk about these things."

Even with Clemente no longer batting ahead of him in the lineup, Stargell fashioned one of his finest seasons in '73. He led the National League with 44 home runs, 119 RBIs, 43 doubles and a career-high .646 slugging percentage. Stargell also posted a .299 average, his highest since 1969.

Stargell's all-round offensive game placed him in serious contention for the National League's MVP Award. Clemente had won his lone MVP in 1966—his 12th major league season. Stargell hoped that he might take home his first MVP in what was also his 12th season. Much like he did in 1971, Stargell watched another player, Cincinnati's Pete Rose, win the MVP. Snubbed by the writers in the voting, Stargell did receive a significant award during the off-season. The Pirates named him the winner of their newly-formed "Roberto Clemente Memorial Award," given to the Pirate player who best represented the high standards set forth by the late right fielder.

Stargell's leadership abilities, which Joe Brown had discussed prior to the 1973 season, became officially recognized in the spring of 1974. Danny Murtaugh, who had returned to the Pirates' managerial post after Bill Virdon's 1973 late-season firing, acknowledged Stargell's leadership by naming him team captain. Stargell became the Pirates' first captain since Bill Mazeroski, who had served in that role from 1962 until his retirement prior to the 1973 season.

On April 11, 1974, Commissioner Bowie Kuhn presented Stargell with major league baseball's annual "Roberto Clemente

Award." The award, distinct from the Pirates' "Roberto Clemente Memorial Award," honored the player that best exemplified Clemente's qualities, particularly off the field. Stargell topped the voting, beating out 47 other major leaguers who had been nominated. "Of all the awards, this ranks No. 1 with me," Stargell told *The Sporting News,* "because it identifies with Clemente, who always tried to help people."

For years, Stargell had impressed the baseball world with his success in hitting home runs and driving in runners; now, baseball officials had taken notice of Stargell's Clemente-like willingness to assist others. Among his most notable causes, Stargell had successfully mobilized public awareness of an illness that had received very little publicity in the 1960s: sickle cell anemia, a disease that attacks blood cells, mostly in African-Americans. "So many people know so little about this disease," Stargell had told the *New York Times* in 1971. "These people live a short, miserable life. We need the help of everyone."

Stargell had also established the Pittsburgh-based "Black Athletes Foundation," an organization dedicated to helping African-American athletes earn better contracts and endorsement opportunities while also addressing problems that affected the black community at-large. Such efforts resembled those of a man named Clemente, who had tried to help Latin American players and the Hispanic community throughout his own major league career.

On the whole, Clemente's death produced a devastating effect on the Pirates' organization. After a disastrous 1973 season, the Pirates managed to return to the playoffs in 1974 and '75. The additions of Dave Parker and Richie Zisk to the outfield, the continued presence of Al Oliver and Willie Stargell in the everyday lineup, and the pitching of newcomers like Jerry Reuss and Jim Rooker, bolstered the club in several areas. Yet, both post-season runs ended quickly, as the Pirates lost to the Dodgers in four games and to the eventual world champion Reds in three games. If Clemente had lived, and if he had continued to play at an All-Star level, the outcomes might have been different. After all, Clemente had proved himself as a great post-season performer. He had become *the* player the other Pirates looked to under the spotlight of October.

Stripped of their most forceful leader and finest all-around player, the Bucs did not return to the World Series until 1979, when Stargell finally won the MVP and spearheaded the victory against the Orioles in the season of "We Are Family." It had taken nearly the rest of the decade—seven years after the death of Roberto Clemente Walker—for the Pirates to once again attain the glory of the Fall Classic.

26

Honors

Unfortunately, full appreciation for Clemente did not arrive until after his death in 1972. Luis Mayoral recalls a telling conversation he had with a Pirates' executive shortly after the New Year's Eve plane crash. "Joe Brown got to Puerto Rico after the accident," says Mayoral. "I was a commission scout representative for the Pirates. He said very quietly, 'Roberto will now get more media attention forever, than he ever thought he'd get.'"

"I really think after Clemente died, I think a lot of people realized, this guy wasn't a bad player," says former teammate Richie Hebner, using a slice of intentional understatement. "He played 18 years in the big leagues, had a lifetime average of .317. If this guy played in New York, Chicago, or LA, he would have walked on Lake Michigan." More than anything else, Clemente displayed a knack for winning. "I mean I had the privilege of playing four years with the man," Hebner says. "I tell ya, he did a lot of things right to win ballgames. He made very few mental mistakes. Not the flashiest guy, didn't hit 35 home runs a year, but he could beat you in a lot of ways." In describing Clemente's impact, Hebner offers an interesting cross-sport comparison. "He was like a guy up where I live [in Walpole, Massachusetts] that I watched for a long time—Larry Bird. Larry Bird could do a lot of things to win games. Clemente was the same type of player."

Immediately after his death, a few Pirate fans campaigned to have Three Rivers Stadium renamed "Roberto Clemente Memorial Stadium." George Wintner, an employee for a local law firm, and Harry Dunn, a student at Allegheny Community College, started an immediate petition, obtaining 10,000 signatures on New Year's Day alone. The chairman of the Pittsburgh Stadium Authority announced that his committee would hold a meeting to consider the change. Unfortunately, the history of the Authority had indicated that such a change was unlikely. In 1970, the Authority had rejected efforts to have the new stadium named in honor of any athletic or political figures. To this day, the ballpark in Pittsburgh remains "Three Rivers Stadium."

Other honors did not fall through. In 1971, major league baseball began awarding a new honor called the "Commissioner's Trophy." At first, the award had no direct affiliation with Clemente, but that would change within a couple of years. Unlike most awards that solely recognize a player for his on-field performance, the commissioner's award was designed to honor the player who best represented the game, both on and off the field. The criteria included sportsmanship, charitable efforts, community involvement, and contributions to one's team. Each of the 24 major league clubs nominated one player for the prestigious award.

During the 1971 All-Star Game festivities, San Francisco Giants' outfielder Willie Mays, Clemente's one-time teammate with Santurce in winter ball, received the first "Commissioner's Trophy." The following summer, the award went to Baltimore's Brooks Robinson, the man who had praised Clemente so effusively after the '71 World Series.

In 1973, Luis Mayoral petitioned the commissioner's office to create an award that would honor Clemente. "I had befriended Bowie Kuhn and most his staff in New York, including Joe Reichler," Mayoral recalls. "About a month, a month and a half after [Roberto's] death, I wrote a letter suggesting that a Clemente Award be instituted. In March of that year, the first "Roberto Clemente Award" was presented by the commissioner's office to Al Kaline at the governor's banquet that they had in Florida in spring training." Rather than form a completely new award, Kuhn decided to rename the "Commissioner's Trophy" as a way of commemorating Clemente.

"We created an award in his honor called the 'Roberto Clemente Award,' for some player each year who had so distinguished himself in terms of public service," says Kuhn. "That was done because we were aware of Clemente's public service. He was a very selfless man."

Although Clemente himself did not win the commissioner's award during its first two years of existence, his involvement with the youth of Puerto Rico and other philanthropic efforts typified the meaning and spirit of the award. After the 1995 season, major league baseball renamed the award, but kept the Clemente affiliation. Now known as the "Roberto Clemente Man of the Year Award," the honor is selected from an even larger group of nominees. Each major league team now nominates three players; from that group, a local winner is chosen to represent each team. The overall winner is then chosen and announced during each year's World Series. The following is a complete list of the award's winners through the 2001 season.

1971	Willie Mays	1987	Rick Sutcliffe
1972	Brooks Robinson	1988	Dale Murphy
1973	Al Kaline	1989	Gary Carter
1974	Willie Stargell	1990	Dave Stewart
1975	Lou Brock	1991	Harold Reynolds
1976	Pete Rose	1992	Cal Ripken, Jr.
1977	Rod Carew	1993	Barry Larkin
1978	Greg Luzinski	1995	Ozzie Smith
1979	Andre Thornton	1996	Kirby Puckett
1980	Phil Niekro	1997	Eric Davis
1981	Steve Garvey	1998	Sammy Sosa
1982	Ken Singleton	1999	Tony Gwynn
1983	Cecil Cooper	2000	Al Leiter
1984	Ron Guidry	2001	Curt Schilling
1985	Don Baylor		
1986	Garry Maddox		

In six of its first seven years, the award went to a future Hall of Famer, leading some to suggest that it carried a connotation of lifetime achievement. In more recent years, award winners have varied from potential Hall of Famers to those who might be considered very good players. The roll call of players who have earned the Clemente Award includes some of the game's most respected personalities: courageous men like Eric Davis, who successfully returned from stomach cancer to participate in the 1997 post-season; the affable Kirby Puckett, one of the game's great ambassadors; the ironhorse Cal Ripken, Jr., noted for his involvement with charity work in the Baltimore area; the gentlemanly Dale Murphy, recognized as one of the game's truly nice people during his playing career; and the deeply religious Andre Thornton, whose powerful Christian beliefs guided him after the loss of his wife and daughter in a horrifying car accident.

The list of winners reflects the prestige of the award. Although the annual announcement of the winner receives relatively little publicity from the national media, the award carries special significance in the baseball world. For those who remember Clemente, and the kinds of causes he stood for in his short life, the award represents the highest level of recognition a player can receive for his accomplishments off the field.

At the same time that major league baseball changed its "Commissioner's Trophy" to pay respect to Clemente, Luis Mayoral proposed a plan for a second Clemente designation to Commissioner Kuhn. "I asked Bowie for permission to present a Clemente award to a Latino player within the 'Latin American Baseball Players Day' presentation I did at different stadiums throughout the major leagues," Mayoral says. "He obviously put a seal on it, 'You can go ahead and do it.' My award was based simply on trying to keep the name of Clemente alive among Latino ballplayers." Like the major leagues' award, Mayoral placed an emphasis on the player's character and integrity. "It was mostly presented to individuals who were not necessarily great players like Clemente, but were good players who also tried to keep alive the image of righteousness that Roberto had projected." Mayoral presented the award for 25 years, concluding it with the 1997 presentation.

The origins of a third Clemente award can also be found in 1973. That fall, the Pittsburgh chapter of the Baseball Writers' Association of America handed out its own "Roberto Clemente Memorial Award." The annual award is presented to an active member of the Pirates who "most exemplifies the standard of excellence established by the late Roberto Clemente." The award is the first one listed in the Pirates' media guide. The complete list follows:

Year	Player		Year	Player
1973	Willie Stargell		1987	Andy Van Slyke
1974	Al Oliver		1988	Andy Van Slyke
1975	Dave Parker		1989	Bill Landrum
1976	Bill Robinson		1990	Doug Drabek
1977	Dave Parker		1991	Barry Bonds
1978	Dave Parker		1992	Andy Van Slyke
1979	Willie Stargell		1993	Jay Bell
1980	Mike Easler		1994	Not Awarded-strike
1981	Bill Madlock		1995	Orlando Merced
1982	Jason Thompson		1996	Jeff King
1983	Tony Peña		1997	Tony Womack
1984	Lee Lacy			Kevin Young
1985	Rick Reuschel		1998	Jason Kendall
1986	Johnny Ray		1999	Brian Giles
			2000	Brian Giles

When the Pirates reported for spring training in 1973, they noticed that a special plaque had been attached to the door of Clemente's dormitory room. At the end of spring training, the Pirates announced that each player would wear a special patch on the sleeve of his uniform. The circular patch featured Clemente's No. 21 in black lettering, with a white background surrounded by a black border. On Opening Day, the Pirates officially retired Clemente's uniform number.

Over the years, more than 30 schools throughout the United States have announced plans to rename their institutions after Clemente. Two hospitals in Puerto Rico have been named in his memory. In 1984, the United States Postal Service issued a Clemente stamp on the 50th anniversary of his birth. Five hundred thousand stamps were purchased in Pittsburgh on the first day of issue.

Having already been elected to the National Baseball Hall of Fame in 1973, Clemente gained election to another Hall of Fame 18 years later. In 1991, the newly formed Puerto Rico Professional Baseball Hall of Fame opened its doors to Clemente and nine other stars. Six of Clemente's teammates in winter league play, including Willard Brown and Bob Thurman, entered the Hall. The inaugural class of Puerto Rican Hall of Famers also included the native father-son combination of Pedro "Perucho" Cepeda and Orlando Cepeda.

In 1993, the Puerto Rican legislature unanimously approved a proclamation to commemorate Clemente each August 18th, the date of his birthday in 1934. Unfortunately, it had taken the government in Puerto Rico over 20 years to pass legislation honoring one of the country's true national heroes.

The Pirates afforded Clemente a special honor in 1994, when they unveiled a 12-foot bronze statue of "The Great One" outside of Three Rivers Stadium. The statue, which depicts Clemente at the completion of one of his majestic swings, was funded by donations from the general public. Numerous Pirate fans made contributions in the amount of $21, the number that Clemente wore during his years in Pittsburgh. "There was even a school where the children donated 21 cents, and they pooled all their money together," says Sally O'Leary. "And another school, [the students] read books, and they got 21 cents for each book that they read."

In 1998, tributes to Clemente continued. The Topps Card Company inserted reprints of Clemente cards in its 1998 card set. The Sports City in Carolina hosted a Clemente celebration as part of its fundraising efforts. The National League named Vera Clemente its honorary captain for the All-Star Game, marking the first time a woman has received the honor. The National Baseball Hall of Fame unveiled a bilingual exhibit (the first in the history of the museum) honoring Clemente 25 years after he became the first Latino immortalized in Cooperstown. In addition, the Hall of Fame hosted live multi-media presentations on Clemente as part of its "Sandlot Stories" series. The Hall's Museum also issued its customers a special commemorative ticket, depicting Clemente artifacts and memorabilia, as part of a year-long celebration of "The Great One."

27

The Sports City

I f Clemente had not perished in the crash of the DC-7, how much longer would his playing career have lasted? In a 1972 spring training interview, Clemente had laid out a timetable. "There is no way I can play more than this year and next year," Clemente told Ira Miller of UPI. "No way." In other words, Clemente had indicated that the 1973 season would be his last.

Opinions gathered from those close to Clemente differ on what might have been the extent of his playing career. Some believed that he would have played just the one more season and retired; others felt that his youthful body and love of the game would have motivated him to play for four or five more years.

During the 1970 season, Nellie King had asked Clemente how much longer he planned to play the game. "It's almost tragically prophetic. This goes back to an interview I did with him the final game at Forbes Field," says King. "He didn't play the final game [at Forbes]. He played the first game—it was a double-header. I had him on between games and I said, 'How long would you like to play, Roberto?'

"He said, 'You know, I would like to play as long as I can. You know, Nellie, I would like to play until I get 3,000 hits.'" When Clemente died, King remembered almost immediately what Roberto had told him only two years earlier. "It's an interesting interview, taped at the stadium," says King, who still has the cassette of his conversation with Clemente. "It was so prophetic, you know? I got goose bumps when I thought about when he died. I would like to play until I get 3,000 hits...To him, that's all he desired."

Clemente's sudden death has also led to inevitable speculation about his potential post-playing career. If he had lived, would he have continued to work in baseball, either as a coach or a manager? Or might he have left the game completely? Although Clemente had managed in the Puerto Rican Winter League, his public comments and private conversations gave no indication that he would have pursued a managerial career after his playing days. "No," King says about Clemente's desire to manage. "He said, 'I'd like to go around working with younger players, maybe in the minor leagues, perhaps as a batting instructor.'"

Still, King remains skeptical about Clemente's hints that he would have stayed in baseball after his playing days. "You know, I think he had such a social conscience that he'd have gotten involved with either a social or political kind of thing. I just don't thing he'd stand around and see things not be done right—socially, you know."

Clemente's list of heroes had included a number of social and political figures. "He admired John F. Kennedy, mostly for the Peace Corps movement," Luis Mayoral says. "Luis Muñoz Marin, too. He was then, and could well be the greatest political figure in Puerto Rico, because under his direction, Puerto Rico became a commonwealth of the United States, which is something like a colony or a territory, but with a lot of benefits for its people. Muñoz Marin believed in the independence of Puerto Rico, but when he saw in the thirties and forties that we were almost Third World, he sacrificed that principle of independence for Puerto Rico. For the betterment of society overall. That's a man who Roberto said gave our people food, who put shirts on our back, and shoes on our feet. More than a politician, he was a great social worker."

During the 1970 season, rumors had swirled that Roberto himself might run for office after his playing days. At least one observer had suggested that he run for mayor of Carolina, his birthplace. Although the idea appealed to him, Clemente had worried that he might be elected solely on his popularity as a ballplayer, rather than on the basis of a legitimate political resume. Clemente did not want to be elected to an important political office on such terms.

As King sees it, Clemente's genuine interest in others would have continued to steer him in humanitarian directions. "He loved people," King says flatly. "He said, 'I love all kinds of people. Being taught about other people.' I really believe he would have been actively involved in social change. He was a strong man."

In a 1966 interview with Myron Cope of *Sports Illustrated*, Clemente discussed his desire to help youths by stoking their interests in sports. The final words of that article provide an eerie foreshadowing of Clemente's fate. "I like to work with kids," Clemente told Cope. "I'd like to work with kids all the time, if I live long enough."

Clemente's death prevented him from working directly with children, but it did not destroy his dream of improving their courses in life. One of Clemente's most cherished goals—the building of a "ciudad deportiva," or "sports city" that would provide both an opportunity and a training ground for young Puerto Rican athletes— would be realized soon after his death. "The Roberto Clemente Sports City was founded in papers the 26th of January, 1973," says Luis Mayoral. "The lands (233 acres) were given by the government of Puerto Rico, but they were wetlands, so it took maybe 10 or 12 years to refill that area, to really start the construction."

Mayoral has visited the facility, as has Marcos Breton. "There's a long driveway leading on to the grounds. At the foot of the driveway, there is a statue of Clemente," says Breton. "It's very striking." Once inside the Sports City, which has grown to 303 acres since its opening, visitors will notice four regulation-sized baseball fields, two softball fields and a smaller field for Little League players. A baseball stadium, named after major league catcher Benito Santiago, provides a centerpiece to the grounds.

Sports other than baseball are also featured at the Sports City. The complex includes three courts for basketball, four courts for tennis and four for volleyball. It also contains an Olympic swimming pool, with an access ramp for disabled persons, and a track and field stadium. The Sports City also has a recreational park and a building that houses the complex' offices. Future plans include the completion of a museum depicting Clemente's life and career, which is currently under construction.

After initial difficulties caused by the poor quality of the land, recurrent financial problems have threatened the existence of the Sports City, which requires over $100,000 in annual operating expenses. "It's never received, I think, the importance from people in Puerto Rico and/or the government," says Mayoral. "Yes, there have been monies poured into it, but I think the [wetlands] area alone has hindered the correct development of the Clemente Sports City." The Pirates tried to help by staging a series of annual exhibition games, with all proceeds given to the Sports City. The Pittsburgh Jaycees also contributed with fundraising efforts. In the continuing economic struggle, the Clemente family has put some of its own money into the Sports City to keep it a viable enterprise for the youth of Puerto Rico.

Economic problems aside, Clemente intended the Sports City as a place to bring families together in an athletic setting while providing a stage for Puerto Rican youngsters, particularly the underprivileged, to participate in athletics. During his stay in Carolina, Marcos Breton learned more about the Sports City's mission. "We had the pleasure of meeting and interviewing and photographing Vera Clemente, his widow," says Breton. "The emphasis, as it was related to us, is that while they want to help these kids develop their athletic skills if they have them, they were far more interested—and they kept using the same words over and over again, whether it's Mrs. Clemente or the people who work at the Sports City—in trying to build good citizens. They want the children there to be good people and good citizens above everything else." Under the direction of Vera Clemente, who became the project's president and executive director in 1993, the Sports City has done just that.

Vera's work, in successfully following through with the plans of her late husband, has not gone unnoticed by those in the baseball community. "After he died," says Bowie Kuhn, "she showed that she had the ability to step up and support the things he believed in, particularly anything having to do with helping kids." Since its inception, over 100,000 children have enrolled in the Sports City.

The Clementes' project has also had an unintended benefit, by helping a number of standout baseball players in the early years of their development. As youngsters, future major league stars like Roberto and Sandy Alomar, Jr., Carlos Baerga, Juan Gonzalez, Orlando Merced, Ivan Rodriguez, Benito Santiago and Ruben Sierra— the city's first big league graduate—all profited from the facilities and instruction provided by "The Great One's" dream: the Roberto Clemente Sports City.

28

The Legacy

What kind of a legacy did Roberto Clemente want to leave after his playing days? A reporter, anticipating Clemente's inevitable retirement, once asked him that question. "I would like to be remembered as a player who gave all he had to give," Clemente responded. Baseball fans should remember him for that—and so much more.

When Clemente first donned a Pirate uniform in 1955, only five other Puerto Rican players played in the major leagues. A total of 29 Latin Americans played that season. In 1972, the final year of Clemente's career, Puerto Rico's representation in the major leagues had jumped to 23, while the overall number of Latinos had risen to 83. By 1997, a quarter century after Clemente's death, the number of Puerto Rican players had grown to 42. The overall number of Hispanics had climbed to a staggering 201 players—or nearly 20 percent of all major league players. In 1998, the list of professional Latin American players includes Clemente's own nephew, Edgard Velazquez, a prospect in the Colorado Rockies' organization. As a tribute to his late uncle, the young outfielder decided to change his name to Edgard Clemente for one season.

How much of a role has Clemente's success and legacy played in the growth of the Latin American presence in the major leagues? "Well, I think that you have to put it in context. I think that there are a lot of forces that have contributed to the explosion of Latin players now that have nothing to do with Clemente," says Marcos Breton, who points to the availability of finding inexpensive talent throughout Latin America as one of the key reasons for the explosion. "But, these kids who are coming now, particularly the ones in Puerto Rico, have grown up with Clemente being the ideal. Clemente and others like him—Juan Marichal and people who played in his era—really showed the way. They pointed the way toward Latin America. And so in that way, he is indirectly responsible and he proved that he could play, and play very very well. His memory keeps that path lit to this day, and keeps people going back. I've heard more than one Latin scout say that an American general manager or a scout supervisor in the United States will tell them, 'Find me a Clemente.' That's an awful tall order. But maybe in the process of looking for that ideal, they find an awful lot of talent along the way. In that way, he's really helped, by encouraging people to keep going back to look for someone like him."

Clemente's legacy has inadvertently created some problems for young players trying to follow in his path. In the late sixties and early seventies, one of the Pirates' top prospects drew such strong comparisons to Clemente that some scouts dubbed him the "Little Clemente." Angel Mangual, a talented Puerto Rican outfielder, resembled Roberto both facially and physically. The Pirates ended up trading him to Oakland in the deal that brought Mudcat Grant to Pittsburgh. After a successful rookie season with the A's, Mangual fell into mediocrity. In 1997, Mangual was arrested for drug trafficking.

"The sad thing that has taken place since Clemente's death," explains Breton, "is that there have been several players who have been burdened with being compared, or being called the 'next Clemente.' And the one who really jumps to mind is Ruben Sierra, who really showed a lot of promise in the late eighties and early nineties, and then his career has just flamed out in the nineties. I'm not suggesting that carrying the burden of being compared to Clemente did him in; he obviously has had other problems to deal with. But it's a heavy burden to carry. It's comparable to an American kid being called the next—you know, who knows—the 'next Ted Williams.' Those types of labels—it's very difficult."

Yet, there are players who do remind observers of Clemente. "The one who jumps out to mind, who isn't Puerto Rican, but is Dominican, is Raul Mondesi," says Breton. "Raul Mondesi is a right fielder the way Clemente was; he has a cannon for an arm the way Clemente had. When he is on the field, he goes all-out on every play, in every game, in every inning, all the time. And that's the way that Clemente played." Another player is Pirates' right fielder Jose Guillen, whose arm strength is reminiscent of "The Great One" and who wears a Clemente T-shirt under his game uniform.

In the years that have passed since his death and election to the Hall of Fame, Clemente's life and career have been explored in a host of books, newspaper and magazine articles, and video documentaries. An underrated player during his lifetime, Clemente has received more fitting respect for his talents in the years since his death. Yet, in 1997, the year that marked the 25th anniversary of his passing, he received relatively little publicity. Luis Mayoral had hoped that major league baseball would officially pay homage to Clemente that season, but another anniversary overshadowed him. "It was a bit sad because the Roberto Clemente family wanted a little patch to appear—at least on Pirate uniforms and maybe on other clubs—as to the 25th anniversary of his death," says Mayoral. "But that [anniversary] was overshadowed by Jackie Robinson. I said, 'Well then, that's bad timing in a way, that the 50th anniversary of Robinson coming into baseball and the 25th anniversary of Roberto's death came that same year.'"

With 1998 representing the 25th anniversary of Clemente's election to the Hall of Fame—and no other anniversaries preempting him—Clemente figures to receive more appropriate national recognition and remembrance. "I know how people should remember him and this is very relevant, I think, in 1998," says Bowie Kuhn. "They should remember him as not only a great ball player—he was a great ball player—but they should remember him as a ball player who struggled in every way he possibly could to give a complete count of himself on the field. And to fulfill that obligation which players should feel to the people in the stands who adore them and support them. And I say that's pertinent because I can't help but feel that today's athletes do not have that sense of obligation to anything like the degree that Clemente did. Clemente will always be a beloved figure, whether the people know it or not, for that reason. He gave everything he had and looked for something more or beyond that to give. That is not the image that professional athletes, by and large, create today in any sport. In professional sports, there is a tendency to see something that appears less than maximum effort. That is the legacy which I think he would have wanted to leave primarily, as a great professional who gave everything. Beyond that I'm sure he would want to leave the legacy that there is an obligation, further obligation, to be a role model. We hadn't used that phrase in talking, but he was a marvelous role model, not only as a player but also as a human being and what he did for people. You could not find a greater athlete in terms of what he stood for and the impact he had on people than Clemente."

In the city of Pittsburgh, the Clemente legacy has remained strong with Pirate fans ever since his death. "Well, they certainly never forgot him," says Sally O'Leary, who still resides in the Pittsburgh area. "I don't know how many times during the season they show a video about him on the scoreboard at the stadium. No matter how many times they show it, there's always a loud, resounding applause; they've never forgotten what he did for this city and what he did for the game of baseball. They've never forgotten that what he really wanted to do in life was to take care of the poor children and the poor people in his country."

"He's become a mythic figure in Puerto Rico," says Marcos Breton. "There's no way that you can understate that. People who were around at that time, at the time of his death, recall it the way we here in the mainland would recall, say when Kennedy was assassinated—President John Kennedy was assassinated—or when the space shuttle blew up. You remember; it becomes a touchstone event in your life. The people in Puerto Rico who were around at that time can tell you exactly where they were when they heard that his plane had gone down on the waters right off of San Juan. And to the younger generation, they've grown up hearing the stories and seeing the videotape. He, to the younger generation, becomes a mythic figure—which is good and bad. When I say bad, I wasn't lucky enough to have been around in the sixties when he was playing, but have had the pleasure and privilege of meeting a few people who knew him and who played with him and against him; he was a very human man. He was a father, and a husband. Had his faults just like anybody else did, and I think that to make him such a mythic figure in a way [makes] people forget the acts that he did, the generosity and the kindness and the courage that he showed. Not just in rushing food and other supplies to the victims of earthquakes in Nicaragua—which is what cost him his life—but just the everyday things that he did."

Perhaps the impact of Clemente's legacy is best illustrated through recent developments in Nicaragua, the country that he had so nobly tried to aid during the earthquake of 1972. For years, the shack-inhabiting residents of the small, isolated village of La Reforma—located about three hours from Managua—lived without local medical care. No doctors, no nurses, no hospital. Since most of the 500 poverty-stricken families did not own cars, they had no access to transportation that could take them to faraway medical facilities.

In response to the crying need for a medical clinic, members of the Pittsburgh Rotary Club spearheaded a fundraising drive. At first, money came in slowly. When it was decided to name the prospective medical facility after Clemente, donations poured in briskly from residents of Pittsburgh and its surrounding areas. As a result, La Reforma now has a medical facility—the "Roberto Clemente Medical Clinic."

"They facilitated fundraising by naming the clinic after Clemente," explains John Steigerwald, a KDKA sports anchor who attended the dedication of the clinic in March of 1998. "The place is here because of what a hero Roberto Clemente was. Clemente made it possible."

Any time you have the opportunity to accomplish something for somebody who comes behind you and you don't do it, you are wasting your time on this Earth.

—Roberto Clemente, 1971

A Tribute to Clemente
by John W. Horne, Jr.

Roberto was born in Puerto Rico in 1934.
It wasn't long before it was baseball he would adore.

He had speed, poise and a lot of charm,
Not to mention a great bat and a powerful arm.
We know what Jackie went through to change the game.
As a Latino, Roberto experienced much of the same.

He started with the Pirates in '55,
But it wasn't until '60 that his bat came alive.
They won the '60 Series thanks to the homer by Bill.
For Roberto Clemente that was quite a thrill.
In the locker room, he was nowhere in sight.
It was the fans he would celebrate with that night.

As he got older he never seemed to tire.
His batting average kept getting higher and higher.
As for the World Series, the Pirates weren't done.
They went again in '71.
Clemente rose to the occasion and hit .414,
And his throws were the greatest ever seen.
The Pirates took the Series four games to three.
Roberto was far and away the MVP.

His 3,000th hit came in September of 1972.
Who knew that it would be his final adieu?
Organizing a relief mission for a devastating earthquake
He was in a plane crash—his life it would take

It was people he loved as much as the game,
Which rewarded him with a place in the Hall of Fame.

Index

A

Aaron, Hank, 45, 65, 74, 140-142, 162, 171, 189, 216, 223-25, 281, 284, 298
Abrams, Al, 56, 157, 161, 192, 242, 325, 330
Acosta, Eduardo "Ed," 230
Allen, Maury, 285
Alley, Gene, 117, 142, 147, 156, 208, 214, 226, 230, 264
Alomar, Roberto "Robbie," 151
Alomar, Sandy Jr., 264
Alou, Felipe, 155, 218, 219, 232
Alou, Jesus "Jay," 232
Alou, Matty, 129, 146, 156-57, 162, 166, 202, 207, 209, 230-31
Altman, George, 148
Amoros, Sandy, 16, 19-21, 25, 27, 31-33, 69-70
Anderson, Sparky, 200, 202
Antonelli, Johnny, 109
Aparicio, Luis, 108, 224
Arecibo (Wolves), 130, 205
Arlin, Steve, 228
Arroyo, Luis, 95
Ashburn, Richie, 73
Atlanta Braves, 155, 164, 171, 187, 196-97, 199, 232, 334
Avila, Roberto "Bobby," 111

B

Badillo, Herman, 236-37
Baerga, Carlos, 348
Bailey, Bob "Beetle," 159
Baker, Gene, 119
Baltimore Orioles, 39, 49, 164, 203, 249-62, 264-77, 280, 283, 286-87, 336, 340
Bando, Sal, 250
Bankhead, Dan, 16
Banks, Ernie "Mr. Cub," 104, 286
Bartirome, Tony, 196-97, 214, 227, 316
Bauer, Hank, 164
Bavasi, Buzzie, 18, 26, 30-31
Baylor, Don "Groove," 341
Belanger, Mark "The Blade," 249, 252-54, 257, 260, 263, 267-68, 275-77
Bell, Jay, 343
Bench, Johnny, 201-02, 225, 303, 329-30
Bennett, Dr. Richard, 113
Berra, Yogi, 90-91, 93, 96-97, 99, 135, 212
Biederman, Les, 15, 17, 47, 52, 82, 104, 111, 118-19, 122, 127, 134-35, 137, 141, 149, 152, 160, 167
Billingham, Jack, 301
Bird, Larry, 340

Black, Joe, 16, 18-24, 27, 32
"Black Maxes," 153
Blair, Paul "Motormouth," 260-63, 265
Blandford, Fred, 201
Blass, Karen, 279
Blass, Steve, 122-123, 160-61, 163, 174, 177, 192, 216, 221-22, 230, 234, 241, 244-45, 253, 258, 267, 272-79, 286-87, 301, 316-17, 320, 322, 329, 331-33
Blount, Roy, Jr., 193
Blue, Vida, 224, 250
Bond, Walter, 121, 142
Bonds, Barry, 343
Bonds, Bobby, 243-45
Boston Braves, 12
Boston Red Sox, 117, 141, 169, 171, 180, 224
Boswell, Ken, 295
Bowa, Larry, 294
Bowen, Rex, 294
Boyer, Clete, 29, 95, 97-98
Boyer, Cloyd, 29
Boyer, Ken, 29, 104, 128
Boys Town, 68
Bragan, Bobby, 53, 55, 59-65
Breton, Marcos, 48, 125, 151, 278, 347-48, 350-52
Brett, George, 299
Brett, Ken, 204
Briles, Nelson "Nellie," 207-08, 210, 211, 216, 236, 243, 253, 264-65
Bristol, Dave, 161-62
Brock, Lou, 230, 341
Broeg, Bob, 110
Brooklyn Dodgers, 9-10, 14-19, 22-27, 29-32, 35, 41-43, 47, 53, 64, 69, 70-72, 76, 79, 267
Brosnan, Jim, 59-60, 87-88, 95
Brown, Joe L., 46, 53, 56, 61-64, 67, 109, 113, 117, 119-122, 126-127, 131-133, 141, 147, 148, 156, 159-60, 165-66, 172-74, 182-83, 189, 192-93, 196, 203, 207-09, 229, 291, 315-16, 320, 322, 335, 339
Brown, "Downtown" Ollie, 75
Brown, Willard "Home Run," 9, 12, 343
Brunet, George, 207-08
Bryant, Ron, 211, 243
Buckner, Billy, 228
Buffalo, 20
Buford, Don, 252-53, 264-65, 267-68, 273-77
Bunning, Jim, 174
Burdette, Lew, 65
Burgess, Smokey, 67, 91, 95, 99
Buso, Dr. Roberto, 131-32, 134, 147

C
Caguas (Criollos), 61, 205, 213
Callison, Johnny, 141
Cambria, Fred, 203
Campanella, Roy, 16, 21, 32-33
Campaneris, Bert "Campy," 250
Campanis, Alex "Al," 9-11, 24-26, 29-30, 43, 84, 99
Canel, Buck, 237
Caray, Harry, 136
Cardwell, Don, 117
Carew, Rod, 327, 341
Carey, Max, 184
Carlton, Steve "Lefty," 185, 230, 235, 294-95
Carmona, Emilio, 3
Carolina (Puerto Rico), 64, 235, 237, 323, 346
Carrasquel, Chico, 124
Carroll, Clay "Hawk," 200, 303
Carroll, John, 35
Carter, Gary "The Kid," 341
Carty, Rico, 197, 199
Cash, Dave, 186, 197, 199, 201, 203, 211, 213-14, 216, 224, 232, 243-45, 252, 257, 261-62, 269-70, 273-74, 276-77, 284, 305, 307, 317-18, 330
Cash, Norm, 108
Cassini, Jack, 27
Cepeda, Orlando "The Baby Bull," 9, 20, 108, 112-113, 121, 123, 130, 169-70, 256, 343
Cepeda, Pedro "Perucho," 343
Cerv, Bob, 94
Chaney, Darrel, 303
Charleston (Charlies), 332
Chass, Murray, 186, 259
Chevalier, Jack, 246
Chicago Cubs, 29, 44, 59-60, 84, 111, 115-16, 128, 133, 135-37, 141, 148, 151, 164, 171, 194, 198, 201-02, 230, 332
Chicago White Sox, 74, 159, 332
Christine, Bill, 16, 118, 184, 242
Christopher, Joe, 67, 68, 83, 105, 110, 169, 196
Chylak, Nestor, 273
Cimoli, Gino, 19, 27, 94-95, 97
Cincinnati Reds, 44, 61, 63, 67, 82, 88, 110, 112, 128, 133, 137, 149, 161-62, 173, 184, 187, 194, 198-99, 200-03, 205-06, 215, 224, 231, 294, 301-03, 307, 330, 335-36
Clarkson, James Buster "Buzz," 12, 13, 33
Clay, Cassius (Muhammad Ali), 163
Clemente, Ana Iris, 1
Clemente, Andres, 1
Clemente, Edgard (see also Edgard Velazquez), 350
Clemente, Enrique, 185, 327
Clemente, Luis (Roberto's brother), 1, 37

Clemente, Luis (Roberto's son), 320, 327-28
Clemente, Luisa Walker, 1-6, 16, 327
Clemente, Matino, 1, 52
Clemente, Melchor, 1-5, 11, 16
Clemente, Oquendo, 1
Clemente, Osvaldo, 1
Clemente, Roberto
   All-Star Game (final appearance in 1971), 224-25
   Birth, 1-2
   Death, 314-24
   First professional contract, 11-12
   First winter league season, 11-14
   Hall of Fame election, 324-25
   Hall of Fame induction, 325-27
   Minor league season, 17-28, 30-31, 33-34
   MVP Award (1966), 152-57
   MVP Award snub (1960), 83, 103-05
   National League Championship Series (1970), 199-203, 206
   National League Championship Series (1971), 241-47
   National League Championship Series (1972), 301-05
   Nicaraguan earthquake involvement, 310-14
   Rookie season in major leagues, 37-53
   Three thousandth hit, 294-300
   Signs with Brooklyn Dodgers, 16
   World Series (1960), 88-103
   World Series (1971), 249-87
Clemente, Roberto Jr., 150, 238, 314, 320, 327-28
Clemente, Rosa Maria, 1
Clemente, Vera (see also Vera Cristina Zabala), 126, 129, 150, 173, 180, 185, 271, 284, 289, 311, 313-15, 318-20, 322-23, 326-27, 344, 348
Clendenon, Donn, 112, 117, 141, 167, 184
Cleveland Indians, 72, 111, 255
Cline, Ty, 200, 202
Clines, Gene "Roadrunner," 212, 232, 234-35, 265, 269, 273, 330-31
Cloninger, Tony, 164, 202
Coates, Jim, 88, 98-100, 103
Cobb, Ty, 168, 325
Coimbre, Frank, 142
Colavito, Rocky, 72, 74-75, 107, 255, 268
Colborn, Jim, 204
Colon, Rafael Hernandez, 237, 321
Colorado Rockies, 349
Colosi, Nick, 201
Connors, Billy, 148
Coombs, Danny, 226
Cooper, Cecil, 341
Cooperstown, 227, 325, 344

Cope, Myron, 101, 147, 239, 347
Cox, Billy, 32
Coyle, James, 148
Craft, Harry, 14
Crosby, Bing, 260
Crowe, George "Big Daddy," 33, 45
Cruz, Jose, 235
Cuellar, Mike "Crazy Horse," 203-05, 249, 257-59, 272-76
Cumberland, John, 242
Cuyler, Kiki, 82

D

Dal Canton, Bruce, 207
Daley, Arthur, 146, 152
Daniel, Dan, 89
Davalillo, Vic, 207-08, 212, 231, 236, 244, 263, 269-70, 330-32
Davis, Eric, 341
Del Greco, Bobby, 56
DeMaestri, Joe, 97, 100
Demeter, Don, 72
Detroit Tigers, 72, 130, 171, 174, 193, 224, 255
Dickson, Murry, 43
Dierker, Larry, 175
Dietz, Dick, 243-44
Dihigo, Martin "El Maestro," 327
DiMaggio, Joe, 82
Ditmar, Art, 88, 90-91, 93, 95
Dobson, Pat "Snake," 249, 261-62, 269, 275
Donoso, Lino, 66
Donovan, Dan, 3, 301
Dorsey, Phil, 50-51, 129, 319
Douglas, Mike, 309
Douglas, Charles "Whammy," 67
Doyle, Charles, 59
Drabek, Doug, 343
Dressen, Chuck, 49
Dreyfuss, Barney, 149
Drum, Bob, 103
Drysdale, Don, 118, 163-64
Dunn, Harry, 340
Dunston, Shawon, 74
Duren, Ryne, 91
Durocher, Leo "The Lip," 30, 64, 164
Durso, Joe, 290

E

Easler, Mike "Hit Man," 343
Easter, Luke, 9
Ellis, Dock, 162-63, 174, 200-01, 216, 223-24, 226, 228, 231-32, 234-35, 242, 252-53, 260, 279
Ermer, Cal, 130
Erskine, Carl, 16
Etchebarren, Andy, 255, 261-62

F

Face, ElRoy "Roy," 37, 89, 91, 94-95, 97, 100, 110
Falls, Joe, 171-72
Father Flanagan, 68
Feeney, Charley, 62, 101, 172, 180, 183, 185, 190, 203, 209, 215, 251, 254, 271, 284, 289, 295-96
Feller, Bob, 325
Fernandez, Chico, 18, 21-22
Fernandez, Ruth, 310-11
Finegold, Dr. Joseph, 181, 227
Fingers, Rollie, 250
Flaherty, Peter, 324
Flood, Curt, 285
Flynn, Errol, 51
Ford, Whitey, 88, 93-95
Foster, George, 303
Fox, Charlie, 243, 245
Fox, Larry, 138
Franks, Herman, 33-35
Fraser, Ron, 310
Frau, Miguel J., 130
Freehan, Bill, 171
Freese, Gene, 42
Fregosi, Jim, 297
Frick, Ford, 108
Friend, Bob, 37, 45, 50, 57, 88, 96, 100, 116, 163
Fryman, Woodie, 232
Fuentes, Tito, 241-44
Furillo, Carl, 16, 25, 28, 31, 33, 71-72, 74, 75-76

G

Galbreath, Dan, 322
Galbreath, John, 195, 247, 291, 317
Gallagher, Alan "Dirty Al," 243-44
Gandhi, 8
Garcia, Arturo, 181, 198
Garland, Mr. Stanley, 50
Garland, Mrs. Stanley, 50
Garrett, Wayne, 187
Garvey, Steve, 341
Gehrig, Lou, 211, 322, 325
Geronimo, Cesar, 303
Gibbon, Joe, 202
Gibson, Bob "Hoot," 109, 139, 171, 198, 230-31, 235-36
Giles, Warren, 81, 118
Gilliam, James, "Junior," 16, 32-33, 216
Giusti, Dave, 163, 192-93, 197, 201, 208, 213, 216, 229, 231, 234, 236, 245, 247, 263-65, 268-69, 303, 316-17
Gomez, Ruben, 9
Gonder, Jessie, 162
Gonzalez, Juan, 140, 348

Gonzalez, Tony, 168
Gordon, Sid, 23
Gotay, Julio, 117
Gowdy, Curt, 272
Grady, Sandy, 172
Grammas, Alex, 200
Granger, Wayne, 202
Grant, Jim "Mudcat," 199, 223, 228-29, 236, 250, 350
Grasso, Mickey, 29
Grimsley, John, 200-01
Groat, Dick, 37, 57, 63, 83, 85, 89-91, 93, 95-97, 99, 102-05, 111, 117, 120, 152, 154, 156
Grygiel, George, 201
Guidry, Ron, 341
Guilfoile, Bill, 190-92, 227, 281, 283, 290, 300, 315-316, 322
Guillen, Jose, 351
Gullett, Don, 202

H
Haak, Howie, 17, 24-29, 74-75, 84, 142, 271, 282, 284
Haddix, Harvey, 67, 88, 95, 100
Hafey, Chick, 82
Hall, Dick "Turkey Neck," 119, 269, 275
Hall, Donald, 13
Hall, Tom "The Blade," 301
Hallahan, John, 160
Haller, Tom, 228
Hamilton, Steve, 243
Haney, Fred, 40-47, 49, 53
Harvey, Doug, 297
Havana (Sugar Kings), 20
Hebner, Richie, 196-97, 203, 211, 216, 223, 226, 232, 235, 243-45, 255, 260-62, 264, 267, 269-70, 281, 298, 339
Heiling, Joe, 136, 165, 280, 324
Heilmann, Harry, 168
Heller, Bernard, 148
Helms, Tommy, 202
Henderson, Ken, 241, 243
Hendricks, Elrod "Ellie," 204, 252-54, 265, 268, 276-77
Hernandez, Jackie, 207, 211, 223, 232, 235, 244, 252, 262-63, 265, 267, 269-270, 273, 276-79
Hernandez, Ramon, 235
Hernon, Jack, 40, 56, 60, 108-10
Herrera, Juan "Pancho," 117
High, Andy, 14
Hill, Jerry, 313-14, 320
Hoak, Don, 67, 74, 91, 95, 97, 102-05, 117, 120
Hodges, Gil, 16, 42
Hoffberger, Jerry, 280

Holtzman, Jerome, 266
Horne, John W. Jr., 354
Hornsby, Rogers, 142, 168-69
Houston Astros, 75, 142, 173, 175, 177, 192, 195, 221-22, 231-32
Houston Colt 45s, 118, 121
Howard, Elston, 91
Howe, Art, 73-75, 77, 155, 220, 292, 333-34
Hunter, Billy, 255, 268
Hunter, Jim "Catfish," 250

I
Irvin, Monte, 5, 15

J
Jackowski, Bill, 117-18
Jackson, Bo, 75
Jackson, Grant "Buck," 262-63
Jackson, Joe, 74
Jackson, Reggie, 204, 224-25, 250, 277
Jamie (deaf child), 183
Jenkins, Ferguson, 152
Jeter, John, 230
Johns Hopkins, 113
Johnson, Bob, 229-30, 243-44, 253, 267, 304, 318
Johnson, Dave, 249, 253, 257, 260, 262-64, 267-69, 273, 277
Johnson, Jerry, 245
Johnson, Tom, 195
Jones, Cleon, 187
Jordan, Michael, 293
Juncos baseball team, 11
Juncos, Ferdinand, 8

K
Kaese, Harold, 102, 246
Kaline, Al, 72, 224, 255, 340-41
Kansas City Athletics, 29
Kansas City Royals, 193, 207
Keck, Harry, 66, 81
Kennedy, John F., 346, 352
Kessinger, Don, 198
Kibler, John, 270, 295
Kienzl, Ray, 62
Killebrew, Harmon "Killer," 225
Kiner, Ralph, 108, 156, 160
King, Clyde, 136, 138-40, 219
King, Jeff, 343
King, Jim, 29
King, Joe, 64, 80, 81
King, Martin Luther, 125-26, 172-73
King, Nellie, 34, 39-40, 48-49, 52, 57, 58-60, 62, 65, 76, 82, 98, 102, 109-10, 115-16, 162-63, 168-69, 174-75, 183, 194, 221-22, 228, 239, 250, 291-96, 303-05, 307-09, 321, 345-47

Kingman, Dave "King Kong," 242
Kiseda, George, 61-64
Kison, Bruce "Sweetie," 207, 253, 260-63
Korean War, 52
Koufax, Sandy, 139, 153-54, 189, 324
Kubek, Tony, 90-91, 95-97
Kubiak, Ted, 236
Kuhn, Bowie, 179, 180, 257, 260, 278, 283-84, 315, 322-24, 326-27, 335, 340, 342, 348, 351

L
Labine, Clem, 42-43
Lacy, Lee, 343
Landes, Stan, 201
Landrum, Bill, 343
Lang, Jack, 324-25
La Reforma (Nicaragua), 353
Larkin, Barry, 341
Lascheid, Vince, 280
Lasorda, Tommy, 19-20
Law, Vernon, 37, 57, 63, 88, 90-91, 94, 96-97, 104, 126, 138
Leja, Frank, 14
Leonhard, Dave, 265
Leppert, Don, 261, 295, 297
Liddle, Don, 43
Lisker, Jerry, 166
Littlefield, Dick, 56
Livingston, Pat, 14, 26
Lolich, Mickey, 224-25
Lonborg, Jim, 205
Long, Dale, 37, 43, 55, 57, 77, 89, 100
Lopez, Hector, 91
Los Angeles Dodgers, 14, 64, 72, 83, 115-16, 118, 127, 139, 152-53, 159, 163, 177, 197, 214, 228, 293, 336
Lown, Turk, 59
Lozano, Rafael, 313
Luzinski, Greg "The Bull," 341
Lynch, Jerry, 135, 137

M
Macon, Max, 19, 23-24, 26-27, 30-31, 33
Maddox, Garry, 341
Madlock, Bill "Mad Dog," 343
Magallanes, 36
Managua, 310-13, 353
Manati, 11
Mangual, Angel, 350
Mantle, Mickey, 88, 90, 92, 94, 100, 128, 189, 219, 283
Marichal, Juan, 123, 151, 155, 162, 243-44, 327, 350
Marin, Roberto, 6-8, 11, 84, 298
Maris, Roger, 88, 90-91, 96, 98, 100, 283
Marshall, Mike, 214-15
Mathews, Eddie, 65

Matias, Francisco, 313, 321
Matlack, Jon, 296-98
Mauch, Gene, 141, 164
Maxvill, Dal, 230
May, Jerry, 207, 256
May, Lee, 200
May, Milt, 230, 232, 256, 263, 330
Mayaguez, 130
Mayoral, Luis, 2-3, 6, 8, 25-26, 29, 33, 36, 48, 49, 50, 104, 105, 111, 112, 116, 124, 125, 126, 129, 140, 142, 143, 155, 176, 186, 278, 282, 293, 296-99, 308, 310-13, 318, 322, 339-40, 342, 346-48, 351
Mays, Willie, 13, 15, 28, 30, 33-36, 44, 58, 72, 80, 89, 104, 108, 112, 128, 134, 139-40, 142, 150, 172, 189, 216, 219, 222-23, 241-42, 244-46, 281, 284, 290-91, 297-98, 340-41
Mazeroski, Bill "Tree Stump," 38, 57, 62, 82, 90-91, 95, 100-01, 103, 123, 155, 163, 167, 213, 216, 238, 242, 245, 269, 282, 298, 307-08, 334-35, 354
McAndrew, Jim, 199
McBean, Alvin, 121, 138, 162
McCarver, Tim, 256
McCool, Billy, 149
McCovey, Willie "Stretch," 241, 243-45
McDaniel, Douglas, 284, 311, 319
McDaniel, Lindy, 104
McDougald, Gil, 91, 93, 95, 100
McHugh, Roy, 46, 83, 84, 102, 176, 195, 200, 205, 212, 227, 257, 266, 274
McLain, Denny, 130
McNally, Dave, 249, 252-253, 264-265, 269, 277
McRae, Hal, 303
Mejias, Roman, 38-41, 47, 49-51, 63-64
Menke, Denis, 196, 303
Merced, Orlando, 343, 348
Merchant, Larry, 152
Merritt, Jim, 184, 201
Meyer, Russ "Monk," 47
Michael, Gene "Stick," 159
Miller, Bob "Monk," 207, 229, 231-32, 242, 269-70, 304
Miller, Ira, 345
Miller, Marvin, 322
Milwaukee Braves, 14-17, 45, 64-65, 84, 138, 141
Miner, Albert, 238
Minnesota Twins, 121, 130, 141-42, 155
Minoso, Minnie, 124
Molitor, Paul, 154
Mondesi, Raul, 351
Montemayor, Felipe, 38, 40, 43, 51
Montreal Expos, 187, 198, 214
Montreal (Royals), 18-23, 25, 27-31, 33, 41, 48, 150

Monzant, Ramon, 36
Moon, Wally, 72
Moose, Bob, 159, 174, 187, 202, 254, 267-68, 301, 303
Morgan, Joe, 221, 301
Morgenweck, Hank, 201
Mota, Manny, 117, 137, 162
Mr. Earl, 127
Munoz Marin, Luis, 346
Munson, Thurman, 325
Murphy, Dale, 341-42
Murray, Dr. Charles W., 199
Murrell, Ivan, 226
Murtaugh, Danny "The Irishman," 64-65, 82, 94, 96-98, 118-119, 133, 165, 189-90, 195, 198-99, 200, 202-03, 210, 228-29, 231-32, 234, 236-37, 242-45, 252-54, 256, 258, 260, 262-64, 267-69, 271-72, 275, 277-78, 281-82, 317, 322, 335
Musial, Stan "The Man," 81, 136, 142, 168, 219, 260, 324-25
Musick, Phil, 82, 173, 228, 242

N
Napp, Larry, 108
Nelson, Jim, 194
Nelson, Rocky, 67, 96, 98, 100
Newcombe, Don, 16, 32, 47
New York Giants, 3, 14-15, 30, 33, 35-36, 42, 44, 57-58, 76,
New York Mets, 115-16, 138, 164, 187, 194, 198-99, 202-03, 210, 215, 223, 236-38, 290, 295-97, 299
New Orleans, 40
New York Yankees, 14, 82, 88-100, 103, 128, 173, 190, 232, 258, 283, 325, 327
Nicaragua, 310-16, 318, 322, 324, 353
Niekro, Phil, 341
Nieves, Heriberto, 237
Nitschke, Ray, 259
Nixon, Richard M., 299, 324
Nolan, Gary, 200
Norman, Fred, 228
Northey, Ron, 118
Nover, Sam, 2, 38, 83, 126, 174, 302
Nunn, Bill, 102, 104

O
Oakland A's, 75, 224, 229, 250, 350
O'Brien, Johnny, 53
Oceak, Frank, 84, 92, 258, 275
Odom, Jim, 255, 258
O'Leary, Sally, 129, 194, 227, 290, 295, 319, 344, 352
Oliva, Tony, 121, 142, 151, 155, 224

Oliver, Al, "Scoop," 200, 202-03, 208-09, 216-17, 223-24, 232, 242, 244-45, 253, 257, 261, 263, 267-70, 316, 333, 336, 343
Oliveras, Max, 205
Olivo, Diomedes, 160
Olmo, Luis, 14, 34-35
O'Malley, Walter, 69-71
Osborn, Don, 265
O'Toole, Andrew, 23, 62, 102, 126, 139, 175
Ottawa (Athletics), 20

P
Pafko, Andy, 45
Pagan, Jose, 12, 129, 162-63, 182, 201, 252-53, 257, 262, 265, 269, 275-76, 313, 322
Pagliaroni, Jim, 117, 145
Palmeiro, Rafael, 151
Palmer, Jim, 249, 251-53, 267-68
Paris, Jose Antonio, 314
Parker, Dave "The Cobra," 332-33, 336, 343
Patek, Freddie "The Flea," 203, 207
Patterson, Daryl, 334
Pena, Orlando, 193, 208
Pena, Tony, 343
Pendleton, Jim, 67
Perez, Tony "Tany," 130, 202, 303
Perry, Gaylord, 241-42, 244-45
Pesky, Johnny, 141
Philadelphia Phillies, 43, 46, 73, 115, 117-18, 133, 148, 152, 162, 164, 168, 174, 194, 197-98, 214-15, 223, 229, 232, 285, 294-95, 326-27
Pinson, Vada, 110
Pittsburgh Pirates, 22-25, 27-28, 37, 40-41, 43-44, 49-53, 55, 56, 57-67, 72-74, 76-77, 79-85, 88-105, 108, 111, 113, 116-120, 122-124, 126-29, 131-139, 141-143, 145-49, 151-53, 155-57, 159-68, 171-75, 177, 179, 180-83, 185-99, 200-03, 207-17, 219-24, 226-37, 239, 241-45, 247, 249-54, 256-67, 269-84, 287, 289-99, 300-05, 308-09, 315-17, 319-20, 322, 325-27, 329-37, 340, 342-44, 348-51, 353-54
Pizarro, Juan, 9, 64, 129-30, 159, 161
Podres, Johnny, 42-43
Ponce Leones (Lions), 142
Pont-Flores, Rafael, 156
Powell, John "Boog," 249, 257, 260, 264, 267-269, 273, 275, 277
Power, Tyrone, 51
Power, Vic, 205
Powers, Johnny, 67
Prince, Bob "The Gunner," 66, 278-79, 296, 308
Puckett, Kirby, 341-42
Pulli, Frank, 295

Purkey, Bob, 82, 127-28

Q
Quay, Luke, 183, 295-96, 308

R
Ray, Johnny, 343
Reberger, Frank, 211
Reese, Harold "Pee Wee," 42
Reichler, Joe, 340
Rettenmund, Merv, 249, 253-56, 260, 267, 269-70, 273-76, 278
Reuschel, Rick, 343
Reuss, Jerry, 230, 336
Reynolds, Harold, 341
Rhodes, Dusty, 57
Ribant, Dennis, 162
Rice, John, 261
Richardson, Bobby, 90-91, 94, 97, 100, 103
Richman, Milton, 51, 204, 213, 233, 247, 250, 279, 285, 297
Richmond (Virginias), 19-20, 23
Ricketts, Dave, 163, 234
Rickey, Branch "The Mahatma," 22, 24, 28-29, 36, 40, 53, 57, 61, 84, 91
Rickey, Branch, Jr., 55
Rigney, Bill, 35
Ripken, Cal Jr., 341-42
Rivera, Arturo, 313-14, 321
"Roberto Clemente Sports City," 68, 327-28, 347-48
Roberts, Curt, 39, 51
Robertson, Bob, 159, 202, 209, 216, 219, 230-32, 242-45, 252, 258-59, 262-64, 267, 269, 272-73, 275, 277-78, 282, 304-305, 330
Robinson, Bill, 343
Robinson, Brooks "Vacuum Cleaner," 249, 252-253, 257-258, 260, 262-265, 270, 273, 283, 287, 340-41
Robinson, Frank "The Judge," 112, 203-04, 216, 219, 225, 249, 252-54, 257, 260-61, 263-67, 269-70, 273, 276-78, 286-87
Robinson, Jackie, 12, 15-16, 22, 25, 31-33, 39, 50, 64, 351, 354
Rochester (Red Wings), 20, 24-25
Rodgers, Andre, 129, 162
Rodriguez, Ivan "Pudge," 348
Rogers, Thomas, 237
Rooker, Jim, 336
Rose, Pete "Charley Hustle," 161, 187, 200, 202, 299, 301, 335, 341
Ross, John, 205
Roush, Edd, 82
Rudolph, Ken, 198
Russo, Jim, 251, 273

Ruth, Babe, 289, 325

S
Sada, Pepe, 129-30
Saffell, Tom, 40-41, 43
St. Louis Browns, 12
St. Louis Cardinals, 14, 46-47, 53, 56, 81-82, 84, 110, 117, 128, 133, 135, 171, 192-95, 199, 207-08, 230-31, 234-36, 256, 259, 285, 300
San Diego Padres, 183-84, 214, 226, 228, 230
Sands, Charlie, 228
San Francisco Giants, 89, 112, 115, 117, 121, 123, 134, 140, 146, 155, 156, 162, 177, 197, 211, 222-23, 229, 241-46, 290-91, 298, 340
Sanguillen, Manny, 129, 159-61, 163, 203, 211, 223-24, 226, 230-32, 235-36, 244-45, 251-52, 260, 262-64, 268, 270, 272, 275, 277, 280, 286, 302-03, 313, 318, 320, 322, 330-32
San Juan Senators, 5, 129-30, 170, 203-05, 209, 213, 215, 325
Santiago, Benito, 347-48
Santiago, Jose "Pantalones," 10, 169-70
Santo, Ron, 171
Santurce Cangrejeros (Crabbers), 9, 12-13, 28, 33-34, 36, 61, 140, 203-05, 213
Saturday Night Live, 48
Savage, Ted, 117
Schmidt, Mike, 284
Schneck, Dave, 297
Schoendienst, Red, 230
Schofield, Dick, 134
Seaver, Tom "Tom Terrific," 198, 295
Secory, Frank, 108
Shantz, Bobby, 92, 97-98
Sheehan, Tom, 14
Shepard, Larry, 174, 182
Shopay, Tom, 263, 268, 276-77
Shuba, George "Shotgun," 31
Sierra, Ruben, 348, 350
Simmons, Ted, 230
Singleton, Ken, 203, 341
Sisk, Tommie, 174
Sisler, George, 56, 107
Sixto Escobar Stadium, 9, 34, 113
Sizemore, Ted, 230
Skinner, Bob, 57, 85, 90, 96-98
Skowron, Bill "Moose," 88, 91, 93, 97-99
Smith, Earl, 40-42
Smith, Hal, 84, 99, 101
Smith, Red, 119
Snider, Duke, 16, 25, 31, 33, 71-72
Smith, Ozzie, 341
Spahn, Warren, 65, 84, 138-39
Speier, Chris, 241, 243-44
Stafford, Bill, 96-97

Stargell,Willie, 75, 116-17, 123, 135, 137, 141, 145, 162-63, 167-68, 184, 192, 198, 202-03, 209, 211-13, 215-17, 220, 223-24, 226, 230-32, 234, 244-45, 250, 252, 258, 261-63, 268-69, 272, 275-79, 282, 309, 316-17, 330, 334-36, 341, 343
Staub, Daniel "Rusty," 296
Steadman, John, 268
Steigerwald, John, 353
Steiner, Mel, 201
Stengel, Casey, 90-91, 93, 97, 103
Stennett, Rennie, 207, 232, 235, 307, 318
Stewart, Dave, 341
Stockton, Dick, 181
Stone, Steve, 211
Stoneham, Horace, 15, 33-34
Stuart, Dick "Dr. Strangeglove," 84, 88, 90, 96, 101
Sukeforth, Clyde, 22-24, 27-29, 64, 84, 94
Surkont, Max, 45
Suro, Rodrigo Otero, 204
Sutcliffe, Rick, 341
Sweet Georgia Brown, 162
Syracuse (Chiefs), 20

T
Tappe, Elvin, 108
Taylor, Carl "Hawk," 193
Temple, Johnny, 88
Terry, Ralph, 94, 100
Texas Rangers, 50, 126, 140, 186
Thomas, Frank, 37, 40-42
Thompson, Don, 31
Thompson, Jason, 343
Thornton,Andre, 341-42
Thurman, Bob "Owl," 12, 34, 36, 343
Tolan, Bobby, 201-02
Toronto (Maple Leafs), 20
Torre, Joe, 230, 259
Traynor, Harold "Pie," 81-82, 157, 184, 256, 293
Trouppe, Quincy, 14
Turley, Bob, 92-93, 96
Tutko, Dr.Thomas, 259
Tuttle, Dennis, 74-75, 333
Twombly,Wells, 283

V
Valentine, Ellis, 75
Van Slyke,Andy, 343
Veale, Bob, 139, 141, 174-75, 229, 232
Velazquez, Edgard (see also Edgard Clemente), 349
Versalles, Zoilo, 150-51, 155
Vietnam War, 195
Vigoreaux, Luis, 310-11

Vilella, Sanchez, 169-70
Virdon, Bill, 56, 90-91, 94, 96-98, 100, 209, 215, 223, 295, 298, 300, 317, 322, 331-32, 330, 335
Vizcarrondo High School, 8

W
Waco (Pirates), 40
Wagner, Honus, 142, 168, 294, 300, 325
Walker, Harry "The Hat," 133-37, 141, 145-48, 152-53, 156-57, 162, 165-66, 222-23, 238, 322
Walker, Luke, 201, 230, 233, 235, 260-61, 265
Walsh, Davis J., 62, 64
Waner, Lloyd "Little Poison," 157
Waner, Paul "Big Poison," 142, 298
Washington Senators, 49, 173
Watson, Bob "The Bull," 221
Watt, Eddie, 263, 269, 275
Ways, C.R., 309
Weaver, Earl, 224, 252, 262-63, 267-69, 273, 275-77
Whitman, Dick, 19, 25, 27
Wickersham, Dave, 173
Wilcox, Milt, 202
Williams, Billy, 128
Williams, Charlie, 290-91
Williams, Dick, 31
Williams, Ted, 80, 136, 141, 168, 218, 325, 351
Wills, Maury, 107, 157, 159, 162, 167, 173, 216, 228
Wilson, John, 222
Winfield, Dave, 75, 341
Wintner, George, 340
Wise, Rick, 197
Wolf, David, 259
Womack,Tony, 343
Wood,Wilbur, 159

Y
Yake, Byron, 315
Yastrzemski, Carl, 171, 224, 299
Young, Cy, 153
Young, Dick, 9-11, 29, 164-65, 181, 238, 255, 259, 274, 280-81, 286
Young, Kevin, 343

Z
Zabala, Vera Cristina, (see also Vera Clemente), 120, 128
Zimmer, Don, 33
Zisk, Richie, 207, 336
Zorrilla,Pedro "Pedrin," 8-9, 11-16, 26, 30, 33, 61, 84, 159